ECONOMIC ROLE OF TRANSPORT INFRASTRUCTURE

ECONOMIC ROLE OF TRANSPORT INFRASTRUCTURE

Theory and Models

CLAUDIO FERRARI
University of Genoa, Genoa, Italy

ANNA BOTTASSO
University of Genoa, Genoa, Italy

MAURIZIO CONTI
University of Genoa, Genoa, Italy

ALESSIO TEI
Newcastle University, Newcastle upon Tyne, UK

ELSEVIER

Elsevier
Radarweg 29, PO Box 211, 1000 AE Amsterdam, Netherlands
The Boulevard, Langford Lane, Kidlington, Oxford OX5 1GB, United Kingdom
50 Hampshire Street, 5th Floor, Cambridge, MA 02139, United States

Notices
Knowledge and best practice in this field are constantly changing. As new research and experience broaden our understanding, changes in research methods, professional practices, or medical treatment may become necessary.

Practitioners and researchers must always rely on their own experience and knowledge in evaluating and using any information, methods, compounds, or experiments described herein. In using such information or methods they should be mindful of their own safety and the safety of others, including parties for whom they have a professional responsibility.

To the fullest extent of the law, neither the Publisher nor the authors, contributors, or editors, assume any liability for any injury and/or damage to persons or property as a matter of products liability, negligence or otherwise, or from any use or operation of any methods, products, instructions, or ideas contained in the material herein.

Library of Congress Cataloging-in-Publication Data
A catalog record for this book is available from the Library of Congress

British Library Cataloguing in Publication Data
A catalogue record for this book is available from the British Library

ISBN: 978-0-12-813096-4

Publisher: Joe Hayton
Senior Acquisition Editor: Brian Romer
Editorial Project Manager: Joshua Mearns
Production Project Manager: Bharatwaj Varatharajan
Designer: Christian J. Bilbow

Typeset by TNQ Technologies

CONTENTS

PREFACE

A traditional handbook on transport economics teaches policy-makers and students that infrastructure policy consists of two components, i.e., infrastructure investment and charging users for infrastructure costs. The latter is part of the levy imposed on the transport users for the marginal external cost that they cause. An even important issue is how authorities should approach decision-making on investments in transport infrastructure.

It all starts with a correct definition of transport infrastructure investments. It not only concerns investment in new infrastructure but also improvement works, repairs, and maintenance. Just have a look at the national accounts to see how huge amounts of money are involved. From a scientific point of view, the economic decisions about transport infrastructure expenditures must always be analyzed in the same way: the investment should only be made as long as the benefits outweigh the costs.

But we all know that in reality this simple rule is not always followed by (often politically influenced) decision-makers. In the past, transport infrastructure investments have been a preferred instrument for policy-makers and politicians. Still these days those infrastructure investments are often used, or should we say abused, to reach targets outside the transport sector. Typical examples are linked to general economic policy, regional policy, to reach social objectives, or even linked to the agricultural and/or military business. In those situations, the real economic role of transport infrastructure for the welfare of the society and its actors has been forgotten and/or neglected.

I consider this book on the economic role of transport infrastructure a welcome reaction, as it complies with a continuous need for information about how transport infrastructure should be used and evaluated. It also contributes to a critical evaluation and systematization of the available scientific knowledge on the link between transport infrastructure and economic activity. The authors work in an interdisciplinary way, combining transport economics and regional economics. Their main aim is to provide a book that not only focuses on the economic role that transport infrastructures play but also stresses the techniques of projects' assessment and how to investigate the wider economic impacts of transport infrastructure.

This book not only fills a scientific and policy gap. Being dedicated to Professor Ugo Marchese, it reminds me how much this great Italian scholar influenced the transport economics scientific world, including myself. This book contributes to Ugo's heritage. I'm grateful for that.

To conclude this preface: this book is a must have!

Prof. Dr. Eddy Van de Voorde
Department of Transport and Regional Economics (TPR)
University of Antwerp, Belgium

CHAPTER 1

Introduction

> *"A system which is efficient in the static sense at every point of time can be inferior to a system which is never efficient in this sense, because the reason for its static inefficiency can be the driver for its long-term performance."*
>
> ***J. A. Schumpeter.***

Writing a book is a risky venture. One has the feeling that there is always something else to read, study, learn, and discuss; that his toolbox is not adequately equipped to complete the task.

Nevertheless, sometimes one is requested to try this adventure. This is what happened to us. After the publication in 2014 of our joint paper titled "Ports and regional development: A spatial analysis on a panel of European regions" on the journal *Transportation Research—Part A*, we were asked to reflect on the opportunity to write a book on the economic role of transport infrastructure.

We are well aware of the existence of some masterpieces which deal with the economic impact of transport infrastructure; indeed, we have learnt a lot from them as students and we have still been using them in our university graduate and postgraduate courses. Despite this, in the past two decades, economic theory has deeply reconsidered the role played by transport infrastructure in fostering economic activity and growth, and, moreover, the set of economic models and tools that are nowadays available to researchers has been incredibly enriched. Thus, we felt that there were sufficient novelties in the literature to warrant at least an attempt to critically evaluate and systematize the available scientific knowledge on the link between transport infrastructure and economic activity. Readers only are entitled to judge if we have achieved this goal.

This book focuses on the economic role of transport infrastructure, thus combining the disciplines of transport economics with regional economics. This means that some important issues related to the economics of transport infrastructure have not been deliberately considered. In fact, the present volume does not claim to cover all possible issues associated with transport infrastructure investments; indeed, it would be a challenge well beyond our capabilities. In particular, issues related to the financing and regulation of transport infrastructures go well beyond the aims of this book; similarly, the

Economic Role of Transport Infrastructure
ISBN 978-0-12-813096-4
https://doi.org/10.1016/B978-0-12-813096-4.00001-9

industrial organization issues (e.g., the possible introduction of competition for the market and in the market, or the vertical relationship between airports and airlines, or the de-verticalization process in the railways sector, etc.) or the political economy of transport infrastructures have been largely neglected. Readers interested in these other important issues may easily find several valuable contributions in the literature.

Our main purpose is that of providing our readers with a book that focuses on the economic role that transport infrastructures play, and, in particular, on the most popular techniques of projects' assessment as well as on the several econometric techniques that exist in the literature to investigate the wider economic impacts of transport infrastructure.

This work has been written primarily for postgraduate students interested in applied economics and in particular in transportation and regional studies. Some notions of micro- and macroeconomics are requested as well as a basic knowledge of econometrics. Notwithstanding this *caveat*, this book may be read by a large public, and in our intentions it could represent a useful tool to inform policy-makers interested in the subject, as well as practitioners and spatial planners. In this sense, this book facilitates "cherry-picking" readers because each chapter is self-consistent and autonomous as much as possible.

This book is divided into three parts. The first part is formed by two chapters that, in some sense, provide the background of this book; indeed, the two chapters deal with the economics of transport infrastructure and with the recent models that provide the theoretical framework to think about the possible "transmission" mechanisms through which transport infrastructures might influence economic activity and growth. In this part, readers are introduced to the infrastructural elements that characterize the transportation system. For every transport mode, the main economic characteristics are presented; in particular, the chapter focuses on the lumpiness of supply and the role of scale economies that make transport infrastructure multiuser plants. These characteristics, coupled with the agglomeration economies associated with the infrastructural endowment, make this sector strategic for governments. Then the chapter focuses on the economic benefits, and how they change, during the life cycle of transport infrastructures. It concludes with some reflections on how transport infrastructures will evolve in the near future in accordance with the concept of "smart transport". The following Chapter 3 presents the theoretical literature that has analyzed the role of transport infrastructure investments on economic activity. After briefly describing classical exogenous and endogenous growth models, the main contributions of the New Economic Geography (NEG) literature are surveyed. NEG models analyze the interaction between agglomeration and dispersion forces and the role played by changes in transport costs associated with improvements in the transport system. Recent NEG models suggest that reductions of trade/transport costs produce uneven spatial developments that are accompanied by faster growth in all regions.

The second part of this book is dedicated to the appraisal process of infrastructure and their impact on the economic system. It consists of three chapters dedicated to the quality of available data, the techniques that are typically employed in ex-ante impact assessment of infrastructure projects, and the econometric models that are instead generally employed in the academic literature to conduct ex-post impact assessment evaluation of transport infrastructure, respectively. The quality of data is extremely important because it affects the quality of results of the empirical analysis. In most cases, data refer to some quantitative characteristics of transport infrastructure, as the rail or road length, the number of seaports or airports, or the amounts invested in infrastructure works. In turn, the production of qualitative data is still limited and, sometimes, the quality is again expressed in quantitative terms; by way of example, the road network is sometimes split into highways and normal roads or paved and unpaved roads. Chapter 5 is dedicated to the assessment of infrastructure. It presents and discusses the three widely adopted techniques for infrastructure assessment: Cost—Benefit Analysis, multicriteria analysis, and input—output techniques. This part of the book concludes with the presentation (Chapter 6) of the econometric approaches that have been used in the literature to ex-post evaluate the impact of transport infrastructures on growth and other economic outcomes. It starts discussing the role played by economic theory in informing the empirical analysis and then considers the econometric tools that have been used in recent years, such as panel fixed effects, Generalised Method of Moments (GMM), spatial econometrics, Vector Auto Regressions (VAR), and counterfactual impact evaluation methods. Finally, it provides a brief discussion of the level of analysis at which studies have been conducted, from macroeconomic to regional, industry, and firm level.

The last part of this book is devoted to discuss the empirical evidence on the economic effects of transportation infrastructure networks by leveraging on a series of meta-analyses as well as on a selected group of very recent studies that apply state-of-the-art econometric methods. Although much of the literature is focused on the impact of transport infrastructure on production, Chapter 7 also explores the role played by transport networks on other relevant dimensions of economic activity that have received increasing attention in recent years, such as employment and population, productivity, firm dynamics, and trade. The evidence from both the meta-analysis and the "targeted" short literature review drive the discussion on a tentative conclusion on the economic effects of transport infrastructures associated with different modes of transport. This third part of the book concludes with Chapter 8 that is dedicated to the description of the transport planning process, providing examples of some of the main international transport network strategies. Thus, while the previous chapters discuss theoretical studies that investigate the impact of the transport network on economic activity, this chapter focuses on the planning process of some of the main infrastructure initiatives, linking the planning activities to the assessment process. Given the growing role of alternative funding solutions, the chapter presents also a section dedicated to public–private partnerships, discussing their role in the achievement of wider regional benefits.

Final considerations and issues for further research are outlined in the concluding pages (Chapter 9).

We are highly indebted to several colleagues that contributed to this book by inspiring us with their valuable comments, suggestions, and fruitful discussions. The list of names would be so long that we prefer to avoid to explicitly mention them, but their names recur frequently in the list of references. We only mention one of them, Professor Ugo Marchese who introduced the discipline of Transport Economics in the graduate programs of the University of Genova in the 1960s and was among the founders of the Italian Association of Transport Economists.

Lastly, this book is dedicated to our wives, husband, and children (also the boy who was born while we were typing this introduction). We are extremely proud of their continuous support, patience, and encouragement that allowed us to steal them a lot of time, hopefully not in vain, to work on the manuscript. We are extremely grateful for this.

CHAPTER 2

The Economics of Transport Infrastructure

Contents

The infrastructure system is a network made of several routes connecting a number of terminals. This system together with the vehicles that circulate on it and the load of vehicles—passengers or cargo—forms the transportation system; i.e., the combination of transport supply and demand (Blauwens, De Baere, & Van de Voorde, 2008). According to Quinet, Touzery, and Triebel (1982), it is useful to distinguish the transport system into two subsystems—infrastructures and services—to analyze the specificities that characterize the two.

Under an economic perspective, transport infrastructures are essential facilities for the production and the consumption function of the economic agents. They positively impact on the economic system raising the productivity of private inputs, reducing the cost of production, and raising the rate of total factor productivity growth.

These effects derive from the traffic that use the system of infrastructure; nevertheless, in the following we will focus on the economics of the infrastructural system, i.e., the opportunities offered to people to move or to purchase goods and services from a point to another and not on the transport services or the traffic (that represent the result of these opportunities).

Economic Role of Transport Infrastructure
ISBN 978-0-12-813096-4
https://doi.org/10.1016/B978-0-12-813096-4.00002-0

This is the essence of transport infrastructure: to make the economic and physical space narrow and in consequence to provide the opportunity for a different plot of economic and social relations among the connected areas.

Nowadays, the infrastructure system is always made of physical assets; the sole exceptions are represented by the maritime and air transport modes that use natural (not manufactured) routes—water and air, respectively; but terminals are manufactured assets for all transport modes.

2.1 THE ELEMENTS OF THE TRANSPORT NETWORKS

In general, any network is made of links and nodes. In the transport system, the nodes are the terminal facilities—i.e., the geographical points where trips start and end—whereas the links are the transport infrastructures. There is also an additional element characterizing the transport networks that is the mode of transport: air, sea—and, where it is possible, riverine—rail, road, and pipeline transport. Therefore, it is possible to distinguish a transport network for each transport mode, and in many cases the literature and the policies are focused on a single mode of transport; but terminal facilities make it also possible to switch from a mode to another giving rise to transport intermodality. It is noteworthy that intermodality is something more than the mere spatial overlapping of two (or more) modal transport networks, it is instead the organization of a single voyage through two or more transport modes without any breaks of bulk, in case of cargo movements, or with acceptable transit times in case of passengers, with the final goal to improve mobility and the efficiency of the whole distribution process (Bektas & Crainic, 2007). This definition of intermodality implies that it effectively takes place when not only the voyage is arranged to use a multiplicity of modes, where each of these modes may have a different transport carrier responsible for it, but also when intermodal transport means are involved (such as the ro-ro and ro-ro-pax ferries in maritime transport). In practice, it is usual to refer to multimodal transport when the cargo utilizing several transport modes is moved under a single contract or bill of lading.

Then, it is possible to distinguish the main infrastructural components for each transport mode, as follows:

- Air transport
  - Airport runways
  - Terminal facilities
  - Air navigation assets

- Seaborne and riverine transport
  - Dock and terminal facilities
  - Accessibility to surface infrastructures
  - Harbor approaches
  - Navigation aids
  - Channels
- Rail transport
  - Tracks
  - Signaling
  - Interchange
  - Rail stations
- Road transport
  - Carriageways
  - Interchanges
- Pipelines

Adopting a territorial approach, the notion of transport corridors emerges. Following the first definition by Priemus and Zannoveld (2003) they are "narrow bundles of infrastructure that connect two or more regions dispersed over a certain space" (Drewello and Scholls, 2016). This notion has rapidly acquired success, namely due to its multiscalar and multidimensional nature, and now it informs, for instance, the infrastructure policy of the European Union[1].

Another possible classification of transport infrastructure refers to the kind of services it serves. According to Martin and Rogers (1995), the infrastructure network is composed of domestic infrastructure serving domestic business (and impacting on firms location) and international infrastructure serving the international business and trade.

Either one considers the single elements or different combination of elements of the infrastructural network they require to be measured both in physical terms—namely the length of railways or roads or the volume of traffic they can serve—and in monetary terms, i.e., the stock of money invested in infrastructures.

2.1.1 The Infrastructural Endowment

The transport systems is the backbone of the global economy (Schuckmann, Gnatzy, Darkow, & von der Gracht, 2012), and its infrastructural component contribute—under specific conditions that will be further analyzed in the book—to the economic growth (Banister & Berechman, 2001). Due to the importance of the economic benefits deriving from infrastructures to people and firms located in a particular region, the infrastructural endowment has always been investigated to understand the relation between infrastructural investment and GDP growth and where and when infrastructural investments are needed. While the relation between investment in public infrastructures or core public infrastructure (something more closely related to transport infrastructure) will be analyzed in the following chapter, in what follows the focus is on the analysis of the infrastructural endowment (or infrastructure supply) that usually precede any transport planning process.

Looking at the infrastructural endowment, the very long life span of infrastructures (that will be discussed further), means the adoption of a long-run perspective that aims at assuring to the economic agents the same opportunities of welfare, thus avoiding any consideration about the short-run fluctuations of the demand of transport. Moreover, because the transport demand, in general, has exhibited a growing path in the last two centuries, it makes sense to concentrate the attention on supply and postpone the balance between transport supply and demand to any specific infrastructural project. Last, in a normative approach to infrastructures, expansion of infrastructural supply may be decided to accommodate the economic development (actual or expected) or overcome current bottlenecks or even to stimulate lagging regions (Rietveld & Boonstra, 1995).

Therefore, it is necessary to have a set of possible measures of the infrastructural endowment that will refer to its capacity or to the volume of people or firms that may be benefited in terms of lower prices (consumers), higher jobs (people), or higher profits (firms).

The several measures used in practice may be grouped into the following:

- physical/quantitative measures;
- qualitative measures;
- accessibility measures.

Physical or quantitative measures consider the physical length of the different routes (such as the length of railways or roads). Therefore, the most common measures of infrastructural endowment refer to the ratio of the length of railways and road routes to the population, or alternatively the surface, of the region they pass through. Table 2.1 shows some figures referred to a sample of countries considering this kind of physical measures.

Figures reported in Table 2.1 clearly show that this way of measuring infrastructural endowment is highly affected by several factors, such as the size and shape of countries, their geographical location, and also the stage of development and the GDP level. The combination of these factors

Table 2.1 Rail and road infrastructural endowment—ratios on surface area

	Rail	Road		Rail	Road
	km/000 sqkm	km/000 sqkm		km/000 sqkm	km/000 sqkm
Algeria	1.8	36.8	Korea, Rep.	36.4	829.8
Argentina	9.0	25.0	Latvia	28.7	228.1
Austria	60.3	1592.7	Lithuania	27.1	1107.2
Azerbaijan	23.9	309.3	Luxembourg	106.2	1119.3
Bangladesh	19.1	13.6	Macedonia, FYR	27.2	374.7
Belarus	26.3	359.6	Malaysia	6.8	351.2
Belgium	117.2	3947.4	Mexico	13.6	70.0
Bosnia and Herzegovina	20.0	379.3	Moldova	34.2	261.0
Brazil	3.5	25.0	Mongolia	1.2	3.1
Bulgaria	36.2	173.3	Morocco	4.7	92.1
Cameroon	2.1	8.6	Mozambique	3.9	7.9
Canada	5.2	41.6	Norway	10.8	196.7
Chile	7.3	24.0	Pakistan	9.8	232.5
China	7.0	361.2	Poland	60.6	897.8
Congo, Dem. Rep.	1.6	1.2	Portugal	27.6	773.1
Cote d'Ivoire	2.0	20.2	Romania	45.2	209.2
Czech Republic	119.9	1656.7	Russian Federation	5.0	54.3
Denmark	49.5	1728.9	Saudi Arabia	0.7	22.1
Egypt, Arab Rep.	5.2	126.6	Serbia	43.1	316.9
Estonia	17.5	230.5	Slovenia	59.6	1923.3
Finland	17.6	147.7	South Africa	16.8	130.4
France	54.7	1873.0	Spain	33.3	1350.3

Continued

Table 2.1 Rail and road infrastructural endowment—ratios on surface area—cont'd

	Rail	Road		Rail	Road
	km/000 sqkm	km/000 sqkm		km/000 sqkm	km/000 sqkm
Gabon	3.0	4.1	Sudan	2.3	2.3
Georgia	22.6	274.2	Swaziland	17.3	62.1
Germany	93.6	1805.9	Sweden	21.7	302.7
Greece	17.0	313.4	Switzerland	87.4	1731.0
Hungary	84.8	828.6	Syrian Arab Republic	11.6	340.5
Indonesia	2.5	148.1	Tunisia	23.4	90.2
Iran, Islamic Rep.	4.9	91.9	Turkey	12.9	449.6
Iraq	4.9	137.0	Turkmenistan	6.4	97.5
Ireland	27.3	1366.5	Ukraine	35.7	275.2
Israel	54.1	841.2	United Kingdom	60.7	1619.1
Italy	56.5	1618.4	United States	23.2	437.8
Jordan	5.7	80.6	Uzbekistan	9.4	168.8
Kazakhstan	5.3	32.0	Vietnam	7.1	448.2

Source: The World Bank (for railways length and surface area); CIA Factbook (for length of paved roads).

explains, for instance, why the United States registers values well below those of countries with lower levels of GDP per capita. For instance, according to the World Bank statistics, the United States registered in 2015 a value of GDP per capita (expressed in constant values 2011 and in Purchasing Power Parity, PPP) of 52,704$ against 38,865$ of United Kingdom and 10,911$ of Tunisia, nevertheless the US railways and road endowment compared with these countries is approximately 1:3 and 1:4 in respect of United Kingdom, and 1:1 and 1:2 in respect of Tunisia, respectively.

Similar considerations may apply in case the infrastructural endowment is calculated on the population instead of the surface area, as shown for the same set of countries of the previous table in Table 2.2.

It is noteworthy that the above data give the impression that both the road and rail transport systems have been developed without any forms of coordination. The Spearman correlation coefficient calculated on figures presented in Tables 2.1 and 2.2 shows, in fact, only a weak correlation (equal to 0.154 in case of infrastructural endowment measured in respect to surface area and equal to 0.295 in case of endowment measured in respect to population). Effectively, the actual road and rail networks are the result of different investment decisions happened over almost two centuries and made by several actors—private and public ones—at different level of governments—regional, national, and more recently also supranational (as the European institutions). Namely at the beginning of their respective history investment were made without any form of coordination; as happened in United Kingdom in the mid-19th century during the so-called "railways mania" (Ferrari, 2016; Odlyzko, 2010).

In the case of transport terminals, the supply measures are given by their capacity, i.e., the maximum flow of passengers, vehicles, or cargo that these terminals can move in a period of time maintaining a good level of service. Possible measures for airports may refer to the air terminal or to the runways, whereas in the case of seaports they may refer to the port terminals or to the port access channels.

All these kind of physical measures of the infrastructure endowment do not take into account the quality of the infrastructures; they implicitly consider that the economic effects and the condition of transport services are exactly the same in case of using an unpaved road or a highway. For instance, in the railways system, the possibility that two different places are connected by a single-track rail lane (with trains passing both upward and downward) or a double-track rail lane (with any truck dedicated to a single

Table 2.2 Rail and road infrastructural endowment—ratios on population

	Rail	Road		Rail	Road
	km/000 inhab.	km/000 inhab.		km/000 inhab.	km/000 inhab.
Algeria	0.11	2.25	Korea, Rep.	0.07	1.65
Argentina	0.58	1.61	Latvia	0.93	7.38
Austria	0.59	15.64	Lithuania	0.60	24.65
Azerbaijan	0.22	2.81	Luxembourg	0.49	5.21
Bangladesh	0.02	0.01	Macedonia, FYR	0.34	4.64
Belarus	0.58	7.87	Malaysia	0.08	3.88
Belgium	0.32	10.73	Mexico	0.21	1.10
Bosnia and Herzegovina	0.27	5.09	Moldova	0.33	2.48
Brazil	0.14	1.03	Mongolia	0.62	1.65
Bulgaria	0.56	2.66	Morocco	0.06	1.21
Cameroon	0.04	0.18	Mozambique	0.11	0.23
Canada	1.47	11.69	Norway	0.81	14.75
Chile	0.31	1.02	Pakistan	0.04	1.00
China	0.05	2.53	Poland	0.50	7.39
Congo, Dem. Rep.	0.05	0.04	Portugal	0.24	6.85
Cote d'Ivoire	0.03	0.29	Romania	0.54	2.51
Czech Republic	0.90	12.41	Russian Federation	0.59	6.45
Denmark	0.38	13.20	Saudi Arabia	0.05	1.54
Egypt, Arab Rep.	0.06	1.41	Serbia	0.53	3.93
Estonia	0.60	7.93	Slovenia	0.59	18.91
Finland	1.09	9.15	South Africa	0.38	2.94
France	0.45	15.47	Spain	0.36	14.70
Gabon	0.48	0.65	Sudan	0.11	0.11
Georgia	0.42	5.13	Swaziland	0.24	0.85

Germany	0.41	7.96	Sweden	1.00	13.97
Greece	0.21	3.80	Switzerland	0.44	8.73
Hungary	0.80	7.81	Syrian Arab Republic	0.11	3.36
Indonesia	0.02	1.11	Tunisia	0.35	1.34
Iran, Islamic Rep.	0.11	2.05	Turkey	0.13	4.54
Iraq	0.06	1.69	Turkmenistan	0.59	8.96
Ireland	0.42	20.80	Ukraine	0.47	3.66
Israel	0.15	2.26	United Kingdom	0.23	6.10
Italy	0.28	8.02	United States	0.72	13.50
Jordan	0.07	0.97	Uzbekistan	0.14	2.46
Kazakhstan	0.83	5.04	Vietnam	0.03	1.63

Source: The World Bank (for railways length and population, data refer to 2014); CIA Factbook (for length of paved roads).

direction) makes the capacity of the double-track lane more than twice the capacity of a single-track lane. At the same time, two single-track rail lanes connecting the same two places following different paths may result in a higher potential capacity if each of them is dedicated to a specific direction. These effects are lost when the infrastructural endowment is simply measured by the length of rail tracks.

It is then necessary to introduce measures able to represents some qualities of infrastructures. To make comparable physical data referred to qualitatively different infrastructures belonging to the same transport mode, it is possible to apply suitable coefficients (to take into account the differences in quality). Alternatively, the infrastructural endowment measures may be restricted to the part of the network that is considered more advanced. In fact, it is quite common to find comparisons solely based on the high-speed railways length, or the length of highways, i.e., the best infrastructural elements per mode.

The third way to measure the infrastructural endowment is represented by accessibility measures. From the seminal definition of accessibility as a potential of opportunities deriving from interactions (Hansen, 1959), the transport and regional economics literature, and planners too, have proposed several and different definitions and operationalizations (Geurs & Östh, 2016) of this concept. According to Geurs and van Wee (2004), we consider accessibility measures as "indicators for the impact of land-use and transport developments and policy plans on the functioning of the society in general." In particular, we refer to measures interpreting the possibility offered to people and firms to reach a particular infrastructure within specific times or the physical distance from the infrastructure (or the travel cost to be borne). These kinds of measures are specifically advisable for transport terminals; they assume the following forms: number of citizens (or firms) living within 100 km or within 1 hour of travel from an airport or from a seaport; number of people that can access to highways or railways, covering a limited number of kilometers or in limited number of minutes, etc.

All the above measures of infrastructural endowment are widely used in the current transport planning and inform most of the current transport policies.

2.1.2 The Lumpiness of Supply

Apart from the way adopted to measure the supply of transport infrastructures, an important characteristic of the system is the rigidity of supply, namely in the short run. This is simply the consequence of the difficulty to immediately and significantly change the length of rails or roads or the capacity of a transport terminal. Moreover, when this occurs it takes several time—therefore, it is essential to plan the expansion of infrastructures well in advance—and usually it determines a significant increase of capacity. In fact, the effects deriving from a marginal increase in the infrastructure endowment are quite negligible (for instance, some kilometers of a new road lane), whereas the effects of doubling a railway or of opening a new port or air terminal are potentially much more important. These indivisibilities result in a supply curve displaying some discontinuities. Therefore, the necessity to take into account the long lead-time necessary to change the transport system and the indivisibilities of capacity expansions, together with the long-run increase of transport demand, determines the lumpiness of the supply curve.

For the abovementioned reasons, for traffic volumes close to the maximum capacity of the infrastructure in the short run, the supply curve becomes rigid as shown in Fig. 2.1.

Only in the medium-long term, it may move on the right in consequence of (possible) additional capacity. The long-run supply curve, as usual, is the envelope of the lower parts of the short-run curves (Quinet & Vickerman, 2004), as shown in Fig. 2.2. The figure also shows the discontinuity that characterizes the provision of infrastructures over time.

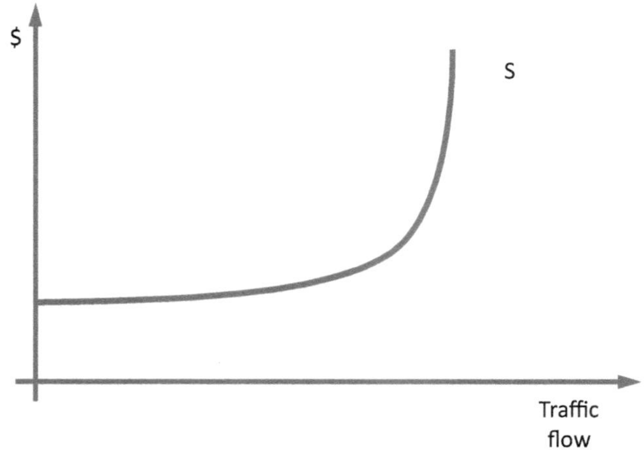

Figure 2.1 The supply curve in the short run.

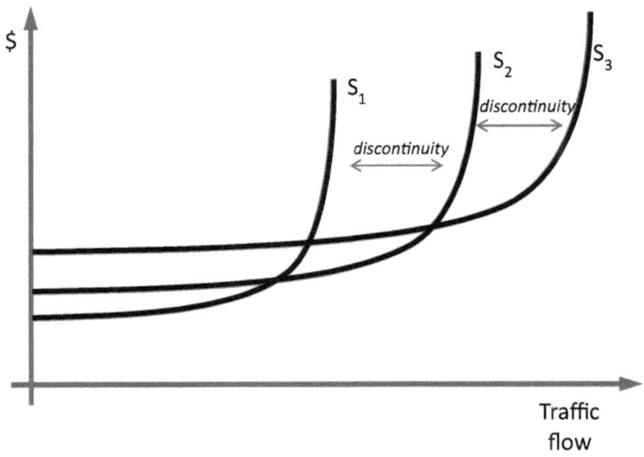

Figure 2.2 The long-run supply curve.

2.1.3 The Public Role of Infrastructures and the Role of Public in Infrastructure Planning

Transport infrastructures represent the fixed component of the transport system (Button, 1982) and determine a wide range of scale and scope economies; therefore, as underlined by Rietveld (1994), they are usually supplied as a collective input into production. It is quite common that transport infrastructures serve a multiplicity of users—in Rietveld and Bruinsma (1998) this same characteristic of infrastructures is referred to as *polyvalence*. For instance, either passenger together with cargo or, in the case of transport of passengers, the same infrastructure is used for leisure travels as well as for commuting, etc. When infrastructure serves a specific user (as in the case of a port terminal serving an industrial plant), they are strictly managed to maximize the profit of the industrial plant and the magnitude of the external impacts is limited or even null. Therefore, in this book we will concentrate on common infrastructures. Terminal facilities serve a multiplicity of users too; even if some cases of dedicated terminals are more common to be found. This is the case of some port or air terminals dedicated to a specific segment of transport demand (such as containerized cargo or cruise passengers) or also some airports in United States, but also in these cases they rarely are dedicated to a single transport operator.

Transport infrastructures determine the accessibility degree of locations and regions, thus contributing to their differentiation in the localization decision process of firms and families. Both will be more attracted by regions and locations with a higher degree of accessibility due to the possibilities of transforming accessibility into value.

The two abovementioned characteristics contribute to generate agglomeration economies (Rodrigue, Comtois, & Slack, 2006); such economies attenuate rapidly with distance (Rosenthal & Strange, 2003). This results in the formation of clusters, thus an uneven regional distribution of the economic agents. In consequence, if transport infrastructure investments, in general, determine positive economic benefits, not all regions impacted by the same infrastructure receive the same benefit, in some cases the effects may be even negative (in terms of reduction of jobs, localization disadvantages, etc.) for some regions. This kind of consequences will be further discussed in Chapter 3.

It is also in relation to these characteristics that investment in infrastructure usually involves public capital, and governments have a high interest in controlling the level of supply. Even in periods of poor public finance, the leading role of governments in infrastructure providing remains strategic for several reasons. First of all, only governments have the necessary long-run vision to engage in projects that will have possible returns well far in time; moreover, only governments have the right size to afford the important financial efforts needed by most of the infrastructural projects. In addition, the relevance of the macroeconomics effects of transport infrastructures makes them a leading tool for the development of the economics and industrial national and regional plans.

Under an economic perspective, infrastructures in several cases behave as natural monopolies (i.e., the average cost curve is subadditive) or their "high cost of provision, longevity and scale economies (...) create tendencies towards monopoly control" (Button, 1982).

In spite of the just-mentioned features, governments proved to be not the best actors for the efficient management of transport infrastructures (Nijkamp & Rienstra, 1995). That is why the deregulating and privatizing processes that took place since the late 1970s in the transport service sector progressively interested also the management of the already existing infrastructure networks. This process began in the United States with the liberalization of air transport (Kahn, 1988) and went on in Europe, mainly under the forms of privatization and deregulation processes, interesting the railways and air transport sectors—and later on, the urban transport sector. Afterward, it progressively interested several other countries and world regions. These processes went hand in hand with the enforcement of regulations and the strengthening, in some cases the birth, of regulating agencies (Button & Keeler, 1993; Friebel, Ivaldi, & Vibes, 2010).

Moreover, the lack of public finance has forced the governments to find forms of private involvement in financing infrastructural project, such as project financing contracts or more in general public—private partnerships (PPPs). Although in the former the project's cash flow guarantees the financial provisioning and the government assumes some risks linked, for example, to the duration of the planning and adoption stage of the project, in the latter, PPPs represent multiactor forms of collaboration based on shared risks, competencies, and benefits between governments and private companies (Klijn & Teisman, 2003) even if this same concept assumes different country-based meanings (Roumboutsos, 2016).

All the above features founding the intervention of governments in the provision and management of infrastructure may be grouped into three, according to Annema (2013): market failures, equity reasons, and the generation of revenues.

2.2 THE COST STRUCTURE OF TRANSPORT INFRASTRUCTURE

The costs associated with transport infrastructures may be distinguished, as usual, in fixed and variable costs but their analysis may be conducted under the view point of the subject that bears the different cost items. Concerning this latter perspective, costs can be differentiated among the following:

- Costs borne by the public (tax financed) or costs related to a private entity that manages the infrastructure and the costs due to the existence of a level of traffic that use the infrastructure (i.e., management-related costs and traffic-related costs)
- A further component is given by the externalities that both the infrastructure and the traffic flows generate on the society.

Considering the distinction among fixed and variable costs, it is noteworthy that, due to their nature, transport infrastructures present an important gap between marginal and average costs generating a time-inconsistency problem (Bergantino & Goetz, 2013). In fact, among the fixed costs are the construction costs that are extremely more expensive than the cost that annually is necessary to bear in order to maintain efficient the same infrastructure. Following relevant literature (e.g., Helm, 2009; Tsamboulas, Verma, & Moraiti, 2013), different modal infrastructures have different categorization among costs and their ratio.

Nevertheless, investment (i.e., construction) and renewal costs are the main fixed cost for any infrastructure, whereas maintenance and operation costs represent the main categories of the variable costs.

Just to have an idea of the variety of construction costs per single mode, Table 2.3 presents figures concerning the kilometric cost for some rail and road European infrastructures.

Table 2.3 shows several examples of transport infrastructure construction costs. The main difference among the provided examples is the division among nodal infrastructures or terminals (e.g., ports and airports) and connecting infrastructures (e.g., rail and road). The investment costs within the two categories are comparable but they normally differ in terms of other costs. Nevertheless, the construction of every element (or its renewal) represents the highest part of every investment plan. Differences are related to the operating costs of different alternatives. For instance, in 2015 the average rail operating cost in European Union was about 30€/train-km (with high fluctuation of more than 60€/train-km in France and about 6€/train-km in Hungary), of which about 30% related to the infrastructure management. This normally ends up with fares that cover only partially the overall operating and infrastructure historical costs. For instance, high-speed trains in France registered in 2015 an average price per pax-km of about 0.3 euro that makes approximately 152€/train-km for a full loaded train. In China, for instance, price per pax-km are about 0.07€ (with an occupancy ratio of about 70%) despite the comparable investment costs occurred in the two countries (Olivier, Songhi, & Zhou, 2014). It is important to underline that traditionally HSR do not have high densities, making difficult to cover capital costs related to the initial investment.

Also in consequence of the abovementioned reasons, often transport infrastructures are, at least partially, publicly subsidized (e.g., main national lines normally do not cover full cost with their revenues) given their social value. Fig. 2.3 shows as main literature (e.g., Button, 1982) normally represents the traditional cost infrastructure problem. Fig. 2.3 represents this problem in a graphical way.

Fig. 2.3A shows the investment cost (independent to traffic generation and then to be considered a fixed cost) of a hypothetical infrastructure and the related operating cost (the main variable cost component). Operating costs are relatively low in comparison to investment costs apart in the case of the saturation of the infrastructure capacity that generates higher operating costs (e.g., maintenance cost increases). This variable/fixed cost relationship affects the average/marginal cost development (Fig. 2.3B).

Table 2.3 Some examples of cost per kilometer of rail and road infrastructure

High-speed railways (HSR)		
Historical cost	**Country**	**€/km**
• South-East; Atlantique; Rhone Alpes; Northern Europe; Paris Interconnections; Mediterranee	France	10 M
• East European; Perpignan-Figueras; Rhine-Rhone; Nimes-Montpellier; Sud Atlantiques		13 M
• Madrid-Barcelona; Madrid-Seville	Spain	9 M
• Madrid-French border; Malaga-Costa del Sol; Valladolid-Madrid; Madrid-Alicante-Murcia		15 M
• Florence-Rome; Rome-Naples; Turin-Novara	Italy	32 M
• Novara-Milan; Milano-Bologna; Bologne-Florence; Milan-Venice;		45 M
• 350 km/h high-speed links (e.g., Shijiazhuang—Zhengzhou)	China	13 M
• 250 km/h links (e.g., Nanning—Guangzhou)		9 M
• Seoul-Gimpo (airport link)	Korea, Rep.	91 M
Highways		
Estimation of new infrastructure	**Country**	**€/km**
New highways	UK	7.5 M
North Marmara motorway (government estimation)	Turkey	13.5 M
New highways	Poland	9.6 M
New highways	Norway	18 M
New highways	Spain	6.7 M
New highways	Lithuania	4 M
M4—Gojra–Shorkot	Pakistan	3 M
Nodal infrastructure		
Project	**Country**	**€**
Maasvlakte 2 (Port of Rotterdam)	The Netherland	3 billion
Calgary airport	Canada	1.8 billion

Source: Own elaboration on various websites.

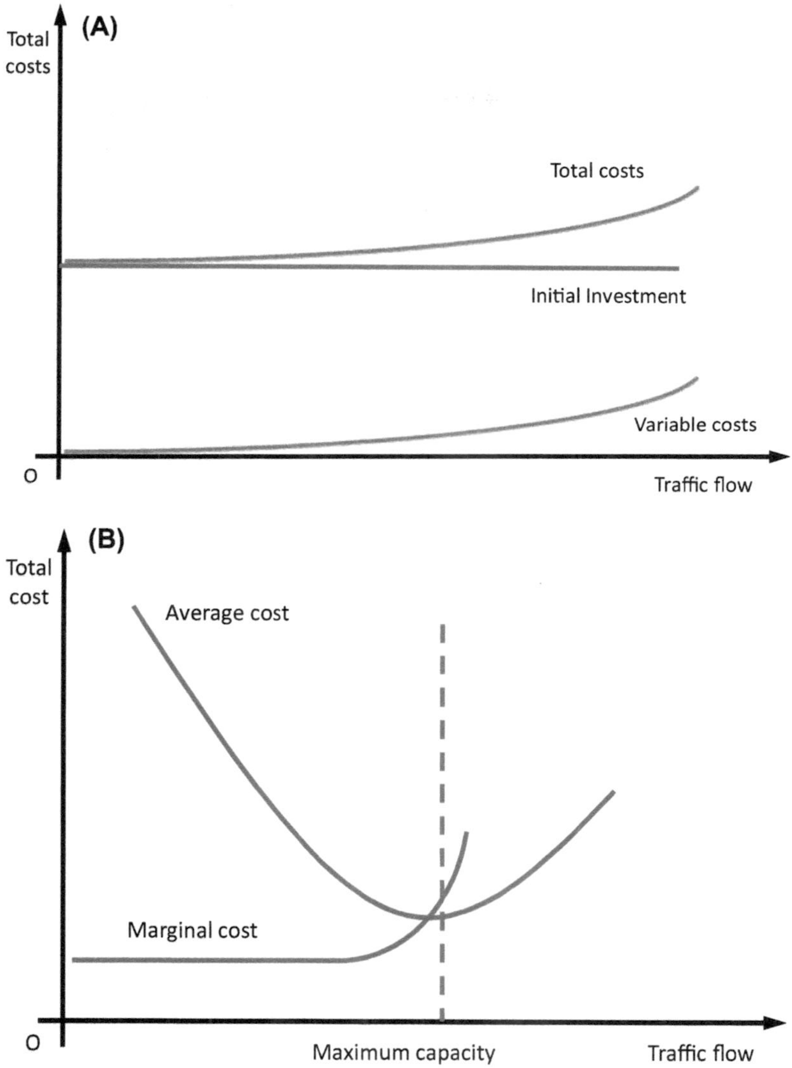

Figure 2.3 Total (A), average and marginal (B) cost curves.

The average cost is the overall cost per unit of traffic (i.e., the total cost divided per traffic units), whereas marginal costs are normally defined as the cost of the additional inputs needed to produce an additional unit of output (Box 2.1). Thus, given the abovementioned trend for fixed and variable costs, average costs are initially high for the infrastructure managers (due to high fixed costs), and they progressively reduce depending on the traffic volume. On the other hand, marginal costs are generally low (thanks to the

Box 2.1 Scale economies in transport infrastructure: evidences from the literature

The transport and industrial organization literatures have empirically investigated the cost structure of transport nodes such as airports and terminal ports. In the case of airports, a very recent literature review (Bottasso & Conti, 2017) has highlighted that small airports clearly operate with a technology characterized by scale economies: this might suggest that small airports might incur in financial problems because of marginal costs might fall short of average costs, which in turn requires nonmarginal cost pricing or subsides that could be justified (under appropriate cost benefit analysis) as long as airports deliver wider economic benefits to the surrounding areas in terms of additional trade and productivity, as discussed in Chapter 7. By way of contrast, the empirical evidence suggests that larger airports are more likely to enjoy smaller-scale economies (as found, for a sample of large international airports, by Martin and Voltes Dorta (2011)) or constant or even diseconomies of scale (as reported, for the largest UK airports, by Bottasso and Conti (2012)). Indeed, as the scale of operations grows, more stringent environmental constraints, land scarcity, and difficulties in running large airports might generate diseconomies of scale. After all, as noted by Gillen (2011), "doubling throughput more than doubles the space needed so there may well be diseconomies of scale with terminals."

In the case of seaports, there are several attempts to measure the efficiency of port terminals and the existence of increasing returns to scale both by using data envelopment analysis (DEA models) and stochastic frontier analysis (SFA). For instance, Cullinane and Wang (2006) comparing 69 European container terminals found that "a large scale of production is more likely to be associated with high efficiency scores." This is in line with results found by Barros and Athanassiou (2004) for Greek and Portuguese container ports and also with Bottasso et al. (2011) that analyzing a small sample of Italian container terminals through an SFA found a slight increasing return to scale. Moreover, Total Factor Productivity seems positively impacted by technical and scale changes as also confirmed by Chang and Tovar (2014) studying a sample of Chilean and Peruvian seaports. It is worth noticing that considering containerized trades the scale economies of port terminals may be induced by the evolutionary trend characterizing the liner shipping industry and in particular the deployment of ever bigger containerships that obviously need a corresponding evolution of terminals to appropriately serve the calling ship.

Finally, there is also a literature on scale economies in the management of highways and railways infrastructures. In the case of railways, Benfratello, Iozzi, and Valbonesi (2003) analyzed the cost structure of 20 Italian highways concessionaries and found mixed evidence. Indeed, they report evidence of scale economies for a network of up to 2000 km; however, if the largest

Box 2.1 Scale economies in transport infrastructure: evidences from the literature—cont'd

concessionaire is excluded from their sample, economies of scale seem to be exhausted for a network of about 300 km. Interestingly, returns to density are never exhausted, i.e., for a given network size, an increase in users is always associated with a less than proportional increase in costs. In the case of railways infrastructure management, Smith (2006) reports positive returns to density but diseconomies of scale for the United Kingdom and notes that previous US evidence is broadly consistent with constant scale economies, whereas most EU studies found diseconomies of scale. It is, however, important to recognize that the railways industry is complex to analyze because of the vertical integration between the operations of passenger and freight services on one side, and the management on the infrastructure on the other side, which leads to the necessity to study scope economies deriving from vertical (dis)integration.

operating cost trend), and they increase only when the infrastructure is achieving its saturation. This relation often generates deficit for the infrastructure manager (Fig. 2.3B shows that if the tariff for the use of the infrastructure is set equal to the marginal cost, unless the transport flow is close to the maximum capacity of the infrastructure, revenues will be lower than costs[2]). Thus, it is necessary for the public sector to invest in transport infrastructure (at least subsidizing major projects) or to regulate the sector (since it is often observed a tendency to monopolistic market organizations). Often, this need is connected to the idea that transport serves a social purpose and—to some extent—transport infrastructure should be treated as public good, namely nonrivalry good, i.e., a good "which all enjoy in common in the sense that each individual's consumption of such a good leads to no subtraction from any other individual's consumption of that good" (Samuelson, 1954).

Another characteristic of the infrastructure investment is the production of externalities. Apart from monetary factors, transport infrastructure generates different kind of external costs and benefits. Blum (1998) underlines how public investment in transport infrastructure provision is often related to the creation of positive externalities or—at least—the possibility to reduce negative externalities currently present in a specific region.

Despite this approach, many authors (e.g., Bocarejo & Oviedo, 2012; Holl, 2004a,b) register divergent opinions on the actual value of the generated transport infrastructure externalities. Main categories of positive and negative externalities related to transport could be summarized as follows:

- *Utility*, an increase of connectivity can generate more than proportional effects on the utility perceived by an infrastructure user, generating induced demand or other location effects (e.g., increasing tourism);
- *Accessibility*, a transport infrastructure investment can normally assure a higher degree of accessibility, influencing further investment in a given region or a reduction of both consumption and production costs. Nevertheless, Rietveld and Bruinsma (1998) register the presence of also costs related to an increase of regional accessibility, such as a major threat to local production activities;
- *Environment*, transport infrastructures are normally characterized by high impact on the environment in both the construction phase (e.g., landscape, modification of the natural environment) and during the infrastructure operating life (e.g., air and water pollution, noise). Nonetheless, given the different impacts of the several transport modes, the correct planning could help reducing current level of external transport cost on the environment (e.g., reduction of road transport pollution through a new investment in rail connection);
- *Society*, transport investment could generate indirect cost–benefit to the society due to the different characteristics of both the transport infrastructure and of the existing alternatives. Among the externalities related to this category, congestion, risk, and safety and security issues could be accounted as main generated costs.

Those external effects influence both the perceived private costs of the transport service (and then the perceived value of the infrastructure investment) and the real overall generated effects of the transport infrastructure on a given region. These two categories of elements—together with the high fixed costs—normally explain the intervention of public authorities in the investment appraisal and in the market regulation. For instance, main externalities are included in the different infrastructure investment evaluation processes (e.g., Beria, Giove, & Miele, 2012), mainly using a monetization of the different impacts to be added to the usual financial items.

Concerning the first category of effect (i.e., the different perceived value of transport activity between the private user and the real social generated costs), this is due to the difference between the cost of transportation for the private user, that is connected to the simple transport costs (i.e., fuel, vehicle, toll, insurance) and that is borne by the society that either partially

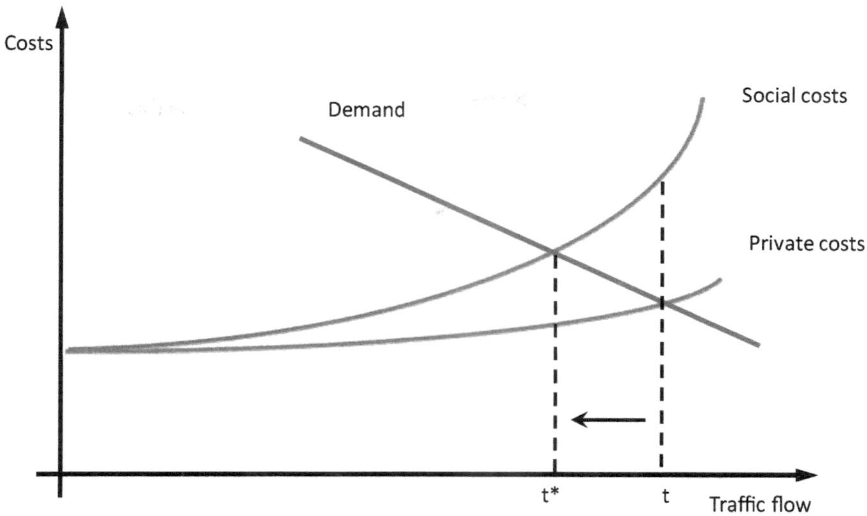

Figure 2.4 The Pigouvian approach.

pay the infrastructure (e.g., subsidize) to lower down the access fee or is paid in terms of external costs (e.g., congestion, air pollution generated by the transport). Thus, in both the investment planning and in the infrastructure management, the user perceives only a part of the overall generated cost. A particular example is given by the Pigouvian approach (Fig. 2.4) applied to transportation problems (Knitter & Sandler, 2015; Rothengatter, 2015) in which, following the theory introduced by Pigou (1929), it is shown how the internalization of the overall social cost within the private user cost would reduce the transport demand (and in accordance with Pigou approach this tax could be further used to either reduce negative externalities or increase better performing solutions).

The difference between private and social cost appears fundamental in both public subsidization activities and in transport planning activity. In fact, often highest cost infrastructure (e.g., railways) could either generate less negative externalities in comparison to cheaper solutions (e.g., road transport) or account for higher positive externalities. For instance, while NIMBY (not-in-my-backyard) syndrome characterizes all main infrastructural investment projects (Tillema, Hamersma, Sussman, & Arts, 2012), this is particularly important for transport infrastructures, mainly in relation to the difficult estimation of externalities in the overall project evaluation (and then in a precise estimation of overall social costs and benefits).

Related to this latter element, the second category of factors to be linked to the cost-related externalities of transport investment is their monetization process. In fact, several government bodies (e.g., Profillidis, Botzoris, & Galanis, 2014) estimate the local values of projects to be associated with specific costs (e.g., landscape, natural environment, risk, congestion, pollution) generated from transportation-related activity (both at investment and service level). This is normally included in every assessment exercise. These evaluations, which should normally be developed at local level, can be considered highly volatile and are not easy to be generalized, even at regional scale. The evaluation methodology is normally included in national and international guidelines (e.g., Maibach et al., 2010; World Bank, 1998) and distinguished per different category, transport mode, and technologies. This differentiation is normally linked to the performance of a determined vehicle (e.g., truck vs. city car) in respect to the environment in which the effect is created (e.g., high density populated area vs. countryside). For this reason, landscape costs related to a new bridge in a remote region could be different from the "same" landscape costs of a new bridge within a city centre or in an environmentally protected area.

In relation to the abovementioned division of transport infrastructure cost, it is important to underline that often part of the costs connected to the investment phase are to be considered sunk costs, i.e., not recoverable. This issue is mainly related to the fact that part of the activities (e.g., project, administration, and capital costs) occurred independently on the evolution of the investment and are not directly connected to potential modifications of the overall project. Thus, although some cost items could be recovered if the project fails or it is modified, sunk costs are still generated, also influencing the future land use of the infrastructure area (e.g., Litman, 1995). Moreover, a part few cases of railways lanes transformed into bike or pedestrian routes, in general, when infrastructures are dismissed there are no alternative uses.

For the abovementioned characteristics, historically both private and public bodies have funded transport infrastructures, depending on the capability of transport facilities to generate enough revenues or to be linked to general public purposes (e.g., Helm & Thompson, 1991). Despite this, because transport infrastructures are highly capital intensive, starting from the XX century, public authorities were heavily involved in the transport investment project, all over the world. Starting from the last two decades of the XX century, this tendency has been radically modified mainly in relation to the growing public debts of many countries and the research of technological know-how of many developing economies (e.g., South America). These new tendencies push governments to promote different managerial solutions, normally linked to Public–Private Investments, as defined by the World Bank (2016). These agreements normally assure to the actors involved a reduced risk in the investment and the possibility to share cost and know-how, limiting the managerial difficulties related to the initial high investment cost (Tsamboulas et al., 2013).

2.2.1 The Cost of Transport in Relation to Distance

The transport modes differ for several characteristics, in particular we refer to flexibility and size of vehicles.

The road transport presents the narrowest range of size of vehicles. In case of transport of passengers, it ranges from one person (the driver) to some decades of passengers when people take the bus, whereas in case of freight transport, the range goes from small urban van to trucks that can load at best two TEU (Twenty Equivalent Unit, the unit of measure of containerized cargo). Nevertheless, road transport is the most flexible mode, and the cost of access to road network is quite negligible. For this reason every voyage starts and ends using a road transport mean.

In railways transport the size of vehicles is bigger than in road transport. A passenger train can move hundreds of people—the exact number depends on the type of service (high-speed trains, commuters, or regional trains), but it is not so easy to be accessed and in case of high-level services, as the high-speed trains, the cost of access is higher as only a limited number of rail stations are served by this type of service. In the case of freight transport, the capacity of a freight train depends on the physical and technical characteristics of the infrastructure that define the length of the train. In Europe, a train 650 m. long can move approximately 5,200 tons. The cost of loading and unloading a train is higher than the same cost for the road transport, due to the biggest volume of passengers or cargo and also due to the necessity to tranship passengers or cargo from road to rail transport.

The seaborne transport is the mode presenting the highest range of sizes, the biggest vessels in passenger transport are the cruise ships that reach even a capacity of more than 5000 cruisers, whereas in the freight transport the biggest full containerships reach a nominal capacity of 19,000 TEU and the biggest dry bulk carriers belonging to the "Capesize" category have a DWT (dead weight tonnage) capacity of more than 80,000 tons. Nevertheless, the seaborne transport presents a multitude of small and medium vessels, which makes this mode of transport extremely flexible in terms of vessels capacity. Notwithstanding, this mode may be accessed only through a sea/river port terminal, then the access cost is the highest in the whole transport system due to the cost of loading/unloading the vessel and due to the fact the ports are almost scattered in space.

The air transport behaves similarly to seaborne transport, namely in case of passengers. The vehicle size does not reach the number of the biggest ships, but they are impressive too. For instance, the Airbus 380 can host from 525 to 853 passengers depending on the seats configuration, and the biggest cargo airplane can carry heavy cargo weighing up to 250 tons. Airports as ports are scattered in place and the cost of access to them coupled with the cost of loading and unloading vehicles is high.

Infrastructures contribute to the cost of transport with two components: the first is the cost of entering (the terminal cost) and using the infrastructure system and the second is represented by the cost of accessing a specific infrastructure. The overall cost of transport is achieved adding to these components the cost associated with the use of a transport mean. This cost grows with the distance covered by any specific user or vehicle. Therefore the function of total cost of transport (TCT) in respect to distance (expressed in kilometers) is

$$\mathrm{TCT}(d) = AI + ACV \cdot d$$

where, AI is the cost to access the infrastructure (not dependent by the distance traveled) and ACV is the kilometric cost of the vehicle and d is the traveled distance.

Any transport mode has its own TCT curve that differs both for the different cost of accessing the infrastructure and also for the kilometric cost of the vehicles used. Fig. 2.5A represents the TCT curves for the road, rail, and seaborne transport mode, whereas Fig. 2.5B shows the respective average curves (derived from the curves of Fig. 2.5A). The different size of vehicles available in each transport mode, and consequently their economies of scale, contributes to reduce the average cost with the increase of distance covered.

It is then clear how any transport mode has a range of distances for which it should be preferred to the others. In particular, the road transport is the mode that due to its flexibility and low cost of access is preferred for short trips. At the opposite, the seaborne transport—and the air transport, that behaves similarly—is preferred for the long (mainly international) trips. The railways stay in the middle, and they compete with road transport for

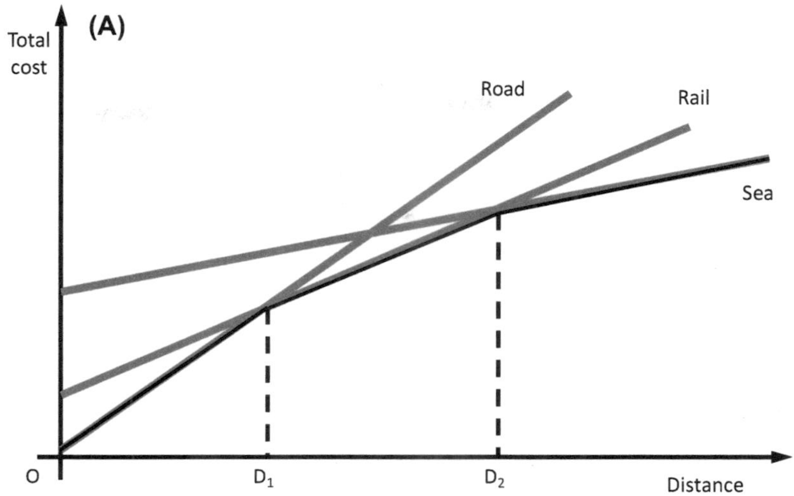

Figure 2.5A Total cost in respect to distance for three transport modes.

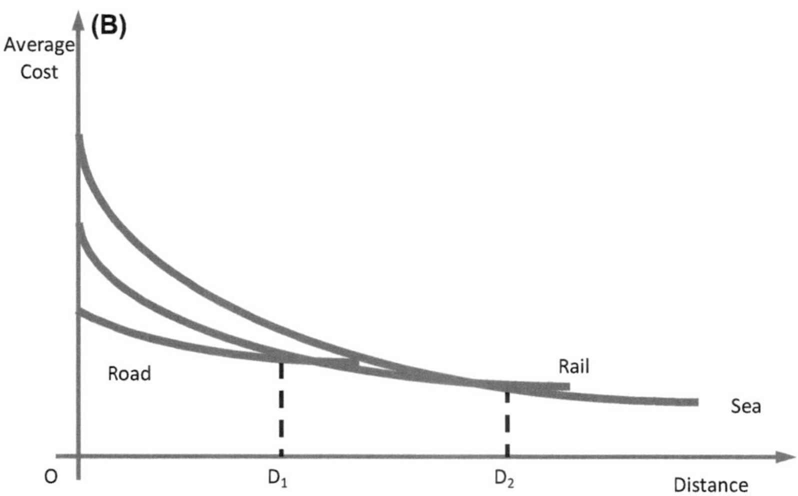

Figure 2.5B Average cost in respect to distance for three transport modes.

short trips and when trips become much longer they may be replaced by the sea transport (as the short sea shipping services). (Box. 2.2)

2.3 THE LIFE CYCLE OF TRANSPORT INFRASTRUCTURE

Transport infrastructures have a very long life span. They are subject to periodical adjustments or revamping, but when we run a railway or a road it

Box 2.2 Infrastructure access and charges

The peculiar shape of cost curves of transport infrastructure together with their nature of essential facilities introduces the problem of the most convenient way to both guarantee a fair access to the infrastructure to a plurality of potential operators and charging its use.

Concerning the charging policies, on the one hand, because most infrastructures operate in a monopolistic environment, the monopolistic price guarantees that all costs are recovered by revenues. Nevertheless, this result implies a reduction in the transport flow and prevents infrastructure to spread all of its (possible) positive external effects. On the other hand, an infrastructure charged at the marginal cost fixes the traffic flow when the transport demand encounters the marginal cost curve, but unless the infrastructure is heavily congested marginal cost is below average cost (due to the economies of scale typical of infrastructure), and then the infrastructure manager operates with losses. In this case, the infrastructure is managed to maximize the traffic flow, and the difference between average and marginal cost may be covered through a subsidy.

Apart from these two opposite criteria to determine the right charge for infrastructure use, the economic literature proposes several other methods to determine a charge that balances the purpose of recovering the operating costs and the goal of maximizing the demand served (i.e., the traffic flow). Among different alternatives, the social marginal cost pricing includes in the infrastructure cost also the external costs (due to accidents, pollution, contribution to global warming, etc.), thus increasing the cost for the users—in respect to the (private) marginal cost price—and reducing the traffic flow. Another alternative is the two-part tariff proposed as infrastructure charge in which users pay a fixed tariff that covers the fixed cost and a variable tariff that is proportional to the infrastructure use (e.g., the number of journeys or the distance covered). The sum of the two-part tariffs for all the users covers all the costs of the infrastructure manager. Similar to a two-part tariff is the Ramsey pricing method that sets the variable part of the two-part tariff inversely proportional to the demand elasticity; in this way the fully recovering of the infrastructure cost is obtained with the minimum reduction of transport flow (i.e., users). The Ramsey rule recalls the principle of "charging what the traffic can bear" that means that as transport is demanded for something else—to reach a place, a market or a production plant—the price for the use of an infrastructure must take into account the value that users gain from it (Jansson & Shneerson, 1979; Marchese, 1996); at the same time the Ramsey rule may allow for market abuse toward customers with a low elasticity; therefore, the consequences of its adoption should be well considered.

Often charging strategies are connected to the rules that apply for operators to access the infrastructure. In fact, charges are normally related to the possibility for transport users to exploit the transport services, such as for the payment of the bus tariff or the price of having access to the motorway.

Box 2.2 Infrastructure access and charges—cont'd

A connected issue is represented by the possibility to have access to a certain infrastructure from a transport operator point of view. In this situation, the rules (and prices) are referred not to the final user of the transport service but to the operator that will exploit the use of the transport infrastructure to provide the transport service itself. Access to infrastructure is therefore a key element for understanding the potential impact of transport on a certain region, given its connection with both the final transport charge and with the generated flow. For this reason, access policies are often connected to the regulation of the transport infrastructure (e.g., public, private, PPP, franchise system, dedicated infrastructure) as well as to the possibility for a plurality of operators to operate within the same infrastructure or the need of having an exclusive use. Relevant examples are both the rail and the airport sectors in which slot charges represent the way to assign a time period in which operators can use the needed infrastructure (as discussed by Adler et al. (2014) for the liberalization of Asian airport sector and by Sentence (2003) in terms of desirable auction process). In most cases, the infrastructure is managed by specific operators after a tendering process (e.g., as in the case of concessions for the port sector (Pallis, Notteboom, & De Langen, 2008); and in the case of most motorway systems (Albalate & Bel, 2009)), and this tendering process establish access rules and—in some cases—users' charges as well. In this case, the main goal of the infrastructure access policy is to guarantee a fair use of the infrastructure, optimizing the management of the transport infrastructure and regulating the users' tariffs based on the rate of return or imposing a price-cap.

The connection between users' charges and access strategy is well represented by the multipart tariffs used in the railways sector for determining the access to infrastructure use (Crozet, 2004); two-part tariffs often used for determining the users' charge are peculiar examples of the multipart tariff. In few cases, the costs borne by the infrastructure operator are recovered through a shadow-toll that is not paid directly by users but by a public body to the infrastructure manager. In this way, the toll does not impact on the users' transport choices but the infrastructure is operated without monetary losses. This kind of charge was introduced in Portuguese motorways in the late 1990s (Santos & Santos, 2012) and later abandoned to move to a toll system. In this case, toll system is sometime connected to different alternatives that might discriminate differentiated users, such as in the case of differentiated tariffs between cars, motorbike, and truck within several motorways systems.

Lastly, several regulations (as in the case of the rail sector in Europe (Nash, 2005) and transport authorities (as Acciaro & Vasileios (2018) discuss for Port Authorities) introduced environmental and social aspects in the access charges, adding either the environmental risk of using the infrastructure or the generated environmental costs to the tariff paid by the operator to access to the infrastructure.

is quite common to pass on something that was projected and built even several decades (sometimes centuries) before.

This aspect is even more common in the case of specific kinds of infrastructure, such as tunnels and channels. For instance, the Panama Canal, that represents a strategic node in the maritime transport network, was initially opened in 1914 and it was recently enlarged in 2016, i.e., one century afterward. Similarly, Suez Canal was first opened in 1869 and renewed in 2016. Not only maritime infrastructures are normally characterized by such great life span; for instance, the AlpTransit rail tunnel, opened in 2016, has replaced the Gotthard rail tunnel—bridging Italy and Switzerland beneath the Alps—originally opened in 1882. Similarly, although main roadways are often under maintenance, main structures are normally everlasting infrastructures (e.g., Roman road system, part of the Chinese silk road).

The long life span of a transport infrastructure, from the planning stage to its replacement, may be usefully split into six stages, as summarized in Table 2.4.

The first stage is the period of time that is necessary for the planning of the infrastructure. The duration of this period depends on several factors: in particular the complexity of the infrastructure and/or of the project and the complexity of the bureaucratic procedure and the number of analyses that are necessary for the formal approval of the project (for example, in Europe, projects for new railways or highways need the environmental effects assessment, whereas less relevant projects are exempted or follow

Table 2.4 The stages of infrastructure life cycle

Stage	Main features
1. Planning	This stage contains the evaluation process of the projected infrastructure and its alternatives
2. Building	This stage contains the capital investment in infrastructure
3. Start-up	In this stage the cash flow of the infrastructure is progressively positive even if the capacity exceeds the demand
4. Maturity	In this stage the infrastructure is adequate to the level of demand and its economic effects are at the highest level
5. Obsolescence	In this stage the infrastructure is out-of-date and it often is congested
6. Renewal/ Replacement	The infrastructure is replaced by another one (in some cases it may change its original purpose) or it is revamped to start a new life cycle

simplified procedures). In this stage, the main risk is associated with the political goodwill to carry on a specific infrastructural project and the duration of the bureaucratic course.

The second stage is the period of time taken by the infrastructure building. Its duration depends on the complexity of the project (as in the case of the channel tunnel linking France to United Kingdom beneath the English Channel) or on the length of the path in the case of road or rail infrastructure. But it may also vary in accordance with the availability of financial resources. In this stage, the risk due to the lack of finance—i.e., the possibility that the construction work will be delayed or that they will be interrupted—is progressively reduced.

The third stage (start-up) starts when the infrastructure begins to serve the transport demand. Initially, the infrastructure presents an overcapacity since the traffic is well below the maximum capacity. This is due to its long life and therefore the necessity to plan any infrastructure improvement staring at the transport demand forecasted in the long run. In this stage also revenues are quite low, but increasing, and the cash flow is turning positive in respect of the previous stages. The duration of this stage depends on the evolution of transport demand and also on the way the infrastructure interacts with the other elements of the transport network.

The fourth stage is the stage of maturity. It occurs when the infrastructure serves the demand at its maximum level. In this stage also the external effects of transport infrastructure are the highest. This stage usually lasts for several years, sometimes decades, and its duration may be extended by extraordinary maintenance or by adopting some technological innovation (i.e., deepening the use of capital in the production function). For instance, in the railways sector, the adoption of ERTMS/ETCS (European Rail Traffic Management System/European Train Control System) may increase the rate of utilization of rail trucks and the safety of rail traffic, thus permitting to continue to serve a growing demand for rail transport services without investing in new rail lanes. In this stage, some cases of congestion may occur, but they are still sporadic.

When the infrastructure becomes overutilized and congestion periods are more frequent, then the service level for passengers and freight downgrades. It means that the infrastructure is entering the obsolescence stage. The duration of this fifth stage depends on the willingness to cope with this deficiency of the transport infrastructure and also on the availability of financial means to renew or replace the old infrastructure.

The infrastructure life cycle ends with a sixth stage that may assume a twofold meaning. In fact, people in charge of deciding when and how to invest in infrastructure may preliminary choose whether to renew the congested (or out-of-date) and already existing infrastructure—for instance, building an additional lane on a highway or removing possible bottlenecks limiting the capacity of the infrastructure—or to replace the old infrastructure with a new one. In both cases, this stage causes a new cycle in the life of the infrastructure.

Fig. 2.6 summarizes how costs and revenues associate with the construction and management of infrastructure move during its life cycle.

The abovementioned life span description is strictly linked to the cost structure. Although investment costs are concentrated in the first two stages, operating costs and revenues are distributed along the following three stages. During the sixth stage both operating and investment costs could occur, depending on the decision-making process for the further infrastructural development.

A fundamental issue in the transport infrastructure investment topic is the phenomenon of path dependence. According to Puffert (2002) "a path-dependent economic process is one in which specific contingent events—and not just fundamental determinative factors like technology,

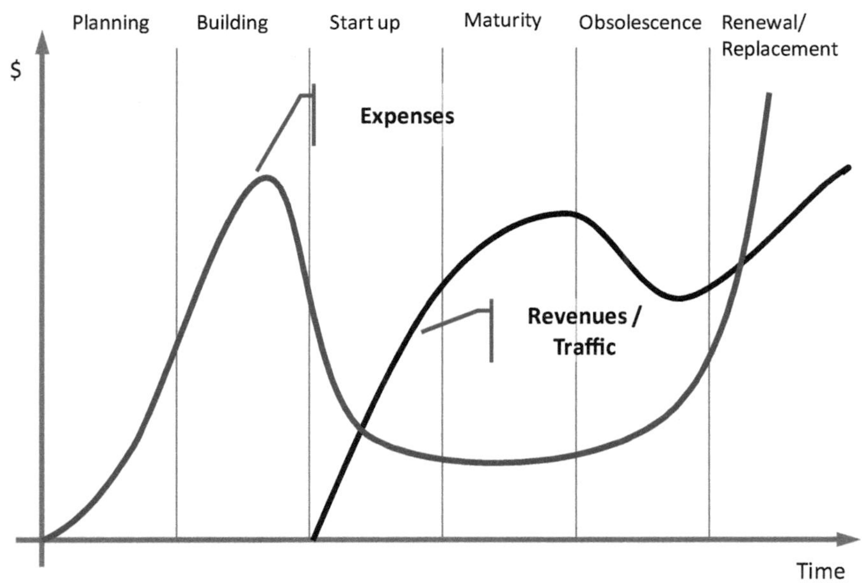

Figure 2.6 Expenses and revenues along the infrastructure life cycle.

preferences, factor endowments, and institutions— have a persistent effect on the subsequent course of allocation". This element is well spread in transport studies because the strategic investment choices in transportation elements have a strong influence in the future transport policy. A relevant example of this element in transport investment is both the alternative decision of improving specific infrastructure typologies (e.g., motorway system, unpaved roads) and the persisting adoption of certain standards. An example could be identified in the rail gauge standardization process. Historically, different rail companies adopted different gauge measures, whereas now almost 60% of the rail network adopts the so-called Stephenson gauge (1,435 mm). Both the persistency of the differences and the adoption of a standard cannot be explained by specific determinative factors but only through the repetition of contingent events. Thus, apart from specific supranational events (e.g., TransEuopean Network in Europe, One-Belt-One-Road strategy in Asia), rail gauge appears as a persistent factor, despite technological or economic-driven factors that could lead to different outcomes. Similar issues happen in the regional transport planning (Xie & Levinson, 2013) and in the infrastructure governance (Notteboom, De Langen, & Jacobs, 2013). Thus, once an infrastructure—and its characteristics—is planned, it has to take into account the context in which it is embedded and it will influence the future planning of the given region, not only in terms of capacity (or externalities) but also considering the adopted technology and the general regional endowment. The transport planning is then linked to a sequence of events in which each choice will promote a subsequent action. In the markets characterized by path dependence, even in cases of not optimal choices, it is costlier to modify the adopted solutions than using suboptimal ones.

Apart from the phenomenon of path dependency, a correct planning activity is also connected to the Braess paradox (1968) in which the author stated that "it is indicated by an example that an extension of the road network may cause a redistribution of the traffic which results in longer individual running times", this is because transport flows are normally not only linked to the infrastructure provision as a whole but to at least other three elements: competing transport alternatives, bottlenecks, and flows distribution. Thus, in certain conditions, an additional transport infrastructure could turn to increase congestion (on a specific transport mode) and negative externalities instead of improving the general transport scenario.

Transport infrastructure should be then studied as part of the integrated transport network, and investments should always consider the effects of the new infrastructure in both time (i.e., path dependence) and space (e.g., Braess paradox).

2.4 TOWARD SMART INFRASTRUCTURES

In recent years, any process is of no value if it cannot benefit from the adjective "smart". And as correctly pointed out by Glancy (2015), "smart cities require smart transportation".

So in the final part of this introductory chapter on transport infrastructure, we will investigate what is usually meant with smart transport or smart infrastructures, what changes this concept is going to have on the current transport network, and current expectations on the changes the infrastructure network will have in the future.

The main concept behind the term "smart" is a strict and continuous interconnection among infrastructure and vehicles, based on the massive adoption of new technologies that ultimately will reduce, or even avoid, the human intervention in driving vehicles or in controlling and managing traffic flows.

If the currently modern infrastructures are usually referred to as "intelligent infrastructure" due to the adoption of Intelligent Transport Systems (ITS) operating in a "vertical" sense, i.e., favoring interconnection between infrastructure and vehicles within a specific transport mode (as, for example, the dynamic messages signs already installed in many highways or interstate roads enabling drivers to change their behavior in accordance to the service level of the infrastructure they are using), the next evolutionary stage will be characterized by a dramatic increase of technology in both infrastructures and vehicles that will allow the full integration of the different transport modalities.

This modal vertical integration—i.e., a close connection between infrastructure and vehicles—is a matter of fact for railways. In fact, automated metropolitan trains are a reality and the most advanced rail lanes—as the high-speed rail networks—highly rely on technology in the sense trains adapt their speed based on the information they instantaneously receive from the rail tracks and if the train driver does not change the speed in accordance with the message received the locomotive will automatically change it. This is, in short, how the European Rail Traffic Management System (ERTMS) operates through the information exchange between the locomotive and tracks using the GSM radio system. This system, or similar ones, will progressively be adopted on the whole railways networks.

The other transport modes will follow the same path, and probably will go even further. Namely the road system has recently accelerated this process. Along with the development of electric vehicles the automobile producers have been heavily investing in ITS, enabling drivers to be more conscious of their driving (checking for pedestrians, detecting the blind spots, measuring the distance in respect of the in front vehicles, etc.) all of them finalized to the introduction of fully automated cars and trucks. Manyika et al. (2013) consider that the advent of automated vehicles will represent a future disruptive technology, as it surely was the advent of railways in the first half of the 19th century and the motorization in the 20th century.

Several are the possible advantages deriving from this future scenario. First of all, when the surface transport systems—road and rail—will be operated by automated vehicles, everyone expects that the rate of incidents and fatalities will dramatically drop. At the same time, being the traffic flows more, or even completely, homogeneous the capacity of infrastructure will increase without any physical expansion of the infrastructure, i.e., without any (additional) land request (Bagloee, Tavana, Asadi, & Oliver, 2016). This result will also be favored by a greater use of public transport for urban mobility needs made possible by an improvement in the efficiency of public services and the replacement of part of the current transport demand by forms of digital mobility and a wide use of shared forms of mobility. This in turn will have also positive effects on the environment.

In this future scenario characterized by a transport driverless system, in which even the transport path is automatically selected to minimize the generalized transport cost (based on real-time data and not on a predefined scenario as currently happens with most car navigators), also the value of time spent in travel will completely change due to the real possibility to use travel time for different purposes, as leisure or work or else.

Moreover, the most important effects could derive from the interconnection of infrastructures. An integrated (instead of sectorial) approach to infrastructures will contribute to optimize the investment for additional capacity, redistributing traffic flows to take into account the externalities (in particular, environmental effects) and at the same time to optimally use the transport capacity available. This should definitively increase intermodality thanks to the choice of the right mode and transport path in respect of the infrastructural and service conditions existing when the demand of transport rises. These positive effects need a completely change in the approach to transport infrastructure problems toward a greater cross-mode (or cross-sectorial) coordination of interventions and a unique policy to transform the current mode transport systems into a "system-of-systems" (Hickford et al., 2015). In this scenario, the so-called synchromodality could realize, this implies that the choice about the transport mode or vehicle to be used to move cargo is based on the set of vehicles or modes available in real times, i.e., at the same moment in which a transport demand rises. Synchromodality should optimize the trade-offs between the quality and cost aspects of multiple modalities adding flexibility to the supply chain (Tavasszy, Behdani, & Konings, 2015).

The current infrastructural system needs huge investment to realize this plausible scenario, in particular in Information and Telecommunication Technology (ICT), to be ready to satisfy the increasing transport demand and to exploit its potential benefits.

To sum up with a slogan: the increasing transport demand may be faced not exclusively with more infrastructure but above all with qualitatively better infrastructure.

CHAPTER 3

Transport Infrastructure and Economic Activity: Theoretical Issues

Contents

Transport infrastructure investments are one of the components of transport policies, together with price instruments and regulation. Such investments can take the form of new infrastructure works, upgrading existing endowment and improving transport services. The main objectives of transport policies include boosting growth, reducing disparities, improving social inclusion and sustainability; their effectiveness depends on several factors, not only associated with changes in agents' expectations and incentives but also linked to the implementation of complementary non-transport policies that enable transport policies to fully convey their effects.

The immediate impact of an expansion in transport network capacity (or an improvement in its quality) is to lower transport costs by reducing distance, congestion, and travel times. As a result, production costs drop, factors productivity increases, and output grows (provided that private capital investments are not crowded out).

In a nutshell, these are the predictions of traditional growth theoretical models (exogenous and endogenous growth models), which, however, do not provide specific microeconomic foundations.[1] Indeed, real effects of transport infrastructure investments stem from different possible transmission mechanisms and processes activated by agents' response to

[1] A comprehensive survey of growth theory is found in Barro and Sala I Martin (2004).

Economic Role of Transport Infrastructure
ISBN 978-0-12-813096-4
https://doi.org/10.1016/B978-0-12-813096-4.00003-2

monetary and time savings, which have been analyzed by the New Economic Georaphy (NEG).

According to the NEG literature, trade and location choices taken by workers and firms are the main economic decisions that are able to explain the wider economic effects associated with transport infrastructure investments. Such decisions are significantly affected by barriers to mobility of goods and factors, mainly related to transport infrastructure inefficiency.

The improvement in transport infrastructure, by reducing travel time and costs, increases markets accessibility and favors trade, thus enlarging relevant markets for firms and allowing the exploitation of comparative advantages and scale economies. Interregional and cross-country trade expansion generate output growth and induce productivity, enhancing competitive pressure that affects firm dynamics, economy restructuring, and improvement in the quality of production factors. Moreover, higher intraindustry trade supports the diffusion of technology and knowledge, thus promoting innovation and growth.

Turning to location choices, improved transportation may lead to the agglomeration of firms and workers that cluster to take advantage of economies of scale, thicker markets, higher backward and forward intra-industry and interindustry linkages, larger varieties of goods, better information, and knowledge spillovers. The concentration of economic activity generates pecuniary and nonpecuniary externalities that promote growth. However, firms and worker reallocation generates also dispersion forces associated with congestion, increase in the price of nontradable goods and land rents. The balance of these forces endogenously determines the spatial distribution of economic activity.

Most NEG models suggest that when transport costs decrease from high to medium, agglomeration becomes more likely, while further reductions reduce the advantages of concentration because proximity becomes less important. Hence, declines in transport costs may produce a bell-shaped curve of spatial development, associated with a rise in regional disparities in the early stage of the process and a reduction in later stages, thus generating a trade-off between growth and regional equality in certain frameworks. Such trade-off needs to be taken into account by policy-makers, together with considerations on long-run potential negative externalities associated with a more intensive use of the transport system, such as congestion and pollution issues because short-run policy objectives might conflict with long-run ones. More importantly, it is crucial to understand if alternative spatial distributions of economic activity are associated with overall growth or to reorganization, with some areas growing at the expense of other areas; to this aim, it becomes crucial to conduct general economic equilibrium type of analysis.

Other issues make the study of the economic impact of transport infrastructure investments a complex task, both from a theoretical and empirical point of view. In fact, their effects present significant heterogeneity that is related to different contexts, different perspectives of the analysis, and different ways of measuring a similar phenomenon.

For example, the scale of analysis requires the consideration of alternative elements because agglomeration and dispersion forces that matter on a local basis (city) are often different from those acting at regional or national level. Although commuting and congestion costs are crucial in urban economics, transportation costs for goods and interregional mobility costs for production factors shape the distribution of economic activity across regions.

Another important factor that affects the analysis is the degree of development of a country/region: economic conditions, political and institutional characteristics, investment conditions can significantly affect the working of the expansive transmission mechanisms predicted by theoretical models.[2] Moreover, some issues such as inclusion, poverty, health, and education generally gain relevance when considering less developed countries.

Similarly, structural features that characterize different countries introduce some constraints into the analysis: the lower mobility of workers in Europe with respect to the United States makes it difficult to apply predictions of theoretical models that assume perfect mobility of factors.

Modeling the economic effect of transport infrastructure needs to take into account also industries heterogeneity, for example, in terms of intensity of use of different transport services, and infrastructure heterogeneity, not only related to the different modes (road, railways, etc.) but also associated with their quality and efficiency of use. Additionally, the network characteristic of transport infrastructure shapes the analysis; the degree of centrality of a node (infrastructure) within a transportation network matters for location decisions and network externalities determine the diffusion process of growth enhancing mechanisms.

[2] Also the existing infrastructure endowment might determine the extent of the returns on infrastructure investments because there might be diminishing returns over a certain threshold.

It is evident that modeling such complexity in a unifying framework is unfeasible; however, the theoretical literature surveyed in this chapter has made significant progress in this direction. After briefly sketching the role of transport infrastructure investments within classical exogenous and endogenous growth theory models, this chapter deals with theoretical models that analyze the spatial distribution of economic activity; in such a framework, the role of transport infrastructure becomes fundamental and sometimes generates unpleasant results. This chapter describes the main characteristics of the basic core-periphery model proposed by the NEG literature and the most important extensions developed from relaxing some of the assumptions of the original model. The last paragraph discusses recent NEG contributions that jointly model location decisions and growth. These models introduce localized innovation activity that generates technological externalities and knowledge spillovers as engines for growth.

3.1 EXOGENOUS GROWTH MODELS

In the Solow growth model, aggregate production (Y) can be expressed as a function of aggregate capital (K) and the number of workers (N) in the economy:

$$Y = F(K, N) \tag{3.1}$$

The shape of the function F depends on the state of the art of technology. Under the hypothesis of constant returns to scale and of decreasing returns to capital and labor, the aggregate production function can be simplified as a relation between production and capital per employee:

$$\frac{Y}{N} = f\left(\frac{K}{N}\right) \tag{3.2}$$

Moreover, the level of production in each year determines savings, investments, and depreciation, which in turn affect the future level of capital.

In this framework, for a certain rate of growth of population, increases in per capita production can be generated by an increase in capital (via an increase of the saving rate). However, given the hypothesis of diminishing returns to capital, the expansion of capital cannot sustain the growth of production forever. Hence, variations in the stock of capital are associated with transitory higher production growth rates, which, however, will be exhausted as soon as the economy reaches a new equilibrium characterized by a higher level of production and a zero rate of growth in per capital income. In growth models, such situation is defined as a *steady-state* equilibrium.[3]

The Solow model can be extended to account for the role of exogenous technical progress. By assuming that technical progress can improve the amount of services provided to consumers, it can be included as an augmenting factor (A) in the aggregate production function:

$$Y = F(K, A, N) \tag{3.3}$$

By assuming that technological progress is labor augmenting, the aggregate production function can be expressed in term of "effective labor" (AN):

$$\frac{Y}{AN} = f\left(\frac{K}{AN}\right) \tag{3.4}$$

All the other assumptions of the general model still hold and imply that the steady-state rate of growth of production is equal to the rate of technical progress and does not depend on the rate of saving, which only affects production levels. Again, as in the base model, an increase in the rate of savings induces a temporary rise in the growth rate of capital and production which will stabilize around a higher steady-state level of capital and production. However, technical progress makes the growth path of the economy upward sloping and not flat as in the base model.[4]

Transport infrastructure might be included in the Solow model either by considering them as a separate component of capital or by assuming that they provide an improvement of the amount of services provided to consumers. In the first approach, the stock of transport infrastructure can be considered as an additional input in the production function. Indeed, adding transport infrastructure as a further factor of production implies assuming that their services are pure nonrival public good with services proportional to the stock of capital. Moreover, such infrastructures are often

[3] The hypothesis of exogenous saving rate is discarded in growth models where the consumption and saving decisions are determined by optimizing households and firms that interact in competitive markets (Ramsey, 1928; Koopmans, 1965). In such models, saving rates affects the speed of convergence to the steady state.

[4] In more recent versions of the Solow model, also human capital accumulation is included, but the main results of the model do not change.

funded by the government, and their unit cost are not determined by the market so that it becomes difficult to suppose that such factor is remunerated according to its marginal product (Duggal, Saltzman, & Klein, 1999). These arguments cast some doubts on the theoretical accuracy of such approach.

Alternatively, it might be assumed that transport services are a determinant of technical progress which shift the aggregate production function upward and boost the marginal productivity of private inputs. However, as it will be explained in Chapter 6, under the assumptions of Cobb–Douglas production function and neutral technical progress, both approaches generate the same estimating equation so that from an empirical point of view it becomes difficult to distinguish them.

As we have briefly discussed, in the theoretical framework of exogenous growth models, transport infrastructure investments might generate expansive *level* effects on production but cannot sustain growth. However, these models are not able to explain how such effects are produced and cannot provide microfoundations for such predictions.

3.2 ENDOGENOUS GROWTH MODELS

Around the end of the 1980s, some economists suggested a new class of growth models where the main factors driving growth become endogenous. The simplest endogenous growth model (Romer, 1986), so-called AK model, by discarding the hypothesis of diminishing returns to capital, can predict positive long-run per capita growth, even without technical progress (e.g., as a consequence of higher saving rates). The assumption of constant returns on capital is justified by considering that capital comprises physical and human capital (the latter thought of as skills embodied in a worker). Moreover, by allowing for the possibility that physical and human capital are produced by different technologies (e.g., Lucas, 1988), the production of human capital may generate long-term growth, similarly to improvements in technology. Several extensions of the original model include optimizing agents choosing consumption, savings, and the optimal level of R&D activity, which in turn enhance technical progress and growth (e.g., Romer, 1990; Aghion & Howitt, 1992). Alternatively, to eliminate the assumption of diminishing returns to capital, the existence of learning by doing is introduced (e.g., Romer, 1986).

Within the framework of endogenous growth models, the role of infrastructure has been treated by including either infrastructure expenditures (flow) or infrastructure capital (stock) in the aggregate production function. The fundamental model is the one by Barro (1990).

Barro (1990) assumes that the government buys a flow of services (e.g., transport) from the private sector that corresponds to the input g of the following aggregate production function:

$$\frac{y}{k} = \theta\left(\frac{g}{k}\right) \tag{3.5}$$

where y is output per worker, k is capital per worker, and g is per capita government purchase of goods and services. By assuming a Cobb–Douglas functional form, the production function becomes

$$y = Ag^{\alpha}k^{1-\alpha}, \quad \text{with } 0 < \alpha < 1 \tag{3.6}$$

With A representing the productivity component. Given the assumption on α, the function exhibits constant returns to scale; moreover, by defining η as the elasticity of production with respect to g, the marginal product of capital is as follows:

$$f' = \frac{\partial y}{\partial k} = \theta\left(\frac{g}{k}\right)\left(1 - \theta'\frac{g}{y}\right) = \theta\left(\frac{g}{k}\right)(1 - \eta) \tag{3.7}$$

Assuming that government purchases are financed with distortionary taxes T (τ is the tax rate), a budget constraint is added to the model:

$$g = T = \tau k \theta\left(\frac{g}{k}\right) \tag{3.8}$$

The second main component of the model is the consumption (C) growth rate equation (γ) derived by solving an intertemporal utility maximization problem for consumers characterized by a utility function with constant elasticity of substitution σ:

$$\gamma = \frac{\dot{C}}{C} = \frac{1}{\sigma}(f' - \rho) = \frac{1}{\sigma}\left[(1 - \tau)\theta\left(\frac{g}{k}\right)(1 - \eta) - \rho\right] \tag{3.9}$$

where ρ is the discount rate. When T and g and y grow at the same rate, γ will be constant, so that in steady-state equilibrium consumption, capital and output per capita grow at the same rate that depends on the marginal productivity of capital. As expected, taxes and purchases have opposite effects on growth; an increase in government purchases positively affects the marginal productivity of private capital and sustains higher growth, whereas an increase in financing public expenditures with taxes reduces per capita growth. The latter effect dominates when government size is big, whereas the expansive effect prevails with a smaller government. To maximize growth and consumers' utility, the tax rate must be equal to the elasticity of aggregate production with respect to public services, that is, when the ratio of expenditures on production (g/y) matches the share it would get if the services were provided by competitive markets as production inputs. Such threshold level determines if purchases in infrastructure services positively affect growth.

The model suggested by Barro (1990) has been extended to account for possible rivalry and excludability of certain infrastructure, like transport ones (e.g., Ott & Turnovsky, 2006).[5]

Another modeling approach that allows to account for such infrastructure characteristics suggests to include service infrastructure as a factor input in the production function. Barro and Sala I Martin (1992) model public services as an input to production in the framework of the AK model and obtain the same predictions of the Barro (1990) model; the relation between the size of the government and the per capita growth rate is U-shaped. A similar approach has been followed by Fernald (1999), whose model allows to investigate the effect of transport infrastructure (roads) on more vehicle-intensive sectors; furthermore, the network nature of transport infrastructure is accounted for by the model, together with possible congestion effects. See Box 4 in Chapter 6 for some details on the Fernald (1999)'s work.[6]

Similarly, Agenor (2010) includes public infrastructure capital as input of the production function, together with private capital and "effective" labor, defined as the product of the quantity of labor and a productivity index, which in turn depends on the availability of health services provided by the government. This specification implies that greater access to health services boosts workers' productivity, and therefore output. Moreover, it is assumed that greater access to health reduces time preferences so that agents become less impatient; this, in turn, raises savings and promotes physical capital accumulation and growth. Given that infrastructure improves the

[5] Such models suggest that congestion raises the optimal income tax and lowers the optimal user fees.

[6] A related issue is the existence of spillover effects between infrastructure endowments of close countries. For example Cohen and Morrison-Paul (2004) model a cost function of the manufacturing sector in US states that include both each state public capital stock and geographically connected states one.

economy's capacity to provide health services, the growth rate depends on the interactions between public infrastructure, health, savings, productivity, and private physical capital. Furthermore, the author posits a nonlinear relation between the stock of public capital and its efficiency, as a consequence of external network effects so that the model can generate multiple equilibria depending on the initial position of the economy in terms of the stock of capital per worker and on expectations of private agents.

In most of the cited theoretical literature, the interaction between public infrastructure investments and private capital influences economic growth. The key assumption underlying this relation is that infrastructure investments affect private capital accumulation. Indeed, the accumulation of both types of capital (private and public) is assumed to reflect technological progress needed to offset diminishing returns to capital so that technological knowledge and capital accumulation are combined together.

Alternatively, capital infrastructure may be included in the aggregate production function by assuming that they affect growth by directly improving technical progress, hence shifting the production function upward and rising the marginal productivity of factor inputs. Within this framework, Shioji (2001) suggests a dynamic model of economic (regional) growth with public capital where the Cobb–Douglas aggregate production function is modified to include public capital G in the productivity component.

$$Y = AK^{\alpha}L^{1-\alpha} \tag{3.10}$$

where Y represents production, K is private capital, and L is labor input, which is assumed constant over time. Technical progress A depends on local productivity B and on public capital G; c is a nonnegative parameter:

$$A = B\left({}^{G}\!/\!_{L}\right)^{c} \tag{3.11}$$

By combining Eqs. (3.10) and (3.11), the production function becomes

$$Y = BK^{\alpha}L^{1-\alpha-c}G^{c} \tag{3.12}$$

Building on previous growth theory, the author develops an open economy model with capital mobility across regions, adjustment costs for investment and public capital. The cost of investment for firms is as follows:

$$I\left(1 + \frac{\zeta}{2}\frac{I}{K}\right) \tag{3.13}$$

where I is the investment and ζ is a positive constant. By maximizing firms' discounted value of net cash flow over an infinite time horizon, it is possible to obtain first-order conditions and steady-state equations of the model. Interestingly, the steady-state output per capita can differ across regions because of differences in the stock of public capital per capita (G/L) and in the local productivity (B). Moreover, in steady state the long-run elasticity of output per capita with respect to public capital is $c/1 - \alpha$, that is larger than c. Indeed, as the author suggests "public capital augments output in the long run not only through its own productivity effect but also by attracting private investment to the region."[7] Hence, the model shows that public capital not only has a direct effect but also contributes to subsequent growth by encouraging private capital accumulation.[8]

As just briefly sketched, the basic hypothesis of endogenous growth models is that growth is the outcome of rational decisions of agents with regard to the accumulation of physical (Romer, 1986) and human capital (Lucas, 1988), the allocation of resources to R&D activities (Romer, 1990), or public expenditure on infrastructure (Barro, 1990). These decisions are able to increase the productivity of production factors, which in turn generates growth.

Growth models discussed above do not deal with the issue of the spatial distribution of economic activity. Indeed, the growth process is accompanied by significant structural changes, such as variations in demand, industries and employment composition, human capital, financial development, institutions and organizations, and infrastructure endowment. Such changes affect location choices of firms and people, which in turn interact with the process of growth. Jointly modeling growth and the spatial distribution of economic activity is a hard task that has been tackled only recently by the NEG literature, that models the trade of goods and the mobility of production factors in a general equilibrium framework.

[7] Similarly, Duggal, Saltzman & Klein (1999) includes the stock of infrastructure as a determinant of technical progress and suggests that infrastructure improves productivity by lowering production costs.

[8] Again, when the Cobb–Douglas functional form is adopted, the direct and indirect impacts of infrastructure investments on production cannot be empirically disentangled.

3.3 THE SPATIAL DISTRIBUTION OF ECONOMIC ACTIVITY

The location of economic activity is strictly related to both physical and economic geography. The unequal distribution of economic activity across space is obviously linked to natural characteristics (endowment of resources), but other "second nature" forces are at work in shaping such outcome. Starting from the 1990s, understanding the mechanisms underlying these processes has gathered greater attention in the economic debate aimed at explaining regional and urban growth disparities. This debate has remarkable implications from a policy perspective, given that a significant share (one-third) of EU budget is devoted to the reduction of spatial inequalities.

The comprehension of the geographical pattern of economic activity and of its dynamics is the object of analysis of the NEG that hinges on spatial economics, trade theory, growth theory, and urban and regional economics ideas.[9] The fundamental concept of NEG models is that the spatial distribution of economic activity is jointly determined by the interaction of self-enforcing centripetal (agglomeration) and centrifugal (dispersion) forces, that changes over time and whose nature can vary depending on the spatial scale of the analysis (local, regional, or international). The outcome of such interaction can be significantly uneven and persistent so that it becomes crucial to understand the underlying economics.

Increasing returns to scale, monopolistic competition, transport costs, and external economies are the main ingredients of early NEG models.

The hypothesis of increasing returns to scale, deriving from the existence of some forms of indivisibilities, is a key element for explaining geographical distributions of economic activities[10] because it generates the incentive to concentrate production in space to exploit savings associated with larger scale of production. Such hypothesis is crucial to the explanation of agglomeration patterns, but implies that traditional perfect competition Arrow—Debreu approach to general equilibrium modeling cannot apply (it relies on convex technology set). Increasing returns to scale leads to a market structure characterized by imperfect competition, and the Dixit and

[9] In this century, one of the first economists dealing with the advantages of geographical concentration of economic activity is Marshall (1920) who explains which factors induce small-scale concentration of firms within specific sectors.

[10] Scotchmer and Thisse (1992) call this "the folk theorem of spatial economics."

Stiglitz (1977) model of monopolistic competition represents a starting point for several NEG models.

Monopolistic competition involves horizontally differentiated products and constant elasticity of substitution (CES) utility functions, so that consumers love variety; each firm produces a single version of the good and fixes its price acting as a monopolist in its market. The size of the market is limited by the presence of other firms producing different varieties of the product, but no strategic interactions take place among firms; moreover, barriers to entry and exit are absent and the number of firms is high in equilibrium.

Another ingredient of the NEG modeling strategy is the assumption of transport costs. Indeed, for space to be relevant to location choices, transport costs must be positive. Even when transport costs decrease and become low, location choices turn out to be more sensitive to small differences among locations because firms' and workers' incentive to move change in response to variations in transport costs. NEG models assume that transport costs take the form of "iceberg" costs as suggested by Samuelson (1952). Under this assumption, goods are freely shipped, but a share of their value melts down during transit; such modeling strategy eliminates the need for describing the transport industry. The level of transport cost affects location decisions of workers and firms.

3.4 THE CORE-PERIPHERY MODEL

The milestone model proposed by Krugman (1991a) shows how large-scale agglomerations can emerge from the interaction of increasing returns and transport costs in the presence of firms and productive factors mobility. The model is like a $2 \times 2 \times 2$ model of trade theory, with two regions, two production sectors (manufacturing and agriculture), and two type of workers (farmers and workers). Agriculture produces a homogeneous good in a competitive framework, under constant returns to scale, using farmers as the only input. The manufacturing sector produces horizontally differentiated goods, each produced by a single firm in a monopolistic competition market, under increasing returns to scale (with positive fixed costs and constant marginal costs) and using workers as the only input. Contrary to farmers that are uniformly distributed across regions, workers are mobile between regions; moreover, only the trade of manufactured goods involves iceberg transport costs, whereas agricultural goods are costless to transport.

The utility function of individuals has the consumption of both goods in its argument:

$$U = C_M^{\mu} C_A^{1-\mu} \tag{3.14}$$

where C_M and C_A represents the consumption of the manufacturing and agriculture goods, respectively. Consumers do not prefer one product to the other, but they prefer variety. The aggregate consumption of the manufacturing good is modeled as a CES function to reflect symmetry and preference for variety:

$$C_M = \left[\sum_{i=1}^{N} C_I^{(\sigma-1)/\sigma} \right]^{\sigma/(\sigma-1)} \tag{3.15}$$

where N is the number of potential products and $\sigma > 1$ is the elasticity of substitution. Solving the maximization problem for consumers shows that the share of expenditure devoted to manufacturing goods is μ and that the elasticity of substitution is constant. Moreover, the model assumes that the share of workers employed in manufacturing (L_M) is exogenously given and equals μ.

When the number of products is high, the elasticity of demand is constant and matches the elasticity of substitution, so that firms maximize profits by setting a constant markup over marginal costs. However, given the free entry assumption, profits are null in equilibrium and each firm produces the same amount of output (independently from the wage rates) that is negatively correlated to marginal costs and positively correlated to fixed costs and elasticity of substitution. The number of manufacturing goods (i.e., the number of firms) is proportional to the number of workers and is inversely correlated to fixed and marginal costs.

The general equilibrium of the model is obtained by optimizing consumption for each good in each region, while taking into account the movement of workers induced by real wage differentials: if a region offers higher real wages and there is no incentive for firms to locate where there is no manufacturing, all workers will be concentrated in that region.

In the model, the immobility of farmers acts as a centrifugal force because they consume all type of goods, whereas the centripetal force is generated by a circular causation of forward linkages (the preference of workers to be close to the producers) and backward linkages (the convenience of producers to cluster in larger markets).

In fact, when a higher number of firms establishes in a region, a larger variety of good will be produced, thus attracting more consumers/workers; the increase in the number of workers creates a larger market with respect to the other region, thus generating the so-called *home market effect.*[11] Competition in the local labor markets should favor higher nominal wages; moreover, the price index of that region will decrease so that real wages will rise and more workers will be induced to move there. The existence of scale economies generates the incentive to concentrate production in one region and the existence of transport costs encourages firms to produce in the region with a larger market, so that more varieties of the goods will be produced; in this way the agglomeration process is self-powering.

If forward and backward linkages counterbalance the centrifugal force induced by immobile farmers, economic activity will show a *core-periphery* pattern where all manufacturing activity is clustered in one region. Such pattern is more likely when transport cost are low enough, when economies of scale are more significant (i.e., low elasticity of substitution), and when products are sufficiently differentiated. Indeed, Krugman shows that if transport costs are sufficiently high, firms do not find convenient to concentrate in one region, given that it is too costly to serve periphery from the core region, and the global economy shows a symmetric regional distribution of production. The Krugman (1991a) core-periphery model allows for the possibility of either convergence or divergence between regions according to values assumed by the critical parameters of the model. Indeed, even small changes in these parameters can induce dramatic changes in the general equilibrium outcome; however, regional disparities arising from the model are stable equilibria based on precise theoretical microfoundations so that spatial structure emerges from invisible hand processes.

3.5 EXTENSIONS OF THE BASIC MODEL

The Krugman (1991a) model has been extended along different dimensions, and very interesting results have been obtained by relaxing some of its assumptions. In particular, the introduction of additional mechanisms driving dispersion and agglomeration of economic activity has allowed researchers to analyze more complex agglomeration patterns.

[11] The home market effect predicted by models of trade is the tendency for large countries to become net exporters of goods with high transport costs and significant scale economies (Hanson, 1998).

In the baseline model, the immobility of farmers acts as a centrifugal force, whereas the centripetal force is associated with forward and backward linkages. Transport costs do not have a univocal impact on these forces. Indeed, additional factors can be responsible of dispersion or concentration of economic activity. A (partial) list of other forces at work as summarized in Table 3.1 (Krugman, 1998).

In the left column are reported the *Marshallian* sources of external economies, usually called agglomeration economies, and that are generated by close and intense economic interaction. A larger local market generates both backward and forward intraindustry and interindustry linkages; moreover, it enables access to a larger variety of goods and services. Industrial concentration supports thick labor markets, especially for specialized skills, that allow better matching of workers to firms' skill needs; the clustering of economic activity generates externalities such as knowledge spillovers, i.e., improvements of the diffusion of information due to proximity. The first two externalities are defined as "pecuniary," as they are mediated by markets, whereas the third one is defined as "nonpecuniary" as it is associated with nonmarket interactions. Although these nonmarket mechanisms are more relevant for small-scale agglomerations (cities and industrial districts), pecuniary externalities become more important for explaining larger-scale concentration patterns.[12]

The right column of Table 3.1 shows the main dispersion forces that shape the spatial distribution of economic activity. The immobility of land, natural resources, and people (in the case of an international framework) do not favor the concentration of production because dispersed factors might create dispersed markets. Higher demand for land induced by clustering of economic activity rises land rents, thus slowing concentration; the same results stem from increased congestion associated with concentration of people and firms.

All cited factors affecting geographical concentration and dispersion operate simultaneously in the real world; however, for analytical reasons

[12] Duranton and Puga (2004) classify the effects associated with agglomeration economies in three categories: sharing, matching, and learning. Sharing is related to the higher availability of public goods provided in more densely populated areas and to the higher accessibility of intermediate and business services. Matching is linked to the improvement of the matching process between employers and employees in thicker markets. Learning effects derive from knowledge spillovers generated by proximity and associated with the nonrival and (partially) nonexcludable nature of knowledge.

Table 3.1 Factors affecting geographical concentration and dispersion

Centripetal forces	Centrifugal forces
Market size effects (linkages)	Immobile factors
Thick markets	Land rents/commuting
Knowledge spillovers and other pure external economies	Congestion and other pure diseconomies

NEG models typically focus on a subset of them and provide different predictions in term of spatial distribution of the economic activity.

For example, Livas-Elizondo and Krugman (1996) add commuting costs that depend on the distance from the center and introduce housing/farming as space consuming activities so that land rents counterbalance commuting costs. These elements reduce the likelihood of agglomeration. The supply of nontradable services, like housing, and congestion issues represent dispersion forces also in the model suggested by Helpman (1998). In this model, contrary to Krugman (1991a), decreasing transport costs may trigger the dispersion of economic activity. Such results are particularly relevant for explaining the distribution of economic activity on regional and local scale, where competition for land is a stronger issue with respect to a larger-scale perspective.

Turning to centripetal forces, by observing that agglomeration of economic activity takes place also in contexts characterized by very low labor mobility, some authors suggest additional mechanism associated with proximity that may drive such process. Different works by Krugman and Venables (1995, 1996) focus on the role of input/output vertical linkages between firms; as the output of one firm can be the input for another, upstream firms benefit from higher proximity to their customers and downstream firms benefit from being closer to their suppliers. The main novelty of these models, with respect to Krugman (1991a), is the assumption of two monopolistically competitive industries that are in a vertical relationship and no labor mobility.[13] Different distributions of the economic activity can emerge depending on transport costs; when transport costs decrease from high to medium, agglomeration becomes more likely, while further reductions lessen the advantages of concentration because

[13] In Krugman and Venables (1996) each industry produces an output that can be used for consumption and as an input so that intraindustry linkages acquire relevance together with interindustry linkages.

proximity becomes less important. Transferring the predictions of these models to a larger scale can explain country specialization and patterns of industrialization. As explained by Fujita, Krugman, and Venables (1999) "declining trade (transport) costs first produce, then dissolve the global inequality of nations." Thus, economic integration among countries, by reducing trade cost, may generate a bell-shaped curve of spatial development, associated with a rise in regional disparities in the early stage of the process and a reduction in later stages.[14]

Another interesting extension of the baseline Krugman (1991a) model is related to the introduction of more than two regions. The generalization proposed by Krugman (1993, 1994) suggests that transport costs and economies of scale can generate multiple agglomeration in equilibrium that tend to keep away from each other.

It is important to stress that theoretical models surveyed so far do not provide realistic quantitative versions able to explain the welfare implications of production factors movements and locational changes of economic activity. Indeed, from a policy perspective, it is crucial to understand if relocation of economic activity associated with certain policy interventions, like infrastructure investments, generates growth or reorganization.

Some authors have adopted an alternative approach that generates models more suitable for empirical investigations, based on the new international trade literature hypothesis of endogenous cross-country productivity distribution. This literature shows new mechanisms bringing gains from trade, either under perfect competition (e.g., Eaton & Kortum, 2002) or in the presence of noncompetitive markets (Melitz & Ottaviano, 2008).[15]

Within this framework, an interesting contribution is the study by Donaldson (2018) who analyzes the economic effects of the network of railroads built in colonial India and shows that railroads reduced trade costs and allowed regions to gain from trade.

The author proposes a Ricardian trade model that includes many regions, many commodities, and costly trade. Geographical heterogeneity

[14] Fujita and Thisse (2013) survey several extensions of the core-periphery model able to generate such patterns. Tabuchi, Thisse, and Zhu (2015) revisit NEG models by focusing on technological progress as an agglomeration force.

[15] For example, Combes, Duranton, Gobillon, Puga, and Roux (2012) expand the model by Melitz and Ottaviano (2008) to allow for agglomeration economies driven by technological externalities.

generates productivity differentials across regions and across commodities, so that comparative advantages can be exploited through trade. A reduction in bilateral trade costs generated by the creation of new connections among regions generates an expansion of trade that induces specialization based on comparative advantages. The complexity of the model induced by the assumption of product heterogeneity is reduced through the adoption of the approach suggested by Eaton and Kortum (2002). Authors model the amount of variety of a commodity that can be produced with one unit of land in each region as the realization of a stochastic variable drawn from a Type-II extreme value distribution, whose parameters vary across regions and commodities. These random variables are drawn independently for each variety, commodity, and region.

The model provides four important results: (1) Regional price differentials among identical commodities are due to trade costs. (2) Bilateral trade flows take the "gravity equation" form. (3) Railroads increase real income levels. (4) Once local productivity is controlled for, the impact of the railroad network on welfare in a region is captured by its impact on the share of that region's expenditure that it sources from itself.

A more general model is proposed by Redding (2016), with an arbitrary number (n) of regions indexed by i, $n \in N$ where locations differ in terms of land supply, productivity, amenities, bilateral (iceberg) trade costs, and their relative geographical location. Land and labor are the two factors of production; workers are mobile, love varieties, and have heterogeneous preferences across locations. Transport costs, increasing returns to scale, and love for variety generate pecuniary externalities that act as agglomeration forces.[16]

The author models consumer preferences, production, expenditure shares, price indices, and residential choices.

Preferences for worker ω resident in location n depend on good consumption (C_n), residential land use (H_{Un}), and an idiosyncratic amenity component $b_n(\omega)$ drawn independently across locations and workers from a Fréchet distribution.

[16] Another study by Redding and Turner (2015) proposes a model of economic geography that includes many locations, transportation costs between and within locations, and commuting costs within locations. Goods' variety depends in their availability in space and are produced in perfectly competitive markets. Transport infrastructure investments reduce trading and commuting costs thus affecting wages, trade shares, land prices, and population; however, workers' mobility stops when real wage are equalized across locations, so that the welfare effect is the same everywhere.

$$U_n(\omega) = b_n(\omega)\left(\frac{C_n(\omega)}{\alpha}\right)^{\alpha}\left(\frac{H_{Un}(\omega)}{1-\alpha}\right)^{1-\alpha} \quad 0 < \alpha < 1 \tag{3.16}$$

The good consumption index is defined over the endogenous number of horizontally differentiated varieties supplied by each location (M_i)

$$C_n = \left[\sum_{i \in N} \int_0^{M_i} c_{ni}(j)^{\rho}\right]^{\frac{1}{\rho}} \tag{3.17}$$

where the CES parameter (ρ) determines the elasticity of substitution between goods ($\sigma = 1/(1-\rho)$). This preference structure implies that expected utility for each location is decreasing in its population.

Varieties are produced in a monopolistic competition setting with increasing returns to scale. Production costs include a fixed component F and variable costs in terms of labor that depend on each location-specific productivity A_i that in turn is independently drawn across goods and locations from a Fréchet distribution.

Profit maximization implies that equilibrium prices are a constant markup over marginal cost, and that equilibrium employment for each variety is equal to a constant. Labor market equilibrium entails that the number of varieties supplied by each location is proportional to the number of workers choosing to locate there. This condition implies that trade shares between different location depend also on relative local population L_i, besides wages (W_i), productivity A_i, and the elasticity of trade to trade costs ($\sigma - 1$). Equilibrium values for prices for each variety, employment, and trade shares enable to derive the consumption goods price index P_n.

Residential choices depends on the idiosyncratic amenity component b_n, on income v_n, on the consumption goods price index P_n, and on the land rent r_n of each location. Equilibrium in the land market implies that land rent derives from the equality between land income (labor income and expenditure on residential land) and expenditure on goods, as expenditure on residential land is redistributed lump sum to residents.

The general equilibrium of the model is defined by the number of workers (L_n) in each location, the share of each location's expenditure on goods produced in other locations (trade shares p_{ni}), the wage in each location (W_n), and the Fréchet shape parameter for amenities ε.

Given the land area, productivity, and amenity parameters (H_n, A_n, B_n) and quasisymmetric bilateral trade frictions (d_{ni}) for all locations, the equilibrium configuration may be obtained from a two-equation system that determines the equilibrium population and trade share of each location as a function of the parameters of the model.

Comparative statics analysis suggests that locations with higher productivity, higher land supply, and better amenities relative to other locations (i.e., better goods market access to other locations) have higher populations and a higher number of varieties produced, which in the presence of trade costs acts as an agglomeration force. These characteristics raise the price of land until expected utility, conditional on living in each location, is the same across locations. However, regions that are more attractive are more populated and pay higher wages and house prices. Under some parameter restrictions, the dispersion forces dominate the agglomeration ones, and the model provides a unique equilibrium distribution of economic activity. Moreover, higher trade costs to all other locations decreases the equilibrium population of that location.[17]

Model-based counterfactuals can be carried out based on the system of equations derived for general equilibrium to generate predictions on the reallocation of labor across locations following a change in trade costs, productivity, or amenities. Redding (2016) shows that the common change in welfare across locations consequent to such changes can be written as a weighted average of the change in real income in each location, where the weights depend on location population shares or, alternatively, as the weighted average of the changes in domestic trade shares and populations of each location.

The model is able to explain the effects of variations in trade (transport) costs on the reallocation of economic activity, thus providing a useful complement to reduced-form regressions that analyze the impact of transport infrastructure investments. Moreover, it allows to distinguish between reallocation effects from the creation of new economic activity,[18] a topic that will also be addressed in Chapter 7.

In all models reviewed so far, when the concentration of productive activities prevails in an area, the conditions for cumulative local growth are

[17] The trade elasticity ($\sigma - 1$) and the labor supply elasticity with respect to income (ε) influence the sensitivity of equilibrium population values to variation in these characteristics.

[18] The author simulates the model and shows that an improvement in transport infrastructure has a positive impact on population, wages, land rents, and a negative effect on the price index, with significant heterogeneity between treated and nontreated locations associated with the degree of trade costs and to heterogeneity on workers' preferences.

generated; however, such models are static and do not model the growth process. Nevertheless, they allow to compare different steady-state equilibria reached by the economy after significant changes in critical parameters (e.g., a reduction in transport costs).

3.6 GROWTH AND GEOGRAPHY

Recently, in the theoretical literature a set of dynamic models where location choices and growth are jointly determined have been proposed. The link between endogenous growth models and regional location models stems from the assumptions that not only do production activities but also knowledge production tend to be geographically concentrated. These models introduce localized innovation activity that generates technological externalities and knowledge spillovers. Knowledge spillovers are localized in the sense that the cost of R&D in one region also depends on the location of firms (stock of knowledge capital). Such externalities, together with pecuniary ones, induce the agglomeration of innovation activity and production in one area and a cumulative causation process that generates endogenous growth. By *regionalizing* the processes of knowledge creation, accumulation, and diffusion, NEG dynamic models shed some light on the interaction between geographical space and growth.

Indeed, Grossman and Helpman (1991) have already shown that with free trade and localized knowledge spillovers, the increasing returns activity concentrates in one location. However, models of endogenous growth and trade (which involves capital) do not all imply that free trade leads to divergence (Goh & Olivier, 2002).

One of the first models that tries to link growth and geography has been proposed by Walz (1996), who extends a framework with vertical linkages and costless migration by adding the endogenous expansion of product variety; however, the model generates unrealistic results. Black and Henderson (1999) show that urbanization entails localized knowledge spillovers, thereby affecting the endogenous growth of the economy. A major limit of the model is the assumption of a city developer managing the migration process.[19]

[19] Some urban economics models describe the interactions between growth and the size distribution of cities and suggest that localized externalities induce aggregate increasing returns. In these models, agglomeration triggers growth and growth leads to agglomeration (e.g., Duranton, 2007).

Fujita and Thisse (2002, 2003) combine a core-periphery model with a Grossman–Helpman growth type model with horizontally differentiated products. They assume that firms fixed cost are represented by patents produced by mobile skilled workers. When transaction costs are sufficiently low and patents are tradable, the model generates a core-periphery equilibrium, with the R&D sector and most of the manufacturing clustered in one region; hence, localized spillovers favor growth. If patents are non-tradable, only higher trade costs can sustain the core-periphery pattern. Indeed, authors do not study details of the transition process of economic activity location.

Baldwin and Martin (2004) summarize the main results of the models proposed by Baldwin (1999), Martin and Ottaviano (1999), Baldwin, Martin, and Ottaviano (2001) and Baldwin, Forslid, Martin, Ottaviano, and Robert-Nicoud (2003). In these models growth impacts on geography by generating cumulative causation processes because centripetal forces induce the accumulation of human, physical, and/or knowledge capital in one region, which in turn spend a share of their income locally; "growth poles" and "growth sinks" characterize aggregate growth that is driven by factor accumulation in a subset of regions. As Fujita and Thisse (2002) suggest "agglomeration can be thought as the territorial counterpart of economic growth." In these models lower transaction costs on goods have an effect not only on industry location but also on the growth rate and these effects can be "catastrophic" or not, depending on the mobility of capital.

The rise of regional disparities is counterbalanced by faster growth in all regions; however, the agglomeration process definitely improves welfare in the core regions but has ambiguous effects on the welfare of the periphery regions. Thus, these models suggest the existence of a possible spatial equity-efficiency trade-off.[20]

Minerva and Ottaviano (2009) present a two-region (North–South) model and analyze the link between geography and regional growth in the presence of trading goods costs (transport costs) and barriers to ideas transfer (communication costs). In particular, authors focus on the effects of

[20] Localized spillovers are not the only way that geography can affect growth. Martin and Ottaviano (2001) generate a feedback between growth and agglomeration by assuming vertical linkages rather than local spillovers in innovation. Because the innovation sector uses manufacturing goods as an input, the location of manufacturing affects the cost of innovation through trade costs. Yamamoto (2003) presents a similar model with circular causation between growth and agglomeration coming from the vertical linkages between the intermediate goods sector and the innovation sector.

infrastructure investments on such costs and their consequence on growth and agglomeration patterns.

The North and the South are equally populated by Q immobile workers and have an identical stock of knowledge capital K_o that can freely move and is produced by R&D laboratories (financed through bonds with riskless return r(t)). Workers consume a traditional good Y, produced in a perfect competition setting with constant returns to scale, and a horizontally differentiated good D, produced in a monopolistic competition market structure with increasing returns to scale (fixed costs are represented by knowledge capital and marginal cost are β). The total number of varieties (N) depends on the aggregate knowledge capital stock $K^w(t)$. Preferences are modeled with a Cobb–Douglas utility function:

$$U = \int_{t=0}^{\infty} \log\left[D(t)^{\alpha} Y(t)^{1-\alpha}\right] e^{-\rho t} dt \tag{3.18}$$

where D(t) represents a CES consumption basket with elasticity of substitution σ greater than one. The maximization of the utility function provides the optimal share of consumption and expenditure of each good.

Trade flows of differentiated goods face iceberg transport costs that differ across regions, being lower in North with respect to South; moreover, within-regions transport costs are lower than interregions ones. Given that all firms bear the same marginal costs and face the same σ, they have constant markups ($\rho = \sigma\beta/(\sigma - 1)$) and the same producer price so that final consumers price reflect transport costs differentials. Solving the profit maximization problem generates the following expression for the price index:

$$P(t) = pN(t)^{\frac{1}{1-\sigma}}[\delta_N \gamma(t) + \delta_R(1 - \gamma(t))]^{\frac{1}{1-\sigma}} \tag{3.19}$$

where $\gamma(t) = n(t)/N(t)$ is the share of firms located in the North and $N(t) = K^w(t)$ is the total number of firms, which equals the total stock of knowledge capital. The parameters δ_i reflect transport costs differentials.

The stock of knowledge capital $K^w(t)$ is produced by perfectly competitive profit maximizing R&D laboratories. The R&D production function, accounting for localized knowledge spillovers and intermediate business services, is specified as a constant return to scale technology like

$$\dot{K} = A(t) \left[\frac{D(t)}{\varepsilon}\right]^{\varepsilon} \left[\frac{Q_I(t)}{1 - \varepsilon}\right]^{1-\varepsilon} \tag{3.20}$$

where $\dot{K} = dK(t)/dt$, $Q_l(t)$ is the share of labor employed in R&D activity, D(t) is the basket of business services (the same of consumption basket), ε (bounded between zero and one) is the share of business service in R&D, and A(t) is the region-specific level of productivity in R&D. The productivity is modeled to account for knowledge spillovers whose diffusion is hindered by communication costs:

$$A(t) = AK^{w}(t)^{\mu}[\omega_N \gamma(t) + \omega_R(1 - \gamma(t))]^{\mu} \tag{3.21}$$

where A is a positive constant, ω measures communication costs (the higher is ω, the lower they are), and μ measures the intensity of knowledge spillovers. The expression for the marginal cost of producing knowledge suggests that it is lower in the area that hosts a higher number of firms (North); thus, the existence of transport and communication costs induce a concentration of the R&D activity where production is clustered so that the area will drive the growth process.

Market clearing conditions for products and labor markets close the model and show that the relation between growth and location is circular. On the one side, more agglomeration reduces the cost of innovating and brings faster growth; on the other side, faster growth increases the share of expenditure of the area where innovation takes place so that more firms locate there. Thus, agglomeration and growth are jointly determined; in particular, the model predicts that when only transport costs affect the cost of innovation, a reduction of interregional and intra-North costs promotes agglomeration and growth in the North, whereas a reduction of intra-South transport cost induces agglomeration form North to South but reduces growth.

As Minerva and Ottaviano (2009) suggest "*The result of our paper is a unified framework that summarizes the main insights of NEG on the relation between infrastructure, economic growth and agglomeration. (1) There is a tradeoff between growth and regional equality as improved infrastructure in developed 'core' regions fosters agglomeration and growth, which are instead hampered by improved infrastructure in developing 'peripheral' regions. (2) Better interregional connections may increase rather than decrease regional inequality as improved transport and communication infrastructure between core and peripheral regions may foster not only growth but also agglomeration.*"[21]

Another group of theoretical models has tackled the issue of considering more than two locations, to investigate more complex patterns of economic

[21] Fujita and Thisse (2003) confirm these insights when also labor is mobile.

activity that are closer to reality. Indeed, this is a complex task because economic agents should forecast the distribution of economic activity over space and time. To reduce such analytical complexity, Desmet and Rossi-Hansberg (2014) present a dynamic model of spatial development and assume that allocation paths do not affect return of agents' current decisions even if they are forward looking.

The model has four main ingredients. First, there is a continuum of locations on a line and firms produce in manufacturing or in the service sector.[22] A constant return to scale technology is assumed, with land and labor as inputs; moreover, land is fixed so that there may be congestion. Second, when firms trade goods and services they face iceberg transport costs; labor is freely mobile and can relocate every period until utility is equalized in equilibrium. To produce, firms bid for land and can improve its productivity by innovating (even if land rents bid profits away). Third, firms invest in innovation by acquiring a probability of drawing a shift in technology. Because technology diffuses spatially, locations can get access to "spatially discounted" versions of technology from innovating neighbors. In particular, it is assumed that the benefits from innovation last for only one period because they are incorporated into land rents; as a result, in equilibrium investments in technology stem from a current profits maximization problem.[23] This assumption drastically simplifies the model without reducing its explanatory power.

Authors set initial conditions such that firms operating in the manufacturing sector are more productive, are bigger, and innovate more. This implies that locations hosting a high number of manufacturing firms face higher relative service prices and have the incentive to import them from nearby locations where prices are lower; such locations tend to specialize in service and attract workers. The reallocation of workers toward location specializing in services endogenously incentives higher innovation so that both manufacturing and services improve productivity and lead the country to a balanced growth path. Thus, the coagglomeration of services and manufacturing provides an additional source of local growth accommodated by trade.

In the model, the spatial distribution of economic activity interacts with the structural transformation of the economy. When the service sector starts

[22] This implies that locations are ordered geographically and both transport costs and technology diffusion depend on distance.

[23] Factors and goods markets clear sequentially.

innovating and improving productivity, it also starts attracting workers and employment becomes higher. Hence, the model predicts a positive relation between employment density, innovation, and productivity growth.

Focusing on transport costs, the model predicts a negative relation between them and static welfare, as higher transport costs reduce the incentive to specialize. However, higher transport costs increase the benefits from producing in concentrated locations and induce further agglomeration. In fact, departing from clustered locations, relative prices of manufacturing goods will rise because of transport costs, so that service producers located close to manufacturing area grow and have higher incentives to innovate; once innovation starts, it improves productivity also in nearby locations and leads to higher aggregate growth. Moreover, with higher transport costs the increasing labor share of the stagnant sector will become more densely clustered, leading it to start innovating earlier.

These results are not fully consistent with standard economic geography models; the static loss associated with higher transport costs may be counterbalanced by higher incentive to innovate in some locations, so that overall growth and welfare might improve.

Indeed, under certain critical values of the parameters, in the core-periphery models increased transport costs lead to higher dispersion (it becomes too costly to cluster production and ship products to periphery); insofar agglomeration favors growth, these models predict a negative impact of transport costs on growth. In the Desmet and Rossi-Hansberg (2014) model, higher transport costs induce agglomeration, whereas in core-periphery models induce dispersion.

Similarly to Desmet and Rossi-Hansberg (2014), other authors have proposed dynamic growth models with a continuum of locations. Quah (2002), Boucekkine, Camacho, and Zou (2009) and Brock and Xepapadeas (2008, 2010) are some examples. A common assumption is that each point in space is isolated but there are spillovers or diffusion; they do not include transport costs, national goods markets, and factors mobility to maintain mathematical tractability. Furthermore, they do not model spatial interactions so that the latter are not suitable to provide interesting patterns of location of economic activity.

3.7 CONCLUSIONS

A significant amount of resources is devoted to investment in transportation around the world every year. These investments are designed to promote development and growth as well as to reduce spatial disparities and favor convergence. The comprehension of the economic mechanisms underlying the effect of transportation investments on the economic activity is intrinsically linked to location choices made by firms and workers, as well as to the movement of goods across space.

During the last 30 years, much effort has been dedicated to study such issues and a major contribution has been offered by the NEG literature.

NEG models analyze the interaction between agglomeration and dispersion forces and the role played by changes in transport costs associated with improvements in the transportation system. The first generation of NEG (static) models suggests that transport costs reductions generate agglomeration of the economic activity, whereas further reductions favor its dispersion across space. Thus, economic integration among countries, by reducing trade cost, may generate a bell-shaped curve of spatial development, associated with a rise in regional disparities in the early stage of the process and a reduction in later stages. However, agglomeration of firms and workers in one area may not represent a win—win equilibrium and spatial disparities may arise and persist over time.

In more recent NEG (dynamic) models, location choices and growth are jointly determined. Forces that foster the location of industry in a region also encourage the accumulation of human, physical, and/or knowledge capital. Localized knowledge spillovers reduce the cost of innovation and generate a cumulative causation process that sustains endogenous growth.

In most of these models, reductions of trade/transport costs produce uneven spatial development, so that the expansion of economic activity in the core area takes place at the expense of other peripheral areas; however, the emergence of regional disparities is accompanied by faster growth in all regions. Hence, such models imply a trade-off between static losses associated with relocation of economic activity and dynamic gains due to faster growth.

Such result has important policy implications, given that interventions aimed at reducing regional inequalities might conflict with the pursing of long-run growth objectives. Indeed, the theoretical results reached by recent NEG growth models through the *regionalization* of the processes of knowledge creation, accumulation, and diffusion, represent a significant improvement in the comprehension of the interaction between geographical space and growth.

However, it is important to note that most NEG models can generate very different results in terms of the economic impact of variations in transport costs, depending on the values assumed by critical parameters of the models and on the role assumed by different agglomeration and dispersion forces. Hence, it becomes crucial not only to further develop research on this issue but also to carefully analyze the results of the empirical literature that are discussed in Chapter 7.

CHAPTER 4

Data Issues

Contents

4.1 INTRODUCTION

When Weber (1929) first introduced his theoretical work on the effect of distance—and related transport costs—on the optimal location of the economic activity, one of the main received critics was the simplification related to the evaluation of the transport costs, mainly in connection with different regional characteristics (and potential transport infrastructure elements). This issue was highlighted by many authors (e.g., Fujita & Krugman, 1995; Fujita, Krugman, & Venables, 1999) with the definition of the limitations of different modeling approaches whenever spatial elements—and related infrastructure endowment—are used within applied models.

The selection of appropriate variables for the interpretation of economic phenomena has been always a challenging task, mainly in relation with the correct interpretation of the collected elements and the related results. Similarly, the collection of reliable and representative data for the transport sector has been proven even more critical because the effectiveness of the analysis of the transport system is normally related to the correct representation of the spatial environment. In fact, although—as in every economic model—several alternative statistical values may represent the same kind of phenomenon, the choice among different transport variables can substantially change the results of the analysis. For instance, in the road sector, the capacity of an infrastructure might be represented by either a plurality of static values, like the length of the road network, length per lane of road network, and number of vehicles before achieving congestion. Alternatively, dynamic ones can be used, like the number of cars possibly using the road network over a year or over a day or number of cars considering either average commercial speed or maximum speed over a

Economic Role of Transport Infrastructure
ISBN 978-0-12-813096-4
https://doi.org/10.1016/B978-0-12-813096-4.00004-4

certain period of time. Moreover, those variables might also be affected by the quality of the infrastructure as well (e.g., paved or unpaved roads). Obviously, the different interpretations of "capacity" affect the real usability of the correct variable.

Thus, data choice and collection in the transport assessment exercise are normally linked to a series of criticalities: (1) the same situation can be represented by a plurality of variables that are not strictly interchangeable among each other; (2) it is often very difficult to check the quality of the data; and (3) some variables may represent different aspects associated with infrastructure, depending on the methodology used. Furthermore, because the transport network is normally represented by both nodes and arches, certain data might have a reduced meaning if they are only linked to one of these elements (e.g., assessing congestion of a motorway not considering the number of entrance/exits of the motorways, the origin/destination matrix, or the different lanes of the motorway itself).

Table 4.1, for instance, shows a few examples in relation of variables used to describe port infrastructure endowment by different authors (1). As it is possible to see, depending on the goal of the analysis, port capacity and related terminal activities have been represented using financial, reputational, operational, and physical values.

Thus, the assessment of transport infrastructure and its characteristics is strictly linked to the choice of relevant data and measures that should be able to represent the problem of interest. Moreover, some values are normally used to represent either business (i.e., related to the companies that use the infrastructure, such as in the case of revenues or financial elements) or economic (i.e., related to the general transport market or to the macroeconomic elements, such as in the case of capital investment or market prices) characteristics of the transport sector. Despite the inclusion of these elements, most of the abovementioned variables hardly have an operational meaning in terms of actual infrastructure endowment, not directly assuring a certain level of traffic or productivity. The possibility to find and evaluate relevant and meaningful data is then crucial for the representation of the regional capital endowment.

Although the choice of a given variable might be connected to the final aim of the analysis developed by the researcher, a further critical element often encountered by scholars is related to the discrepancies in collecting information on the quality of the network (2). Indeed, potential inconsistencies arise when comparing different statistical sources, or even when comparing data for different regions within the same database.

Table 4.1 Example of data used to represent port infrastructure endowment

Reference	Paper title	Data used to represent ports
Park & Seo (2016)	The impact of seaports on the regional economies in South Korea: Panel evidence from the augmented Solow model	Port throughput, container traffic, port investment value
Perez, Trujillo, & Gonzalez (2016)	Efficiency determinants of container terminals in Latin America and the Caribbean (LAC)	Port connectivity index, length of quays, storage facilities, number of cranes
Serebrisky et al. (2016)	Exploring the drivers of port efficiency in Latin America and the Caribbean	Mobile cranes, STS cranes, port area, throughput, berth length
Song & van Geenhuizen (2014)	Port infrastructure investment and regional economic growth in China: Panel evidence in port regions and provinces	Capital stock, port traffic
Wanke (2013)	Physical infrastructure and shipment consolidation efficiency drivers in Brazilian ports	Berth number, warehousing area, yard area
Wilmsmeier & Hoffmann (2008)	Liner Shipping Connectivity and Port Infrastructure as Determinants of Freight Rates in the Caribbean	Connectivity indexes, port area, number of services, number of ships served, number of companies calling at the ports, size of the vessels
Asteris & Collins (2007)	Developing Britain's port infrastructure: markets, policy, and location	GDP, stakeholders' reports, handling capacity
Haralambides (2002)	Competition, Excess Capacity, and the Pricing of Port Infrastructure	Investment costs, traffic, handling capacity
Notteboom, Coeck, & van Den Broeck (2000)	Measuring and explaining the relative efficiency of container terminals by means of Bayesian Stochastic Frontier Models	Centrality index with respect to hinterland served, number of cranes, terminal area, quay length, workers

Table 4.2 sums up the statistics of different countries within the Latin America region, including details of their transportation systems. The table shows how countries belonging to a certain region could be—in principle—compared using the overall network length but also assessing specific networks' quality characteristics (such as paved, unpaved, or length of expressways) as well as the density of those infrastructures. Nevertheless, not all the countries publish the same kind of data (e.g., length of expressway), thus reducing the possibility to develop consistent comparisons and related assessments.

This issue is even more important if linked to the level of geographical accuracy of different variables. For instance, many countries just publish statistics at Federal or State level, affecting the quality of the data used. An example is included in Bottasso, Conti, Ferrari, and Tei (2014) in which some of the used variables are declared to be only at NUTS2 level, whereas others can be found at NUTS3 level, where NUTS is the "*Nomenclature des unités territoriales statistiques*" and therefore the size of the statistical geographical unit (in which NUTS2 represent bigger regions than NUTS3). Similar geographical aggregation issues might be also encountered with the OECD's TL region (Box 4.1).[1]

Moreover, as assessed in Ducruet & Lugo (2013) and Calatayud et al. (2016), transport infrastructure is now often studied using network-related variables in which some specific variables (e.g., the transport flow) are often used as proxies for both demand (e.g., cargo using an infrastructure) and supply (e.g., level of connectivity and accessibility), depending on the methodology used (3).

In particular, the use of aggregated indexes, such as the Logistics Performance Index (World Bank, 2017), the Doing Business Indexes (World Bank, 2018a), and mode specific indexes (such as the Liner Shipping Connectivity Index promoted by UNCTAD (2018)), represents a further attempt to homogenize transport data worldwide, even though it seems to reduce the possibility to assess regional-specific situations. This latter element is mainly linked to the fact that aggregated indexes are normally developed at macroregional or country level, not allowing for comparisons among local units.

[1] Refer to http://ec.europa.eu/eurostat/statistics-explained/index.php/Glossary:Nomenclature_of_territorial_units_for_statistics_(NUTS) for a definition of NUTS level and to http://www.oecd.org/cfe/regional-policy/regionalstatisticsandindicators.htm for TL regions.

Table 4.2 Example of different length values to represent roadway network data

	Brazil	Argentina[a]	Chile[a]	Colombia	Venezuela	Peru	Ecuador
Total roadway network (km)	1,580,964	231,374	77,764	206,500	96,189	140,672	43,670
Paved (km)	212,798	69,412	18,119	n.a.	n.a.	18,699	6,472
Unpaved (km)	1,368,166	161,962	59,645	n.a.	n.a.	121,973	37,198
Unpaved/paved	6	2	3	n.a.	n.a.	7	6
Paved/Area	0.025	0.025	0.024	n.a.	n.a.	0.015	0.023
Unpaved/Area	0.164	0.059	0.080	n.a.	n.a.	0.095	0.134
Area (sq. km)	8,358,140	2,736,690	743,812	1,038,700	882,050	1,279,996	276,841

[a]expressway data also available.
Source: Authors' elaboration from the CIA factbook, 2016.

Box 4.1 The geographical units

Every country and international organizations use specific methods to organize regional statistics, normally forming standardized geographical units for registering economic and social indicators. The most common systems used for international analyses are the ones used for the OECD Regional Statistics (i.e., Territorial Levels [TL]) and for the Eurostat database (i.e., *Nomenclature des unités territoriales statistiques* [NUTS]). Interestingly, all the geographical units are organized through a hierarchical aggregation method, with several levels that represent bigger and smaller regions. For instance, Eurostat system is based on four geographical levels in which NUTS0 represents countries, NUTS1 represents macroregions within certain countries [i.e., NUTS0], NUTS2 represents regions within certain NUTS1, and NUTS3 represents provinces within certain NUTS2. Similarly, TL system contains three different levels (i.e., states, first administrative tier, and second administrative tier). Despite this common structure, different systems normally use different methods in the definition of relevant regions: for instance, although OECD uses an administrative division, Eurostat prioritizes the homogeneity of certain characteristics (i.e., population) to guarantee the comparability of relevant statistics. This difference generates inconsistent data among the two main international data sources, at least for some of the common studied countries.

Similar differences can be found in other international and national databases, such as for the different definition of the metropolitan areas by the OECD and other regional institutions.

The elements underlined above raise a problem of data acquisition and of correct measurement of certain elements that normally affect transport analysis. This chapter discusses the correct approach to measurement of transport system taking into account data collection issues.

4.2 MEASUREMENTS OF TRANSPORT SYSTEMS

As for the famous "problem of measurement" concept that characterize quantum mechanics, also transport systems are characterized by a defined difficulty in accounting for measurements that can lead to a good representation of the intended outcome, especially when this measurement has to be included in a formal mathematical model. This problem is linked to the impossibility of unanimously representing the regional endowment in terms of needed transport infrastructure or the impossibility of clearly quantifying the optimal use (i.e., efficiency and productivity level) of a given transport system. This fact has been underlined by a multitude of contributions, for instance, assessing transport efficiency from different points of view (e.g., Janic, 2007; Gutierrez, Monzon, & Pifiero, 1998). The difficulties underlined above generate several problems for the assessment of transport investments that will be discussed in Chapter 5. Current sections will instead focus on the problem of finding relevant measures to describe transport endowment of a certain region (e.g., Torrisi, 2009).

In many policy papers (e.g., EU, 2017; World Bank, 2018b), the problem of determining the need for further infrastructure investment is often linked to the definition of a sufficient level of endowment in terms of both transport infrastructure and services. Thus, an important element in evaluating transport infrastructure is not just the quantity of the transport network (e.g., length of railway) but also the level of service guaranteed by that network (e.g., frequency of trains, passengers per km) and the possibility to increase the level of accessibility of a region. Hence, while from a statistical point of view certain measures could be representative of a particular level of infrastructural endowment, the representation of the network and the connectivity of different nodes of the network are relevant information to be discussed and included in the transport measurement problem.

Therefore, whereas for a static assessment of the network, the quantity and quality of the infrastructure are key parameters, endowment is often assessed in terms of density of the infrastructure, the level of connectivity guaranteed by the network, and the population served by the transport service. For instance, during the railway investment phase, new stations and rail lines were built either trying to connect most populated areas or essential production facilities (e.g., mines, factories) and trade nodes (e.g., ports). The definition of *density* then covers an articulated subject that should consider both the regional extension and the population distribution. Therefore, density is normally considered a proxy for the capillarity of the transport network. This element has caused a hierarchy among different infrastructures with roads that often offer higher density levels than railways (but the density could vary depending on the specific infrastructure typology because expressways are normally less widespread than traditional roads). Similarly, ports are normally more numerous than airports.

The role of flow variables in representing transport infrastructure is a key element of several transport studies. Transport activity is characterized not only by variables that measure the activity over a certain period of time (e.g., pax for the studied year) but also by variables related to the distance covered by the relevant flow. Measures of pax (/cargo-kilometer (or -mile)) are common measures that combine the quantity with the distance covered within a certain period of time. This unit of measure is particularly important for the transport business as it gives an idea of the potential use of the vehicles during the given period of time. For instance, the same airplane used for shorter routes could serve more passengers than it is employed on longer routes—within the same period of time and with the same payload—just because of the length of the route. Obviously, this might affect both the frequency of the service and the number of vehicles needed to transport the same quantity of either passengers or cargo.

On the other hand, graph theory is normally applied to better understand the need for further infrastructure in connection with a measure of centrality of a certain node (e.g., a city, a port, a region, or any other point that might be connected) in a given network (e.g., Derrible & Kennedy, 2011). A general centrality degree is normally given by the "speed" with which a node is connected to the others; a higher centrality degree then reflects a higher number of nodes directly connected to the studied one. Among different measures, eccentricity, closeness, and betweenness are the most commonly used indexes to measure the level of connectivity of a given node. According to Jalili et al. (2016) "*Betweenness centrality is based upon the frequency with which a node lies between the shortest communication path of all other possible pairs of nodes within a network and highlights the gatekeepers of communication within the network. Eccentricity centrality of a node is calculated as the reciprocal of the maximum of shortest path lengths from that node to all other nodes in the network. In contrast the closeness centrality is measured by the reciprocal of sum of the geodesic distances from that node to all other nodes in the network.*" Thus, while centrality can be used as a measure of connectivity of different points within a region, different measures can be used to determine the role of this node within a certain network, as well as the effect of a problem occurred to the studied node on the other parts of the network, planning relevant solutions (Box 4.2).

Together with their general role of nodes within a network, transport terminals are normally measured through quantitative factors, at financial, operative, and physical levels. Table 4.3 sums up the main quantitative statistics normally used to describe main terminal infrastructures.

It is important to point out that many of these variables are found in differentiated versions, independently from the mode, and can be evaluated using gross and net values. For example, the container traffic is often

Box 4.2 Measures of connectivity

Graph theory helps understanding the role of different nodes within a given network, as the one represented in Graph 4.1 below. Given the different positions of the nodes and the distance (given by the squared value on each node) while X is the only node connected to every other destination (i.e., registering higher centrality degree), the shortest path to every other node is guaranteed by node C (i.e., betweenness). Both C and X have equivalent values in terms of closeness degree. This situation generates different values for the different centrality indexes of the network, increasing potential misunderstanding in finding useful measures to represent it.

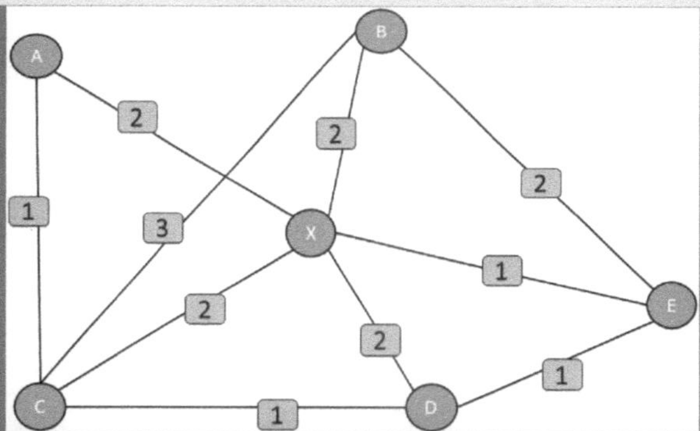

Graph 4.1 General network.

published in tonnes, TEUs or FEUs[2] and such alternative measures are strongly affected by the conversion rates used, thus affecting their level of comparability (but it a matter of fact that moving a 40-feet container is completely different from moving two 20-feet containers in terms of time spent, energy cost, etc.). Moreover, some of these values (e.g., exchange rates/purchase power for financial elements; representation of density levels for physical factors; level of productivity for operational elements) do not always follow the same level of regional representation. For instance, while

[2] For instance, several logistics operators and ports release data in terms of either TEU (i.e., twenty equivalent units) or tonnes even if two-third of their traffic is composed by FEU (i.e., forty equivalent units), applying a standard conversion rate between TEU and tonnes (that varies from 9 tonnes per TEU to 15 tonnes per TEU) affecting the exact amount of cargo handled.

Table 4.3 Example of quantitative variables used to describe the transport network

	Physical	Financial	Operational
Ports	Draft, yard area, berths, quays, equipment (e.g., cranes)	Investment, import/export, income, link with relevant economic sectors, cost of transport, capital stock	Labor force, connected maritime services, direct calls, hinterland connectivity level, throughput, number of pax, number of ships, ship size, custom procedures, time of operations
Airports	Length of runways, number of runways, terminal area, gates	Investment, income, import/export, cost of transport, capital stock	Slots, labor force, connection with the "hinterland," time of operations, number of flights, number of pax/cargoes, service frequency, number of connected airports
Railways	Length of the tracks, gauge, number of tracks, rail park equipment (e.g., cranes), station characteristics	Investment, income, cost of transport, capital stock	Labor force, weight and length of the train, number of wagons, height of trains, tunnels and other constraints, stations characteristics, slots, speed, time of operations, number of trains, number of pax/cargo, service frequency
Roads	Length of the road, number of lanes, capacity of lanes	Investment, income, import/export, cost of transport, capital stock	Speed, vehicles characteristics, time of operations, frequency, number of vehicles, number of pax/cargo

all nodal infrastructures (e.g., ports and airports) are "locally embedded"—and so are the related variables— it is not always true for network infrastructures (e.g., capacity over a region is normally linked to the entire network and then shared by multiple regions). Moreover, while physical characteristics hardly change over short periods of time and they are characterized by lumpy effects (see Chapter 2); financial and operational characteristics vary considerably over short periods of time, generating different infrastructure "endowment" data even if the infrastructure is not physically varied (i.e., the airport capacity might change because of a better distribution of slots even if the characteristics of both terminals and runways remain the same).

Similarly, the transport flow (e.g., number of vehicles per hour in a given part of the network) is normally considered an essential performance measure for the transport planning and to identify the level of potential congestion of the network itself. Concerning this element, and especially for network infrastructure, the assessment of potential bottlenecks is a strategic measure for understanding the regional infrastructure endowment.

In addition to the "quantity", transport infrastructure is often characterized by a certain level of quality that strongly affects the evaluation of the regional endowment. The definition of quality has changed over the time and it is normally dependent from the technological level of a given region.

A good example of the "quality" element in transport network is given by the railway sector. While the length of the network is often a homogenized information worldwide, several characteristics differentiates the railways in different parts of the world. The simplest way is the gauge system, i.e., the spacing between the rail tracks; as it is well known that—at least for the passenger—the larger is the gauge, the more comfortable is the rail journey. Nonetheless, the quality of the infrastructure can also be represented by the electrification rate or the possibility to increase either the quantity of transported goods (i.e., the weight of the wagons or the length of the trains) or the speed (i.e., introduction of high-speed train networks). High-speed networks, in particular, registered a quite interesting development. First high-speed trains have been introduced in Japan in 1964 with the first Shinkansen service and further developed in France (1981) with the first TGV rail link. Starting from the 1990s, several countries introduced high-speed trains, but some of them decided to include mix rail networks for both traditional trains and high-speed ones (despite some technological and organizational challenges). Currently, China has the most extended dedicated network, opened in 2007 and currently still under development;

Chinese high-speed rail network overpasses the 22,000 km (with further plan of doubling the value). Plans for the expansion of a dedicated high-speed rail network are also under discussion in many other countries (e.g., United Kingdom) and also for connecting wider economic areas (e.g., European Union and Asia). The quality of a network is not only given by the "speed" factor but also by other characteristics. In the rail sector, for instance, the standard gauge defines train constraints as well as the possibility to interoperate between different parts of the network. While the standard gauge is becoming more and more common worldwide, specific narrower or broader networks are still present in several world regions (mainly within the former Soviet republics, with differentiated gauges, and in some African and Asian countries, mostly due to their colonial past). This issue caused a series of problems in the possibility to introduce international trains, for instance, slowing down the effectiveness of Asia—Europe train links. Many international initiatives are currently under development for introducing standard measures and increasing the rail performance, nonetheless differences still persist. Table 4.4 sums up main railway characteristics in a sample of countries.

Most of the differences in terms of infrastructure standards and qualitative elements still persist because the perception of quality is often linked to the transport governance structure and to regional characteristics. Indeed, transport is a part of public common capital endowment, quite common in

Table 4.4 Rail network characteristics (in km) in main world countries

	Standard gauge (1.435)	Other gauges	Electrified	High dedicated speed network	Total
Canada	77,932	0	0	0	77,932
United States	293,564	0	3	0	293,564
United Kingdom	16,534	303	5357	0	16,837
Germany	43,209	259	20,052	1	43,468
France	29,473	167	15,624	2	29,64
Italy	18,77	1412	13,167	1	20,181
Russia	0	87,157	40,3	0	87,157
China	124	0	80	22	124
Japan	4,8	22,511	20,534	2764	27,311
India	0	68,525	23,654	0	68,525

Source: Authors' elaboration from CIA data (2017) and rail network operators.

continental Europe and in most Asian countries, whereas the transport sector is mostly privatized in the Anglo-Saxon tradition, such as in United Kingdom, United States, and Australia. While the former element plays a great role in the perception of the public/private stakeholders and their willingness in investing for upgrading the network, the latter factor heavily affects the possibility to make some investments. For instance, most countries that do not have an electrified railway network are normally characterized by less dense populated areas (and then by a needed service frequency and length size of trains that do not justify the investment for electrification) or environmental challenges (e.g., special climate conditions, mountains, islands). Thus, the comparison among networks should normally incorporate those characteristics to assess their "quality."

Similarly to gauge and electrification, other transport networks are often characterized by specific characteristics, such as the pavement percentage of roads and airports' runways or the inclusion of specific services within the infrastructure (e.g., parking slots, storage areas). Moreover, special characteristics (e.g., pavements, information services) are normally linked to an upgrade in terms of infrastructural goals, such as the possibility to reduce accidents or to increase the productivity of the network.

Starting from the 1990s, several national policy interventions in the transport sector have been determined in view of achieving better environmental performances (EEA, 2018). For this reason, the capability to shift transport flows from road to less pollutant transport modes (e.g., railways, sea) has been considered a key element for the development of an advanced transport system as well as the energy efficiency of the network itself. From the former measures, the presence of logistic parks—in which to perform the modal shift—and the adoption of smart technologies to increase the smoothness of transport (e.g., virtual checking points within motorways section, clearance gates, tracking systems, and sensors) have been the most commonly used infrastructure upgrades all over the world. On the other hand, energy efficiency measures—together with other environmental investments—have been pushed in many transport networks. A good example for this is the increased investments in new bunkering stations at port level (e.g., to substitute traditional fuels with LNG) as well as the possibility to include both wind and solar generation plants within the port structures, decreasing the pollution generated by ship operations (e.g., Arduino et al., 2013). Thus, measures connected to infrastructure characteristics are now linked to the environmental performance, such as noise and emissions, increasing the role of the external elements (together with accessibility and accidents) included in the transport network measurements.

Moreover, starting from the introduction of the just-in-time strategy around the 1970s, the interoperability and the technological readiness of transport infrastructure became a key element in the evaluation of the regional transport system. Endowment is now not just a matter of length of the network or of the specific characteristics of the service, but it is also connected to the possibility to include technological innovations or to perform advanced logistics services. Measurements are now including also the reliability of the operations as well as the capability of the single infrastructure to be interconnected with a plurality of transport modes. This is particularly relevant for nodal infrastructures, such as ports, logistics parks, railway stations, and airports. Focusing on seaports, in accordance with Notteboom and Rodrigue (2008), dwell time[3] and the reliability of cargo-handling operations in terms on inbound and outbound flows are key factors in the maritime industry to choose the port in which to call at. Thus, while the physical characteristics of ports might be similar, the possibility to consistently perform well in terms of dwell time and to efficiently be connected with trucks and rail is becoming a key element to compare ports, more than just the connectivity indexes or other physical characteristics (e.g., draft).

Eventually, while for measuring the transport infrastructure, quantity and quality variables are often used to describe and assess the network—representing the supply of transport—a different viewpoint is normally given in assessing the demand of transport. Measures of demand are normally associated with the costumers of a given transport infrastructure, thus being defined by the flow passing through the infrastructure (e.g., passengers, cargo handled, number of vehicles).

Table 4.5 shows an example for the airport sector, including the main 10 worldwide airports for traffic. Although the overall capacity of these airports is greater than the registered traffic (and probably mixed between passenger and cargo), the flow establishes a measure of demand. Despite this consideration, as also mentioned above, flows are often used to represent both the demand and the supply, depending on the analysis and the methods.

[3] Dwell time is the time that the cargo has to spent in the port area before either be loaded on a ship (in an export flow) or be able to leave to port gate (in an import operation) after all the port activities have been concluded.

Table 4.5 Airport statistics worldwide

	Cargo (2017 data)			Passengers (2016 data)	
	Airport	**Tonnes**		**Airport**	**Pax**
1	Hong Kong, HK	4,881,075	1	Atlanta, US	104,171,935
2	Memphis, US	4,307,050	2	Beijing, CN	94,393,454
3	Shanghai, CN	3,703,431	3	Dubai, AE	83,654,250
4	Incheon, KR	2,791,739	4	Los Angeles, US	80,921,527
5	Anchorage, US	2,689,306	5	Tokyo, JP (HND)	79,699,762
6	Dubai, AE	2,651,467	6	Chicago, US	77,960,588
7	Louisville, US	2,442,331	7	London, GB	75,715,474
8	Tokyo, JP (NRT)	2,272,612	8	Hong Kong, HK	70,305,857
9	Taipei, TW	2,233,493	9	Shanghai, CN	66,002,414
10	Frankfurt, DE	2,110,670	10	Paris, FR	65,933,145

Source: Authors' elaboration from Airport council international, 2018.

In assessing transport networks, the abovementioned measures are normally linked to relevant economic (e.g., GDP, Trade, foreign direct investments) and business (e.g., revenues, labor characteristics, company investments) related variables. While the choice of which variable should be used is normally methodology driven, the accordance between the geographical aggregation of the transport network characteristics (e.g., city, province, region, nation) and the related economic variables is normally a challenge, often affecting the reliability of the assessment. For instance, it is often not easy to find trade or investment data for smaller geographical units, whereas it is relatively easier to collect them at regional or national level. Thus, the problem of measurement is often not just linked to the choice of the right variables but also in terms of the spatial level, as also briefly discussed in Bottasso, Castagnetti et al. (2013) and Bottasso, Conti et al. (2013).

4.3 DATA FOR SYSTEMS' EVALUATION

If the problem of choosing the right measure to perform a transport analysis can be considered relatively hard but it is normally research driven, the provision of worldwide and regional transport data is even more challenging, given the scattered source of information. In fact, while every country is normally providing reliable data, that information is not perfectly consistent if the goal is an international comparison. Nonetheless, they might be quite useful in terms of specific regional and local assessments.

International database, as mentioned, are relatively uncommon and—in their attempt to provide comparable datasets for a variety of countries—they often provide conflicting information with national statistics providers.

Table 4.6 lists a series of international sources that provides regional information and transport network characteristics.

The use of national datasets is normally the optimal choice for comparing different infrastructure systems, given the level of detail often

Table 4.6 Main worldwide database

	Transport network	Economic variables	Link
General database			
CIA Factbook	☆		https://www.cia.gov/library/publications/the-world-factbook/
World Bank—LPI	☆		https://lpi.worldbank.org/
World Bank—DB	☆	☆	http://www.doingbusiness.org/
World Bank		☆	https://data.worldbank.org/
IMF		☆	http://www.imf.org/external/index.htm
UNCTAD	☆	☆	http://unctadstat.unctad.org/EN/
Regional sources			
OECD	☆	☆	http://www.oecd.org/cfe/regional-policy/regionalstatisticsandindicators.htm
IDB	☆	☆	https://data.iadb.org/Datacatalog/Dataset
ECLAC	☆	☆	http://www.cepal.org
Eurostat	☆	☆	http://ec.europa.eu/eurostat
ADB	☆	☆	https://www.adb.org/data/statistics
Public Industry sources			
AAPA—ports	☆		http://www.aapa-ports.org/
ESPO—ports	☆		https://www.espo.be/
ACI—airports	☆		http://www.aci.aero/Data-Centre
IATA—airports	☆		http://www.iata.org/services/statistics/
UIC—railway	☆		https://uic.org/statistics

included in local databases. Nevertheless, the inclusion of data from different sources always generates inconsistencies in the treatment of relevant statistics. This is particularly true for the assessment of transport infrastructure, whenever the counting of the same variable could be done applying different methods. Table 4.7 shows an example of the discrepancies that can be highlighted in the port sector in relation with the traffic variable. Eurostat and ESPO (European SeaPort Organization) offer statistics on the majority of the EU ports, but the collection methods differ considerably, generating inconsistencies in the availability of updated data (in the table below the last common year is 2015), the unit of measure (for the containerized cargo tonnes, handled boxes, and TEUs are commonly used to register port traffic), and the overall values, especially in comparison with official port statistics or national accounting systems. Moreover, while national accounting systems are normally updated for major ports, they register delays in collecting data for medium–small ports, reducing the availability of information of the most recent months (or years, in some cases). As mentioned in ESPO's website (2018), main differences then rely on the fact that "*Eurostat relies on data from the National Competent Authorities*

Table 4.7 Comparison among different statistical source of the same data

Source	Eurostat	ESPO	National statistics (or port when national accounting is not present)	
Data	2015, TEU	2015, TEU	2015, TEU	Last available
Antwerpen	9,370,000	9,653,511	9.653.511	122,969,439 (Tonnes, 2017)
Hamburg	8,848,000	8,821,481	8,821,481	8,815,469 (TEU, 2017)
Genova	2,079,000	2,242,902	2.242.902	2,297,917 (TEU, 2016)
Gioia Tauro	3,030,000	n.a.	2.546.805	2,762,000 (TEU, 2016)
La Spezia	1,579,000	1,300,442	1.300.442	1,272,425 (TEU, 2016)
Rotterdam	11,577,000	12,234,535	12,234,535	13,700,000 (TEU, 2017)
Felixstowe	4,043,000	n.a.	n.a.	24,764,000 (tonnes, 2016)

The inconsistency of data is often causing interpretation problems, provoking limits in the possibility to generate time series merging data coming from different database. In fact, as shown in Table 4.7, while average discrepancies could be considered marginal (around 3%–4%), some years could register differences of more than 20% (e.g., La Spezia) causing a general distortion in the use of mixed datasets.

Source: Authors' elaboration from different statistical sources, 2018.

(NCAs). The source of ESPO data are the port authorities themselves. Eurostat disseminates figures on the gross weight of goods handled in the ports (excluding the tare weight of containers and RO-RO units). However, ESPO ports use the gross-gross weight of goods (including the tare weight of containers and RO-RO units). Eurostat figures on number of TEUs handled only cover Lo-Lo containers (Lifted-on Lifted —off). Ro-Ro containers (Rolled-on Rolled-off) are counted as Ro-Ro units. ESPO data reports number of containers in TEU independently of the kind of vessel transporting them." Thus, collection methods and different interpretations of same elements generate differences within the same variable.

CHAPTER 5

Investment Appraisal

Contents

Investment appraisal is really a hard matter, namely when it regards infrastructure. This is due to the fuzzy boundaries on this kind of exercise. In fact, the impacts of transport infrastructure are geographically, temporarily, and socially dispersed and diversified.

Nevertheless, it is important to have a tool, even an imperfect one, that can inform decision-makers, especially when resources—and especially public resources—are scarce.

This chapter is devoted to analyzing the monetary and nonmonetary techniques that economists have proposed to perform ex ante transport investments appraisal. We will deal in particular with the Cost—Benefit Analysis (hereinafter CBA), the MultiCriteria Analysis (hereinafter MCA), and the Input—Output Analysis (hereinafter IOA). None of these techniques is optimal *in re ipsa*, but each presents strengths and weaknesses with respect to the others.

Before exploring the methodologies and technicalities of the approaches just mentioned, it is noteworthy to discuss the rationale of the *ex-ante* evaluations and which goals they try to achieve.

Economic Role of Transport Infrastructure
ISBN 978-0-12-813096-4
https://doi.org/10.1016/B978-0-12-813096-4.00005-6

5.1 THE GOAL(S) TO BE ACHIEVED

The definition of the goal to be achieved through an investment in infrastructure is not as irrelevant or even neutral (with respect to results) as it could appear at first. In fact, it assumes that the subject entitled to take this decision has been clearly defined. In this book, we assume that this subject is a public entity, either the central government or a local institution, i.e., someone interested in maximizing the welfare for a certain community. But in case of a private investment, the subject who invests his money is interested—only or mainly—in the possibility to gain some profits from the investment.

The private and public points of view differ for the number and volume of the effects that enter in the appraisal process. An example will clarify this difference. Imagine a new tolled highway connecting two sites already connected by a no-tolled road. Adopting a private point of view, that of a private company investing in the new highway, all the vehicles using the new infrastructure will contribute to the benefits of the investment, whereas on the side of costs will be considered only those effects determining a monetary expense. Otherwise, adopting a public or social point of view among the benefits will enter only those users that decide to move only in consequence of the new infrastructure—the users that move from the old road to the new one are not considered if their generalized transport cost (GTC)[1] does not change—whereas the costs are represented not only by those effects determining a monetary expense but also by some nonmonetary items as the impact on pollution, safety, and time spent by users on traveling.

As anticipated above, we will adopt a public perspective interested in the maximization of a social goal, but the interest of private investors could be considered as a specific case of the more general rules of the appraisal process because it considers only what impacts on the private sphere of the investors. We agree with Cole (2005) who states that: "A social cost benefit basis is a comprehensive evaluation of modal options, where all relevant impacts are taken into account using social, rather than the private, benefits and costs."

In general, utility is assumed as the unit of measure for collective welfare, and this kind of analysis takes into consideration the variations of

[1] The generalized transport cost is the sum of the monetary and nonmonetary (i.e., the value of time, the comfort of transport services) cost of transport.

collective welfare, i.e., the usefulness or enjoyment that individuals get from using a resource.

In general, the appraisal process is based on the principle of compensation introduced by Kaldor (1939) and Hicks (1940) that, being less stringent, overcomes the so-called "status quo tyranny" due to the Pareto's efficiency notion. In short, this is the rationale of the CBA that gains and losses in consumer surplus resulting from a particular intervention may be summed up and compared, concluding in advising the decision-maker to take the investment if the former exceeds the latter. According to Mishan (1972), if the algebraic sum of compensating variations is positive, the intervention will realize “a potential Pareto improvement”.

Two important assumptions are implicit in this way of conducting the appraisal.

The first one refers to the final goal of the analysis or the criteria of decision; measuring variations in consumer surplus assumes efficiency as the leading criterion. But other criteria could be used as effectiveness, that is the capacity of an intervention to achieve a specific goal as, for instance, the reduction of fatalities, or equity, that implies the fairness of an intervention. Following the previous example, fatalities may be reduced also adopting strict speed limits, but this measure will impact on the efficiency of the transport system. Therefore, the three criteria—efficiency, effectiveness, and fairness—may conflict each other and the maximization of one of them may impact on the others. At the same time, when the decision-maker has to choose among several options, it is often the case that the ranking of the options changes with the decision criterion.

The second assumption regards winners and losers of the intervention: it is not relevant who wins and who losses and how benefits are spread among users or territories that are crossed by the infrastructure; moreover, in the CBA, it is also not relevant if the Kaldor–Hicks compensation is effectively paid. In other words, any distributive effect is simply not considered, even if distributive considerations may be included in the analysis afterward.

It is also relevant to take into account the private or public nature of winner and losers; Little and Mirrlees (1974) suggested to weigh the benefits discriminating between public and private gains because “raising tax revenue creates distortions” (Little & Mirrlees, 1991).

In transport infrastructure projects, changes in accessibility are considered a good measure of the effects on welfare deriving from a project; the economic literature stresses that accessibility has got strong relationships with economic efficiency and equity (Geurs, Boon, & van Wee, 2016;

Rietveld, 2003; Banister & Berechman, 2001). In fact, an accessibility improvement may result in lower logistics costs for firms and lower GTCs for travelers, but a transport infrastructure, as described in Chapter 3, may even result in a competitive advantage of a region with respect to its neighbors.

Even if the adoption of utility (i.e., the consumer surplus) as the variable to be maximized by infrastructure investment is generally accepted and supported by central and local institutions in their guidelines about transport investment appraisal, other goals (or variables to be optimized) have been suggested. Rawls (1971) proposes to look at the individual holdings of primary social goods, a mixed of means (as freedom of movements, thought, etc.) and resources (i.e., income) (Brighouse & Robeyns, 2010), whereas Sen (2000) suggests to maximize the individual capabilities[2] and therefore he criticizes traditional CBA because it lacks to evaluate personal freedoms and because it is based on market valuations. Moreover, as highlighted by Yard (2012), Sen conceives freedom also as a process thus focusing on the discussion on the various investment alternatives. On this issue, some steps forward have been done at least in some countries opening the discussion on projects to anyone interested in, as in France with the voting of law N 2002-276 that introduced the *debat public*.

The utilitarian perspective that gives CBA an ethical foundation (van Wee, 2012) adopting a general vision irrespective of the individual positions raises several concerns about:

- The degree of democracy of the transport planning process. van Wee (2011) stresses in his book that "democracy has to be concerned both with majority rule and the rights of minorities", but there could also be cases in which the benefits are concentrated among few agents and costs are spread among a larger number of agents and if benefits exceed costs—and these costs are widely dispersed so that they are almost negligible for any single subject—the minority imposes its will.
- The applicability of some principles of justice to the transport planning process. In most countries (for instance, the European Union) mobility

[2] "Capability" is a term coined by the Nobel prize Amartya Sen. As he states:
"A person's 'capability' is represented by the set of n-tuples of functionings from which the person can choose any one n-tuple. The 'capability set' thus stands for the actual freedom of choice a person has over alternative lives that he or she can lead and reflects a variety of factors including personal characteristics and social arrangements" (Sen, 1990).

is perceived like a right; in particular circumstances, as in rural contexts this right must be balanced with the inability of infrastructural investment to fully recover their cost, hence the need to balance the acknowledgment of a right (mobility) with a loss of resources.

Also deontology perspective should inform the CBA process. In particular, because transport investment changes accessibility, it is particularly important to take care of the impacts on social values (Geurs et al., 2009)—as public health, personal safety, forced relocation, historical and cultural resources, etc.—other than economic and environmental ones.

5.2 THE COST–BENEFIT ANALYSIS

The CBA consists in the comparison of costs and benefits—direct and indirect—deriving from a specific intervention. Its theoretical foundations may be found in utilitarianism and the Marshallian's concept of consumer's surplus and afterward in welfare economics. The practical adoption of CBA became popular in the United States during the 1930s (during the so-called Roosevelt's New Deal) after the approval of the Flood Control Act in 1936. It recommended this technique for water-related developments and soon afterward CBA began to be applied to several other kinds of investment.

It is a monocriterion decision process; it means that all costs and benefits are expressed through a single unit of measurement: money. This implies that for any item of cost or benefit who is in charge of performing the analysis has to evaluate the magnitude of the impact (positive or negative), resulting from the difference of a particular indicator before the investment (the so-called "do-noting scenario") and after its implementation, and then assigning to that impact a monetary estimation.

The monetary estimation of costs and benefits needs unit prices. There are two possibilities:

- Cost and benefits that are exchanged in the market against a price.
- Costs and benefits that have no price because they refer to elements that are not exchanged on the market. It is the case of nonmonetary items as the time savings or the reduced rate of incidents or the mortality reductions due to an improved transport infrastructure, but also the impact of

pollution and so on. In addition, pure public goods have no market price. All these are usually referred to as intangible effects[3].

Instead, the former case refers to tangible effects, i.e., goods and services whose price is determined by the market. Welfare economics suggests that their prices measure the real value of resources if they are determined in (perfectly) competitive markets; otherwise the market price should be opportunely changed to eliminate distortions due to the reduced competition in the market or due to the existence of externalities or information asymmetry. The result is a shadow price that represents the "social opportunity cost of the resources used" (Drèze & Stern, 1990). In general, shadow prices are in the form of conversion factors to be applied to the market prices. Shadow prices should also be used in case of input rationing (as the case of labor market in the short run) and when the sum invested is so important to have a potential impact on the market price of some resources. In these cases, the shadow prices assume the form of factor of correction of market prices.

In the case of intangible effects (as public goods), it is impossible to determine a shadow price due to the absence of a market price to be opportunely changed; then their value must be estimated through the willingness to pay of consumers (i.e., the consumer surplus). In literature, several methods have been proposed to estimate two of the most important intangible elements mainly concerned with infrastructural investment: human life and the environment.

It is really difficult to determine the economic value of human life, nevertheless it is necessary. Otherwise CBA assumes implicitly that its value is zero. Until the 1960s, estimation of the value of life was based on the discounted sum of expected future income (Brady, 2008). This method is questionable for its implicit implications—the value differs in relation to age, gender, and kind of job—even if it is seldom used to calculate compensations due to injury or death. The willingness to pay approach is suitable to estimate the value of reducing the risk of death or damage, thus deriving not the value of statistical life but the value of reduction of the statistical risk (Sunstein, 2004).

The economic literature proposes also several methods to infer a monetary price for environmental nonmarketed effects that may be classified in direct and indirect approaches. Although direct approaches allow to

[3] In Economic literature, an intangible good is a good or service not market exchanged. It does not matter if it has physical characteristics or not.

estimate the willingness to pay, indirect approaches "measure the relationship between the 'dose' (e.g., pollution) and the non-monetary effect (e.g., health impairment)" (NSW, 2016).

To the first group (direct approach) belong the following methods of estimation:

- Stated preference (SP) surveys; they try to simulate a market by placing hypothetical valuations of real improvements in specific environments.
- Revealed preference (RP); this method has the same goal of SP, but information on the economic importance of an environmental externality is obtained looking at changes in market price of production affected by that externality.
- Contingent valuation; it is a technique aiming at estimating through the observation of the peoples' behaviour the willingness to pay for a benefit or conversely what they would like to receive as a compensation for a damage or a loss.
- Conjoint analysis; it obtains the same result of contingent evaluation asking directly peoples their preferences.

Indirect approaches consider the following methods of estimation:

- Travel cost method. It assumes that the travel cost borne by consumers to visit a specific site (as a recreation or touristic site) proxies its price and thus it derives the consumers' surplus. This approach, firstly suggested by Hotelling in 1946, is applicable only to existing amenities and it is highly site-specific.
- Hedonic prices method. It assumes that environmental features impact on the economic value of residential sites then infers the value of environmental changes analyzing the changes in the rental market. Hedonic prices are used to estimates the value of environmental effects as noise and air pollution as well as costs and benefits due to changes in accessibility. As stated by Henneberry (1997) also the relationship between transport investment and property values is site-specific.
- Mitigating measures. In this case the environmental effect is measured through the cost of replacing or restoring a damage or loss, or through the cost incurred by actions needed to avoid a possible damage (as, for instance, the cost of moving some activities that are too close to an inland terminal treating hazardous goods).

All the abovementioned methods and techniques present pros and cons that are widely discussed in literature due to the possibility of biases in direct surveys, the implications (and the assumptions) of the methods used to aggregate information, and the concrete possibility to generalize results; notwithstanding they allow the nonmonetary effects to enter into the CBA process and contribute to determine its final result.

5.2.1 Benefits Deriving From Infrastructure Investment

Benefits deriving from an infrastructure investment are captured by changes in consumer surplus in the transport market. Effects on other markets may be left out if transport demand is appropriately defined and there are not market imperfections (Jara-Diaz, 1986; Mohring, 1993), otherwise they would represent a double-counting[4].

The positive impact due to an infrastructure improvement results in a lower GTC (due to a reduction in transport time or in transport cost or a combination of both) for users.

In case of improvements to an already existing infrastructure, it is useful to distinguish the users looking at their behaviour into three components:

- Existing demand; travelers and goods that already moved on the same infrastructure (before the improvement) and find even more convenient to go on moving on that infrastructure;
- Diverted demand; travelers and goods that already moved on the same corridor but using a different infrastructure and after the interventions decide to change the transport mode or the infrastructure used in consequence of a lowered generalized cost; and
- Generated demand; travelers and goods that decide to move only in consequence of the lowered generalized cost.

Existing and diverted travelers (and goods) enter in the CBA only if the investment determines a reduction in the GTC. In this way, the benefits represent the advantages they gain with the investment. Otherwise, if the general transport cost does not change, the benefit deriving from the investment is zero[5].

The gains for infrastructure users are measured through the "rule of half" that assuming that the transport demand is linear consists of multiplying the difference between the GTC of the marginal user (before and after the investment) for the sum of the preexisting and the new traffic flow

[4] This is a critical point due to the extremely strict hypothesis. In the real world, made of imperfect markets, effects on other markets may be considerable, leaving room to the so-called wider economic benefits. They are discussed further in the text (see Section 5.2.6).

[5] In literature this is known as the Downs–Thomson paradox (Mogridge, Holden, Bird, & Terzis, 1987). It happens when the level of congestion in the transport system is so high that an infrastructure improvement is not able to reduce the generalized transport cost for users due to the high volume of diverted and added demand that "vanishes" the investment (i.e., after a period of adjustment the level of the generalized transport cost becomes equal to the initial one).

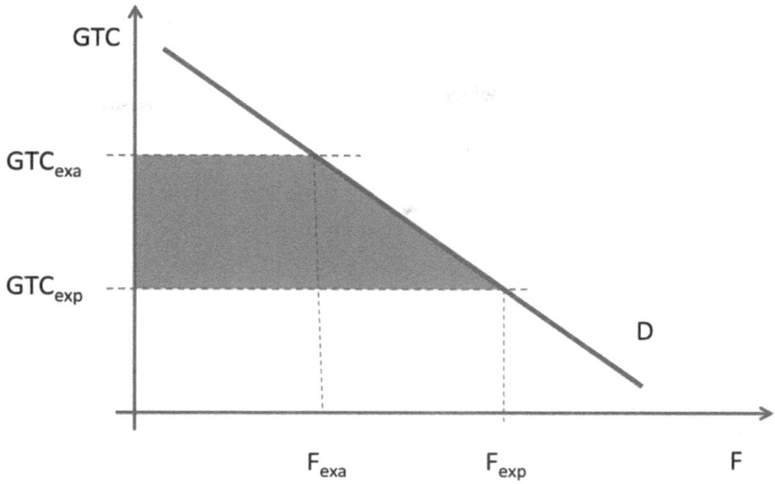

Figure 5.1 The variation of consumers' surplus.

and dividing by two. Fig. 5.1 gives a graphic representation of the formula (Eq. 5.1). In Eq. (5.1) CS stands for consumer surplus and F for the traffic flow; moreover, *exa* stands for ex-ante (the investment) and *exp* for ex-post (the investment).

$$\Delta CS = (GTC_{exa} - GTC_{exp}) \bullet F_{exa} + 1/2\,(GTC_{exa} - GTC_{exp}) \bullet (F_{exp} - F_{exa})$$

$$\Delta CS = 1/2\,(GTC_{exa} - GTC_{exp}) \bullet (F_{exa} + F_{exp}) \qquad (5.1)$$

As already stated, the rule of half approximates the gains in consumer surplus and it is widely accepted in CBA practice. Nevertheless, it cannot be applied in case of the introduction of a completely new mode of transport and when the infrastructure investment is so important to determine a dramatic change in the GTC (Economic Commission for Europe, 2003).

5.2.2 Infrastructure Costs

A transport infrastructure project entails three different kinds of costs: the investment cost, the operation cost, and the maintenance cost[6].

[6] The report written by ECORYS and CE Delft (2005) for the European Commission contains a detailed list of cost items for infrastructure in five different modalities—road, railways, maritime, air, and waterways transports.

In case of building a new asset—either a linear infrastructure, like a road or a railway, or a nodal point, like a port, a station, or an airport—the investment cost represents the greatest part of the overall costs. This item includes the costs due to the planning and reclamation of the area that will be occupied by the infrastructure and the costs due to the building and approval of the asset. These cost items include the financial cost of capital recruited in the financial market and more in general the cost opportunity of capital.

To the monetary costs listed above should be added also some nonmonetary cost items: as the impact on the environment determined by the works of construction and by the existence of the infrastructure asset for its entire life. All these cost items appear (or begin to appear) in the first years of the life span of the asset under construction making the cash flow negative.

Once the asset is built and ready to operate, other cost items appear: the cost associated with the operation and management of the asset. In general, these costs are fully covered by the benefits accruing by the ordinary utilization of the asset (either monetary revenues or nonmonetary gains if the asset is offered to users for free).

The third cost item is represented by the maintenance costs, which, in turn, may be split into routine maintenance costs and periodic maintenance costs. They are essential to maintain the asset efficient along its entire life span. Although the former costs are almost constant over the lifetime of the transport asset, the periodic maintenance costs are more relevant and in some cases they are so important to determine a change in the sign of the annual cash flow (therefore, sometimes they are labeled as renewal costs, thus meaning that these costs are necessary to prolong the lifetime of the asset).

5.2.3 How to Compare Benefits and Costs

Costs and benefits appear along a long period of time; the extremely long life span of infrastructure means that also the effects due to their existence (and use) last for really a long time. Despite this, the CBA usually considers costs and benefits that happen within a period of time that is no longer than 30 years. The last year of analysis coincides with the year of estimation of the remaining capital value, i.e., the residual value of the infrastructure other than the period of analysis (Box 5.1).

Box 5.1 On the residual value of infrastructure

In most cases the life span of infrastructure investment is longer than the period of time taken into account by the appraisal exercise. In these cases, in the last year of the period of analysis appears the residual value among the benefits. In theory the residual value represents "the value of the infrastructure at the end of its project lifetime and the value that the asset generates over time" (Jones et al., 2014). In practice it is often calculated discounting the net benefits expected beyond the analyzed period or more simply as the nondepreciated amount of the asset.

The estimation of the residual value is critical under several perspectives. Actually, the residual value should express not only the depreciated value (as a sort of sales value) of the asset, but this evaluation should take into account the changes in the transportation scenario (occurring in the same and also in the competing transport modes) beyond the time span considered in the analysis. It is not by chance that transport infrastructure expenditures may fall into the category of sunk costs when there is a low value for alternative uses (Helm and Thompson, 1991; Szymanski, 1991; Sánchez, 2000).

In theory, the optimal time period of analysis should coincide with the entire life cycle of the infrastructure (including the period of time necessary to its project and building), but a rule of thumb widely accepted suggests to avoid to exceed 30 years. In fact, it is extremely difficult to foresee what will happen after 30 or more years—one should imagine what will be the future socioeconomic scenario that determines the demand for transport, how it will be shared among the different modes and infrastructures; the costs for the maintenance of the infrastructure, and so on—with a high risk to make some mistakes; but anyway whatever will costs and benefits be estimated, once they are discounted to the first year of analysis, their value will result very small, i.e., they are ineffective with respect to the final result of the analysis.

More practically, the guidelines of the national or supranational agencies suggest the proper extension of the period of time to take into consideration for the different transport sectors or kinds of infrastructure, as shown in Table 5.1.

Then, costs and benefits cannot be immediately compared with each other. It is necessary to discount all costs and benefits applying an opportunity discount rate.

Table 5.1 Reference period of analysis per transport sector (years) for a sample of Countries

Sector	European Union[a]	Australia[b]	UNECE[c]
Railways	30	50	30
• rail sleepers (concrete)		20	
• rail sleepers (timber)			
Roads	25–30	40	
• concrete road pavement			
Ports and airports	25		
Urban transport	25–30		
Control systems (IT system)		5	

[a]ANNEX I to Commission Delegated Regulation (EU) No 480/2014 (EU 2014).
[b]Transport for New South Wales (2016).
[c]UNECE (2003).

From a theoretical point of view, the discount rate should reflect the opportunity cost of money invested in the infrastructure. According to Burgess and Zerbe (2011), economic literature proposes three different approaches to determine the discounting rates: the Social Opportunity Cost of capital (SOC) that reflects the economic value for giving up to invest the same money for the same time in another asset; the Social Time Preference (STP) that adopts a shadow price to take into account the displacement of capital; the Marginal Cost of Funds (MCF) that uses different discount rates between- and within-generations to take into account the need to cover any budgetary expenses due to the investment.

It is worth noticing that the discount rate is a critical factor because it is not neutral to the net result of the comparison of costs and benefits; in fact, a high rate reduces the impact of what happens in the last years analyzed, whereas on the opposite a low discount rate reduces the impact of what happens in the first years considered[7]. As transport infrastructure are characterized by high costs in their first stage of life while benefits emerge only after the construction stage, the adoption of a (relatively) high discount rate may be considered a prudential choice, since it gives more importance to what happens in the first years of the infrastructure project when the flow of costs and benefits may be estimated more accurately. Due to the relevance of the discount rate on the goodness of the analysis, a reference value is often suggested by the institutions interested in supervising public

[7] It is important to note that a discount rate equal to zero makes costs and benefits happening in different years immediately comparable.

investments; notwithstanding analysts may adopt a different discount rate on justification.

5.2.3.1 The Net Present Value

The first mathematical way to compare costs and benefits is summing the difference between the discounted flow of costs and benefits, as shown in Eq. (5.2).

$$\mathrm{NPV} = \sum_{t=0}^{n} (C_t - B_t) \times (1+i)^{-t} \tag{5.2}$$

If the Net Present Value (NPV) is positive (NPV > 0), it means that the benefits deriving from the transport infrastructure exceed the costs, then the infrastructure deserves to be done. The opposite happens if the NPV is negative (NPV < 0).

If NPV = 0, it means that the infrastructural investment is not able to increase the utility in the system and in this situation it is a better choice to avoid to go on with the infrastructure project.

The NPV depends on the choice about the discount rate, as already discussed in this chapter, and on the time span considered by the analysis.

Regarding the choice of the discount rate it is important to consider that the NPV is an inverse function of the discount rate i used in Eq. (5.1), as shown in Fig. 5.2 illustrating that the higher the interest rate, the smaller the net present value.

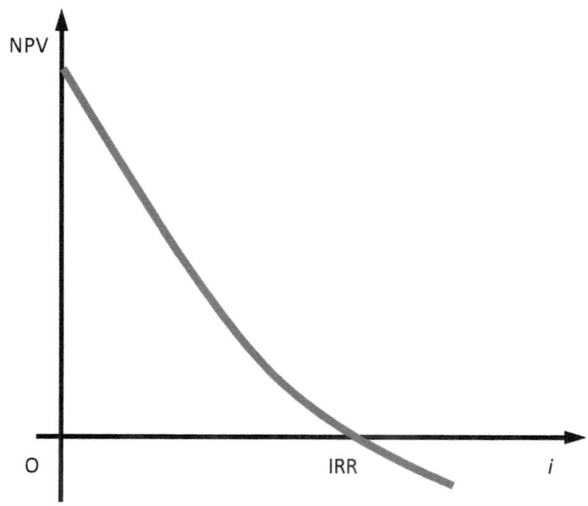

Figure 5.2 Net present value in the function of discount rate.

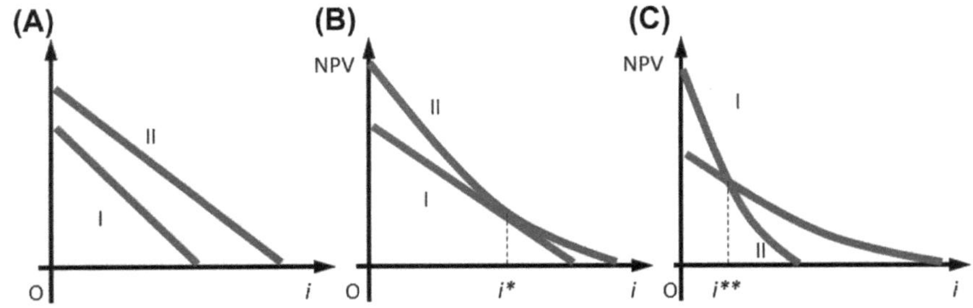

Figure 5.3 Net present value in case of two alternative projects (I and II). (A) alternative II is always better than I; (B) alternative II is always better than I but for a specific rate of interest (*i**); (C) if the rate of interest is lower than i** the best alternative is I; if the rate of interest is upper than i** the best alternative is II.

Moreover, in case of a comparison among several mutually exclusive investment alternatives, the NPV gives a precise rank order only if the discount rate is univocally determined. Otherwise, the analysis may fall into one of the three cases shown in Fig. 5.3 where the relationship between NPV and the discount rate (i) is compared for two alternatives (labeled I and II, respectively).

In Fig. 5.3, in the case sub (A) the alternative II is always better than the alternative I—i.e., the NPV generated by the alternatives II is higher than the NPV generated by the alternative I whatever the discount rate (i) is. In addition, in the case sub (B), the alternative II is better than the alternative I, but there is a specific discount rate (i^*) for which the two alternatives generate the same NPV. Evidently, in such situation the alternative II should be preferred to alternative I due to the uncertainty of the effective value of the rate i along the period of analysis. Lastly, in the case sub (C) the alternative II is preferable to the alternative I if the discount rate is higher than i^{**}, whereas the opposite occurs if the discount rate is lower than i^{**}. According to finance literature, in this scenario the rate i^{**} takes the name of Fisher's intersection (Pandey, 2015)[8]. If the discount rate i^{**} is very high or very low—for instance, 30% or 0.02%—then the situation is not so critical because these are discount rates that are not likely to realize during the lifetime of the infrastructure; consequently, referring to Fig. 5.3 case

[8] According to Fisher, assuming two mutually exclusive projects with an equal initial investment need, there is an "equalizing rate (...) such that the present values of the two options would be equal" (Fisher, 1930). Later on Mao (1969) made explicit the conditions necessary for the existence of one (or even more) Fisher's intersection.

(C), alternative II will be preferred if i^{**} is very low and alternative I will be preferred if i^{**} is very high. When i^{**} is a feasible value, i.e., there is a real possibility that it will be the correct real discount rate of the cash flows characterizing the infrastructure investment, then the ranking of the two (as in our example), or more, alternatives is much more difficult and this situation should suggest to refine the analysis to reduce the uncertainty. Something similar happened when the Commission of the European Economic Community compared four alternatives for the Channel Link and, as reported by Button and Perman (1983), a variation in the discount rate (coupled with a high growth scenario) made the single rail tunnel plus a bridge more convenient than a double rail tunnel.

The time period of analysis influences the NPV because as the infrastructure projects in general impose a negative cash flow in the first years and a positive cash flows only some time after its entering into operation, a longer period of analysis includes a bigger number of fiscal years with a positive cash flows than a shorter period of analysis.

The calculation of NPV may pose some problems when comparing several mutually exclusive investment opportunities because it may solve in favor of bigger projects, determining relevant cash flows, instead of minor projects (characterized by low costs and benefits). Moreover, it is important to take into account that in most cases infrastructural investment are (for several reasons discussed in the previous chapters) supported by public subsidies; Bonnafous and Jensen (2005) demonstrate that in the case of transport infrastructure that are partially financed by the users, as in the case of public–private partnership, the best ranking criterion is the ratio of the socioeconomic NPV to the amount of subsidy required.

5.2.3.2 The Internal Rate of Return

The previous section mentioned two possible drawbacks of NPV: its sensitivity to the discount rate and the tendency to favor big projects.

To overcome these weaknesses, a different way to evaluate the profitability of a project derives from the calculation of the Internal Rate of Return (IRR), i.e., the discount rate that equalizes the costs and benefits. This index as argued by Weber (2014) seems "implicit in the work of Böhm-Bawerk (1889) who postulated an investment rule so as to maximize the net cash flow for each invested dollar. [While] Keynes (1936) terms the IRR therefore the marginal efficiency of capital".

Turning to Fig. 5.1, the IRR is the rate i that equals NPV to zero. The calculation of IRR is expressed in Eq. (5.3) solving for r.

$$\sum_{t=0}^{n}(C_t - B_t) \times (1+r)^{-t} = 0 \tag{5.3}$$

It is important to stress that IRR presents the merit of avoiding any choice about a discount rate, being determined only by the cash flow generated by the investment; therefore, it is particularly used when there is the necessity to rank several projects. Due to its immediate meaning and the easiness to communicate it to a large public, IRR is largely used by practitioners. This despite some concerns on the theoretical ground. The most important is that the calculation of NPV and IRR for several alternatives determines inconsistent rankings if the cash flows of projects are different, as it happens when a public body has to choose how to allocate a certain budget to a multitude of transport investments. In literature this problem is debated since the 1950s, and it is known as reinvestment assumption. It deals with positive cash flows happening during the lifetime of the investment and how to calculate, and at which interest rate, the possible reinvestment (Kalhoefer, 2010; Kalhoefer, 2010). The finance literature offers some indexes or approaches to overcome the NPV-IRR inconsistency—as, for instance, the "selective IRR" (Weber, 2014) or the modified IRR—but in our view they lack the easiness to communicate (and make its meaning understandable to a large public) that characterizes IRR.

Another concern refers to the possibility that Eq. (5.2), being a root of a polynomial, gives more than one result, thus generating an ambiguity of results. In fact, the Descartes' rule defines the maximum number of real roots of a polynomial, determined by counting the number of sign changes in the sequence formed by the annual cash flow (i.e., the polynomial's coefficients).

In case of a simple infrastructure investment as the construction of a tolled bridge presenting negative cash flows in the first years, due to the costs incurred to build the bridge, followed by positive cash flows determined by the tolled raised by the vehicles passing over the bridge (leaving aside any other kind of costs and benefits), the IRR polynomial presents only a change in sign and the IRR is univocally determined. But if we add during the lifetime of the bridge the necessity of periodic maintenance works imposing to close the bridge for some months, there is the possibility that in that particular year the cash flow will turn negative, and then the IRR polynomial will present three roots. For the economic significance of

IRR, negative roots are trivial, but a multiplicity of positive roots represents a problem. It should be mentioned that this is more a theoretical problem than an operational one; in fact, as remembered by Ben-Horin and Kroll (2012) "confusing multiple IRR solutions are only possible under unrealistic large fluctuations of the cash flows", nevertheless this problem casts doubt on IRR as a proper tool to select among several projects.

Lastly, the significance of IRR depends on the capital discount rate. In fact, either in case of a multiplicity of projects ordered by IRR or in case of a single project and assuming that there is not a budget constraint, it is necessary to decide, in the former case, which projects are to be financed and in the latter case if the project is sufficiently profitable for society. In both cases, IRR should be compared with the cost of capital (or capital discount rate). Then, IRR is not able to completely avoid any consideration about the cost of capital, i.e., the main criticality of NPV that the promoters of IRR wanted to solve[9].

To conclude, both instruments—NPV and IRR—are useful to understand the ability of investments to add value and may be considered complementary to each other. Notwithstanding the scientific literature is fairly unanimous in favor of the superiority of NPV with respect to IRR (Osborne, 2010).

5.2.3.3 Other Indicators

A further indicator that is often used to present and summarize the CBA results is the ratio between the discounted flows of benefits and costs (benefit-to-cost ratio). Its significance is immediate, because a value higher than unit means that the benefits deriving from the investment are higher than its costs, then the investment is able to increase welfare. At the same time being a ratio, it may focus the attention of decision-makers on small interventions that are able to generate immediate benefits instead of large investment characterized by a lower benefits–costs ratio but also able to generate a large volume of benefits.

Another indicator is the payback period, i.e., the number of years necessary to the full recovery of the initial investment. It is calculated cumulating annually the difference between benefits and costs (either discounted or using their current values). This indicator is not useful to rank

[9] A clear example is found in the French project evaluation tradition that, according to Bonnafous and Jensen (2005), in the 1980s considered approved any project with an IRR of at least 8% (*taux d'actualisation du Plan*).

alternatives but it adds useful information especially when private capital is involved in the investment. According to Blauwens, De Baere, & Van de Voorde (2008), this indicator may be misleading because it does not take into account what happen, in terms of the net cash flow, beyond the recovery of the initial investment.

5.2.4 Sensitivity Analysis

The aim of this kind of analysis is to highlight which variables of a specific project are critical. This in the sense that a change in the magnitude of the critical items (either cost or benefit) have a great impact on the final results; even to change the final result turning the NPV from positive to negative or vice versa.

In the assessment process of big projects, consisting in a huge number of cost and benefit items, this analysis selects a subset of variables that are relevant with respect to the final results and therefore are worthy of a special consideration in their estimation.

From a practical point of view, for each alternative, all the independent variables should be detected. This means, for instance, that for infrastructural projects whose benefits are mainly represented by traffic revenues, this positive item should be divided into its two independent components: traffic volume and traffic yield. Revenues in fact may change due to a change in one or both of these components. Then percentage changes are imposed to any independent variable and if the impact on the final results is greater than the initial change then that variable may be considered as critical.

A common way to pursue the sensitivity analysis is the calculation of the so-called switching values, i.e., the percentage change that an independent variable should undergo to completely dissolve the NPV or reduce it under a predefined acceptability threshold.

Moreover, it is important to understand the impact on NPV due to changes in more than one variable; for instance, what happens to NPV if the time for building a new airport doubles together with a decrease in the expected demand. Therefore, it is advisable the construction of some (optimistic and pessimistic) scenarios based on the extreme but realistic lower and upper values for each critical variable.

5.2.5 Risk Analysis

As already mentioned at the beginning of this chapter, the infrastructure assessment is a process that deals with the dynamics over a rather long period of time of a multiplicity of variables that after their monetary evaluation become cost and benefits whose combination gives an overall result (in general, an NPV or an IRR). Therefore, it should be taken into account that the future could be different from what we expect at present.

In literature, there are not so many papers investigating this important topic. Among the most referred to is Flyvbjerg, Bruzelius, & Rothengatter (2003) that reviews a large set of infrastructure projects (grouping cases from several countries) finding a relevant gap between estimated and effective costs and also between estimated and actual benefits. Other papers focus on the overestimation of benefits due to optimistically forecasts of demand (Flyvbjerg, 2007; van Wee, 2007) that in the case of urban rail transit projects, as reported by Pickrell (1990), may exceed 50% of the actual transport demand. On the costs side, Cantarelli et al. (2010) reviews some large-scale infrastructure projects findings a general costs overrun and this is coherent with the results found by Makovšek (2014), whereas for Nijkamp and Ubbels (1999) the most important reason for cost overruns are political decisions to amend or extend the projects.

This gap between preinvestment and the ex-post evaluations may be due to several reasons: mistakes in the estimation of costs or benefits or a change in the scenario considered for the analysis, or as found by Beria et al. (2018) in the case of the Spanish and Italian high-speed rail networks due to projects deliberately designed and planned out-of-scale.

According to Quinet (1998), mistakes may be due to the inadequacy of the model structure or to the inaccuracy of the current data. Even strategic behavior of some actors may results in benefit overestimation (Trujillo, Quinet, & Estache, 2002).

Nevertheless, more often when dealing with transport infrastructure characterized by a very long lifetime, differences are due to changes in the scenario—or the uncertainties on the exogenous variables according to Quinet (1998)—described in the moment the decision on the project is taken. They may be caused by changes in demographic, social, and economic conditions, as well as changes in policies and the regulation set of the market, but also technological changes that can completely modify the scenario in which the infrastructure is embedded.

All the abovementioned criticalities determine an optimism bias that finds its theoretical basis in the prospect theory (Kahneman and Tversky, 1979). According to this theory, the outcome of the project alternatives is uncertain but the associated probabilities are known, therefore "general errors of judgment are often systematic and hence predictable rather than randomly passed errors or biases" (Salling & Leleur, 2012). To deal with the optimism bias, it is recommended the adoption of reference class forecasting that consists of learning from past experiences of similar projects, in particular those that have recorded costs overruns and benefits underruns.

In the project assessment it is of the utmost importance the estimation of the risks associated with any of the existing alternatives, studying the probability distribution of each of the critical variables. Then NPV may be recomputed through a Monte Carlo technique (Salling & Banister, 2009) to associate a probability to the event of NPV reduced to zero or IRR below a reference discount rate; eventually actions to risk prevention and mitigation are to be identified and pursued.

5.2.6 The Wider Economic Benefits

In an ideal world—made of perfect competitive markets, without any information asymmetry, no entry barriers, etc.—that normally informs the CBA process of transport investment, direct effects of an infrastructure investment would be representative enough of all the possible effects. In this scenario, the inclusion of spillovers in the CBA would represent a double-counting (Mohring, 1993), thus confirming the results already found by Jara-Diaz (1986) that "a competitive productive environment makes the transportation consumers' surplus exactly equal to the net economic benefits provoked in the products' markets".

At the same time, there is a consensus in literature on the positive macroeconomic impact of transport investment on economic growth that is not completely captured in the transport forecasts of demand used in traditional microeconomics tools for investment appraisal as the CBA (as shown in Chapter 7).

In particular, the assumption of positive returns to scale and the presence of nonperfectly competitive markets leads to the formation of agglomeration effects. Moreover, when the investment is sufficiently large, traditional forecasting approaches fail "to capture the changes in behaviour of transport users" (Vickerman, 2008). In these conditions, indirect impact may be larger than direct impact leading traditional CBA to suboptimal choices and opening to the debate about the inclusion of this portion of impact in the CBA process and on the robustness of their estimates (Rouwendal, 2012). In literature these effects are referred to as Wider Economic Impacts (WEIs).

WEIs, when they occur, are due to:

- Agglomeration economies. Transport investment may improve accessibility of a particular region favoring changes in localization patterns toward the formation of clusters. Thus proximity may result in a reduction of costs for firms and households (Laird & Venables, 2017).
- Increased competition and productivity gains. Several studies—presented and discussed in Section 7.2.2—have studied the effects of transport investment on productivity growth finding that they are positive but modest (Deng, 2013).
- Changes in the labor market. In particular, improved accessibility due to infrastructure investment may deeply impact on labor market widening its dimension with positive effects on the participation rates, the number of working hours per worker (the reduced transport time may be converted into labor time), the competition, and specialization of workers (Elhorst & Oosterhaven, 2008). Moreover, as illustrated in Chapter 3, such changes prevent "thin" and monopsonistic labor markets (Pilegaard & Fosgerau, 2008).

Nevertheless, the magnitude and the timing of these effects are widely disputed. As reported in Beria and Grimaldi (2013), some reviews on WEIs due to infrastructural projects account for a great portion of direct benefits. In this sense, Zhu, Van Ommeren, & Rietveld (2009) estimate that indirect welfare effects of infrastructure improvement through decreases in overall unemployment are about 10%–20% of the direct welfare effects, but Bonnafous (1987) reviewing some case studies found that WEIs are over estimated in ex-ante evaluations. These uncertainties may explain why several countries' guidelines differ in considering WEIs in the CBA process (Wangsness et al., 2017), notwithstanding their calculation may contribute as an additional information for decision-makers on the potential long-term effects due to infrastructural interventions (Rothengatter, 2017). At the same time, the estimation of WEI could represent the way to broad the scope of CBA for large investment.

Then, it is still valid the suggestion made by Vickerman (2008) about the need for further research to unravel how transport infrastructure influences the decision-making of firms and households.

5.3 MULTICRITERIA ANALYSIS

CBA has been criticized under several perspectives (Cole, 2005). In particular, the adoption of a single unit of measurement, the utilitarian perspective, and the complexity of the process (together with the subjectivity of some choices) represent the most important criticalities of CBA. Moreover, CBA offers to decision-makers and stakeholders a net result that may hide some possible contrasts. In fact, CBA ranks alternatives for the algebraic sum of all costs and benefits, but in reality, some alternatives, even if profitable (i.e., with a positive NPV), could be considered in principle unfeasible by decision-makers and/or stakeholders because their implementation would make some conditions unacceptable; for instance, due to a detriment of the quality of the environment, of public health, etc.

MCA has been proposed as a mean to broad the comprehensiveness of the appraisal process, to compare alternatives in their ability to achieve several different goals avoiding the need to monetize every effect and lastly taking into account uncertainty (Keeney & Raiffa, 1976). Moreover, MCA promotes the active participation of people (stakeholders) in the decision process.

MCA makes use of criteria, indicators, and weights. Criteria or attributes are the dimensions that are to be investigated by the assessment process, i.e., the objectives to be achieved or implemented. In case of infrastructure investment, examples of criteria are impact on accessibility, impact on the environment, impact on the transport safety, etc. Each criterion may be measured through a set of quantitative or qualitative indicators that give information about effects on that criterion due to the implementation of a particular alternative. Weights are numbers that express the relative importance of both criteria and indicators and should reflect preferences and priorities of decision-makers and stakeholders.

The novelty introduced by MCA with respect to CBA is that the objective function to be maximized is case specific (and not unique as in CBA). Moreover, the selection of the criteria to be taken into consideration and their relative importance (weights) may be decided, case by case, by the decision-makers and the stakeholders too.

Once alternatives and criteria have been defined, each impact is measured through one (or more) indicator(s) using its (their) own unit of measurement. Nevertheless, MCA has to come to a conclusive result comparing the different impacts. The comparison is made through the adoption of appropriate weights to be applied to each of the impacts. The definition of weights is the most critical phase in an MCA process, and in literature several methods have been proposed (see, for instance, Nijkamp, Rietveld, & Voogd, 1990) that we will discuss briefly. All MCA methodologies follow a similar approach to the analysis, but they differ in the way they organize and synthesize information in accordance with the specific decision situation (Tsamboulas, 2007).

MCA is a broad concept and it is widely used as a synonym of multiobjective analysis and multiattribute analysis as well. Nevertheless, in operational research literature, they assume different meanings; in particular, multiobjective analysis is a decision tool to select the optimal choice among an infinite set of alternatives, whereas in multiattribute analyses the set of options is finite and the constraints are explicit.

Multiobjective analysis in its turn includes several techniques; the most popular are Goal Programming (GP) and MultiObjective Programming (MOP) that use linear programming to evaluate the alternatives for their capacity of achieving the objectives that may be ranked under some rules (as a lexicographic order or weights). Although in GP each objective has an expected values (the values that the decision-maker wants to achieve), MOP selects a number of nondominated alternatives that are Pareto efficient in the sense that there are no alternatives that achieving the same result for all the objective less one register a better result for this latter objective (Tanino, Tanaka, & Inuiguchi, 2003). These techniques highlight trade-offs among objectives characterizing the "optimal alternatives".

Infrastructure investment decisions probably are much better described by a multiattribute context in which the set of feasible alternatives is finite and also the set of goals to be achieved is clear enough for decision-makers.

Based on the aforementioned assumptions, a performance matrix (or evaluation or even project–effect matrix) is compiled in which each row describes an alternative and each column describes the performance of the alternatives against each criterion. In this way, the dominated alternatives—i.e., the alternatives that do not present a better performance for at least one criterion all the others being equal—may be rejected. To select one among the remaining alternatives, several approaches have been proposed in literature and in practice. We will discuss briefly some of them referring the interested readers to the vast literature available (for instance, Triantaphyllou, 2000).

Even if MCA recognizes the influence of several objectives or criteria in the decision process, notwithstanding this does not imply that all criteria have the same importance. They should then be ranked according to some rules. The most popular methodologies, that in the practice are increasingly mixed each other, are the following:

- Analytical hierarchy process. This method was initially proposed by Saaty (1988) and adapted to make it applicable to transport projects.

It bases the scores of criteria and objectives as well on pairwise comparisons.

- Outranking methods. Originally proposed by Roy (1975) in a seminal paper, this methodology adopts the concept of dominance not in a strict way but assigning each of the criterion a specific weight and defining appropriate preference, indifference, and veto thresholds[10]. Therefore, in case of comparing two alternatives—A and B—alternative A is preferred to B if A is at least as good as B on a majority of criteria and if it is not significantly bad on any other criteria.
- Concordance and discordance sets. Based on a pairwise comparison, the concordance set is made of the criteria (appropriately weighted) for which an alternative is better than (or equal to) another, whereas the discordance set is made of the weighted criteria for which an alternative is worst than another. The weighted sum of the two sets of criteria gives the concordance and the discordance indexes that measure to what extent one alternative is more attractive than another.
- Fuzzy sets express the relative importance of alternatives and criteria with fuzzy numbers[11]. They try to capture the uncertainty, imprecision, and incomplete information as well, especially when linguistic variable are used—e.g., in case of binary choices or when in a survey respondents use categorical variable (as "too much", "fairly", "not much", etc.)—regarding most of the criteria included in the analysis (Pedrycz, Ekel, & Parreiras, 2011). For each criterion, a membership function is applied to identify a degree of belonging to a specific set.

The results of MCA (as those obtained by the CBA) need to be corroborated by a sensitivity analysis before informing the decision-makers.

Even if the several methodologies of MCA were not explained in details, it should be clear that they are not exempt from a subjectivity bias (Medda & Nijkamp, 2003). Despite this, in favor of MCA is the fact that subjectivity refers to the weights assigned to criteria (or objectives) and attributes—and not on the evaluation models as in the CBA—moreover,

[10] In this way, this methodology takes into account qualitative and quantitative differences among the preferences of stakeholders with respect to the alternatives. Alternatives that do not exceed the veto threshold should be rejected and the choice will fall on one of the remaining alternatives. The reader will appreciate the difference with respect to the compensation principle adopted in CBA.

[11] "Fuzzy numbers generalize classical real numbers and roughly speaking a fuzzy number is a fuzzy subset of the real line that has some additional properties" (Bede, 2013, p. 51).

they are transparent (and not hidden in the assumption of a particular model or econometric function). It means that biases are in some way more acceptable because they reflect the opinion and ideas of those who decide weights (policy-makers, residents, or someone else), i.e., those who will probably pay the costs of the investment and will gain its benefits.

MCA is increasingly used—as reviewed by Macharis and Bernardini (2015)—and, especially in combination with traditional CBA (as in Gühnemann, Laird, & Pearman, 2012), seems the appropriate tool for the appraisal of large investment or mega projects (Dimitriou, Ward, & Dean, 2016) or in general as a tool for strategic decisions, i.e., when the impacts of the investment have future disruptive consequences. Notwithstanding, the most recent contributions on investment appraisal agree on the importance of combining different assessment methods to overcome the limitations that characterize each of them.

5.4 THE CORRECT "TIMING" OF INVESTMENT APPRAISAL

At the end of this chapter, a reader should have an idea of the different techniques that may be used for the investment appraisal. This phase in the planning process of transport infrastructure is extremely important to inform decision-makers and then reducing possible cognitive limitations and biases affecting the final decision.

This result may be achieved if the investment appraisal is well-timed, but in practice "there is often a risk that CBA enters the planning process too late to play any meaningful role" (Mackie, Worsley, & Eliasson, 2014). On this point, the timing of the investment appraisal in the planning process makes a difference. If it is foreseen too early, when options on infrastructure investment are little more than ideas, the appraisal process may effectively inform the different scenarios and contribute to select the most promising, but at this stage the identification (and measurement) of benefits and costs can only be rough. For example, a project consisting in a new highway in a plain region with a positive NPV may in the construction phase increase its costs if the public opinion obtains that part of the route will proceed in tunnels to reduce the environmental impact. On the opposite, if the appraisal process is postponed and it happens when the selection of alternatives has already been done, the result will necessarily be suboptimal and in most cases the appraisal process will only reinforce a choice already taken by politics (based on different criteria).

The transport literature has found contrasting results on the effectiveness of investment appraisal to select the optimal choice (see, for instance, on the opposite sides, Fridstrøm & Elvik, 1997; Eliasson & Lundberg, 2012). These results confirm that investment appraisal should not be a static exercise, to be conducted only once during the planning process, but should be implemented in a dynamic manner and continuously updated to take into account changes in the project and in the comparative scenarios as well.

5.5 INPUT–OUTPUT ANALYSIS

Input-Output Analysis (IOA) represents a powerful tool for macroeconomic assessment of investment and policies. According to Wassily Leontief (1986), it is "a method of systematically quantifying the mutual interrelationships among the various sectors of a complex economic system".

IOA is a generalization of the national accounts—more precisely, the supply and use tables that feed the insectoral transactions matrix—based on the assumption that the amount of input to obtain a unit of production remains constant irrespective of the volume of production; this rule applies to all industries and it does not change over time (i.e., if four wheels are necessary to make a car; 12 are necessary to produce three cars, and so on; moreover the current ratio will remain the same also in the future). These ratios—$a_{ij} = x_{ij}/x_j$—are usually referred to as technical coefficients because they reflect the structure of the technology adopted in the economic system. Technical coefficients were originally expressed in terms of physical quantities, but for practical reasons they are now commonly inserted in value terms (implicitly assuming prices are fixed). Thus, the whole interrelationships among the industries composing an economic system may be written as follows:

$$\begin{bmatrix} a_{1,1} & \cdots & a_{1,n} \\ \vdots & \ddots & \vdots \\ a_{j,1} & \cdots & a_{j,n} \end{bmatrix}$$

The elements of the above matrix are the technical coefficients (they assume values lower than 1, and their vertical sum is lower than 1 because the value of production of each industry is higher than the sum of its inputs). Then the system of production may be simplified and written as follows:

$$X = AX + Y \tag{5.4}$$

Where X is the vector of production of the x_j industries composing the economic system; Y is the vector of final demand; and A is the square matrix of technical coefficients.

Eq. (5.4) means that the each industry (and production system as a whole) every year has to produce the volume of output necessary to satisfy the final demand (for consumptions, investment, exports, and inventories) and to furnish inputs demanded by the other industries.

Solving Eq. (5.4) for X, we obtain Eq. (5.5), in which $(I - A)^{-1}$ is called Leontief inverse matrix.

$$X = (I - A)^{-1} \cdot Y \tag{5.5}$$

The Leontief inverse matrix tells us how the economic system responds to a unit increase of the final demand. This formulation of the Leontief inverse matrix implies that firms operate with constant return to scale, the technology does not change, and that the inputs supply curves are perfectly elastic (i.e., there is no scarcity of inputs).

In general, Eq. (5.5) is used to estimate effects on the production sector due to a change in the final demand. In fact, assuming that at time 1 the final demand is expected to be equal to Y_1 (different from Y_0, i.e., the demand at time 0), the new level of production will be equal to

$$X_1 = (I - A)^{-1} \cdot Y_1 \tag{5.6}$$

And the effect on production due to the change in the final demand will be

$$\Delta X = X_1 - X_0 \tag{5.7}$$

In case the changes in demand are so important to determine a technological change, Eq. (5.6) may be rewritten as

$$X_1 = (I - A_1)^{-1} \cdot Y_1 \tag{5.8}$$

Similarly Eq. (5.7) becomes

$$\Delta X = X_1 - X_0 = (I - A_1)^{-1} \cdot Y_1 - (I - A_0)^{-1} \cdot Y_0 \tag{5.9}$$

Where A_0 and A_1 represent the old and the new Leontief inverse matrixes, respectively, i.e., including a technological change.

Some simple passages allow to derive the matrix of employment multipliers. First, it is necessary to calculate and diagonalize the vector of coefficients of labor intensity per unit of production. Then, multiplying this diagonal matrix for the A matrix gives a new matrix $_{L}A$ whose elements ($_{L}a_{ij}$) measure the level of labor in industry *i* necessary to accomplish with a unit increase in demand for industry *j*.

Thus, IOA allows for economic as well labor impacts with a sectoral detail determined by the accuracy of the initial supply and use tables[12].

IOA may represent the interdependencies within a particular economic system (i.e., an isolated economic system) as well as the interdependencies and the exchanges among several economic systems. The latter situation is depicted by a multiregional model accounting for the interdependencies existing among one region and the others. In case the multiregional model presents a region representing the "rest of the world," the multiregional system becomes an isolated system. These regional interdependencies assume the form of monetary flows (due to the trade of inputs and/or outputs) moving from a region to the others. In such case, in each region the product of any industry is obtained combining together inputs coming from the same region as well as inputs coming from the other regions and in the model the sum of the total outflows and inflows of inputs and outputs should balance the total shipment of goods moving from any region to the others.

The input–output framework initially used to understand the economic significance of industrial interdependencies and for evaluating the economic impact of changes in the final demand (or in the system of prices or even in the technology applied by industries) has recently been extended to take into account specific (sometimes noneconomic) factors as the environment and the energy use, till arriving to the computation of social accounting matrices (Miller & Blair, 2009).

Also infrastructural investment—and more in general the transport sector—may be evaluated through the IOA under different perspectives.

In case of an investment plan requiring construction works, the I-O framework is able to compute the impact of these works. In fact the construction works will impact the final demand for some industries and the overall effects are the application of the above Eqs. (5.6) and (5.7).

[12] Supply and use tables are important toll of the national accounting system for compiling GDP. For a specific region, usually a country, the supply table describes process of internal production plus imports, whereas the use table shows where and how goods and services are used in that region. The use table also shows how the components of value added (compensation of employees, other net taxes on production, consumption of fixed capital, net operating surplus) are generated by industries. Supply and use tables are necessary to compile a symmetric input–output table.

In addition, changes in regional accessibility may be analyzed. In case of an isolated region, an improvement in accessibility will result in an increase of the final demand (driven by an increase of exports), whereas in a multiregional model, a relative change in regional accessibility will impact on the level of final demand for any regions and in a change in the interdependencies (exchanges) of inputs and outputs among the regions. These changes will happen in the short and medium run, whereas in the long run changes in accessibility determine a relocation process of firms and households that require some particular assumptions before being assessed within an I-O framework.

Even if this approach is not so popular in transport-applied researches, it is worth noticing that Leontief in 1979 (reprinted in Leontief, 1986) used IOA to assess the impact of maritime traffic growth on world ports, whereas the Port Canaveral's investment plan was assessed by Braun (1990). More recently, Coppens et al. (2007) used the I-O approach to estimate the relevance of the Belgian port of Antwerp; this latter work inspired Danielis & Gregori (2013) who used I-O to assess the economic importance of the Italian seaports based on the North Adriatic Sea including port activities in a biregional I-O matrix as a specific industry.

Moreover, I-O matrix may be extended to take into account the interrelationship between value-added and final expenditures, thus capturing the full circular flow of income. When this occurs the matrix is called SAM—Social Accounting Matrix. It is social because it considers distributional features of household sector as well as transactions between different institutions. This kind of tool considering either macro- or mesoeconomic relationships was firstly introduced by Stone (1962).

Lastly, the input—output framework is also used to assess the impact on the economic system of the inoperability of strategic infrastructure. This approach firstly introduced by Haimes and Jiang (2001) allows for accounting the economic impact of the "inability of the system to perform its intended natural or engineered functions" (Haimes et al., 2005) due to external failures of the infrastructural system as, for instance, storms, floods, earthquakes, or even terrorist attacks. In some cases, these failures have a persisting impact on the economic system, especially when the inoperability is due to the destructions of some nodes or arcs of the system (as in case of an earthquake). In other cases, when failures consist in a reduced service level of the infrastructure system (as in the case of the breakdown of a radar in a hub airport), effects are only temporary and the system is able to recover in a relatively short run.

These analyses are very useful to understand the fragility of the infrastructure system and are helpful in evaluating the optimal level of redundancy that the infrastructure system needs to maintain a high level of service even in case of external (negative) occurrences.

This chapter has discussed the main techniques used for the appraisal of transport infrastructure. Although in practice the CBA is largely adopted and recommended, there is not a technique that is intrinsically better than the others. The choice should depend on the goal(s)—as an increase in welfare, a more balanced distribution of welfare and jobs, the social inclusion, the solution of a congestion problem, and so on (as already discussed in Chapters 2 and 3)—to be pursued. In addition, the moment in which the appraisal exercise is done may have an influence on the right technique to be applied. Moreover, also the comparison of different techniques applied to the same intervention may offer relevant hints to improve the investment itself, as well as appraisal processes that go hand in hand with the evolution of infrastructural projects. Lastly, the literature stresses the importance of ex-post analyses necessary to evaluate the effectiveness of transport infrastructure investment.

CHAPTER 6

The Econometrics of Transport Infrastructures

Contents

Noneconometric approaches such as input–output analysis, structural models, or Spatial Computable General Equilibrium (SCGE) modeling play an important role in ex-ante impact assessments of transportation infrastructure investments and, in general, in cost–benefit analysis.[1]

However, it seems fair to say that the modern micro- and macro-empirical literature on the economic effects of transportation infrastructure, which originates from the pioneering work of Aschauer (1989) on the impact of public capital on productivity, largely follows an ex-post evaluation approach based on the econometric estimation of single equations relating transportation infrastructure capital to some economic outcomes. Moreover, summarizing this largely and rapidly expanding empirical literature, some recent meta-analysis (e.g., Bon and Ligthart, 2013 and Melo,

[1] See, for a brief discussion of SCGE models, Vickerman (2008), Sue Wing et al. (2008), and also Proost and Thisse (2015). For transport investment appraisals, see also Chapter 5 and the references therein.

Economic Role of Transport Infrastructure
ISBN 978-0-12-813096-4
https://doi.org/10.1016/B978-0-12-813096-4.00006-8

Graham, and Brage-Ardao 2013) suggest that the empirical estimates of the impact of transport infrastructure capital on GDP are significantly affected by the specific econometric technique considered in each study.

In the light of the above, this chapter seeks to introduce the reader to the econometrics of transport infrastructures since a better understanding of the advantages and limitations of the main econometric approaches can be helpful to both explain the metaanalysis' finding mentioned above and, more broadly, to allow the reader to better appreciate the reliability and robustness of each single study.

In what follows, we will mainly focus on the impact of transport infrastructure on production, because that has been so far the main focus of the literature. However, it is important to recall that in more recent years there has been an increasing attention toward the role that transport infrastructures play on firm dynamics, trade, and, more generally, on the spatial organization of economic activity.[2] Moreover, it is important to stress that the literature we are going to consider can be ascribed to the debate on the productive effects of public capital, of which transport infrastructure is a key component; although in this chapter we largely deal with the economic effects of transport capital, many issues we will consider could be safely deemed as relevant also for the wider literature on the economic effects of public capital.

In Section 6.1, we will discuss in some detail the role that economic theory plays in informing the empirical analysis. Indeed, in some approaches researchers do not impose much economic structure on the data; this is the case, for instance, not only of time series studies based on vector auto regression (VAR) models but also of recent cross section or panel data studies belonging to the counterfactual impact evaluation literature.[3]

By way of contrast, some authors have sought to evaluate the impact of transport infrastructures while imposing some economic structure on the data, as in the large number of papers that include the transport infrastructure variable in a production or cost function framework. In fact, although the production function is a technical relationship between inputs

[2] For a recent survey of the microeconomic literature on the effects of transport infrastructures on the spatial organization of economic activity, see Redding and Turner (2015).

[3] However, in the latter case some studies estimate equations that are reduced-form versions of theoretical models of regional and urban growth that microfound the joint determination of transport infrastructures, employment, and output, as in Duranton and Turner (2012).

and outputs, the cost function is a behavioral relationship as it is based on the assumption that firms minimize production costs.

Similarly, some studies have explored the role of transport infrastructure within a Solow growth model or, more recently, some authors have analyzed the impact of roads on various economic outcomes such as trade, population, production, or employment by estimating equations directly derived from new economic geography type of models.

In Section 6.2, we will analyze the main econometric approaches that researchers have been using in recent years in the empirical literature. It should be stated at the outset that we do not aim to provide a rigorous treatment of those approaches. Rather, we seek to provide an intuitive explanation of their relative advantages and limitations; in particular, we will analyze in some detail various panel data models, focusing on fixed effects and GMM models as well as on the recent spatial econometric techniques.

Moreover, we will describe the approaches that are commonly grouped under the label "counterfactual impact evaluation" methods, such as difference-in-differences and instrumental variable (IV) models with natural experiments, which have been gaining popularity in some subfields of economics in recent years. Although our survey has a largely micro-econometric flavor, we will also briefly consider time series approaches like VAR models.[4]

Finally, in Section 6.3, we will briefly discuss the type of data that are commonly considered in the empirical literature. We do this mainly because the metaanalyses described in Chapter 6 suggest the possible existence of a differential effect of transport infrastructures depending on the level of spatial disaggregation (e.g., country vs. regional level) of the data, possibly because of the role played by spillover effects associated with transportation infrastructure investments.[5] Moreover, the use of industry- and firm-level data might provide researchers with useful identification strategies to deal with the important endogeneity concerns associated with the estimation of the economic effects of transportation infrastructures.

[4] There are also econometric approaches that combine both panel data and time series techniques in nonstationary environments. Recent examples relevant for this chapter are the studies of Canning and Pedroni (2008), Bronzini and Piselli (2009), Bottasso, Castagnetti, et al. (2013), Bottasso, Conti, et al. (2013), and Calderon et al. (2015). In this chapter, we will largely ignore this avenue of the literature.

[5] Moreover, some authors (e.g., Redding and Turner 2015) argue that negative spillovers across regions might occur as well.

6.1 THE ROLE OF ECONOMIC THEORY

The studies that, since the pioneering work of Aschauer (1989), have sought to evaluate the impact of transport and other types of public infrastructure capital on production, have estimated equations like the following one:

$$Y = \alpha TK + \beta X + u \tag{6.1}$$

Where Y is production (GDP in the case of studies conducted at macroeconomic level), TK is transport infrastructure capital, X is a vector of control variables (possibly including lags of the dependent variable, as it is typically the case in the VAR literature), and u is a disturbance term. All approaches seek to consistently estimate α, the impact of TK on Y.

The empirical strategies that various authors have used to estimate the impact of TK on Y differ, depending on the type of data and the econometric approach, which we will discuss in detail in Section 6.2.

In this section, we instead focus on the underlying theoretical framework that has led economists to derive equations similar to Eq. (6.1).

In particular, in some studies, authors have made little use of economic theory to impose some structure onto the data. This is the case, almost by definition, for studies that use VARs, typically conducted on macroeconomic data; the estimated equations are neither derived from an explicit economic model nor do they make use of particular economic assumptions.[6]

A similar case could be made for studies that follow the counterfactual impact evaluation literature. As noted by Gibbons and Overman (2012), studies in this tradition estimate the impact of a policy on a given economic outcome without necessarily a reference to a particular economic theory or model. Nevertheless, it should also be remembered that it has been recently shown (see Redding and Turner, 2015) that equations that are typically estimated in this type of literature can be often reinterpreted as reduced-form versions of structural equations of new economic geography type of models. In this case, economic theory is helpful because it can better clarify why transportation infrastructure is endogenous in equations like Eq. (6.1) and, at the same time, it can motivate the exclusion restrictions (see Section 6.2).

[6] However, economic theory does play a role also in VAR models because it enters in the identification assumptions underlying the estimation of VAR models. See Section 6.2.

By way of contrast, many studies have instead analyzed the impact of transport capital on production within the production function framework. We discuss this approach in detail in Section 6.1.1 because it was by far the typical approach in the 1990s and 2000s, and it is still relatively popular nowadays. In turn, Sections 6.1.2 will consider the cost function approach, whereas in Section 6.1.3 we will very briefly deal with other theoretical frameworks.

6.1.1 The Production Function Framework

A production function with transport capital can be represented as in Eq. (6.2)

$$Y = F(A,\ K,\ L, KT) \tag{6.2}$$

Where Y is GDP, K is private capital, L is labor inputs, A represents the level of technology, and KT is transport capital.[7] In Eq. (6.2), KT is entered into the production function as a conventional private input.

Alternatively, some authors consider a production function as in Eq. (6.3):

$$Y = F(A,\ K,\ L) \tag{6.3}$$

In Eq. (6.3), it is usually assumed that the level of technology depends on KT: $A = BKT^{\gamma}$, where B captures other factors that can explain technology, such as human capital, R&D capital, institutions, etc.

In other words, some researchers do not assume that transport infrastructures enter in a production function like a conventional input that firms combine together with private ones to obtain output, but rather they consider a conventional production function and assume that the level of technology (i.e., the level of total factor productivity) depends on the amount of infrastructure capital that is available to firms as a (quasi) public good. The justification of why the level of infrastructure capital can impact on the level of total factor productivity can be found in Chapter 3, to which we refer.

[7] When Y is defined as GDP or value added, the only private inputs are capital and labor. However, if industry- or firm-level data are used and Y is defined as gross output, then also intermediate inputs (like materials, services, energy) should appear in Eq. (6.2).

The vast majority of studies operationalize Eq. (6.2) assuming a Cobb–Douglas functional form for the production function:

$$Y = AK^{\alpha}L^{\beta}KT^{\gamma} \tag{6.4}$$

Taking logs on both sides yields (where lower case letters denote natural logs)

$$y = a + \alpha k + \beta l + \gamma kt \tag{6.5}$$

In particular, γ denotes the elasticity of production with respect to transport infrastructure capital: $\gamma = \frac{\partial Y}{\partial KT}\frac{KT}{Y}$. From the expression of γ, one can then easily compute the marginal effects of transport capital as $\frac{\partial Y}{\partial KT} = \gamma\frac{Y}{KT}$, which can then be compared with the user cost of transport capital in transport schemes evaluations.

It is easy to see that if we assume that *KT* enters into the production function through its effect on *A*, we derive an identical equation:

$$y = b + \alpha k + \beta l + \gamma kt \tag{6.6}$$

In other words, either we consider that *KT* enters the Cobb–Douglas production function as a conventional private input as in Eq. (6.2) or as a technology determinant as in Eq. (6.3), we end up with the same estimating equation.

In Eqs. (6.2) and (6.3), we have assumed that the level of technology is of the Hicks neutral type. If we assume, as it is typical in most growth models, that the level of technology is of the Harrod neutral type, i.e., labor augmenting, again we end up with a very similar estimating equation that, econometrically, cannot be distinguished from Eq. (6.5):

$$Y = K^{\alpha}(AL)^{\beta}KT^{\gamma} \tag{6.7}$$

By taking logs, we get

$$y = a\beta + \alpha k + \beta l + \gamma kt \tag{6.8}$$

Similarly, in the case of *KT* entering in the production function through *A*, we would have

$$Y = K^{\alpha}(AL)^{\beta}, \text{with } A = BKT^{\gamma} \tag{6.9}$$

By taking logs, we get

$$y = a\beta + \alpha k + \beta l = \beta(\gamma kt + b) + \alpha k + \beta l \rightarrow y = b\beta + \alpha k + \beta l + \beta\gamma kt \quad (6.10)$$

Econometrically, Eq. (6.10) cannot be distinguished from Eq. (6.8). In other words, either you estimate Eq. (6.8) or Eq. (6.10) we end up with the same elasticity of GDP with respect to *KT*. However, the economic interpretation is slightly different. Indeed, γ in Eq. (6.8) measures the elasticity of GDP with respect to *KT*. In turn, this very same elasticity in Eq. (6.10) is given by $\beta\gamma$. In other words, if we assume that the economic model generating our data is that in Eq. (6.10), we can distinguish the effect of TK on GDP that goes through higher A (γ), from this that passes through higher effective labor (β).[8]

Bringing in further assumptions on technology and firm behavior, namely constant returns to scale in private inputs ($\alpha+\beta = 1$), perfect competition in input and output markets, no externalities, as well as profit maximization, it can also be shown that the log level of TFP (obtained as the difference between the log of output and the average of the logs of private inputs, weighted by their respective shares in value added) depends on the level of *KT*.[9] The advantage of this specification is that we do not have to estimate α and β, although we need to impose some structure on the data using theoretical assumptions that might be invalid, such as constant returns to scale in private inputs and perfect competition.[10]

[8] De la Fuente and Vives (1995) show that an equation which is observationally equivalent to Eq. (6.8) or Eq. (6.10) can be derived from a simple regional model where production of the final output depends on production of intermediates and on transport costs, with the latter depending on the region land area and on public infrastructure. The authors show that, assuming a Cobb–Douglas technology for the production of intermediates and perfect mobility of private capital across regions, it is possible to derive an equation which is observationally equivalent to Eq. (6.8) and Eq. (6.10). See also Romp and de Haan (2007) for a discussion.

[9] The assumptions of constant returns to scale, profit maximization, and perfect competition allows one to exploit the equivalence between the observable factor shares in value added and the unobservable factor elasticities.

[10] If one has information on total production costs (including the cost of capital), under a cost minimization assumption and a unitary elasticity of costs with respect to output it is possible to measure the input elasticities without no assumptions on market structure.

Alternatively, one can estimate the production function without public capital, compute TFP residually, and then regress TFP on KT, as in the study by Holl (2016) on the effects of access to highways on firms' productivity in Spain.[11]

The Cobb–Douglas production function has been used several times in the empirical literature. Some of the most recent studies include Bottasso, Castagnetti, and Conti (2013) on a panel of OECD countries; Chen and Haynes (2015) for a panel of metropolitan statistical areas in the United States; and Arbues, Banos, and Mayor (2015) for a panel of Spanish provinces, among the others.

Despite its popularity, the Cobb–Douglas functional form has been criticized because of its restrictive assumptions. For instance, it is well known that, under a Cobb–Douglas technology, the elasticity of substitution between inputs is equal to one. Secondly, returns to scale are forced to take on the same value for all units in the sample, independently from the level of production. This has led some economists to prefer more flexible functional forms that do not impose a priori the above restrictions on the data.

One of the most common in the empirical literature is the translog, which can be considered as a second order approximation to an arbitrary production function and that adds square and cross products of each input. For instance, the analogue of Eq. (6.5) is as follows:

$$y = a + \alpha k + \beta l + \gamma kt + \alpha_2 k^2 + \beta_2 l^2 + \gamma_2 kt^2 + \delta_1 kl + \delta_2 kkt + \delta_3 lkt \tag{6.11}$$

In the case of Eq. (6.11), the elasticity of Y with respect to KT can be derived as follows:

$$\varepsilon = \gamma + 2\gamma_2 kt + \delta_2 k + \delta_3 l \tag{6.12}$$

The elasticity therefore depends on four parameters and on the values of the inputs; this implies that we can have different values for the elasticity at each sample point. It might even be the case that for some observations the elasticity is negative, whereas for others it is positive. This flexibility is

[11] In the equations above, we have not restricted the production function to have constant returns to scale, neither in private inputs ($\alpha + \beta = 1$) nor in across all inputs ($\alpha + \beta + \gamma = 1$). In other words, the production function is compatible with both neoclassical and endogenous growth models. See also Straub (2011) for a discussion of the effects of public infrastructures on GDP at macro level.

important because in samples composed, for instance, by industries in different regions, we are not forced to impose the same elasticity on each data point, in the same way as we are not forced to impose the same value for the returns to scale parameter. Moreover, we can easily test whether the translog functional form is supported by the data or rejected in favor of the Cobb–Douglas, which is nested in it. The potential pitfall associated with Eq. (6.9) is that multicollinearity problems might arise, due to the square products and cross-products terms.

It might be worth to recall that, in the case of the translog, the way *KT* is included in the production function is no longer irrelevant. Indeed, Eq. (6.4) is based on the assumption that *KT* is treated as a conventional private input. However, if we assume that *KT* affects output because it affects TFP, then we obtain different equations depending on the model of technological progress that we consider. For instance, Hicks neutral technological progress would result with an equation like 6.11 without the interaction terms involving *KT*. Eq. (6.11) would instead result only if we allow technology (and *KT*) to be potentially both labor and capital augmenting. In other words, when the technology is of the translog type, the way transport capital enters into the production function is no longer irrelevant.

This reminds us to an important critique to the use of a production function framework to estimate the impact of public infrastructure capital. Duggal, Saltzmana, and Kleinb (1999) in fact argue that including public capital inputs into a production function is valid only as long as there is a market for services of public capital where a price is formed that firms can then compare to the benefits of public infrastructures. If that is not the case, then the estimation of a production function like Eq. (6.2) would be misspecified.

Another possible criticism to the estimation of a production function is that the coefficient γ in Eq. (6.5) should capture the impact of *KT* on *Y*, ceteris paribus. If transport capital and, say, private capital are complements, then one might expect that an increase in the levels of transport capital could lead firms to invest more, which in turn should lead to higher output. Therefore, because private capital acts as a "mediating" factor, γ might capture only the direct effect of *KT* on *Y*, but not the indirect effects that operate through private inputs.

In addition to this, the estimation of production functions poses formidable challenges to the correct identification of input elasticities. Indeed, inputs are chosen by firms simultaneously with the level of output, so that a classic simultaneity problem might arise. Although there are several approaches available in the literature to deal with production function estimation (Van Beveren, 2012), it seems fair to say that input endogeneity can create additional problems to researchers that already need also to take into account the endogeneity of transport capital.

Finally, if the production function is estimated with firm-level data or at the level of small spatial units, another problem can arise. One of the effects of an improvement in transport infrastructure is to reduce the prices paid for intermediate inputs. However, intermediate inputs in gross output production functions are typically deflated using aggregate industry deflators. If the difference between the aggregate deflator and the relevant firm-specific deflator is large, the intermediate input variable would be subject to measurement error causing, under classical measurement error assumptions (Wooldridge, 2010), a downward bias to the intermediate input elasticity; however, because transport infrastructures capital is negatively correlated with the (wrongly) deflated intermediate inputs, then we could have transmitted bias to the elasticity of public capital as well.

The production function is a technical relationship between the amount of inputs that a firm uses and the maximum level of output that can be obtained. As such, it is not based on any important behavioral assumption imposed on producers. However, estimating the impact of transport infrastructure capital on GDP within a production function framework brings about one possible, relatively minor, advantage that should be traded-off with the pitfalls discussed above, namely that researchers impose some "discipline" on the data. The literature contains a wealth of estimates of α and β and, if certain theories or models are correct, one can have a range where estimates of α and β should fall. For instance, under constant returns to scale in private inputs, perfect competition and profit maximization, α and β can be interpreted as the share of inputs in GDP, and values clearly outside the ranges commonly found in the literature for these parameters should act as a warning that parameter estimates might be badly estimated.

6.1.2 The Cost Function Framework

An alternative to the estimation of a production function that has had some popularity in the past is the cost function framework. The cost function is an economic relationship between the minimum cost of producing a certain amount of output, given the price of factor inputs and, possibly, a set of technical variables, such as infrastructure capital, and the production technology. Unlike the production function, the cost function is a behavioral relationship; indeed, it is derived assuming that firms minimize their production costs, given the price of capital and labor, and given the production technology that is used to produce a certain amount of output.

Mathematically, the cost function is the solution to the following optimization problem:

$$\min WX_{X=L,\ K}\ s.t.\ y = F(A,\ K, L, KT)$$

In the above program, firms are assumed to select private inputs X to produce, at minimum cost, a certain amount of output Y, given input prices W, the stock of transportation infrastructures KT, and the production function F. In particular, it can be shown that, assuming a Cobb–Douglas functional form, we can derive a relationship between costs, input prices, output, and transport capital, with the latter that is assumed to be available at zero costs to firms. A similar result can alternatively be obtained by assuming that KT affects the level of technology A.

In some studies, authors have used the variable cost function framework, i.e., they have assumed that firms minimize variable costs only and treat private capital as a quasi-fixed factor, similarly to public capital. In this case, the cost function has the stock of private capital instead of its price as a regressor.

If one considers a Cobb–Douglas technology, it is possible to use the cost function to retrieve the information on technological parameters that could also be available from the estimation of a production function;[12] however, the Cobb–Douglas is very restrictive, as noted in Section 6.1.1. A popular alternative is the translog even if, in this case, it is not possible to retrieve the parameters of the production function from the cost function; in other words, the translog cost function is not "self-dual" with the translog production function. Nevertheless, the translog and other functional forms, such as the Generalized Leontief, have been used in applied works because they are flexible functional forms, as they do not impose strong a priori restrictions on technology.

For example, in the translog case, authors have estimated equations like Eq. (6.13), where lower case letters denote natural logarithms and tc is the log of total production costs:

[12] This can be seen in Mas Colell et al. (1995).

$$tc = a + \gamma_k w_k + \gamma_l w_l + \gamma_y y + \gamma_{kk} w_k^2 + \gamma_{ll} w_1^2 + \gamma_{yy} y^2 + \gamma_{kl} w_k w_{l+} \gamma_{ky} wy$$
$$+ \gamma_{ly} w_l w + \gamma_{kt} kt + \gamma_{ktkt} kt^2 + \gamma_{kkt} w_k kt + \gamma_{lkt} w_l kt + \gamma_{kty} kty \tag{6.13}$$

Although the translog is perhaps the most popular flexible functional form among empirical researchers, other functional forms, such as the Generalized Leontief, have also been considered in the literature. Examples are the studies by Cohen and Morrison (2003) who estimated the impact of airport capital on manufacturing costs for a panel of US states; Cohen and Morrison (2004) who considered the impact of highways infrastructure investments on manufacturing costs and Cohen and Monaco (2008) who analyzed the impact of port infrastructures on the manufacturing costs in the United States. In turn, studies that have used the translog to investigate the impact of public infrastructure capital on costs are Lynde and Richmond (1992), Nadiri and Mamuneas (1996), Aviles-Zugasti et al. (2001), and Rovolis and Spence (2002), among others.

One advantage of estimating a translog (or other flexible functional forms) cost function is that, by Sheppard's Lemma, it is well known that the derivative of total costs with respect to the price of input i gives that input's conditional demand equation,[13] which in turn depends on the output level, input prices, and possibly technical variables, such as transport infrastructure capital.[14]

In the translog case, the derivative of log costs with respect to log prices yields the input shares in total costs. For instance, in the translog cost function in Eq. (6.13) above, we have that, in the case of private capital input:

$$\frac{\partial \ln TC}{\partial \ln W_k} = \frac{\partial TC}{\partial W_k}\frac{W_k}{TC} = X_k^* \frac{W_k}{TC} = \frac{X_k^* W_k}{TC} = S_k^*$$
$$= \gamma_k + 2\gamma_{kk} w_k + \gamma_{kl} w_l + \gamma_{kkt} kt + \gamma_{ky} y \tag{6.14}$$

[13] Sheppard's Lemma is nothing else than an application of the Envelope theorem. If one derives the "optimal" cost function $WX^*(Y, WTK)$ with respect to W_i, where $X_i^*(Y, W\ TK)$ is the conditional demand equation of input i derived from the cost minimization program above, one gets X_i^*; indeed, the derivative would be $X_i^* + W_i \frac{\partial X_i^*}{\partial W_i} = X_i^*$ because X_i^* has been already chosen optimally, and its derivative with respect to W_i is equal to zero by the Envelope theorem.

[14] To be well-behaved, a neoclassical cost function needs to respect a set of conditions that are either imposed before estimation or verified as post. In particular, the cost function needs to be nondecreasing in factor prices and output and linearly homogeneous and concave in factor prices.

In Eq. (6.14), X_k^* is the optimal conditional demand equation for private capital and S_k^* is the relative optimal share equation. Eq. (6.14) can then be used to assess whether and how an increase in the transport capital stock influences the conditional demand for private capital. In turn, the elasticity of total costs with respect to transport capital is derived as follows:

$$\frac{\partial \ln TC}{\partial \ln KT} = \gamma_{kt} + 2\gamma_{ktkt}kt + \gamma_{lkt}w_l + \gamma_{kkt}w_k + \gamma_{kty}y \qquad (6.15)$$

It is possible to jointly estimate Eqs. (6.13) and (6.14) together in a seemingly unrelated regression procedure imposing the relevant cross equation restrictions,[15] which allows in turn to dramatically increase the degrees of freedom and therefore the estimates' precision.

Moreover, the estimation of the conditional input demand equations allows researchers to compute relevant elasticities of substitution between transport infrastructure and private inputs, which in turn make it possible to test whether transport infrastructure and a given private input are complements or substitutes in production. For example, Cohen and Morrison (2003) find that investment in airports tends to increase the incentives to expand the private stock of capital in the US manufacturing sector, suggesting that airport capital and private capital are complements in production.

At this stage, it is important to recall that while in a production function framework we derive the elasticity of output with respect to transport capital, in the cost function case we derive the elasticity of costs with respect to transport capital that, although related, are not the same thing. However, the latter can be used to derive an estimate of the "shadow" value of transport infrastructure; if transport capital is measured in monetary terms, we can use information on the transport capital elasticity, the stock of transport capital, and production costs to derive the dollar reduction in private costs associated with an increase of transport capital by one $. This shadow value of transport capital can then be compared to its user cost (that should in principle consider also the costs arising from the use of distortionary taxation) to compare the marginal benefit of transport capital to its marginal cost. In principle, when the shadow value of transport infrastructure is equal to its user cost, the provision of transport infrastructure is

[15] Economic theory suggests that the coefficient of w_k in Eq. (6.14) should take on the same value as the coefficient of the square of w_k in Eq. (6.13) and similarly for the other coefficients in Eq. (6.14).

optimal, from a societal point of view;[16] in turn, if it is lower (higher), there is instead an over (under) provision of transportation capital.

Finally, it is sometimes thought that the estimation of a cost function is less subject to endogeneity problems. Unfortunately, this is not the case; indeed, input prices, as typically measured in the literature, are not likely to be exogenous, unless one has firm-level data and input prices are derived from price indices at market level in the region where the firm is located and if it is sensible to assume that firms do not have buyer power in their labor market. Moreover, output is unlikely to be exogenous, but selected by firms responding to productivity shocks that are unobserved by the econometrician, which are, however, correlated with production costs. Therefore, the estimation of a cost function is unlikely to be a panacea for the endogeneity problems that plague the estimation of production functions.

6.1.3 Other Theoretical Frameworks

One theoretical framework that has been sometimes considered in this literature is the Solow growth model, discussed in Chapter 3.1. As it is well known, the Solow growth model considers a production function similar to that in Eq. (6.9) with constant returns to scale for private inputs and assumes that countries invest a constant fraction of their income in physical capital accumulation.[17] The steady state of the model is given by (Mankiw, Romer, & Weil, 1992):

$$y = a + \beta s + \mu h + \delta n \tag{6.16a}$$

Where y, s, h, and a are the logs of output per capita, the investment rate in physical capital, the propensity to accumulate human capital and technology, respectively; finally, n represents the growth rate of population.

In turn, researchers might assume that the level of technology depends on transport capital as in Eq. (6.9), yielding an estimating equation of the type:

$$y = a + \beta s + \mu h + \delta n + \gamma kt \tag{6.16b}$$

[16] It goes without saying that investments in other types of capital (human capital, R&D, telecom, etc.) might well have greater returns than investments in transport infrastructure.

[17] In more recent versions of the Solow growth model, also human capital accumulation is allowed for.

An equation similar to this one has been estimated several times in the economic growth literature. An example related to transport infrastructure is the recent paper by Park and Seo (2016) who estimated a dynamic version of Eq. (6.16b) for a panel of Korean provinces to investigate the impact of port infrastructures on output.

An alternative to Eq. (6.16b) is to assume that the total capital stock can be split into private capital and transport capital; in this case, the two stocks could be treated equally, and in Eq. (6.16a) one would have two variables proxying for the investment rate, namely the rate of investment in private capital and the rate of investment in transport infrastructure. The advantage of this formulation is that it might be easier to derive the rate of investment in transport infrastructure than reconstruct a monetary value for the stock through the perpetual inventory method.

Again, the estimation of Eq. (6.16) is not without problems, unless one assumes that s, h, and n are exogenous. Moreover, the steady-state expression of per capita output in Eq. (6.16) is often included in an equation for the transitional dynamics of the economy, yielding an expression for the growth rate of per capita output as a function of the above variables plus the initial level of GDP, which further complicates the analysis because of difficulties associated with the estimation of dynamic panel data models (see Del Gatto et al., 2011 and Section 6.2.2).

A closely related model is that of Shioji (2001) who considers an otherwise standard Cobb–Douglas production function where public capital (expressed in per worker terms) is assumed to influence the level of Hicks neutral technology. He shows that, in the steady state of his growth model (as in that of Solow's), the elasticity of output with respect to public capital is larger than what one would derive from the estimation of the production function (γ) because in the long-run public capital, by stimulating production, leads to more capital accumulation, which in turns leads to higher output, so that the long-run elasticity should be equal to $\gamma/(1-\alpha)$, where α is the elasticity of output with respect to private capital; given a capital elasticity of about 1/3, this means and increase in the elasticity of output with respect to public capital by about 1.5.[18]

Before turning to a description of the econometric approaches, it is worth mentioning the fact that, in recent years, the attention of researchers has somewhat shifted from the estimation of the impact of transport

[18] See De la Fuente (2010) for a review of the effects of public infrastructure on production using the Mankiw et al. (1992) theoretical framework.

infrastructure on production to the role that transport infrastructures plays, as a major determinant of transport costs and accessibility, on trade, population, employment, and, more generally, on the spatial organization of economic activity.

In the case of trade, this literature has embodied transport infrastructure capital (such as roads or port facilities), into gravity equations of trade that, at least since the seminal study by Anderson and Van Wincoop (2003), have been microfounded and derived from models of international trade.[19]

Along these lines, Duranton, Morrow, and Turner (2014) and Duranton (2015) have built a model of trade among cities that host several sectors, each producing its own city-specific variety of a good. The model, which is based on Anderson and Van Wincoop (2003), yields to a two-step estimation strategy. The first step is a classic gravity equation that allows authors to derive a city propensity to export and import, conditional on bilateral distance with trading partners, and importer and exporters characteristics. In the second step, the propensities to import and export (derived from the importer and exporter fixed effects in the first step) are regressed on the extent of the road network within a city. The important point to highlight is that the set of estimating equations is directly derived from a trade model, thus highlighting how economic theory can be used to derive testable predictions about how road construction affects trade.

Similarly, Duranton and Turner (2012) have used the new economic geography theoretical framework to build a model that features the joint evolution of employment and the provision of highways in a system of cities. Along these lines, Redding and Turner (2015) have built a model featuring imperfect competition, many locations, trade within and between locations, and commuting costs within locations and have shown that equations commonly used to estimate the impact of transport infrastructures on urban population, employment, or production can often be rationalized as reduced-form versions of certain structural equations in their model.[20]

[19] We will discuss into some detail the econometric challenges that have to be dealt with in the estimation of gravity equations in Section 6.2.1 where we will analyze the use of panel fixed effects estimators to identify the effects of transport infrastructure on various economic outcomes.

[20] See Chapter 3 for a description of new economic geography and the role played by transport infrastructures.

6.2 ECONOMETRIC APPROACHES

The existing meta-analysis about the effects of transport infrastructure on production by Melo et al. (2013) and Holmgren and Merkel (2017), as well as those on the productivity effects of public capital by Bon and Ligthart (2013) and Nunez-Serrano and Velazquez (2017), which we will discuss in Chapter 7, have found some interesting, albeit somewhat conflicting, patterns on the role played by various econometric approaches on the magnitude of the elasticity of production with respect to transport infrastructures.

This fact, at a minimum, suggests that the econometrics does seem to matter; this result in turn motivates our choice to discuss in some detail the econometric issues underlying the estimation of the effects of transport infrastructure on production and other economic outcomes.

It is important to stress that our aim is not to provide a rigorous treatment of the various estimators, but rather to provide the intuition about their relative advantages and possible limitations and therefore to allow the reader to better appreciate why certain estimators are unlikely to provide robust estimates of the productivity effects of transport infrastructures.

Moreover, we will see that some estimators are likely to be valid only under certain assumptions, whose validity can be justified in some cases but not in others. However, these same estimators have been used in some studies rather mechanically, without much discussion of why the authors believe the assumptions underlying their use are valid in the specific case at hand.

Before dealing with the most important "families" of estimators that have been used in the literature, it is, however, important to clarify why it is difficult to provide a consistent estimate of the economic effects of transport infrastructures.

Let us consider the following equation, where y_{it}, tk_{it}, and X_{it} represent the log of GDP, the log of transport infrastructures, and a vector of control variables (possibly in logs) in region i at year t, respectively:

$$y_{it} = \alpha tk_{it} + \beta X_{it} + u_{it} \tag{6.17}$$

The controls in the vector X may just be the set of (the log of) private inputs in a production function or the investment rate and population growth in an equation of a Solow growth model; a set of time dummies that capture macroeconomic developments common to all units in the sample or just other possible determinants of production, such as capacity utilization, population density, and other regional characteristics.[21] Moreover, tk_{it} might represent either an amount (i.e., the length of roads rather than the value of the road stock) or a simple dummy related to the existence of a given transport project (i.e., the existence of a high-speed rail network).

To be able to consistently estimate the elasticity α with OLS, it is well known that there must be no correlation between tk_{it} and the error term. However, there are several reasons that make the existence of a nonzero correlation very likely.

1. First, it is possible that a network expansion takes place precisely when Y is unusually large, because tax receipts are relatively big and the government has funds to finance the realization of transport projects. In this case, one will find a positive correlation between an extension in the transportation network and GDP, which, however, could be, at least in part, spurious. By way of contrast, if transport infrastructure projects are undertaken in downturns as part of a stimulus package, then one will see a negative correlation between tk_{it} and the error term, because tk_{it} will increase precisely in periods when economic activity is unusually low, impairing a negative bias to the OLS coefficient of α. In a similar vein, if there are time lags in an execution of a project, it might well happen that a project decided in periods of recession is realized during booms, again impairing an upward bias.[22] Interestingly, Duranton and Turner (2012) find that their OLS estimates of the effects of US interstate highways within a metropolitan area on employment growth of that metropolitan area are downward biased; this of course implies that highways tend to be disproportionally allocated to metropolitan areas experiencing a negative employment shock. Using very detailed data they are able to check this assumption by finding a negative (conditional on controls) correlation between employment growth in a city and the growth of the share of population in that city that is employed

[21] The example is referred to a panel data of regions; however, the point that we make is essentially valid also for other types of data, such as a panel of various industries in different countries as well as for firm-level data.

[22] In this example, we consider a panel data model because it has been the type of data most commonly used in the literature; nevertheless, to some extent the above comments can be generalized also to purely time series data. In cross-section data there are other similar issues; for instance, positive transport infrastructure elasticities might simply capture the fact that richer countries/regions have more transport infrastructures precisely because they are richer.

in the road building sector. In other words, if a city experiences a negative employment shock, more highways are allocated to that city, which in turn increases the share of workers employed in the road building sector.

2. Second, models such as those of Redding and Turner (2015), or Duranton and Turner (2012), have shown how, in a city or region, infrastructure provision, on the one hand, and economic outcomes such as employment and production, on the other hand, can be simultaneously determined. For instance, in the Redding and Turner's (2015) model, equilibrium employment (and output) depends on productivity, which is typically not observed and therefore included in the error term. However, the amount of infrastructure provided in a region will depend on productivity, for instance, because higher productivity allows for higher output and larger tax receipts. Similarly, higher employment and output in a region can lead to more congestion and to an increase in demand for transport infrastructures.
3. Third, and more generally, in an equation like Eq. (6.17) there might be omitted variables that explain both a region/country propensity to build a transport network and GDP growth, such as institutions, legal systems, corruption, political connections, etc. By way of example, good institutions that "force" politicians to focus on long-run development might lead some regions to invest more in transport infrastructure; nevertheless, institutions might lead to higher GDP also via other channels, such as certainty of the legal environment, protection of investments, stronger support to R&D expenditure, higher human capital accumulation, etc. Alternatively, if corruption is more widespread in laggard regions, or political economy considerations lead to more infrastructures spending precisely in those regions (Cadot, Roller, & Stephan, 2006; Golden & Picci, 2008), then one could find a spurious negative correlation between GDP and transport infrastructures. Along these lines, if transport infrastructures are measured in monetary terms, in more corrupted areas one would observe higher values of transport capital for a given network extension (because the construction technology is less efficient), again generating another source of correlation between infrastructure capital and the error term. Although some of these omitted variables might be included as controls in the X vector, others will be unobserved and most economists would still see the OLS estimate of α in Eq. (6.17) as unlikely to identify the true elasticity of GDP with respect to transport infrastructures. Moreover, if the control variables

were themselves endogenous and possibly correlated with TK, a bad regressor problem might occur (Angrist & Pischke, 2009), potentially biasing the OLS estimate of α.

4. Finally, if a study is based on firm-level data, an additional endogeneity problem might arise, as more productive firms could self-select into regions with better and more developed transport networks, again potentially biasing the OLS effect of transportation infrastructure on firm level outcomes such as productivity, entry, etc.

In the next subsection, we will describe how some of these issues have been tackled in the empirical literature. One issue that we do not cover at all is the existence of heterogeneous effects of transport infrastructures, i.e., the possibility that the impact of a transport project has a differential effect on treated units. We refer the interested reader to Baum-Snow and Ferreira (2015).

6.2.1 Panel Data

6.2.1.1 The Fixed Effects Model

Let us again consider the panel data model in Eq. (6.17), but let us also assume that the error term has the following structure:

$$u_{it} = c_i + v_{it} \tag{6.18}$$

This yields the following estimating equation:

$$y_{it} = \alpha tk_{it} + \beta X_{it} + c_i + v_{it} \tag{6.19}$$

As we noted above, the OLS estimator (also known as Pooled OLS, POLS, in a panel data context) will deliver consistent estimates of α only insofar as $E(TK_{it}u_{it}) = 0$, i.e., if the so-called contemporaneous exogeneity assumption holds. This in turn requires both $E(TK_{it}v_{it}) = 0$ and $E(TK_{it}c_i) = 0$.

In the light of the discussion above, we see why the POLS estimator is very unlikely to provide a consistent estimate of α; if transport infrastructure increases precisely when GDP is unusually large, then the contemporaneous exogeneity assumption fails because $E(TK_{it}v_{it}) \neq 0$

Moreover, and perhaps even more importantly, the unit-specific component needs to be uncorrelated with transport infrastructures. However, the unit-specific component is likely to capture all time-invariant determinants of GDP, some of which might explain also why transport infrastructure is larger in some country/regions than in others (quality of institutions, corruption, geography, etc.); in other words, it is very likely that $E(TK_{it}c_i) \neq 0$.

It is important that the stringency of the conditions under which POLS can deliver consistent estimates is exacerbated in those studies that estimate production functions because also private inputs can be endogenous and the bias of their coefficients could well be transmitted to that of transport infrastructures.

The most popular way to address some of the pitfalls of the POLS estimator is the use of the so-called fixed effects estimator. The fixed effects estimator deals with the endogeneity associated with the unit-specific error term. It does so by removing it through an appropriate transformation of the model.

Let us define, for any generic variable z, $\overline{z_i} = \frac{1}{T}\sum_{i=1}^{N} z_{it}$ as the average over time of z for unit i. If we take the average over T of Eq. (6.19), we get $\overline{y_i} = \alpha\overline{tk_i} + \beta\overline{X_i} + c_i + \overline{v_i}$. If we subtract this last expression to Eq. (5.19), we get

$$y_{it} - \overline{y_i} = \alpha tk_{it} - \alpha\overline{tk_i} + \beta X_{it} - \beta\overline{X_i} + c_i - c_i + v_{it} - \overline{v_i} \tag{6.20}$$

Eq. (6.20) can be rewritten as follows:

$$\widetilde{y_{it}} = \alpha\widetilde{tk_{it}} + \beta\widetilde{X_{it}} + \widetilde{v_{it}} \tag{6.21}$$

Eq. (6.21) can be estimated by OLS. In other words, through the within transformation of the data one can eliminate the c_i and therefore the possible omitted variable problems associated with unobserved time-invariant heterogeneity that might explain both GDP and transport infrastructures.

However, for this estimator to be consistent, the following important condition needs to be respected (Wooldridge, 2010): $E(TK_{is}v_{it}) = 0;\ \forall\ s,\ t$, which is known as strict exogeneity condition. In words, this condition requires that the level of transport infrastructure in year t is uncorrelated with the past, present, and future values of the error term. This is clearly a more restrictive hypothesis than the simple contemporaneous exogeneity discussed above.

For example, we need to rule out that the government, forecasting a positive shock to GDP in the future, decided in the past to increase transport infrastructure because higher taxes tomorrow will make it easier to service the public debt associated with the transport project, which again would violate the $E(TK_{is}v_{it}) = 0$ condition. Indeed, there would be a correlation between TK_{is} and v_{it} with $s < t$, i.e., between past TK and current v_{it}.[23] In principle, this lack of strict exogeneity could be dealt with by including sufficient lags of TK and interpreting the equation as a distributed lag model, although this procedure might reduce degrees of freedom and it might not be immediate to justify the number of lags to include into the model.

As noted by Wooldridge (2010), it is more problematic a situation where we cannot rule out that, e.g., a negative shock to output in region i as of time t (i.e., a low value of v_{it}) has led the government to react and increase transport infrastructure in year $s > t$, which is quite a plausible scenario, especially if transport infrastructure are realized following a recession and there are important implementation lags; in this case, we would have a negative correlation between v_{it} and TK_{is} with $s > t$.[24]

In other words, the fixed effects estimator solves the unobserved time-invariant heterogeneity issue by eliminating the c_i via the within transformation, but it requires the strict exogeneity condition. It is also important to recall that the fixed effects estimator identifies the parameter of interest by the within variation only, i.e., from changes in Y and KT over time, and discards the cross sectional variation. If the within variation is relatively low, it is possible that the fixed effects estimator will deliver imprecise estimates (with high standard error). Moreover, the within estimator has been criticized for possibly exacerbating measurement error problems; intuitively, this is because the only variation used to identify the effects of KT is the variation within each unit over time and, if KT varies little over time in most units and a large fraction of that variation is due to measurement error, the identified effect might be largely driven by the latter, inducing measurement error bias in the estimate.

[23] Similarly, the government might forecast an increasing demand for transport infrastructure in the future associated with a positive shock to productivity and increase "today" the stock of transport capital.

[24] In general, the bias of the fixed effects estimator if the strong exogeneity assumption is violated, but contemporaneous exogeneity is maintained (the so-called Nickell bias), is a negative function of T. In other words, for a sufficiently long time series, the bias is likely to be small (Wooldridge, 2010). Nevertheless, it should also be recalled that, for sufficiently long T, considerations relative to the time series properties of the estimators and in particular stationarity and cointegration become central to the analysis. For studies that apply time series techniques to panel data to explore the impact of transport infrastructures on production, see Bronzini and Piselli (2009), Bottasso, Castagnetti, et al. (2013) and Calderon et al. (2015), among others.

Various papers have estimated the effects of transport infrastructure on production using the simple fixed effects estimator discussed above. Just focusing on the most recent papers, we can mention Shan, Yu, and Lee (2014) on the growth effects of port infrastructures and Farhadi (2014) on the growth effects of overall transport infrastructure.[25]

At this stage, it is important to remark how the random effects model, where the c_i is not allowed to be correlated with regressors and it is subsumed in the error term and taken care through a generalized least square procedure, is definitely less robust than the fixed effects estimator. This is because the random effects estimator is based on the same strong exogeneity assumption but without the advantage of being robust to unobserved time-invariant heterogeneity.[26]

A closely related approach to deal with the c_i term is to eliminate it via first differencing of the model. The first difference estimator also requires the same strong exogeneity assumption we have just discussed for the fixed effects estimator and, if the latter is valid, the two estimators should deliver the same parameter estimates, although their efficiency can be different.[27] If they do not, then one should worry that the strict exogeneity assumption is violated and, in this case, both first differences and fixed effects estimators are likely to deliver inconsistent estimates.[28]

Wooldridge (2010) suggests that a possible test of strong exogeneity is to include leads of the regressors, in our case transport infrastructures; if leads (i.e., anticipatory effects) are significant, then the strong exogeneity assumption is likely to be violated. In turn, the possible significance of lagged explanatory variables is less problematic because we can interpret the model as a distributed lag one. To the best of our knowledge, this test for the strong exogeneity assumption has hardly been implemented in the

[25] Various recent papers have considered fixed effects models but within a spatial econometrics estimation strategy. We will consider these in Section 6.2.2.

[26] A recent study employing the random effects estimator is Bismark (2014).

[27] If the v_{it} in Eq. (6.18) are serially uncorrelated, then the fixed effect estimator is more efficient than the first difference one; by way of contrast, if the differenced v_{it} are serially uncorrelated, the first difference estimator should be more efficient. See Wooldridge (2010).

[28] If the strict exogeneity assumption is violated, the fixed effects and first difference estimators have different probability limits. Therefore, finding that estimated coefficients are robust across methods can be considered as supportive of the strong exogeneity assumption.

empirical literature on the economic effects of transport infrastructure capital, with the exception of Bottasso et al (2018).

In the empirical literature, some variations of the fixed effects and first difference models have been employed. For instance, when the time dimension is sufficiently long, in some studies authors use a long difference strategy, i.e., considering years at, say, T = 5, 10 year intervals. This might allow estimates to be less sensitive to business cycles and short-run fluctuations. (Box 6.1).

6.2.1.2 Models With Weak Exogeneity and GMM

We noted above that the fixed effects and first difference estimators are based on the strict exogeneity assumption. Sometimes this assumption might be excessively strict. An alternative, less demanding hypothesis is that of *sequential exogeneity*. This can be stated as $E(TK_{is}v_{it}) = 0, \forall s \leq t$. In this case, it is maintained the assumption that past and current values of the regressor should not be correlated to future values of the error term. However, the latter is allowed to be correlated to future values of the regressor. We have noted above that the fixed effects estimator is inconsistent is such a case, although the bias declines as T grows. However, it can be shown that, if the sequential exogeneity assumption holds, there exist IV estimators[31] that can deliver consistent parameter estimates.

To see this, let us first difference Eq. (6.19) to get

$$\Delta Y_{it} = \alpha \Delta TK_{it} + \beta \Delta X_{it} + \Delta v_{it} \tag{6.22}$$

It is easy to see that estimating Eq. (6.22) with OLS does not provide consistent parameter estimates under the sequential exogeneity assumption, which implies that $E(TK_{is}v_{it}) \neq 0, \forall s > t$, which further implies that TK_{it}, which is part of ΔTK_{it}, is correlated with v_{it-1}, which is part of Δv_{it}.

However, we know, under the sequential exogeneity assumption, that past values of TK_{it}, should be valid instruments, i.e., correlated with TK_{it} but not with the error term. Therefore, one could use TK_{it-1} and even TK_{it-2} as instruments for ΔTK_{it}. If among the X vector there is the lagged dependent variable, as in the dynamic version of the Solow growth model (or in some production function studies), ΔY_{it-1} is correlated by

[29] In what follows, we largely follow Bottasso et al. (2018).

[31] See Section 6.2.3 for a very brief discussion of the logic underlying instrumental variable estimation.

Box 6.1 An application of the fixed effects estimator to gravity equations of trade[29]

Recently, the use of fixed effects has become very popular in the estimation of gravity equations of trade. In particular, various trade theories (reviewed in Head & Mayer, 2015) have shown that bilateral trade flows between any two spatial units can be expressed, in a cross-sectional context, as in equation (Box 6.1):

$$T_{ij} = \frac{Y_i}{\Pi_i^{-\phi}} \frac{E_i}{P_j^{-\phi}} D_{ij}^{-\phi} TK_{ij}^{-\theta} \qquad \text{(Box 6.1)}$$

Where Y represents total output of the origin country, E total expenditure in the destination country (both usually proxied by *GDP*), D_{ij} is a vector of drivers of trade costs between any pair of countries, such as distance, common languages or currencies, customs unions, etc. In turn, TK_{ij} represents the product of the stock of transport infrastructure in the couple of countries i and j, whereas Π_i and P_j represents the inward and outward multilateral resistance indexes introduced by Anderson and Van Wincoop (2003) that capture general equilibrium effects. In particular, the authors show that these multilateral indexes, associated with a country market potential and degree of openness to trade, are functions of trade costs (see, for a nice exposition, Fally, 2015).

This has important implications for the econometric estimation of gravity equations. Indeed, traditionally a restricted version of equation (Box 6.1) was estimated, namely one omitting the multilateral resistance indexes. This is, however, problematic because these indices are functions of all often unobserved determinants of trade costs, and their omission might create a correlation between the error term and the included regressors in the vector.

Most of the recent empirical literature has therefore tackled the omitted variable bias affecting the estimation of "naïve" versions of gravity equations by augmenting the latter with origin and destination country fixed effects, as in equation (Box 6.2) below, where d_i and d_j are fixed effects for country i and j, respectively:[30]

$$T_{ij} = Y_i E_j D_{ij}^{-\phi} TK_{ij}^{-\theta} \exp\left(\varphi_i d_i + \varphi_j d_j\right) \qquad \text{(Box 6.2)}$$

Because multilateral resistance terms can be time varying, when panel data are available, regressions with exporter–importer fixed effects, exporter-by-year, and importer-by-year fixed effects have been estimated, as suggested by Baldwin and Taglioni (2006):

$$T_{ijt} = Y_{it} E_{jt} D_{ijt}^{-\phi} TK_{ijt}^{-\theta} \exp\left(\varphi_i d_{it} + \varphi_j d_{jt} + \varphi_{ij} d_{ij}\right) \qquad \text{(Box 6.3)}$$

Where d_{it} and d_{jt} represent country of origin and destination fixed effects that are allowed to vary over time, whereas d_{ij} represent fixed effects for any combination of countries of origin and destination.

Continued

Box 6.1 An application of the fixed effects estimator to gravity equations of trade[29]—cont'd

This fixed effects panel data model is usually operationalized by taking logs of both sides, although Santos-Silva and Tenreyro (2006) have argued that direct estimation of Eq. (6.27) using Poisson quasi-maximum likelihood techniques is preferable on statistical grounds. For an application to the impact of port infrastructures on Brazilian trade, see Bottasso, Conti, Costacurta de Sa Porto, Ferrari, and Tei (2018), who found that an increase in ports infrastructure in Brazilian states is positively correlated with imports and especially exports of Brazilian states.

[30] See Head and Mayer (2015) for other, more "structural", estimation approaches.

construction with Δv_{it}, but Y_{it-2} should not and it might be used as an instrument for ΔY_{it-1}.

For this approach to be valid, it is necessary that the error term in 6.19 is not serially correlated; indeed, in the presence of serial correlation past instruments could be correlated with the differenced error term, making the exclusion restriction invalid.[32]

A similar strategy can be applied in the case of models with contemporaneous correlation between some explanatory variables and the error term; in that case, the orthogonality condition could be stated as $E(TK_{is}v_{it}) = 0, \forall s < t$. In other words, we can allow for correlation between TK and current and past values of the error term, while still requiring no correlation between current values of TK and future values of the error term. In this case, however, TK_{it-1} is no longer a suitable instrument, and TK_{it-2} onward should be used instead.

This first difference IV estimator under sequential exogeneity has been found to perform poorly. A more efficient generalized method of moment estimator due to Arellano and Bond (1991) has been shown to provide more efficient estimates. While we refer to Wooldridge (2010) for an in-depth treatment and to Roodman (2009) for a very useful guide on the practical issues faced by researchers, in this place we can note that the Arellano and Bond estimator exploits more orthogonality conditions, but with the previous estimator shares the idea of using "internal instruments", i.e., past values of the explanatory variables. The Arellano and Bond

[32] In other words, we cannot assume that TK_{it-1} affects ΔY_{it} only through ΔTK_{it}.

estimator is able to do so because it considers a GMM problem specified as a system of equations, one for each time period, where the instruments that are applied in each time period differ because, as more time goes by, more lagged values are available as instruments.

Since this estimator had been found to suffer of a weak-instrument problem because of the quite low correlation between changes and lagged values of the regressors,[33] Arellano and Bover (1995) and Blundell and Bond (1998) proposed a GMM estimator that combines the equation in first differences with an equation in level in a system of equations, from which the name GMM system.

In the level equation, the instruments are differenced to make them exogenous with respect to the fixed effects, which is a valid assumption provided that the change in the regressor is uncorrelated with the fixed effect.[34] If the assumption holds, then lagged changes in the regressor could be used as instruments for the endogenous regressor in the level equation. It is important to note that under this assumption we need to rule out technological catching up across countries (or regions); in fact, if technological progress and efficiency growth are related to the beginning of the period level of technology and efficiency, then it is likely that GDP growth rates are correlated with the unit-specific fixed effects; if we think this to be an important feature of the data, the validity of this estimator breaks down.[35]

All in all, the estimators proposed by Arellano and Bond (1991) and Arellano and Bover (1998) are an improvement with respect to the simple fixed effects estimator. However, they still rely on the assumption that $E(TK_{is}\nu_{it}) = 0, \forall s < t$. What does this assumption imply for the estimation of the impact of transport infrastructure capital on production?

In practice, researchers should be confident that policy-makers do not build a road, a railway, or enlarge a port system today in anticipation of an increase in production that would take place tomorrow because of, say, a productivity boom; if that were indeed the case, then we would have a correlation between lagged values of transport capital and future shocks to the error term, making the GMM estimators discussed so far inconsistent.

[33] This is often the case when the variance of the individual error increases relatively to the variance of the idiosyncratic error term or, in dynamic equations, when the autoregressive component is very close to one. See footnote 54 for a discussion of the weak-instrument problem and for some references.

[34] Both the Difference and System GMM can be run using the xtabond2 routine for STATA.

[35] See Del Gatto et al. (2011) for a discussion.

This assumption seems slightly more defendable than the additional assumption (necessary for the consistency of the fixed effects estimator) that we have also to rule out feedback effects from past shocks to production to current levels of transport infrastructure. Indeed, a past shock to GDP might well motivate a future expansion of the network, when decision and implementation lags are important; the fact that the GMM approaches discussed in this section allow to control for this possibility is reassuring.

Nevertheless, the possibility that forward-looking policy-makers can decide today to improve a transport network because of an expected increase in transportation demand associated with a future increase in production (which might determine $E(TK_{is}v_{it}) \neq 0, \forall s < t$), which could in turn increase congestion, cannot be easily dismissed either as, explicitly or, more often, implicitly has been typicallydone in most applied work.

Related to this, the $E(TK_{is}v_{it}) = 0$ assumption, and the use of TK_{it-2} as instruments for ΔTK_{it}, means that *TK* has only a contemporaneous effect on output; in other words, once we have controlled for the current level of infrastructure, its past values should not have any effect on output. Although this might be reasonable, it is not necessarily always the case. For instance, an increase in the length of motorways in a region might have a contemporaneous effect on output, but it is still possible that past extensions of the motorways continue to have an effect today because of network effects. Moreover, if there are important nonlinearities, it is possible that past additions to the network have a larger effect than current additions. In other words, it is not completely unreasonable that past values of *TK* exert an effect on current output, even if we control for current *TK*. Moreover, if firms need time to adjust to the higher stock of transport infrastructure, we can expect that past values of *TK* have an effect on production beyond the effects associated with its current value.

Indeed, using lagged values of TK_{it} as instruments for ΔTK_{it} is valid provided there is no serial correlation; however, both GDP and transport infrastructure stocks are in general fairly persistent variables which in turn might generate serial correlation in the data. Furthermore, if transport infrastructure is slow moving, lagged levels can be poorly correlated with contemporaneous changes. From this point of view, the GMM-SYS approach might help but, again, its validity is based on a strong identification assumption, namely that contemporaneous changes in transport infrastructure capital never depend on the unit fixed effects; however, the latter can capture unobservables such as institutions, geography, degree of urbanization, etc.

At a minimum, those considerations suggest that caution should be used when employing these GMM estimators whose results, therefore, in our opinion, should not be used as "smoking gun, bullet proof" evidence on the causal effect of transport infrastructure on economic growth.[36]

Despite their limitations, the Arellano and Bond (1991) and Arellano and Bover (1995) type of estimators in this area of empirical research have been proving popular among applied researchers. For instance, Bottasso and Conti (2010) have analyzed the impact of the motorways network for a cross-country panel of industries in the former EU-15 countries; Crescenzi, Di Cataldo, and Rodriguez-Pose (2016) have investigated the relationship between the quality of institutions and the effects of transport infrastructure stocks on GDP for a panel of EU regions; Jiwattanakulpaisarn et al., (2009) and Jiwattanakulpaisarn et al., (2012) who, using a panel of counties in North Carolina, have studied the impact of motorways on employment; and Jiwattanakulpaisarn et al., (2009) and Jiwattanakulpaisarn et al., (2012) who used the same methodology to investigate the relationship between the motorways network and production in a panel of US states.

A final comment on the GMM estimators is warranted. Because one of the original contributions (see Blundell and Bond, 1998) was proposed to estimate (dynamic) production functions, the use of internal instruments has become very popular also as a tool to deal with simultaneity problems in the estimation of production functions,[37] which also explains why studies seeking to estimate the impact of transport infrastructure capital on production have used the GMM-SYS and GMM-DIFF estimators. However, it seems fair to say that recent practice in production function estimation has somewhat shifted toward other estimation approaches, such as those proposed by Olley and Pakes (1996), Levinshon and Petrin (2003), and Ackerberg et al. (2015) (Box 6.2).

6.2.2 Spatial Econometrics

As discussed in Chapter 3, an increase in transport infrastructures in one region can generate positive economic effects in nearby areas if network elements are important. By increasing the stock of highways or railways in region $j \neq i$, transport infrastructure developments might in principle

[36] For a similar opinion, see also the discussion in Crescenzi et al. (2016)).
[37] See, for instance, the literature review of Van Beveren (2012).

Box 6.2 An application of the GMM models

A study which is illustrative of the use of dynamic GMM panel data estimator is Jiwattanakulpaisarn et al., (2012). They evaluated the impact of motorways density on employment using a sample of 100 counties for the state of North Carolina in the United States over the period 1985–97. They estimated an autoregressive-distributed lag model (ARDL) for log employment similar to the following equation:

$$y_{it} = \alpha y_{it-1} + \beta tk_{it} + \gamma tk_{it-1} + \delta X_{it} + \varepsilon X_{it-1} + c_i + t_t + v_{it} \qquad \text{(Box 6.4)}$$

Where c_i is a country fixed effects, t_t is a set of year fixed effects that capture macroeconomic effects common to all counties in the sample, v_{it} is a residual error term, *tk* is the ratio of highways lane miles and the county's area, and X is a vector of controls. The equation in Box (6.4) is an ARDL (1,1) model because it considers both lagged values of the dependent and independent variables. In this model, β represents the contemporaneous effect of highways capital on employment, whereas the long-run impact can be measured as $\frac{\beta+\gamma}{1-\alpha}$. Jiwattanakulpaisarn et al., (2009) assume that $E(TK_{is}v_{it}) = 0, \forall s < t$. In other words, they assume that, conditionally on unobserved heterogeneity, lagged highways and employment, there is no correlation between current highways and future shocks to employment. They estimate the model with both the GMM-DIFF and GMM-SYS estimators. In the latter case, they used TK_{it-2}, TK_{it-3}, and TK_{it-4} as instruments for ΔTK_{it} in the first difference equation, and ΔTK_{it-1} for TK_{it} in the level equation. Although not clearly reported in the paper, tk_{it-1} must have been instrumented, with longer lags, i.e., starting from T-3 in the difference equations and from T-2 in the level equation. They restricted the number of lags to avoid the problem of "proliferations" of instruments that arise in these applications if too many lags are considered. In some specifications, they consider longer lags (e.g., they start from TK_{it-3}) if there is evidence of serial correlation in Box (6.4), which rules out T-2 as a valid instrument for the first difference equation. They do not find evidence of a positive effect of highways density of employment, neither in the short run nor in the long run. In a companion paper, Jiwattanakulpaisarn et al. (2012) use a similar approach to estimate a dynamic production function assuming an ARDL (1,1) specification as in Box (6.4); in that case, also private inputs are instrumented with the same identification assumption used for the motorways density variable: using a panel of US states, they find a positive but small elasticity of output with respect to highways.

remove important bottlenecks and improve the quality of a given link of a wider network, thereby reducing transport costs also in regions others than j, increasing their accessibility. Moreover, it is even possible that, without sufficient investment in nearby regions, a more developed transport infrastructure in region *i* might have little productive effects per se in that region. Similarly, an extension of port facilities in a region, by acting as a gateway for nearby landlocked areas, might have significant externalities on the latter by facilitating their integration with international markets.[38] Furthermore, improving roads in an area might reduce commuting costs to nearby regions, thereby improving the productivity of the latter, for instance, via cheaper access to a large labor market.

It is, however, important to acknowledge the fact that also negative spillovers might arise. This could be the case if the main effect of a particular infrastructure investment in a given region is simply to attract into the region a set of firms located in nearby areas, which are therefore negatively affected by the original transport investment; if transport costs are lower, firms might in fact decide to relocate in that region because it is now better integrated with world markets; moreover, such relocation might foster agglomeration economies and induce further relocations from nearby areas (see Chapters 3 and 7).

The existence of externalities associated with transport infrastructure investments and the scale at which they can be identified (local, regional, of even country level) have important implications for the efficient design and financing of transportation infrastructures; indeed, positive or negative externalities at regional level imply an under- or overprovision of transport infrastructure, respectively. This in turn would call for coordination and possibly cofinancing of new infrastructures at the level where spillovers can be more easily internalized.

The importance that spillovers associated with transport infrastructure investments have for policy-makers, as well as the fact that economic theory does not offer a clear-cut view on their existence, has spurred in recent years the interest of many scholars on the measurement of spatial spillovers associated with transport infrastructure networks.

The issue of spatial spillovers associated with transport infrastructure investments has been generally analyzed, especially in the most recent

[38] See, for instance, Bottasso, Conti, Ferrari, and Tei (2014) who report evidence suggesting that spillovers account for the largest share of total effects of port activity on regional output in a sample of EU regions.

period, within the framework of spatial econometrics; in what follows, we aim to illustrate the motivation underlying the use of spatial econometrics tools and how those have been used in the literature.[39]

The analysis can start from a simple cross-sectional equation like Eq. (6.23) below:

$$y_i = \alpha tk_i + \beta X_i + u_i \tag{6.23}$$

In Eq. (6.27), variables have the standard meaning; y is the log of production in a given region, tk is the log of a transport infrastructure variable, whereas X is a vector containing a series of control variables, such as private inputs, population density, etc., whereas u is an error term.

In a spatial setting, assuming that units are independent makes little sense, even if the nature of the interdependency might be hard to pin down. However, when units can be mapped onto locations, then some structure can be imposed on the degree of interdependence across units in an equation like Eq. (6.23) because researchers can observe the physical location of agents and therefore impose that units far apart have less impacts on their peers than those that are closer.

This is generally done by considering a spatial weight matrix w_{ij}, whose j-element is bigger the closer unit j is to unit i. For instance, in some studies, the j-element is equal to one if the region where unit j is located[40] shares a common border with the region where unit i is located, and zero otherwise, i.e., a contiguity matrix.[41] Other authors prefer instead to use the inverse of distance as a proxy for closeness, so that the typical j-element is equal to $^{1}/_{\text{distance}_{ij}}$, reflecting the so-called Law of Geography, according to which "everything is related to everything else, but near things are more related than distant things." While in the former case only nearby units can have an effect on unit i, in the latter case all units can have an effect, although closer units bear more weight. Similarly, some authors still base the weight matrix on the inverse of distance but include a cut-off threshold

[39] In what follows, we largely borrow from LeSage and Pace (2009) and Gibbons and Overman (2012).

[40] The unit could be the region itself, if the researcher works with regional data.

[41] Various alternatives to this scheme have been used in the literature. For instance, some authors consider a j-element equal to 1 if the distance between units i and j is less than some prespecified distance, such as 150 km (Arbues et al., 2015).

distance (Vega & Elhorst, 2015),[42] so that units after the cut-off get a weight of zero.[43]

The typical spatial econometrics paper considers the linear combination of production in the other regions (y) and the weight matrix w, $\sum_{j\neq i} w_{ij}$, which is known in the literature as spatial lag. When the weight matrix is normalized so that its elements sum to 1, the spatial lag is in turn equal to the weighted average of the dependent variable in Eq. (6.23). Assuming that the impact of the spatial lag on production is linear and identical for each unit (and equal to ρ), the latter is inserted into Eq. (6.23) to give

$$y_i = \rho \sum_{j\neq i} w_{ij} y_i + \alpha t k_i + \beta X_i + u_i \qquad (6.24)$$

The model in Eq. (6.24) is typically rationalized in the literature by noting that in spatial and social interaction processes the value of the dependent variable for one agent is typically jointly determined with those of nearby ones; in other words, when agents assume their utility maximizing decisions, not only do they take into considerations their own characteristics but also decisions of nearby agents, which of course depend on their own characteristics (as well as on the decision of the other nearby agents).

In the case of transport infrastructures, agents in region i would assume their optimal decisions not only by taking their own transport infrastructure (and other characteristics) into account but also the level of production in nearby countries; this is important because, for example, the construction of a new port terminal might reflect growth developments in nearby, possibly landlocked, regions that in turn might use the new port facility; in this case, controlling for the spatial lags might be important per se but also because it might allow researchers to control for biases that might arise from spatial simultaneity.

[42] By way of example, Chen and Haynes (2015) and Arbues et al. (2015) use a contiguity matrix, whereas Bottasso et al. (2014) use a matrix based on the inverse of squared distance. Bottasso et al. (2014) also weight the inverse of squared distance with the product of GDP of region i and j to give more weight to bigger regions. Although Bottasso et al. (2014) use beginning of the period GDP to alleviate possible endogeneity concerns, care should be exercised when using possibly endogenous weight matrices.

[43] In some studies, the matrix W contains parameters, usually associated with the speed of decay of connectivity among units, which are estimated using nonlinear methods or using search procedures alongside other regression parameters. More recently, some authors let W to be estimated directly from the data. See Vega and Elhorst (2015) for an interesting discussion about this recent avenue of research.

Moreover, because transport infrastructures in one region can affect production in that region (if $\alpha \neq 0$), a significant ρ might generate indirect effects in nearby regions through general equilibrium linkages; this suggests that the model in Eq. (6.24) is potentially able to generate a spillover effect because the change in a given explanatory variable in a specific unit tends to affect the dependent variable of that specific unit but, through the spatial lag, also the dependent variables of other units, also those that are not originally connected to the unit where the change in the explanatory variable occurred in the first place.[44]

Of course, the model in Eq. (6.24) might spuriously generate spillover effects if the spatial lag just captures omitted variables that are spatially correlated, such as climatic conditions, institutional quality, or the very same variables contained in the X vector, etc.

Alternatively, spatial spillovers considerations associated with transport infrastructures might be introduced into Eq. (6.23) by allowing transport infrastructures and other variables in nearby regions to have a direct effect on the dependent variable, as in Eq. (6.25) below:

$$y_i = \alpha tk_i + \beta X_i + \gamma \sum_{j \neq i} w_{ij} G_i + + u_i \tag{6.25}$$

According to a terminology popularized by LeSage and Pace (2009), the model in Eq. (6.24) is known as the spatial autoregressive model (SAR), whereas Eq. (6.25) is often labeled as the spatial X model (SLX).[45]

[44] Indeed, LeSage and Pace (2009) note that when the spatial lag of y is included in the model, one can estimate three effects of a particular exogenous variable, namely the direct, indirect, and total effects. The first is akin to the conventional interpretation of a regression coefficient but includes also feedbacks loops across regions, i.e., the feedback effects that are generated by the impacts in nearby regions that are transmitted back in the region where the change in the exogenous variable was originated. The total effect in turn is generally measured as the average impact on the dependent variable of region i of a simultaneous change in the regressor of interest in all other regions. Finally, the indirect effect, which represents the spillover, is the difference between the total and the direct effect. See LeSage and Pace (2009) for a discussion and formal derivation of this result.

[45] See Dal Bo and Florio (2012) and Shan et al. (2014) for a recent application in the case of transport infrastructures, among the others. Interestingly, Eq. (6.25) is that being estimated in studies outside the spatial econometrics framework. See, for instance, Jiwattanakulpaisarn et al. (2012) and Bottasso and Conti (2010) who included the spatial lag of nearby states and countries, respectively, in a production function estimated with the GMM-SYS estimator.

In Eq. (6.25), G is a vector representing the effect of variables in other regions (such as transport networks). As argued by LeSage and Pace (2009), Eq. (6.24) might result from a model where the decision-makers in region i assume their decisions taking into consideration some characteristics of nearby regions, such as transport infrastructure networks, rather than outcomes in nearby regions. Eq. (6.25) is also justified by the "network character" of the spatial economy, which in turn implies that infrastructures in certain regions might have nonnegligible effects in other areas that are connected to the former by a set of historic, economic, geographic, and other social connections, that one hopes to capture with the spatial lags of G. Using also the terminology of LeSage and Pace (2009), in Eq. (6.24) one should capture the possibility that spatial spillovers arise as local as opposed to global spillovers, i.e., not through the general equilibrium linkages that the model in Eq. (6.24) is meant to capture.

In the case of transport infrastructures, one might reckon that it is more natural to think that spillovers tend to arise mainly as local ones. In fact, it is quite natural to look at transport infrastructures as (quasi) public goods (see Chapter 2) that display their effects also in nearby regions. Of course, an equation like Eq. (6.25) might not allow capturing global spillovers. This can be seen more clearly in the case of a weight matrix of the contiguity-type; in this case, an increase in transport infrastructure in region i would not have any effect in region j if that is not contiguous to region i. However, it might be argued that an important transport project might generate an effect also in regions that are far apart because of the general equilibrium linkages captured in the model represented by Eq. (6.24).[46]

Combining the characteristics of the SAR and SLX models, many authors consider the so-called spatial Durbin model (SDM):

$$y_i = \rho \sum_{j \neq i} w_{ij} y_i + \alpha tk_i + \beta X_i + \gamma \sum_{j \neq i} w_{ij} G_i + + u_i \qquad (6.26)$$

In Eq. (6.26), one allows for spatial dependency to arise both from joint spatial determination of outcomes through the spatial lag and though direct externalities arising from spatial effects of relevant characteristics, as in the SLX model. The SDM model has been by far the most popular among

[46] However, a spatial matrix based on distance would not have this property. Nevertheless, see below on the practical difficulties in empirically distinguishing between the SAR and the SLX models.

applied researchers seeking to evaluate the role played by spillovers associated with transport infrastructures, at least for the past 10 years.[47]

In the case of the SDM, indirect spillover's effect of a certain explanatory variable can be derived in a similar way as in Eq. (6.24), but in this case spillovers arise as combination of both global and local ones. Moreover, the SLX and SDM do not share a limitation of the SAR model in Eq. (6.24), namely that the ratio between the indirect spillover effects and the total effect is constant and equal for every explanatory variable, given that spillovers are not generated (only) by the spatial lag term ρ.

From an econometric point of view, the presence of the spatial lags of tk and the other X variables does not pose special problems for the consistency estimation of both the α and γ parameters, although standard errors might be biased.[48]

More complicated is the estimation of ρ. Indeed, the spatial lag is correlated with the error term essentially because of a mechanic link (Gibbons & Overman, 2012); a positive shock to unit i should in fact have an effect on output in a nearby region j, thereby creating an almost mechanical correlation between the error term and the spatial lag, unless $\rho = 0$.

However, under some assumptions (such as normality of the errors, and i.i.d. errors), Eq. (6.24) can be estimated with maximum likelihood. This is not the place to discuss the technicality of the method, but essentially under the above assumptions it is possible to estimate α and β (and the variance parameter) conditionally on ρ, derive the so-called concentrated log likelihood and then find the value of ρ that maximizes the concentrated log likelihood (see LeSage and Pace, 2009 for technical details).

Alternatively, Eq. (6.24) can be estimated by means of Instrumental Variables procedures, where the instruments for the spatial lag are generally the spatial lags of variables contained in the X vector in Eq. (6.24) (Kelejian

[47] The popularity of the SDM is also motivated from the fact that it can be derived by a model that includes spatial considerations only in the error term, also labeled spatial error model (SEM). In particular, the SEM can be derived from a given SDM after imposing a set of appropriate nonlinear restrictions on parameter estimates. See, for papers applying the SDM in the transport infrastructure literature, Arbues et al. (2015), Fageda and Gonzales-Aregall (2017), Chen and Haynes (2015), Yu et al. (2013), and Bottasso et al. (2014).

[48] Provided, of course, that the spatial weight matrix w and the other variables are exogenous. Moreover, as noted in Vega and Elhorst (2015), uncertainty about the true form of the weight matrix might still create estimation issues.

and Prucha (1998)), under the identification assumption that the spatially lagged variables contained in the *X* vector influence the dependent variable only though its spatial lag. In models like Eq. (6.26), where the spatial lags of (some of) the variable contained in the *X* vector plus *tk* (included in the *G* vector) are allowed to directly impact *y*, higher order of spatial lags should be used as instruments, under the identification assumption that those higher orders of spatial lags do not exert a direct effect on *y* (Gibbons & Overman, 2012).

In the case of panel data estimators, authors have generally estimated fixed effects versions of Eq. (6.26) to control for (spatially) time-invariant omitted variables, by allowing the error term to have a unit specific time-invariant component and using a specific quasi-maximum likelihood procedure proposed by Lee and You (2010).[49]

It goes without saying that the assumptions underlying the validity of the fixed effects estimator highlighted in Section 6.2.1 above should be extended to the spatial econometrics setting. Therefore, the use of a spatial econometrics setting is by no means a panacea for the endogeneity of transport infrastructure capital. Although there is recent research ongoing that has been trying to derive consistent estimators of models like that in Eq. (6.26) with endogeneous regressors in a panel data framework with fixed effects, it seems fair to say that the current practice in most spatial econometrics panel data studies is to assume (explicitly or more often implicitly) that transport infrastructure variables are exogenous, conditional on the unit specific fixed effects.[50]

More worrisome is the general critique raised by Gibbons and Overman (2012) to the way the spatial econometrics literature deals with the estimation of the spatial lag of the dependent variable. The corrosive critiques by Gibbons and Overman (2012), in part related to those of Pinske and Slade (2010), are important because they seriously call into question the soundness and robustness of the whole field of spatial econometrics and,

[49] The panel data fixed effects estimator for the SLX, SDM, or SAR models can be estimated using the spxtregress and xsmle routines for STATA. See also Belotti, Hughes, and Piano Mortari (2017).

[50] Bottasso et al. (2014) estimated a model like that in Eq. (6.22) in a GMM-SYS framework, by using appropriate time lags of both the spatial lag of the dependent variable and their main variables of interest, namely regional port throughput as well as its spatial lag. Of course, also in this case the estimates can be criticized in the light of the considerations developed in Section 6.2.1. See also Arbues et al. (2015) for a discussion and a similar analysis.

given the rapid spread of spatial econometrics models in the studies seeking to quantify the spillovers associated with transport infrastructures, we think it deserves appropriate space in this section.

First, Gibbons and Overman (2012) note that the overwhelming use of maximum likelihood to address the endogeneity of the spatial lag in the SAR or SDM models can be criticized. Indeed, maximum likelihood relies on the assumption that the model being estimated is the true data generating process. However, in most applications, the functional form of the model is unknown and the linear form might generate misspecification bias in maximum likelihood applications.

Indeed, as noted by McMillen (2012), there is an important contradiction between the uncertainty surrounding typical spatial econometrics models (in terms of the true form of the weight matrix as well as the functional form for the model being estimated) and the use of maximum likelihood methods, a point forcefully made also in Basile, Durban, Minguez, Montero, and Mur (2014). Moreover, maximum likelihood techniques can be used as long as the determinants of production, such as transport infrastructures, are exogenous, which seems to be a hard to defend hypothesis, in the light of the discussion in the previous sections.

Second, we noted above that the endogeneity of the spatial lag can be dealt with the use of IV methods. However, the validity of the instruments commonly applied in the spatial econometrics literature has been seriously and, in our opinion, persuasively called into question by Gibbons and Overman (2012).

Indeed, in the SDM model one can show that the spatial lag could be predicted by higher orders of the spatial lags of the exogenous variables in the G vector. However, Gibbons and Overman (2012) note that if the exact structure of the weight matrix is unknown, then it is possible that this identification procedure breaks down because the higher-order spatial lags of G might well have a direct effect on the dependent variable, and not only an indirect one through the spatial lag of G. Moreover, even if the exact structure of the weight matrix was known, the various $w'G$, $w'WG$, $w'W^2G$, etc., might be highly correlated, thereby generating a weak-instrument problem because of the little independent variation generated by the various instruments, possibly biasing parameter estimates.

Finally, Gibbons and Overman (2012) note that the reduced form of Eqs. (6.24) and (6.26) (i.e., the equations that one obtains by eliminating the endogenous spatial lag and expressing the dependent variable as a function of the exogenous variables and the parameters) is very similar and in particular little different from the SLX model in Eq. (6.25).

In plain English, although different models and theories of spatial interactions underlie the SLX, SDM, and SAR models, they have very similar reduced forms that differ only in terms of how many spatial lags of the exogenous variables are included and in terms of the way the structural parameters are related to each other. The main consequence is, according to Gibbons and Overman (2012), that it can be very difficult, although perhaps not impossible, at least in principle, to distinguish between these competing models, a critique that is reminiscent of the *reflection problem* first highlighted by Manski (1993) in the case of the peer effects literature.

Gibbons and Overman (2012) suggest that researchers interested in analyzing spillovers should abandon altogether the estimation of the SAR and SDM models in favor of the SLX model.[51] It is true that it can be shown that the SLX model mixes up the effects of global and local spillovers, i.e., these arising from endogenous (general equilibrium) or exogenous neighborhood effects, respectively. However, the overall spillover effect might be interesting as such and, according to Gibbons and Overman (2012), the identification issues are less insurmountable.

Moreover, the estimation of an SLX model makes it easier to credibly identify the effects of spillover variables when they are endogenous, as it is likely to be the case for transport infrastructure capital; indeed, when complications arising from the inclusion of the endogenous spatial lag are avoided, the tools of counterfactual impact evaluation, such as natural or quasi natural experiments, IVs or differences-in-differences, can be implemented.

It is to this set of methodologies that we now turn in Section 6.2.3 (Box 6.3).

6.2.3 Counterfactual Impact Evaluation

We have discussed so far how difficult it is in empirical work to go beyond simple correlations in the data. In particular, we have argued that a positive correlation between, say, the extension of road networks and regional GDP or employment might be entirely spurious. Alternatively, we have noted

[51] See Agrawal et al. (2016) who estimated the effect of highways on local innovation by estimating an SLX model. This paper is also interesting because of the econometric strategy to estimate both the direct and spillover impact of highways.

Box 6.3 An example of spatial econometrics techniques

A typical example of a paper using spatial econometric techniques to estimate the impact of transport infrastructure spillovers on local production is Arbues et al. (2015). They consider a production function with three inputs, namely labor, human capital, and private capital plus the stocks of roads, railways, airports, and ports and estimate it for a panel of 47 Spanish provinces over the period 1986–2006. They consider a spatial panel Durbin model (SDM) similar to that in Eq. (6.26). They consider the spatial lags of all private and public inputs and motivate the inclusion of the spatial lag of output on the grounds that production in nearby provinces might explain fluctuations in the degree of capacity utilization in any given province. The authors consider two types of spatial weight matrix, namely a simple contiguity matrix and another binary weight matrix with values equal to one only in the case of provinces within a radius of 150 km from the centroid of the province of interest. They estimate the model using the maximum likelihood panel fixed effects estimator proposed by Lee and You (2010) as their main approach and they reject both the SAR and the SEM model. They find a positive (negative) and significant direct effect on production only in the case of road (port) infrastructures. In turn, the indirect effects are significant only in the case of the road network, where they account for about one-third of its total effect.

that the observed correlation between those two variables might severely underestimate the true effect of roads on GDP.

We have also argued that the empirical literature has evolved in the past 25 years; the use of panel data and fixed effects is a clear advancement over naïve OLS; in turn, the use of GMM estimators with internal lagged instruments is another example and a potential improvement on the limitations of fixed effects panel data models discussed in Section 6.2.1.

However, and following the practice in other areas of empirical (micro) economics, such as development, labor, and urban economics, over the past years a so far limited but increasing number of studies that are relevant for the study of the economic effects of transportation infrastructure capital have started to put questions about causality at the center stage of empirical analysis.

Indeed, questions such as "what it the causal effect of increasing access to motorways on firms productivity?" or "what is the impact of creating a high speed rail network on economic development of the affected regions?", or, "what is the effect of road network expansion on a city's trade?" have by now become more common in the empirical literature (Duranton &

Turner, 2012; Holl, 2016, & Berger & Enflo, 2017, among the many others).

This is not to say that previous studies did not consider causality issues. Indeed, fixed effects panel data models and GMM methods have been the standard tool to take into account the endogeneity of transport capital stock in empirical works, and their validity clearly depends on identification assumptions. However, the latter have been often put onto the side lines in many studies, rather than appropriately discussed. Moreover, we have noted in Section 6.2.1 above that some of these assumptions can be criticized, or at least should not be taken for granted.

By way of contrast, what is sometimes referred to as the "experimentalist paradigm" in empirical microeconomics (Angrist & Pischke, 2009) has brought questions about causality and identification at the forefront of empirical work.

Very briefly, and referring to Angrist and Pischke (2009) and Imbens and Wooldridge (2009) for an in-depth treatment, the "experimentalist paradigm" considers randomized experiments as the most possible robust identification strategy for a given causal effect of interest.[52] By randomly assigning units to a treatment group, the causal effect can be measured as average differences in outcomes between the treatment and the control group, the latter acting as the counterfactual, which therefore captures what would have happened to the treated units had they not received treatment.

Although in some areas of economics such as labor and development, experiments are rare but possible, in other subfields are surely more problematic, for political or even moral reasons. For instance, it is surely not possible for a central authority, such as the EU, to randomly assign funding for the construction of a highways system in some regions of the European Union, independently from relative levels of development, stage of the business cycle, and so on and so forth. Similarly, the construction of a new airport in a given local area is unlikely to be completely unrelated to considerations relative to tourism, density of population, spatial clusters of economic activity, and so on and so forth.

Hence, the problem with observational data as opposed to data generated by experiments is that the control group, i.e., the units that are not treated (e.g., regions with no high-speed rail) or that have been treated

[52] See, however, the interesting debate in the Journal of Economic Perspectives between one of the main proponents of the experimentalist paradigm (Imbens, 2010), on one side, and more sceptical researchers, such as Deaton (2010), on the other side.

less intensively (e.g., with a less developed high-speed rail network), is generally far from ideal to represent the counterfactual which, as just noted, could be defined as what would have happened to the treatment units had they not been treated. For instance, regions where the highways network increased the most might have been those with the strongest economic growth in the past or with better future perspectives; productivity growth in areas where a new airport was recently opened might simply reflect unobserved determinants that could also explain the demand for air transport services and therefore the very same construction of the airport.

Nevertheless, empirical researchers have identified ways that, under some conditions, can, depending on method, type of study and data, credibly define the counterfactual. In this case, it is possible to identify the effect of a policy or expenditure program as the average difference in outcomes between treated units (or units treated more intensively) and the (valid) counterfactual. It is precisely the emphasis put on the credible definition of the counterfactual, on the conditions under which the selected control group is a valid proxy for it and, more specifically, on the plausibility of the identification strategy of the causal effect of interest from the empirical model, that characterizes the "experimentalist approach"; given the emphasis on the counterfactual, the methods that are applied in this stream of research are also known as Counterfactual Impact Evaluation (CIE) methods.

The typical study in this tradition spends considerable effort in trying to convince the reader that the effect on outcomes of the policy variable of interest (e.g., road network expansion) is identified in the paper only using an exogenous variation in the data; the researcher aims to discuss how her data and research design are such to ensure that units in the treatment and control groups are comparable but for the variation in the policy of interest, and that only the fraction of this variation that is exogenous is used to measure the impact of the policy, which can thus be interpreted causally.[53] Moreover, a deep knowledge of the economics of the sector and of its history and set of policies might, in certain cases, help the researcher to find a credibly exogenous variation in the data, often referred to as a "natural experiment".[54]

In the CIE literature, there are different statistical and econometric tools that are available for researchers; in this chapter, we will mainly deal with

[53] When a research design has these features, it is often said that the policy variable of interest is good as randomly assigned (Angrist & Pischke, 2009).

[54] See also Overmans and Gibbon (2012) for a very clear discussion along these lines.

two such tools that have been gaining some popularity in the literature on the economic effects of transport infrastructures, namely differences-in-differences and IV strategies.

6.2.3.1 Differences-in-differences

Evaluating the impact of a policy or variable of interest X on a given outcome Y by simply comparing mean outcomes in treated and control units is unlikely to be entirely convincing for the many reasons already discussed in the text, such as unobserved systematic differences across treated and control units. Of course, one might control for observable "pretreatment"[55] characteristics, but the analysis is probably unlikely to be fully convincing. In any case, using this approach, the effect of the policy is computed as the average difference in Y between treated and control units.[56]

Alternatively, one could run a "before—after" study; in this case, the effect of the airport on outcome Y is measured by comparing Y for the treated units before and after the construction of the airport; in this case, the units before the construction of the airports act as their own control group. The effect of the airport on Y is measured as the difference in Y before and after the construction of the airport. Again, the analysis might not be very convincing; indeed, there could be omitted variables that vary over time responsible for the growth in Y which, therefore, could be completely unrelated to the construction of the airport.

Differences-in-differences approaches aim to establish causality by combining information of a "before—after" study with that of a treatment and a control group.

[55] By pretreatment we mean characteristics that have been determined before the treatment took place and that therefore are unlikely to be driven by the treatment itself. Let us suppose one wants to use a cross section of data to assess the impact of airports on local development. Controlling for local characteristic is important to make the treatment and control units (e.g., regions with and without an airport) more comparable. However, it is important that these characteristics should not be influenced by the construction of the airport. For instance, culture or levels of corruption are likely to be preexisting conditions, whereas current density of population might well be associated with the presence of the airport.

[56] In regression analysis, this is done after controlling for possible covariates. In matching analysis, the effect is the mean differences across treated and control groups, where each treated unit is compared only to units that are similar along some (pretreatment) characteristics. See Imbens (2014) for a discussion of matching estimators.

By way of example, let us suppose that the government in year T_0 opened up a high-speed rail network but that only few regions were affected. Let us group the interested regions in the group T and the unaffected regions in the group C. Let us also suppose that we are interested in measuring the impact of the high-speed rail network on productivity at the firm level, labeled Y, and that we have information for a period before and after T_0.

A typical differences-in-differences study would identify the effect of the high-speed rail network as the average difference in Y before and after T_0 for firms belonging to regions in group T, minus the average difference in Y before and after T_0 for firms belonging to regions in group C.

In econometric terms, we could run a regression like the following one:

$$Y_i = \beta_0 + \beta_1 T_i + \beta_2 D2_i + \beta_3 T_i D2_i + u_i \tag{6.27}$$

In Eq. (6.27) T_i is a dummy variable equal to 1 for firms located in regions with a high-speed rail network and 0 otherwise; $D2_i$ is a dummy variable for the second period (when the network was in place in the treated regions) and 0 otherwise. In turn, the coefficient of the interaction term T_iD2_i represents the diff-in-diff estimates of the high-speed network, as it measures the effect on Y of the policy for the treated regions. The diff-in-diff estimator in Eq. (6.27) allows researchers to control for both group-specific and time-specific effects and is a significant improvement with respect to simple before—after or treated-control comparisons.

Of course, the regression analysis in Eq. (6.27) can be made more robust by including pretreatment control variables at firm level, such as productivity, sector, age of the firm, etc., that can help make the analysis more robust because they better ensure that treated and controlled firms are more alike.[57] Moreover, examining the pretreatment characteristics of units in the treated versus nontreated regions is important because the more similar the units are, the more convincing the diff-in-diff analysis will be. If some differences across treated and control groups are found, an alternative possibility is to use statistical matching techniques to find comparators for each treated units that are more similar across a set of defined pretreatment characteristics, and then run the analysis on this restricted sample.

[57] It is important to note that the example with firms as units of observations is without loss of generality. The units of analysis might indeed be small local areas, with little change in the analysis. If one has access to more than two periods of data, then one might control also for year dummies.

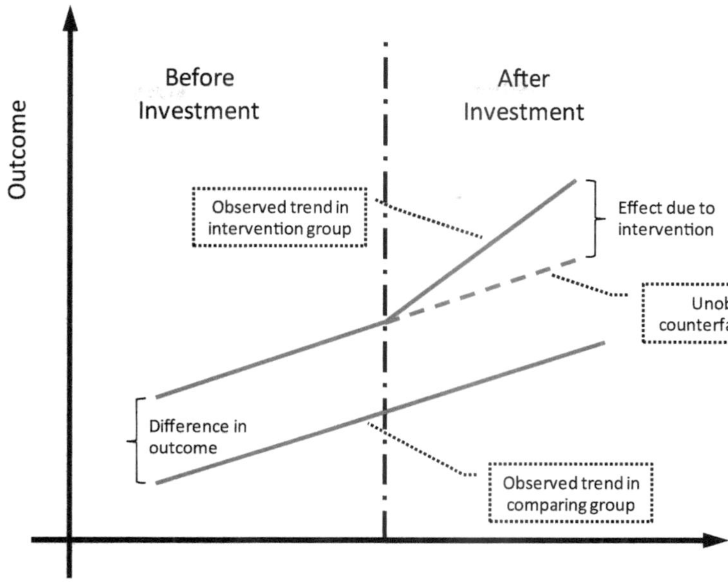

Figure 6.1 The parallel trend assumption in diff-in-diff models.

It is important to stress that the model in Eq. (6.27) is not necessarily a panel, it could just be a repeated cross section of firms.[a] If it is a panel, then one could control for possible systematic differences in treated and control groups by means of unit-specific fixed effects and trends.

Moreover, when the number of years gets larger, it is possible that different regions implement the same policy in different periods; the econometric analysis does not change, even if we should probably call the model a diff-in-diff with staggered implementation, because the parameter of interest is identified also through the staggered implementation of the policy (the opening of the high-speed rail network in this specific example).

For diff-in-diff type of analysis to be reliable, it is important that the so-called "parallel trend assumption" is not violated. This can be understood by looking at Fig. 6.1; in that case, before the intervention the treated and control units were on a similar trend; after the intervention there is a steep change in the treated group, the intervention effect, which would

[a] However, some complications might arise in the case of pooled cross section of firms. Indeed, it is important that firms in the pre-treatment period in the treated (untreated) regions are representative of firms in the post treatment period in the treated (untreated) regions. See, for a discussion, Lechner (2010).

correspond to $\beta_3 > 0$, i.e., a positive effect of establishing a high-speed rail network on firms productivity.

However, unlike in Fig. 6.1, suppose that firms in treated regions are on a steeper increasing trend of productivity (because of some developments in the treated regions we could not control for), whereas in the control group firms are in a more or less static situation. By simple virtue of time, we would find out that, after T_0, firms in treated regions will have higher productivity than those located in the control group, independently from the construction of the high-speed rail network. A positive β_3 might be largely spurious, overestimating the impact of the high-speed rail network on productivity.

Ensuring that the parallel trend assumption has not been violated is a must-do in any good diff-in-diff study. This can be done visually if a sufficient time span is available, by examining whether the data display any differentials in productivity trends in the two groups before T_0.

Alternatively, if a sufficient time span is available, one could include regional-specific time trends into Eq. (6.27) in order to control for possible trend differentials in the various regions. A typical diff-in-diff study is also complemented by a so-called "placebo analysis." This is typically implemented by considering a "fake" T_0, e.g., by assuming, in our example, that the high-speed rail network was opened in the year $T_0 - i$, with $i = 1, 2$.

Finding a significant positive coefficient of β_3 might cast doubts on the identification assumption. Similarly, some authors, following Autor (2003), include leads of the variable of interest. The idea is to test for the existence of anticipatory effects before the actual implementation; in most circumstances, a significant lead is likely to be bad news for the identification strategy because it means that there is something omitted from the model which is driving the results.[58]

Finally, an important point in diff-in-diff models concerns inference. Let us suppose, as in this example, that one has observations at the firm level, whereas the policy is implemented at a more aggregated level, a region in this case; in other words, all firms belonging to a treated region have a value of 1 for T_i. In this case, conventional standard errors are likely to be severely

[58] It is of course possible also to include lags to allow for a dynamic specification. For instance, in Eq. (6.31) one could insert a dummy equal to one only for the first year the high-speed rail network was open and zero otherwise; a dummy equal to one for the second year, one for the third year, and one for the fourth year onward. In this case, one can see when the effect materialized and whether the effect was persistent or not. See Autor (2003).

downward biased (Cameron & Miller, 2015). This can be explained by noting that the actual variation in the data can be much smaller than that implied by the number of observations.

In the example above, the reason is in the fact that our X variable of interest is defined at a more aggregated level (region) than the dependent variable (firm); since the error terms of firms within a single region are likely to be much more correlated than across regions, one additional firm in the sample does not provide "true" additional independent information, and conventional standard errors tend to be "too optimistic".

Similarly, a diff-in-diff model could also be run on variables at the same level of aggregation; in the case of the high-speed rail network, we might have a panel data model where the unit of observation is a region, like the following fixed effects one:

$$y_{it} = \beta_1 HS_{it} + x_{it}^{'} X_{it} + e_i + \delta_t + u_{it} \tag{6.28}$$

In model Eq. (6.28), HS_{it} is a dummy equal to one for those regions in those years when the high-speed network was in place and zero otherwise (the analogue to $T_i D2_i$) in Eq. (6.27), whereas the vector X contains a set of control variables. In this model, there is no need to control for a treated or an implementation period dummy because those are effectively controlled for by the fixed effects e_i and δ_t, respectively, unless the implementation period is heterogeneous across units. In model Eq. (6.28), the regressor HS_{it} is likely to be serially correlated because it is represented by a string of zeros followed by a string of ones for those regions that switch to adopt the high-speed railways. In this case, conventional standard errors are biased.

In both cases, for a correct inference it is necessary to use cluster-robust standard errors that allow for a variance—covariance matrix that does not assume that error terms relative to observation within a cluster (a region in this case) are uncorrelated.[59]

It is important to note that the diff-in-diff model in Eq. (6.28) is a conventional fixed effects one; therefore, the conditions for identification highlighted in Section 6.2.1 above (e.g., strong exogeneity) apply. In

[59] Common statistical software such as Stata has routines that compute cluster-robust standard errors. The main issue in this area is when the number of clusters is small, usually lower than 30—40. In that case, the common practice is that of computing standard errors using bootstrapping techniques, for instance, using the Boottest routine for Stata. See Cameron and Miller (2015) for a very useful and relatively nontechnical survey of this literature.

addition, in this model it is possible to consider the robustness checks for diff-in-diff models discussed above, namely a placebo test, the inclusion of leads (and lags), and the inclusion of unit-specific time trends to make the parallel trend assumption more likely to hold.

To make the research design more credible, some authors, instead than relying on diff-in-diff models, have adopted a diff-in-diff-in-diff modeling strategy. To better appreciate the method, but without loss of generality, let us come back to Eq. (6.27) and let us assume that economic theory suggests that the policy is relevant only for a subset of firms in the region. In our example, suppose that the existence of a high-speed rail speed connection is relatively more important for these firms that are relatively intensive users of rail transport services.[60] Let us suppose also that one could build a dummy U_i equal to one for firms belonging to rail transport user sectors (say with intensity above the median) and zero otherwise. In this case, we could expand Eq. (6.27) as follows:

$$y_i = \beta_0 + \beta_1 T_i + \beta_2 D2_i + \beta_3 U_i + \beta_4 T_i D2_i + \beta_5 U_i D2_i + \beta_6 U_i T_i + \beta_7 U_i T_i D2_i + u_i \tag{6.29}$$

In model Eq. (6.29), the coefficient β_7 of the triple interaction term identifies the causal effect of interest. In model Eq. (6.29), the diff-in-diff-in-diff estimator is equivalent to compute the changes in mean for the firms in the sensitive sectors in the treated regions, and then to subtract both the changes in mean for the firms in the sensitive sectors in the control regions and the changes in mean for the firms in the nonsensitive sectors in the treated regions. In this way one should be able to control both for changes in productivity of sensitive firms across regions that have nothing to do with high-speed rail and changes in productivity of all firms located in the treated regions (possibly due to other policy changes in those regions).

Of course, for β_7 to represent the causal effect of interest it is necessary that the identification assumption is correct, namely that it is true that the impact of high-speed rail is stronger in certain sectors.[61]

[60] For instance, one could see from input—output tables that firms in some industries are intensive users of rail transport services, whereas firms in others are not.

[61] However, simply looking at the input—output tables might be misleading, as firms in some sectors might not buy road transport services but still benefit from a high-speed rail network, such as those depending on tourism. Moreover, by reducing commuting costs, some firms that do not buy rail services might still benefit a lot from the high-speed rail, because their labor market pool will get larger.

A similar empirical strategy could also be implemented in a variant of model Eq. (6.28) using a panel of cross regional—cross industry data:

$$y_{ist} = \beta_1 U_s HS_{it} + x_{ist}^{'} X_{ist} + e_{is} + \delta_{it} + \delta_{st} + u_{it} \quad (6.30)$$

In model Eq. (6.30), we control for region-by-year (δ_{it}), industry-by-year (δ_{st}), and industry-by-region (e_{is}) fixed effects. A positive coefficient for β_1 would tell us that the introduction of high-speed rails tends to increase y relatively more in those sectors that are more intensive users of rail services. It is very important to control for all fixed effects combinations in Eq. (6.30) to have a β_1 that could be interpreted as a the diff-in-diff-in-diff estimate of high-speed rail.

It might be interesting to note that while diff-in-diff models have originally been proposed for binary policies, there is nothing that can prevent us to have a continuous treatment, such as the length of the network. Similarly, the "responsiveness" of a certain sector to transport might not be binary, but a continuous variable, as in Fernald (1999) (see Box 6.4).

Box 6.4 An application of difference-in-differences to estimate the impact of highways on growth

Fernald (1999) used a model in the differences-in-differences tradition to estimate the impact of roads on productivity growth. The idea in Fernald (1999) is quite simple and appealing, although surprisingly little followed in the successive empirical literature (see Li (2017) for a very recent exception). If roads are productive, then industries that use roads more intensively should benefit more from road construction. Indeed, if roads are unrelated to growth and any correlation at the macro level would reflect common trends, there are no strong reasons to believe that the relationship should be stronger in road-intensive industries. Similarly, if the relationship goes from productivity growth to road construction, again we should not find a systematically stronger effect of roads on productivity developments in road-intensive industries.

Fernald (1999) considers a value-added production function $y_i = A_i F(K_i, L_i, T(G, V_i))$, where T represents transport services offered by the stock of roads (G) and vehicles (V). Under standard assumptions (such as cost minimization), the author shows that the unobserved elasticity of output with respect to road services is directly proportional to the elasticity of output with respect to vehicles services, which is observable (and therefore allows him to proxy an industry's road elasticity with an industry's vehicle intensity). He then shows

Continued

Box 6.4 An application of difference-in-differences to estimate the impact of highways on growth—cont'd

that, under some assumptions, the Solow residual for industry i can be expressed as $dtfp_i - dtfp = \theta(s_{vi} - s_v)dg + e_i$. The right-hand side of this equation is the relative difference between the TFP growth rate in industry i relative to the economy wide one; $s_{vi} - s_v$ is the share of vehicle intensity in industry i relative to the economy, dg is the rate of growth of the aggregate stock of roads, and e_i is an error term. Fernald (1999) estimates this equation[62] on US data, for the period 1953–89, for each industry in a system of equations and finds that changes in road growth have a relatively stronger effect in those industries that use vehicles more intensively. He also finds the effects to be stronger in the first half of his sample period; Fernald (1999) argues that this is because the establishment of the first links of a network might well be very productive, but additional ones might be not.

A similar analysis could be conducted by pooling data on industries into a panel and estimate an equation like the following one: $dtfp_{it} = \theta s_{vi} dg_t + u_i + \delta_t + e_{it}$.

One can regress TFP growth in industry i as of time t on the interaction between the vehicle share of industry i and the growth rate of the road stock, controlling for industry and year fixed effects. The vehicle share could be considered time invariant and set at the value at the beginning of sample period to avoid possible reverse causality between roads and the share of road services. A positive θ indicates that an increase in the road stock at country level is associated with higher TFP growth in industries that rely more on vehicles and therefore on road, very much in the spirit of a diff-in-diff approach to identification, where each unit is treated but some are more "exposed" than others. Please note that in this model we identify only the differential effects of roads; we can identify the total effect (multiplying θ by the industry-specific s_{vi} to derive the industry-specific effect and then computing a weighted average across industries) only under the further identification assumption that in sectors that do not use vehicles the effects of roads is zero or at least very small, which is unlikely if general equilibrium effects are substantial. Moreover, note that in the former equation the fact that TFP and g are in growth rate form and that we control for industry fixed effects is analogous to a model for log TFP as a function of log roads, controlling for year effects, industry fixed effects, and industry-specific linear time trends. A similar analysis is undertaken, using firm-level data, in the recent paper by Li (2017) to estimate the impact of roads on productivity in China.

[62] In fact, Fernald (1999) estimates a different nonlinear specification. The equation considered in the text can be obtained from his estimated equation by imposing one restriction on a parameter of the equation.

An identification approach that shares the flavor of the diff-in-diff models, but that is specifically targeted to situations when few units (or even just one) are treated but the time span is sufficiently long, is the synthetic control approach originally proposed by Abadie and Gardeazabal (2003) and implemented in the transport infrastructure impact evaluation literature by Ahlfeldt and Feddersen (2017).

The idea of the synthetic control method is that of comparing the unit that implemented a given policy to a synthetic control, where the latter is a weighted average of other units. Ideally, these units are different from the treated one(s) only because they did not implement the policy; indeed, it is important that, for these control units, the outcome under study (e.g., GDP) be driven by the same structural process occurring in the treated unit, but for the implementation of the policy under consideration.

In particular, the weights for each unit are chosen using matching techniques exploiting similarities between the comparison units and the treated one in terms of a set of pretreatment covariates and/or pretreatment outcomes.[63] With a sufficiently long time period, the researcher can use information before T_0, the period of implementation of the reform or the year when a transport project becomes operative, to construct the counterfactual synthetic control, and then information after T_0 to compare the behavior of the treated unit and the synthetic control (Box 6.5).

6.2.3.2 Instrumental Variables

Although diff-in-diff models can provide a powerful methodology to identify a causal effect of interest, it might still be possible that omitted

[63] In particular, the weights are chosen so that the synthetic control best reproduces the value of the predictors of the outcome under analysis before the policy is implemented. Units that are substantially different from the treated one could receive a weight equal to zero. One advantage of this approach with respect to conventional regression analysis is that the former is less prone to extrapolation bias that occurs when control units are substantially different from the treated one. Moreover, Abadie, Diamond, and Hainmuller (2010) show that if the preintervention period is sufficiently long, then simply matching on preintervention outcomes should allow to control for observed and unobserved factors that explain the outcome. Using the words of Abadie et al. (2014), only units that are similar "in both observed and unobserved determinants of the outcome variable as well as in the effects of these determinants on the outcome variable should produce similar trajectories of the outcome variable over extended periods of time." Indeed, if the outcome variable in the treated and the synthetic control has displayed a similar behavior for a long period before T_0, a possible divergence after T_0 might be attributed to the policy of interest.

Box 6.5 An application of the Synthetic Control Approach

An example of the use of the synthetic control approach to identification is the study by Ahlfeldt and Feddersen (2017) on the economic effects of the openings of the high-speed rail Cologne—Frankfurt. In particular, that high-speed rail features three intermediate steps in small towns of Limburg, Montabaur, and Siegburg. The authors convincingly argue that the openings of intermediate steps in these small towns, as well as its timing, reflected a political, institutional, and bargaining process largely associated with environmental concerns, geographic considerations, and financial costs, and that as such is largely exogenous to current levels and trends of economic development. Authors consider for each of the three intermediate steps a synthetic control made up by three cities, using pretreatment information on economic growth predictors such as GDP per head, population density, shares of various sectors in gross value added, share of university educated workers, and ratio of out-commuters versus in-commuters to construct the weights. In this study, T_0 is 2002 and authors used information between 1992 and 2009. The pre-period was confined to years between 1992 and 1998, when construction works began (and not to the whole 1992-2002 pre-period) because authors believed that the construction of the high-speed rail might have started changing economic behavior even before its actual completion in 2002. The data show that while GDP in the treated units in the period before 1998 closely follows that of the synthetic control, after 1998 there is a clear divergence, with GDP accelerating in the treated units.

variables drive both the policy variable of interest and the dependent variable. For instance, let us consider a panel data of local units as in Eq. (6.28); even if we allow for local units fixed effects, there could still be unobserved time-varying determinants of y_i correlated with, say, the construction of a high-speed rail network . By way of example, planners might have targeted local units with worse (better) growth prospects. In this case, the diff-in-diff analysis would be biased.

Moreover, let us consider the variant of the Fernald's (1999) approach outlined in Box 6.4; suppose that industries relying more on road services were more effective in lobbying for road construction precisely when their future growth prospects deteriorated; in this case, we would have a negative correlation between roads in year t and growth in road-intensive industries in time $s > t$, biasing the diff-in-diff model. In both cases, an IV strategy would be necessary.

IV methods aim to tackle the endogeneity problem, i.e., the correlation between a regressor X and the error term, by using only the exogenous variation in X to identify the impact of X on the outcome variable Y. To do that it is necessary to have at least one variable Z, called "instrument", which needs to have two crucial characteristics.

First, the instrument needs to be sufficiently correlated with the possibly endogenous variable X, otherwise the instrument cannot be used to "extract" any exogenous variation in X. This means that in a regression of the possibly endogenous variable X on the other exogenous variables in the estimating equation and the instrument Z, the coefficient of Z needs to be significantly different from zero.

Second, the instrument needs to affect the dependent variable *Y* only through its effect on X, conditional on the controls included in the original equation; in other words, the only channel through which the instrument can affect the outcome variable is via its effect on the variable X.[64]

If either of these two requirements is violated, the validity of the IV procedure breaks down. Indeed, if the instrument is poorly correlated with the X variable, we have the so-called weak-instrument problem which, especially in small samples, might lead to misleading conclusions.[65] Moreover, the instrument needs to be valid; this is the trickiest point,

[64] Referring to an econometrics textbook such as Angrist and Pischke (2009), the mechanics of IV can be understood as follows: in a first step one regresses the possibly endogenous X variable on the other exogenous variables in the original equation (including the various fixed effects) plus the instrument Z using OLS: this is the "first-stage" equation. In a second step, the outcome variable of interest Y is regressed using OLS on all exogenous variables in the original equation and the fitted values of X in the first step. The coefficient of the fitted values of X is the IV estimate of the effect of X on Y. Indeed, provided the instrument is valid (and the correlation between Z and X sufficiently strong), the fitted values of X capture only the effect on Y due to an exogenous variation in X, i.e., that due to Z. Alternatively, it can be shown that the IV estimator can be derived as the ratio between the coefficient of Z in the regression of Y on Z plus the exogenous controls (the reduced-form equation) and the coefficient of Z in the first-stage equation. IV estimates can be carried out in Stata using the ivregress or ivreg2 routines.

[65] See Angrist and Pischke (2009) for a comprehensive discussion of the weak-instrument problem in IV estimation and the possible statistical tests to detect it. A useful sensitivity check if one suspects a weak-instrument problem is to run the so-called "reduced-form" regression, which is essentially OLS using the instrument instead of the X variable. It can be shown that the coefficient of the instrument in the reduced-form equation is proportional to the coefficient of X in the "structural" equation: if the coefficient of the instrument is not significant or with a wrong sign, then probably there is an important weak-instrument problem and IV estimates might not be reliable. Useful tests for the existence of a weak-instrument problem are available in the routine for Stata ivreg2.

because there is no statistical test to ascertain whether the instrument affects the outcome variable only through the X variable; the validity of the instrument needs to be argued by researchers on a case-by-case basis on the ground of economic theory, historical reasons, etc.[66]

Studies in the CIE tradition do not find IV strategies based on the use of internal instruments (i.e., lagged values) in panel data very convincing for a variety of reasons that, in the case of transport infrastructures, we have already discussed at some length in Section 6.2.1. Similarly, using (higher order) spatial lags of exogenous variables as instruments for the spatial lag of the outcome variable in spatial econometrics studies has been criticized too, as examined in Section 6.2.2.

Researchers following the CIE framework prefer instead to use IVs strategies based on "external instruments" which are found using a combination of economic reasoning, knowledge of history, past policy decisions, and geography.

These studies have a further theme in common, namely the fact that, to exploit the so-called "natural experiments", they need, almost by definition, to focus on samples defined at a much finer level of disaggregation than previous works, such as provinces, counties, cities, small cells (i.e., with a surface of about 100 square km), and census tracts. Nevertheless, this raises a possible concern; indeed, most of the literature on counterfactual impact evaluation is based on the so-called Stable Unit Treatment Value Assumption (SUTVA), which basically assumes away the possibility that the "treatment" received by one unit may affect other units in the sample, which amounts to exclude spillovers and general equilibrium effects. Imbens and Wooldridge (2009) suggest that increasing the level of aggregation can make the SUTVA assumption more plausible. An alternative is to model the interactions among units; with spatial data, the estimation of SLX models might be a tentative way to model such interactions. This is,

[66] When more than one instrument is available, one could test for the validity of the overidentifying restrictions by using the so-called Sargan or Hansen statistics. However, what these tests do is simply to test whether the IV estimates obtained using only one instrument at a time are equal, as they should if the instruments are valid. However, failing to reject the null hypothesis of validity of the overidentifying restrictions might simply reflect that all instruments are in fact endogenous or that they are weak, leading to imprecise IV estimates whose confidence intervals overlap. This explains why in studies in the CIE spirit the validity of overidentifying restrictions is not taken alone as conclusive evidence of the validity of the instruments, which instead should be justified on theoretical grounds.

however, an area where most theoretical research is still ongoing (see Baum-Snow & Ferreira, 2015).

Turning again to the identification strategies found in the empirical literature, following Redding and Turner (2015) it is possible to group them under three main categories:

1. The planned route approach
2. The historical route approach
3. The incidental beneficiaries approach

The planned route approach was pioneered by Baum-Snow (2007) in his study of the effects of the US interstate highways network. The identification strategy is based on a plan for the US highways network in 1947 as a source of quasi-random variation for the way the interstate highways network actually developed in the successive decades. The idea is that, conditional on controls (such as lagged population), the original plan should not have any direct effect on economic outcomes on top of those exerted through the actual development of the network. The plausibility of this assumption is defended on the grounds that the original 1947 plan was motivated by military reasons; it seems reasonable that the unobserved military reasons behind the 1947 plan were orthogonal to (i.e., not correlated with) unobserved determinants of both successive local economic development and, say, the need of future commuters.[67]

A similar analysis is that of Sheard (2014), who studies the effects of airport infrastructure on economic development for US metropolitan statistical areas using the 1944 US National Airport Plan as an instrument for actual airport infrastructures; and that of Berger and Enflo (2017) for Sweden who used two old plans for the development of the first railways network in Sweden as instrument for its actual development.

The historical route approach to identification was in turn pioneered by Duranton and Turner (2012) in their study on the effects of the US interstate highways system on urban growth. In particular, authors propose to use a map of the US railroads network at the end of the 19th century as a source of quasi-random variation for the actual development of the US interstate highways system. The identification strategy is valid provided that, conditional on controls, the unobserved determinants of the configuration of the railways network at the end of the 19th century do not directly affect current economic development beyond their effects

[67] Other more recent papers used the 1947 plan as an instrument, such as Duranton and Turner (2012) and Agrawal et al. (2016).

occurring via the actual implementation of the highways network. Of course, behind the use of this instrument there is the idea that the presence of a railways network might be a good predictor for the successive construction of the highways interstate system; Duranton and Turner (2012) justify this assumption by arguing that the existence of a previous railroad significantly reduces road construction costs for engineering reasons.

Similar identification strategies were used in other papers. Duranton and Turner (2012) used also the routes of major explorations around the half of the 16th century in the modern United States as an instrument for the actual highways network; Garcia Lopez (2015) estimated the effect of highways on suburbanization of Spanish cities and used Roman roads and the 1760 Bourbon roads as instruments for actual highways; Henderson et al. (2015) instrumented actual highways network in China with the 1962 road network; Holl (2016) instrumented distance to highways for a sample of Spanish firms with information on Roman roads and Spanish postal routes in 1760, whereas Percoco (2016) used the network of Roman roads in Italy as a proxy for a highway's exit, among the others.

Finally, the incidental beneficiaries approach rests on the geography of a transport network, which usually is built to connect a few major cities. As a result, some cities that are along the network might have been connected just because they were located near the shortest and least cost line between any two major nodes of the network. In other words, if one excludes the major nodes of the network from the analysis, it might be argued that distance from the network is quasi-random because being connected to the network is unlikely to be due to unobserved characteristics that drive actual economic development, as it would likely be the case for the major cities located in the major nodes of the network.

The first study pioneering this approach was Chandra and Thompson (2000) in their study of the economic effect on rural counties of the US highways system. Other more recent studies following this approach are Ahlfeldt and Feddersen (2017), discussed in Box 6.3, Banerjee, Duflo, and Qian (2012), who used distance from a straight line connecting the historical cities of China to each other and to the city ports constructed at the end of the 19th century; Jedwab and Moradi (2016) on the economic effects of railways in colonial Ghana and who instrumented distance from actual railways lines with distance from a straight line connecting some major centers and Gibbons, Lyytikainen, Overman, and Sanchis-Guarner (2017) who, using very detailed spatial panel data (24-square km on average) for the United Kingdom, estimated the effects of improvements in an index of local accessibility on a series of economic outcomes. Gibbons et al. (2017) deal with endogeneity by focusing on improvements in the accessibility index only in the case of spatial units that are very close to new transport schemes (10–30 km) because the latter are more likely to have been realized with the aim of improving the overall network performance rather than of fostering local economic development at such a small scale.[68]

In Section 6.2.2, we followed Gibbons and Overman (2012) to argue that CIE methods could be used to evaluate the importance of spillover effects; indeed, if the latter are important, it is possible that single equation reduced-form models do not capture the full general equilibrium effects of transportation infrastructures.

In turn, Redding and Turner (2015) suggest that structural models are inherently better suited to capture these general equilibrium effects and in particular to distinguish between the impacts of transport infrastructure on the overall levels of economic activity with respect to the spatial reorganization of it. However, in the light of the discussion in Section 6.2.2, the estimation of an SLX model can provide useful insights on the relative importance of the two effects. Indeed, using data for the US metropolitan statistical areas, Agrawal, Galasso, and Oettl (2017) estimate the impact of interstate highways on regional innovation controlling for highways stock in other areas. They instrument both own and others' interstate highways stock following both the historical route and planned route approach and they found negligible evidence for displacement effects.

Finally, it is worth mentioning that studies using diff-in-diff or IV strategies tend to estimate reduced-form equations, although sometimes derived from economic models of spatial interactions. They might control for additional regressors only if, by doing so, they can make more credible that only the exogenous variation in transport infrastructures is used to identify its impact on various economic outcomes. However, the estimation of production or cost functions has been de facto abandoned. The reason is twofold.

[68] See also Ghani, Grover Goswami, and Kerr (2016) who found positive effects on firm production of a large-scale highway construction and improvement scheme in India. They identified the effect using variation over time in districts very close to the transport scheme with respect to others slightly more far away. They show that their results are robust to using distance from a straight line connecting nodal cities as an instrument.

First, private inputs are endogenous as they are selected by firms reacting to productivity shocks; if this endogeneity is not taken in account, it might be transmitted to the coefficient of transport infrastructures in a production function framework. The identification of the effects of transport infrastructure capital is considered a difficult task per se which can be better accomplished avoiding the complications arising from the existence of additional endogenous variables.

Second, private inputs can act as mediating factors if they are influenced by transport infrastructures; by way of example, if the latter positively affect private capital accumulation, controlling for the stock of private capital captures some of the effects of transport infrastructures on output. Interestingly, a completely different empirical methodology that is based on time series data has been used in the literature to capture both the direct and indirect effects of transport infrastructures, namely VAR, to which we turn in the next section.

6.2.4 Time Series: Vector Auto Regression

VAR is another methodology that has been used in a number of papers in the wider literature seeking to estimate the impact of public capital on GDP. However, it seems fair to say that VAR have been more rarely used in the studies focusing on the narrower concept of transport infrastructures. For this reason, in this section we just provide an intuition of how the methodology works, referring to Hamilton (1994) for a more in-depth discussion and to the relevant studies for recent methodological developments.[69]

A VAR considers time series data for a system of K endogenous variables, such as GDP, transport capital, private capital, and employment. In each equation, a dependent variable (e.g., GDP) is regressed on its own lags and the lags of the other K-1 endogenous variables, plus possibly other exogenous variables, typically using OLS.

The main idea underlying the use of a VAR is that there is not, as in the production or cost function framework, a causal relationship that goes, say, from private inputs and transport capital to GDP, or from output and transport capital to private sector costs. Rather, it is taken into account the possibility that some variables are simultaneously determined, and that there are substantial bidirectional feedback effects between variables. In other

[69] In what follows, we largely borrow from Afraz, Aquilina, Conti, and Lilico (2006) and Pereira and Andraz (2013).

words, transport capital might have an effect on GDP, but transport capital itself might be explained by GDP shocks, e.g., because higher GDP tends to increase the tax base and allows the government to spend more on infrastructures.

Another important feature of VAR is that, unlike in a production or cost function framework, the analysis is not done on a ceteris paribus basis. Indeed, in a production function, the effect of transport capital on output is estimated for any given level of private inputs; similarly, in a cost function the effect of transport capital is estimated for any given level of output (and factor prices). This excludes the possibility that private inputs in the production function or output in the cost function are mediating factors for the effect of transport infrastructures.

In other words, the production and cost function approaches exclude the possibility that important feedback effects exist between private inputs and transport capital and between private inputs themselves. These could arise for a variety of reasons already mentioned when dealing with the motives underlying the endogeneity of transport infrastructures in a production function framework: a higher transport capital stock might increase the marginal productivity of private capital, fostering capital accumulation; nevertheless, it is also possible that some types of transport capital displace private inputs.[70] The dynamics of private inputs and output can in turn affect government policies in terms of transport capital accumulation; higher capital stocks and output can increase the tax base, soften the government budget constraint, and lead to stronger public investment in transportation capital. Similarly, a decline of employment might lead to fiscal packages involving expenditure in transport projects.

If these feedback effects are important, the output elasticity of transport capital estimated in production function studies might not capture the wider, long-run effect of transport capital so that using Pereira and Andraz's (2013) words "a zero elasticity of private output with respect to public capital as obtained for example, from a single equation static production function approach, is neither a necessary nor a sufficient condition for public capital to be ineffective in the long run".[71]

[70] For instance, the construction of high capacity railways might well reduce investment in transport equipment for road transport.

[71] There is a large tradition in the estimation of dynamic production functions. In that case, some feedbacks effects can be "internalized" and a distinction is possible between the short-run and the long-run impacts of transport infrastructure capital on output.

Another relative advantage of VAR is that researchers are not forced to assume that only a long-run cointegrating relationship exists between variables in a system, as in the production function framework. While we refer to Hamilton (1995) for an in-depth discussion, in a nutshell we can note that in time series analysis one variable is considered stationary when the first two moments of its distribution (mean and variance) are constant and the value of the covariance between any two time periods depends only on their distance and not on the exact time. The fact that two or more variables are nonstationary raises important econometric problems (see Hamilton 1995) because a correlation between them could well be entirely spurious.[72] However, it is possible that the relationship between some nonstationary variables whose first difference is stationary (in time series jargon, variables that are integrated of order 1) is, however, stationary, thereby capturing a stable long-run relationship among the variables. While typically in production functions estimated with time series data, or in panels with large T, researchers do not test for the number of cointegrating relationships among output and inputs, there are exceptions, such as Calderon, Moral-Benito, and Serven (2015) and Bottasso, Castagnetti, et al. (2013).

However, there are also limitations in the case of VAR analysis. Indeed, as noted in Pereira and Andraz (2013), a VAR can be seen as the reduced form of a dynamic economic system, whereby public and private inputs are combined to produce output using the available technology, the private sector demands private inputs and the public sector supplies transport infrastructure reacting to developments in the private sector.

However, because no structure is imposed on the data, a causal interpretation cannot be given to the so-called impulse—response functions which are used in VAR analysis to trace the impact of an exogenous shock to one variable onto the other variables in the system.[73]

Therefore, to provide estimates that are more relevant from a policy point of view, researchers necessarily need to use economic theory to impose restrictions on the data. In particular, researchers have to assume a relative ordering for the variables; by way of example, most papers (Kamps,

[72] This was indeed perhaps the main critique raised to the pioneering study of Aschauer (1989), who estimated a production function with time series data with OLS.

[73] When variables in VAR models are stationary but cointegrated, researchers estimate the VAR analogue of Error Correction Models (VECM), to derive a correct interpretation of impulse response functions.

2004) assume that transport capital does not react contemporaneously to a shock to the other variables in the system (i.e., it is considered predetermined), possibly because of implementation lags, and that private capital reacts to contemporaneous shocks to public capital, but only with a lag to GDP and employment shocks, etc.

It goes without saying that these restrictions can be criticized and their validity should therefore be closely scrutinized, as results might be quite sensitive to them.[74] It is interesting, however, that some of these restrictions bear some similarity with the identification assumptions in GMM panel data models discussed in Section 6.2.2.

Among the very few papers that have applied VAR type of analysis to study the impact of transport networks (and not simply public capital) on economic activity, we can mention Ahlfeldt, Moeller, and Wendland (2015),[75] who found that the construction of the rail network in Berlin over the period 1880–1914 influenced economic development, but that transport supply was also influenced by economic development. Other studies include Pereira and Andraz (2005) who analyzed the impact on GDP of public infrastructure investments in various transport modes in Portugal, Pereira and Andraz (2004) who studied the impact of highways in the United States, Meersman and Nazemzadeh (2017) who studied the effect of ports, roads, and railways infrastructures in Belgium, Sturm, Kuper, and de Haan (1998) for the Netherlands, and Tripathi and Gautam (2010) for India, among the others.

6.3 THE LEVEL OF ANALYSIS

In the empirical literature (see Chapter 7), we find studies conducted at various levels of aggregation, i.e., using firm, industry, or macroeconomic data; similarly, some authors have considered the country as the unit of observation, whereas others have used regional, county, or even smaller spatial units.

If one takes a "chronological" point of view, the first wave of studies on the effects of transport and other types of public capital on production was mainly conducted using country-level macroeconomic data (see Afraz et al., 2005). However, since the end of the 1990s, beginning of the 2000s,

[74] See, for instance, the discussion in the recent study by de Jong et al. (2017) on the macroeconomic effects of public infrastructure capital.

[75] The authors used a panel VAR approach which combined the GMM-SYS approach discussed in previous sections with conventional VAR analysis.

a growing number of researchers have started to analyze more spatially disaggregated data, such as US states or regional data in the case of EU countries. The advantage of using more spatially disaggregated data is the availability of panel data, which were not available at the time for the cross-country case,[76] at least if one wanted to go beyond physical indicators and rely instead on monetary values as proxies for the services provided by the stock of transportation infrastructures.[77] Moreover, regional data might be thought to be less prone to the heterogeneity that often plagues cross-country studies which can be relatively more important when a monetary value for the stock of transport infrastructure capital is used, in the light of the different accounting conventions that might exist across countries.

However, the use of regional or even more granular data (such as provinces, counties, etc.) raises an important concern. For instance, the meta-analysis of Melo et al. (2013) and Holmgren and Merkel (2017) on the output effects of transport infrastructures, as well as that of Bom and Ligthart (2013) on wider public capital, find that studies conducted at subnational level tend to identify, ceteris paribus, lower output elasticities with respect to infrastructure capital.

Because in most cases the studies included in the meta-analysis did not control for spillover effects, one could imagine that studies conducted at lower levels of disaggregation do not fully capture these spillovers, unlike what happens in country-level studies. In other words, the difference between country- and regional-level studies is interpreted as evidence of positive spillover effects associated with transport infrastructure investments. This sort of "stylized fact" in turn suggests that, when working with disaggregated data, researchers should carefully think about possible spillover effects and how spillovers could be incorporated into the econometric model (see Section 6.2.2).

Nevertheless, as we will discuss more in depth in Chapter 7, there are various papers that, in some circumstances, have found negative spillovers associated with transport infrastructure investments, casting some doubts on the "spillover interpretation" of the above stylized fact (see also Redding & Turner, 2015).

[76] Of course things have been changing over time. See, for instance, Canning and Pedroni (2008), Calderon et al. (2015)and Bottasso, Castagnetti, et al. (2013) among the others.

[77] See Chapter 4 for a discussion of relevant data in transport infrastructure appraisals.

From this point of view, a fruitful avenue of research would be to compare results obtained at various levels of aggregation (say, at various NUTS levels if working with EU data, or at district, county, metropolitan area, or state if working with US data), although a better treatment of spillovers in the econometric model is probably the only way to obtain reliable evidence both on the existence of spillover effects as well to capture the direct effect of transport infrastructures.[78]

Interestingly, in recent years an increasingly higher number of papers have attempted to evaluate the economic impacts of particular transport schemes using highly disaggregated spatial data, such as the about 10000 electoral wards in the United Kingdom as in Gibbons et al. (2017), the 500 cells for Ghana in Jedwab and Moradi (2016), or the 263 Metropolitan Statistical Areas in the United States in Blonigen and Cristea (2015).

Together with the trend toward the use of more spatially disaggregated data, some studies have gone beyond the use of macroeconomic data and have instead relied on industry-level panel data. In some papers, the same industry (e.g., manufacturing) in various regions was considered, such as in Cohen and Morrison (2003), whereas other researchers focused on industry-level panel data in a single country (as in Fernald (1999), or on cross-country cross-industry panel data as in Bottasso and Conti (2010).

The use of data for a single industry was motivated by considerations related to the endogeneity of transport infrastructure (Cohen and Morrison,

[78] As we have already discussed in Section 6.2.3, Redding and Turner (2015) note that single equation models that correlate outcomes in a local area to the transport infrastructure provision in that area cannot distinguish between a "level" effect and a "reorganization of economic activity" effect associated with transport infrastructures and advocate the use of structural general equilibrium models that would be better equipped to capture the full, general equilibrium effects of transportation infrastructures. Moreover, as we have already noted in Section 6.2.3, the existence of spillovers may be seen as a violation of the SUTVA assumption underlying much work in the CIE tradition. Nevertheless, the inclusion of transport infrastructure variables from nearby regions in the estimated equation could be helpful to get at least some insights on the relative importance of the "reorganization" effect. Alternatively, running regressions with different samples depending on distances from transport improvements schemes might help in checking whether most of the effect associated with the latter is an additive effect or simply a reorganization of economic activity. Moreover, in the case of a spatial organization type of effect, one cannot conclude that there is not an aggregate welfare effect, because a reorganization of economic activity might lead, under some conditions, to higher aggregate output and employment, for example, when comparative advantages are better exploited as the consequence of the transport infrastructure improvement. See also the discussion in Chapter 7.3.

2003; Fageda and Gonzales-Aregall, 2015). The idea is that policy-makers are unlikely to react to developments in the manufacturing sector, which is nowadays a small part of the economy in most advanced countries. However, this interpretation is not very convincing, because it essentially depends on the degree of correlation between the manufacturing sector and the overall economy; if a shock to the wide economy leads the government to react by varying transport infrastructure investment and the manufacturing cycle is closely synchronized to the economy wide one, using manufacturing data does not fully solve the endogeneity problem. Moreover, models such as those of Redding and Turner (2015) clearly show that a better provision of infrastructure capital, by reducing bilateral transportation costs, increases the degree of firm's market access to other regions, which in turn leads to more employment and more output; however, because employment and output in a region depend on unobserved productivity and the latter is likely to influence infrastructure provision, output is endogenous even with manufacturing data, given the crucial role that manufacturing still plays in trade.

By way of contrast, we believe that the use of industry data is interesting for two other reasons. First, the availability of data for various industries allows researchers to estimate rates of returns for transport infrastructure that differ across industries. This can be an important input for policy-makers because they can better appreciate the sectors that might suffer from bottlenecks associated with a possible shortage of transport infrastructures; which in turn can allow policy-makers to anticipate which industries are likely to be the main beneficiaries of a transport expansion program.

Second, and perhaps even more importantly, the availability of cross-industry data might allow researchers, in the spirit of Fernald (1999), to exploit industry-level differences in the sensitivity to services provided by transportation infrastructures as an identification strategy, as discussed at length in Section 6.2.3 and in Box (6.4). If one is able to define a ranking of industries in terms of their sensitivity to transport services, then one should also find a stronger effect of transport infrastructures on output precisely in those industries that rank relatively high in terms of their sensitivity to transport services; industries with low sensitivity to transport therefore act as a control group for industries that are instead "more exposed" to transport, which constitute the treatment group, using the counterfactual impact evaluation definitions.

Finally, in recent years some authors have started using geo-referenced firm-level data to evaluate the impact of transport infrastructures. A recent example is the study by Holl (2016) who used a geo-referenced dataset of Spanish firms to estimate the effect of access to highways (proxied by the inverse of distance from the nearest highway) on firms' total factor productivity. The advantage of having access to a geocoded firm-level dataset is that researchers are able to control for both observed and unobserved firm-level heterogeneities, as well as to allow for heterogeneous effects of transportation infrastructure at industry level, which is not possible using spatial data, however disaggregated they can be.

6.4 CONCLUSION

In this chapter we have introduced the reader to the econometric approaches that have been used in the empirical literature to evaluate the economic effects of transport infrastructures. After highlighting the role played by economic theory in informing the empirical analysis, we have discussed the econometric tools that have been used in recent years in this area, such as panel fixed effects, GMM, spatial econometrics, VAR, and counterfactual impact evaluation methods. While GMM and spatial econometric techniques have been quite popular over the 2000–10 period, counterfactual impact evaluation methods have recently gained popularity among empirical economists. Although this chapter is not a fully fledged introduction to these approaches, we have sought to discuss their advantages and limitations, using actual recent studies as examples. Finally, this chapter also provides a brief discussion of the level of analysis at which studies have been conducted, from macroeconomic to regional, industry, and firm level; while the early literature had a clear macroeconomic flavor, most recent studies are clearly skewed toward more spatially disaggregated type of analysis, with an increasing role played by geo-referenced firm-level type of work. Also in this case, we hope to have highlighted costs and benefits of using data at various levels of disaggregation.

CHAPTER 7

The Economic Effects of Transport Infrastructures: A Critical Review of the Empirical Evidence

Contents

The objective of this chapter is to provide a critical review of the empirical evidence on the economic effects of transportation infrastructure. Because there are already important surveys (e.g., Afraz et al., 2005) and meta-analysis (Melo, Graham, & Brage-Ardao, 2013; Holmgren & Merkel, 2017; Bom & Ligthart, 2013; Nunez-Serrano & Velaszquez, 2017), we do not seek to provide yet another literature review or meta-analysis. Instead, in Section 7.1, we will build on those recent meta-analyses to summarize the existing literature, trying to highlight the reasons underlying the nonnegligible variance that characterizes the distribution of estimates; in particular, we will try to highlight the relative role played by the estimation methodologies, type of samples (e.g., country level vs. industry level), mode of transport, and type of data (e.g., panel data vs. time series). In the light of their importance, we will explore in some detail the empirical evidence on the existence of spillover effects of transportation infrastructures. Indeed, as noted in Chapter 6, the possible existence of spillovers associated with transportation networks, as well as the geographic scale at which they are exhausted, play a key role as far as the efficient financing of transport infrastructure investments is concerned.

Economic Role of Transport Infrastructure
ISBN 978-0-12-813096-4
https://doi.org/10.1016/B978-0-12-813096-4.00007-X

Moreover, in the light of the discussion in Chapter 6, and also taking into account the fact that the meta-analysis and earlier literature reviews largely neglect the impact of transportation capital on economic outcomes other than production and productivity, we think it is also worthwhile to discuss in some greater depth some of the very recent studies that have used state-of-the art econometric methodologies (such as counterfactual impact evaluation methods) to identify the causal effect of transportation infrastructure on various economic outcomes, such as productivity, firm dynamics, trade, employment, output, and population. The studies cover both developed and developing countries as well as all main modes of transport. This material is analyzed in Section 7.2.

In Section 7.3, we will then put together the evidence from both the meta-analysis and our "targeted" literature review to provide a tentative conclusion on the economic effects of transportation infrastructures, distinguishing, when possible, between roads, railways, ports, and airports. We will also leverage on the empirical evidence discussed in Section 7.2 to discuss whether recent studies conducted at local level identify a growth effect of transportation infrastructures or instead point toward a spatial or industrial reorganization of economic activity; this is extremely important because the welfare effects associated with these different scenarios would indeed be very different.

7.1 THE EFFECTS OF TRANSPORT INFRASTRUCTURES ON PRODUCTION: A REVIEW OF SOME META-ANALYSIS

Meta-analysis is a set of statistical techniques that are used to synthetize the results of a large set of previous "primary" studies. The usefulness of meta-analysis rests on the use of statistical methods to identify the main sources of variation in the distribution of the empirical estimates of a given parameter of interest. A meta-analysis is particularly relevant whenever there is large and systematic variation in the empirical estimates; by isolating the factors that, on statistical grounds, contribute to this variation, a meta-analysis helps the researcher to better appreciate the causes of this variation and possibly to focus on the set of results that appear to be more robust on different grounds. Indeed, as noted by Card and Krueger (1995), meta-analysis can be used as a tool to summarize the results of a particular literature "or to evaluate the reliability of the findings in a statistical literature".[1]

[1] For an in-depth discussion of meta-analysis see Stanley (2001).

To better illustrate the power of meta-analysis, an example from the literature on the productive effect of public capital can be useful, as the latter is clearly characterized by large differences in the empirical estimates which, in turn, can be due to a wide arrays of factors.

First, there are differences in the definition of public capital; although some studies use the total value of the public capital stock, others focus on the so-called core public infrastructures (which comprises transport infrastructure and utilities), whereas others concentrate on transport infrastructure only, or even single components of it, such as the stock of roads. In principle, there is no a priori reason that the economic effects of such diverse types of capital such as schools and hospital buildings, roads, airports, or electricity and water grids be homogenous.

Second, when a narrow definition of the public capital stock is considered, either a monetary value or a physical indicator (i.e., the length of motorways) can be used in the analysis.

Third, there are differences in the type of sample considered in each study: some use aggregate country-level data, whereas others focus on more disaggregated data, such as regions, counties, provinces, or even more granular spatial data. Moreover, independently on the level of aggregation, the data might refer to the total economy, to the private sector only, or even to specific sectors. Furthermore, the data might be of the time series, cross section, or panel data type, and, in the latter case, the panel can be short or refer to a sufficiently long time span that allows identifying both a short- and a long-run effect of the public capital stock.

Fourth, in the literature there are important differences in terms of the estimation methodology; for instance, some studies attempt to take into account the endogeneity of public capital using IV or GMM estimators, whereas others do not; in some older panel data studies, fixed effects were not considered; some time series (or panels with long T) studies are based on cointegration techniques[2] and therefore are less likely to capture spurious results, unlike "first-generation" studies which either did not consider nonstationarity issues or simply dealt with it by simply first differencing the estimating equation, thereby ignoring possible long-run relationships between production and public capital.

Fifth, some studies control for possible spillover effects, whereas others impose constant returns to scale for private inputs in the production function. Finally, some studies use the production function approach,

[2] See Section 6.2.4.

whereas others use other theoretical frameworks, such as cost or profit functions, or growth regressions (See Section 6.1).

A researcher might have strong a priori, validated by a careful reading of the literature, on the role played by the estimation method, the type of sample, or the definition of public capital on previous empirical findings; moreover, she could use this knowledge as a "screening" tool to differentiate about "robust" and "less robust" studies. Yet, it might be difficult to derive an objective and generalizable conclusion on what the literature really says about the effects of public capital on production. In this respect, a meta-analysis, by controlling through appropriate statistical tools for the wide range of factors that might impact on the empirical findings, can help a researcher to isolate the factors that impact on the sign and magnitude of an empirical effect in a more objective and transparent way.

The first meta-analysis that we discuss is the study by Bom and Ligthart (2013). Although this study refers to the effects of public capital on production, it provides useful results for transportation capital as well. Moreover, it constitutes a sort of benchmark for other successive meta-analysis, so that we believe its review is important.[3]

The authors consider 578 estimates from 68 primary studies published in the 1983–2008 period.[4] They focus on studies that adopt a Cobb–Douglas production function framework and that consider a monetary definition of the public capital stock; in turn, they do not include in the meta-analysis VAR studies if not based on cointegration analysis. The object of the meta-analysis is therefore to study the determinants of the variation in published estimates of the elasticity of production with respect to the public capital stock. Among the drivers of the empirical estimates that are considered by Bom and Ligthart (2013), we can mention dummy variables for the definition of public capital stock (i.e., total vs. core, vs. transport), the definition of output (i.e., excluding or including the output of the public sector), the existence of controls for spillovers, whether the estimate was a short-run versus a long-run one, the inclusion of unit-specific fixed effects, the date of publication, the type of data (regional vs. country level), whether a

[3] Another recent meta-analysis on the economic effects of public infrastructures is that of Elburz, Nijkamp, and Pels (2017). It focuses on studies conducted at regional and subregional level and is not limited to studies in the production function tradition.

[4] We refer to Bom and Ligthart (2013) for a detailed explanation of the regression equation, the estimation method, and other technical details such as the correction for the so-called "publication-bias."

cointegrating relationship is found in the model, whether the equation is estimated with the variables in levels in time series or panel data without testing for cointegration, whether the model controls for capacity utilization or energy prices, among the others.

The main results in this meta-analysis can be summarized as follows. First, the average elasticity is about 0.11. However, this result hides substantial variation. For instance, the elasticity tends to be higher in the case of public capital that was installed by local governments, in the case of core infrastructure, when the study focuses on private output and in the long run.

Interestingly, studies based on a narrow definition of public capital, namely transport capital, do not find a statistically different result from those based on the wider definition, unlike in the case of studies that analyze the effect of core public capital. This is somewhat puzzling, given that core infrastructure is just transport infrastructure plus the utilities.

Other interesting results highlighted by Bom and Ligthart (2013) is that studies using regional data find lower elasticities, which can be interpreted as supporting the existence of positive spatial spillovers, whereas studies estimating cointegration relationship or featuring variables in long differences are more likely to find larger elasticities. Finally, studies that tackle endogeneity tend to find somewhat smaller elasticities.

All these results that we have just briefly summarized are ceteris paribus results. However, Bom and Ligthart (2013) report some interesting simulations by letting three fundamental study characteristics to vary, namely the time horizon, the definition of public capital, and the level of government that provides the public capital stock. The computation is done by keeping fixed other characteristics; in particular, authors consider studies that correct for endogeneity, that focus on the output of the private economy, that use country-level data, and that do not identify spurious relationships. Authors report elasticities for the wider definition of public capital that vary between 0.083 and 0.145; in turn, for core public capital, the same elasticities range from 0.131 to 0.193. Interestingly, these results are not too far from the conclusions reached in the literature review of Afraz, Aquilina, Conti, and Lilico (2006), who argue that, on average, a sensible range for the output elasticity with respect to public capital is 0.1−0.2.

A similar analysis, but carried out on a substantially larger sample, is undertaken by Nunez-Serrano and Velaszquez (2017), who conduct a meta-analysis of almost 2000 elasticities from 145 papers. Unlike Bom and Ligthart (2013), they do not focus only on production function studies and include estimates based on nonmonetary measures of the public capital stock as well; moreover, they include indicator variables for whether the estimates are from an individual or cross-country study. As in Bom and Ligthart (2013), they differentiate between the level of government that installed the capital stock, the data structure (time series, cross section, panel data), the econometric methodology (i.e., the correction for endogeneity, the possibility of spurious correlation, the control for fixed effects), the definition of public capital (total, core, and transport).

The main results of this meta-analysis broadly confirm those in Bom and Ligthart (2013). Indeed, the average elasticity is 0.13, again with non-negligible variation. As in Bom and Ligthart (2013), elasticities tend to be slightly larger in the long run and slightly lower in the case of estimates likely to suffer from spurious correlation. Interestingly, Nunez-Serrano and Velaszquez (2017) find slightly larger elasticities in the case of estimates derived from cross-country studies or from panel data models.[5] Again somewhat surprisingly, transport capital elasticities are not significantly different from those of total public capital, whereas core productive public capital displays larger elasticities.

While Nunez-Serrano and Velaszquez (2017) and Bom and Ligthart (2013) take a broader view by considering public capital stock, Melo et al. (2013) and Holmgren and Merkel (2017) instead focus mostly on transport infrastructures.

Melo et al. (2013) evaluate 563 elasticities obtained from 33 primary studies. The structure of the econometric analysis is very similar to that proposed by Nunez-Serrano and Velaszquez (2017) and Bom and Ligthart (2013) as the authors control for the econometric methodology (GMM, fixed effects, random effects, and VAR), the use of instrumental variables, the existence of a control for spatial spillovers, the type of sample (regional, cross-regional, cross-country), type of country (high—medium—low income levels), and time frame for the elasticity.

As far as the main results are concerned, there seems to be evidence that panel data models estimated with GMM and/or with fixed effects generally yield lower estimates than simple OLS, whereas US-based studies tend to identify larger estimates than those based on EU samples. In turn, there is

[5] Unlike in Bom and Ligthart (2013), elasticities tend to be lower in the case of public capital installed by local administrations. Morevoer, Nunez-Serrano and Velaszquez (2017) do not find any statistically significant effect associated with the use of instrumental variable techniques.

no evidence that low-income countries are characterized by higher elasticities; although one could expect transport infrastructure to have higher returns in developing countries because of the lower levels of infrastructure, it is possible that the sparser networks and the low degree of connectivity in most developing countries might offset the "scarcity" effect, as observed by Melo et al. (2013). Moreover, it is possible that the efficiency of the public transport system might be lower in developing countries (Berg et al. 2016).

From this meta-analysis, there is in turn again strong evidence that estimates based on regional samples tend to provide smaller estimates, and that long-run output elasticities tend to be higher, whereas the way to measure transport infrastructure (either with monetary or physical indicators) does not seem to matter. Interestingly, the results of Melo et al. (2013) seem to suggest that the productivity impact of roads is larger than that of other modes of transport; in particular, the average elasticity of the other modes of transport is about 0.03, whereas that of roads is about 0.09.

The meta-analysis by Holmgren and Merkel (2017), in turn, focuses again on transport, but it is based on a larger set of estimates (776), derived from 78 studies. The control variables are very similar to those considered in the previous meta-analysis. By using a backward stepwise regression procedure, they end up with a restricted model with about 15 controls that are statistically significant. They find that panel data and time series estimates are generally lower than cross section ones, whereas regional data and production in services are associated with lower elasticities, ceteris paribus. In turn, the type of estimation procedure does not seem to matter much, which is quite surprising, in the light of the evidence in the previous meta-analysis. However, multicollinearity issues might be important, because, especially in recent studies, panel data are very often estimated with GMM; in this case, the lower elasticity associated with the use of panel data might be picking up also the effect of GMM.

The average estimate in the sample is quite large, namely 0.23. Again, as in the first two literature reviews, elasticities based on an aggregate measure of public capital tend to be somewhat larger (0.34). As far as the mode of transport is concerned, there is substantial heterogeneity; moreover, the relative effects of each transport mode seem to differ across industries. Indeed, if we take roads as the baseline, they have average elasticities of about 0.23 in manufacturing and construction, but only 0.16 in services. In turn, in the case of manufacturing and construction, airports seem to display lower elasticities than roads (0.17 vs. 0.23); however, in the case of agriculture and services, the investment in airports seems to impact more on production than the investment in roads, with elasticities of about 0.33 and 0.3, respectively. Similarly, the elasticities of railways are higher than those of roads in the case of the service sectors, but slightly lower in the case of the other industries. Finally, port infrastructures have higher elasticities in the case of agriculture (about 0.33), whereas, as far as the other sectors are concerned, the elasticities are somewhat lower than in the case of roads.

The brief review of these four meta-analyses allows us the first chance to take stock on the effects of transport infrastructure investment. It is important to stress that, although the exact punctual estimates of the average elasticities are not immediately comparable because of differences in the control variables, nevertheless we believe that there are some regularities that emerge from a comparison of these meta-analyses.

- First, in all meta-analysis the elasticity of output with respect to the stock of public capital is positive, with an order of magnitude typically in the 0.1–0.2 range, much lower than the early estimates of 0.40–0.50 by Aschauer (1989)—which opened up the modern debate on the growth effects of public capital—but notably larger than the estimates considered by early reviews during the 1990s (Gramlich, 1994) and more in line with the surveys conducted in the second decade of the 2000s, such as Romp and de Haan (2007) and Afraz et al. (2006).
- Second, all metaanalyses find a nonnegligible degree of heterogeneity across the empirical estimates. Reassuringly, some consistent pattern in the drivers of this heterogeneity seems to emerge across meta-analyses. For instance, there is some evidence that core infrastructure is more productive than the aggregate public capital, ceteris paribus; however, this seems to arise mainly from the nontransport elements of core infrastructure, whereas the elasticities of transport capital are either not significantly different from those of aggregate public capital or even slightly lower. As noted above, this is somewhat surprising, given that, a priori, one would expect transport capital infrastructure to display stronger effects than utilities. In the case of the single modes of transport, roads seem to be more productive than rail and airports (Melo et al., 2013), although according to Holmgren and Merkel (2017), there is significant heterogeneity depending on the final sector considered by the primary studies.
- Third, there is some indication that estimation techniques, more likely to estimate long-run effects, tend to identify a larger impact, which is again a reasonable finding, because most of the (non-Keynesian) productive effects associated with infrastructure capital that have been

identified by the theoretical literature are likely to require some years to fully unfold.

- Fourth, some metaanalyses tend to find lower effects in the case of panel-based estimates; however, whether this is due to the fact that failing to control for individual unobserved heterogeneity leads to upward bias in the elasticity of transport infrastructure (because more productive units tend to invest more in transport because of a stronger demand) or simply to the fact that panel data models are more subject to measurement error bias is not clear.
- Fifth, there seems to be a consensus across meta-analyses that estimates based on greater territorial disaggregation tend to be lower than those based on country-level analysis, which lends some support to the hypothesis that transport networks tend to produce positive spatial spillovers in neighboring jurisdictions.[6]
- Sixth, there is some evidence that more recent studies on average identify lower elasticities. However, it is not clear from the meta-analyses whether this is due to the higher quality of more recent studies, which better take into account endogeneity and spurious correlations in the data, or to possible nonlinear effects of public capital.
- Finally, the measurement of infrastructure capital either in monetary or in physical terms does not seem to matter. This is an important point because authors in the past have often argued in favor or against the use of monetary variables: the fact that it is not possible to identify a systematic effect on the magnitude of estimates is reassuring and might lead in the future to focus more on issues where some disagreements still exist.

One very important issue that the meta-analyses do not seem to have settled refers to the econometric methodology and, in particular, to the use of instrumental variables techniques. Indeed, while Holmgren and Merkel (2017) and Nunez-Serrano and Velaszquez (2017) do not find any systematic effect of using instrumental variables methods, Bom and Ligthart (2013) find strong support for the hypothesis that tackling endogeneity leads to somewhat lower elasticities. In turn, and curiously enough, Melo et al. (2013) report lower elasticities in the case of studies using GMM but higher in the case of estimates based on instrumental variable techniques.

[6] Elburz et al. (2017) also find evidence that the smaller the geographic scale of analysis, the lower the effects of public infrastructures, pointing toward positive spillovers across local areas.

This strikingly different result might in part be due to nonnegligible heterogeneity in the average quality of studies considered by the different meta-analyses and, in particular, to differences in the average quality of instruments (see Section 6.2) in those studies using IV or GMM techniques. If the pool of primary studies differs in terms of reliability of the identification restrictions underlying both IV and GMM estimation techniques, then it is not surprising that different meta-analyses reach different conclusions. If this were true, then simply controlling for the use of IV and GMM in a meta-analysis might not dispense the researcher from taking a position on the validity of the exclusion restrictions, or on the likely existence of a weak instrument problem.

Be as it may, this lack of consensus on this important point is unfortunate, because one is left with no indication on whether the use of IV or GMM has on average any practical effect with respect to simple OLS. Moreover, this lack of consensus across different meta-analysis suggests another consideration. Indeed, some authors argued that an additional primary study, in an already rich empirical literature, might just add "noise" to our knowledge about the state of the world,[7] and that a meta-analysis is precisely the tool that is needed to guide researchers through that "noise": it is somewhat ironic that four metaanalyses might have already rapidly increased that level of "noise," at least for this specific "driver" of empirical estimates.

All in all, the above meta-analyses broadly confirm the results of the surveys of Romp and de Haan (2007) and Afraz et al. (2006). We could summarize the results of the meta-analyses using the words of Afraz et al. (2006), by noting that "the evidence of small albeit positive benefits stemming from public capital and, especially, from transport infrastructure seems to find a broad support in the empirical literature, unlike what earlier literature reviews [...] seemed to suggest" (Afraz et al., 2006). Moreover, as noted by Romp and de Haan (2007) "many studies report that there is heterogeneity: the effect of public investment differs across countries, regions, and sectors."

Furthermore, the metaanalyses shed some light on the reasons of these discrepancies; first, estimators more likely to identify long-run effects tend to find higher elasticities; second, panel data estimators tend to produce somewhat lower estimates; third, when the unit of observation is defined at

[7] See Holmgren and Merkel (2017) for a discussion of this point and some references to the literature.

a lower spatial scale, elasticities are definitely lower, pointing to the existence of spatial spillovers.

In turn, as far as the effectiveness of investments in transport infrastructure is concerned, there is no evidence than transport infrastructures are characterized by higher elasticities than the aggregate public capital stock. However, there is some empirical support for the hypothesis that roads are somewhat more productive than other transport infrastructures (Melo et al., 2013), although with possible heterogeneities depending on the final sector the primary study focused on (Holmgren & Merkel, 2017), with port facilities relatively more productive than roads in the case of the agriculture sector, airports more effective to stimulate growth than roads in the case of services and agriculture and railways with a higher effect than roads only in the case of services.[8]

As noted above, the meta-analyses have been helpful both to confirm the conclusions of previous recent literature reviews, namely the existence of small but positive economic effects of public infrastructure, and to isolate some of the variation in the empirical estimates. However, there are also some shortcomings:

- First, the various meta-analyses have only focused on the impact of public and transport infrastructures on output. However, a majority of studies that we have covered in the meta-analysis embed public capital within a production function framework; as a result, they control for the level of private inputs, which perhaps could act as mediating factors for the effect of public capital on output. As a result, the meta elasticities found in the literature might, to a certain extent, reflect a mix of the impact on (total factor) productivity and output. By way of contrast, in the past few years, several studies have analyzed the role played by the stock of transportation infrastructures outside the production function framework, thereby providing estimates on the effect on production, as well as on other economic dimensions, such as employment, population, production, firm dynamics, productivity, and trade.
- Second, it seems fair to say that, in the most recent period, the literature has been paying more attention to the econometric strategy and to the overall research design, with more studies that have been conducted at a higher level of spatial disaggregation than in the past, when the literature had a much clearer macroeconomic flavor, even when based on regional-level data. As Chapter 6 should have hopefully made it clear,

[8] Elburz et al. (2017) find higher economic effects in the case of road transport.

recent studies belonging to the counterfactual impact evaluation tradition have shown the importance of a careful research design to identify the causal effect of transportation capital on various economic outcomes; however, the meta-analyses have largely neglected these recent studies.

For these reasons, we believe that a careful review of some representative recent works that have reexamined the issue of the economic effects of transport infrastructure is warranted. It is to this type of analysis that we now turn.

7.2 THE EFFECTS OF TRANSPORT INFRASTRUCTURES ON VARIOUS ECONOMIC OUTCOMES: A SELECTED REVIEW OF RECENT EMPIRICAL STUDIES

While the empirical literature in the 1990s and 2000s had a clear macroeconomic flavor, in the past 10 years a series of papers in the regional, urban, and transport economics literature have started to model the impact of transportation networks at a more spatially disaggregated level, such as regions, provinces, municipalities, or even smaller units using georeferenced data.

This trend in part has been reflecting the need to better understand the theoretical mechanisms underlying the relationship between investments in transportation infrastructure networks and local development, which necessarily requires data at local level, as the new-economic geography models have highlighted. Moreover, spatial disaggregated data make it easier to apply counterfactual impact evaluation techniques; indeed, it is not accidental that in the regional and urban economics literature, issues of identification, together with the need to use quasi-natural experiments or cleverly designed instrumental variables, has been gaining momentum and popularity among applied researchers.[9] Finally, new-economic geography has a number of testable predictions as far as it concerns the impact of transportation networks on trade, growth, and productivity.

For these reasons, in this section we focus on a set of very recent studies that have evaluated the impact of transportation infrastructures on various

[9] It is, however, fair to say that some papers employed the spatial econometrics approach which largely neglects the identification issues. Moreover, another strand of the literature has been using internal instruments à la Arellano and Bond (1991). See Chapter 6 for a discussion of the possible limitations of these approaches.

economic outcomes using spatially disaggregated data. However, it is important to note that our survey is by no means exhaustive for several reasons.

First, we focus on studies that have put identification issues at the forefront of their empirical strategy, either by using diff-in-diff techniques or IV strategies with external instruments (see Chapter 6); this means that, with some notable exceptions, we do not cover studies that employed spatial econometric approaches or that estimated panel data models with GMM using internal instruments à la Arellano and Bond (1991).

Second, we do not review studies that have examined the impact of transport infrastructure investments in the 19th century,[10] with few exceptions when they show the long-term impact (e.g., up to the 2000s) of transportation investments on the spatial organization of economic activity.

Third, with some exceptions, we do not cover those papers in the urban economics literature that have analyzed the impact of transport infrastructures on urban sprawl, house pricing, and suburbanization (e.g., Baum-Snow, 2007; Garcia-Lopez, Holl, & Viladecans-Marsal, 2015, among the others). In turn, not only do we focus on studies that have analyzed the impact of transport infrastructures on the level of economic activity in a given local area, measured by GDP, production, employment, or population, but we also investigate the role played by transport investments on trade, firm dynamics (e.g., number of start-ups, employment in young vs. incumbent firms, etc.), and productivity. In particular, analyzing the impact on trade is important because it is perhaps the main channel through which transport infrastructures affect the level of economic activity, the birth (or relocation) of new firms, and even the growth of productivity, by increasing specialization, the division of labor, and by fostering agglomeration economies and the competitive pressures on local producers (see Chapter 3).[11]

It is important at this stage to note an important point. In macrolevel studies, the identification of the economic effect of transport infrastructures is difficult, because of the lack of quasi-natural experiments or credible exogenous instruments. However, if one believes that the identification problem has been solved, it is relatively easy to capture the net economic

[10] Notable examples are Donaldson (2018), Donaldson and Hornbeck (2016) and Hornung (2015).

[11] We also do not consider studies that have assessed the impact of transport infrastructure projects using structural general equilibrium approaches.

effects of transport infrastructures, if there are any. By way of contrast, with spatially disaggregated data, it is perhaps easier to credibly identify the effect on the treated units, but it is by no means clear whether that represents a net growth effect of transport infrastructures or simply the by-product of the spatial or sectoral reorganization of economic activity.

Indeed, let us suppose that some local units, that have been affected by a new transport scheme, experience a boost to employment and GDP relatively to a set of "control" local units (i.e., units that have been not affected by the scheme). It might well be the case that the increase in employment and output is at least in part driven by reallocation of economic activity from the "control" to the "treated" units. Similarly, one study might conclude that a transport scheme has led to a reduction of economic activity in the affected rural areas with respect to other unaffected rural areas (for instance, because the reduction in transportation costs have determined a relocation of economic activity toward the large urban centers outside the sample); again, although this result would be evidence in favor of a reorganization type of effect, one cannot conclude that the overall effect for the country is necessarily zero, because general equilibrium effects might have generated a positive impact for the economy as a whole, which, however, can hardly be measured by a reduced-form empirical model.

Redding and Turner (2015) are indeed sceptical that reduced-form regressions are able to separately identify both the growth and the spatial reorganization effects that may be associated with transport improvements and call for the construction and estimation of structural general equilibrium models.[12] However, also following some insights in Chandra and Thompson (2000) and Redding and Turner (2015), some recent studies have provided indirect evidence on whether a given estimated effect is a "net effect" or rather a simple reorganization of economic activity, and we will discuss them in some detail below.

The remaining of this Section is organized as follows. In Section 7.2.1, we discuss the empirical evidence on trade, whereas in Section 7.2.2 we focus on the effect of transportation infrastructures on productivity and Sections 7.2.3 and 7.2.4 will deal with firm dynamics and with the level of economic development, respectively. In each Section we try to review at least one paper per mode of transport.

[12] Examples of this strand of literature are Donaldson (2018), Donaldson and Hornbeck (2016) and Asturias et al. (2017).

7.2.1 Infrastructure and Trade

One of the first of studies that have investigated the impact of road infrastructure on trade is Duranton, Morrow, and Turner (2014), whose empirical specification directly stems from a theoretical model inspired to Anderson and Van Wincoop (2003). The model considers a set of cities, each producing its own variety of output in different sectors and that trade with each other. Trade is subject to transportation costs; the latter depends on both the amount of interstate highways within city boundaries (which affect the cost of leaving the city) and the distance between any trading cities along the interstate highways network. Moreover, the cost of shipping goods outside city boundaries, which depends on the amount of highways within the city, is allowed to differ across sectors; in particular, Duranton et al. (2014) allow sectors that produce heavier good to have trade costs that are more sensible to increases in the amount of roads within the city boundaries than trade in light goods, which are often goods of higher quality; in turn, authors assume that distances between cities do not have any differential effect on trade costs across sectors, i.e., they implicitly assume that each city chooses its patterns of sectoral specialization depending only on the amount of highways within its boundaries, and not as a function of the amount of highways of their neighbors.[13]

The model provides a set of several testable implications, although we focus only on a subset.[14] First, the model implies that an increase in city highways leads to a surge in exports of heavier goods, whereas the same effect on the value of exports should be positive but smaller. Moreover, the model also predicts a composition effect: following an increase in city roads, employment in weight-intensive industries tends to increase, whereas employment in light-intensive industries tends to shrink. In other words, the model features a comparative advantage story following an increase in highways within a given city; a city with more highways specializes in the production of heavier goods, because the latter is relatively more affected by the fall in transportation costs associated with the expansion in the highways network.

[13] In their model, highways affect trade only by reducing transportation costs. However, the authors acknowledge that highways within a city might affect trade also indirectly by increasing productivity, for instance, because of stronger competitive pressures on local producers derived from a larger pool of competitors or because agglomeration effects.

[14] We refer the reader to the Duranton et al. (2014) for an in-depth analysis.

The model in Duranton et al. (2014) directly leads to an empirical estimation strategy. Indeed, the model yields a gravity equation where trade flows between any two pair of cities i and j are an unknown function of transportation costs, plus two terms related to the economic fundamentals of the two cities, which in turn can be seen as the propensity to trade of city i and j. This leads to an estimable equation as the following one:

$$lnX_{ij} = \delta_i^X + \delta_j^M + O(R_{ij}) + \varepsilon_{ij} \tag{7.1}$$

where δ_i^X is the propensity to export of city i and δ_j^M is the propensity to import of city j, which can be captured by city i and j fixed effects, respectively (see Chapter 6). In turn, $O(R_{ij})$ is an unknown function of road distance between the two cities that Duranton et al. (2014) proxy with a polynomial of different degrees. Within city highways do not feature in Eq. (7.1) because, in the model of Duranton et al. (2014), they simply affect a given city's propensity to trade and, in Eq. (7.1) above, they are subsumed in the exporter and importer fixed effects.

The empirical strategy suggested by Duranton et al. (2014) is therefore a two-step approach. First, they estimate by OLS Eq. (7.1) on a sample of US Commodity Flow Survey Areas, a unit only slightly larger than a US Metropolitan Statistical Areas (MSA), using trade data for 2000. In a second step, they recover the exporter fixed effects and regress them on the number of kilometers of highways within a city boundary plus additional control variables that, in their model, predict a city propensity to trade, such as population, market access, productivity, etc.:

$$\delta_i^X = a_0 + \rho lnR_i + \beta' C + \mu_i \tag{7.2}$$

However, Duranton et al. (2014) correctly acknowledge various sources of endogeneity that make the estimation of Eq. (7.2) by OLS unfeasible. First, a higher propensity to export might lead to the construction of a higher network within a given city boundary; second, there might be variables that are not included in C that drive both highways and a city propensity to export and, finally, the controls might themselves be endogenous. Duranton et al. (2014) resort to instrumental variable estimation. In particular, and referring to the taxonomy discussed in Chapter 6, they follow both the "historical route approach" and the "planned route approach": railroads in 1898 and exploration routes between 1528 and 1850 are the instruments following the historical route approach, whereas highways planned in 1950 is the instrumental variable associated with the planned route approach.[15] Duranton et al. (2014) justify at length the exclusion restrictions underlying the use of these instruments, they discuss why they might fail and include additional controls[16] that are likely to make the validity of the instruments more likely.[17]

Second step results[18] suggest that a more extensive city network is associated with more trade in weight with little difference between OLS and IV results, with an elasticity of about 0.5. In turn, the effect is not statistically significant in the case of the value of exports, suggesting that more roads within a city leads to a specialization that is skewed toward industries that tend to produce heavier goods, as suggested by a series of employment regressions at sector level. Interestingly, the authors test whether their main results hold when one considers trade at different distances; after all, it might well be the case that highways within a city do not matter much for trade between cities that are very far apart from each other (with airways and maybe railways that become more important). Empirical results show that the elasticity for trade in weight is much higher in the case of trade within 1000 km (0.81), whereas the elasticity is much smaller (0.23) and insignificant for shipments traveling more than 1000 km. Interestingly, in the case of short-haul shipping, also trade in value is significantly increased by a more extensive road network.

Interestingly, in a set of auxiliary regressions, Duranton et al. (2014) find a similar result in the case of railways; more railways kilometers within a Commodity Flow Survey area is found to lead to an increase in the weight but not in the value of that MSA's export, with a magnitude that is even larger than in the highways case.

All in all, the study by Duranton et al. (2014) suggests that more interstate highways (and railroads) within US cities lead to an increase in the

[15] Their rationale is extensively discussed in Section 6.2.3 to which we refer.

[16] For instance, if 1898 railroads led to a specialization in manufacturing, and if this specialization persisted, then 1898 railroads might have an effect on trade beyond that operating through a more extensive road network. Similarly, if a large city in 1898 was more likely to receive a railroad and if population is persistent, then again railroads in 1898 would not be a valid instrument. In their IV regressions, Duranton et al. (2014) therefore control for sectoral specialization and population measured well before the beginning of their sample period.

[17] Duranton et al. (2014) show that their results are robust to using only a subset of the instruments; moreover, instruments pass the Sargan test (see Section 6.2.3).

[18] In the first step, they find elasticities of trade with respect to bilateral road distances that are in the range between 1.6 and 1.9 for weight and 1.17 and 1.4 for value.

weight of trade but not in its value, with the exception of short-haul trade, when also the value of trade slightly increases. This suggests that the first-order effect of road construction is to induce a reorganization effect, with cities with more highways specializing in the production of heavier goods, with not much effect on the global value of trade.

A very similar empirical exercise has been conducted by Duranton (2015) on a middle-income developing country, namely Colombia, using trade and road data[19] for 2011. Somewhat surprisingly, using a very similar specification but estimated on Colombian data, Duranton (2015) finds that more roads within a city tend to increase both the quantity and the value of trade with other cities. He finds an elasticity of trade in weight with respect to within city roads of up to 0.4, with a somewhat larger magnitude in the case for the value of trade.[20] In this study, Duranton (2015) uses historical route type of instruments, namely the routes from the era of colonization and the road network in 1938. The justification for their validity is based on the fact that colonial roads were built from reasons unrelated to modern trade and for a country whose local communities were largely autarkic. Similarly, the road network in 1938 was still underdeveloped and trade was still very regional in scope.

The main result of this study is clearly the fact that a more extensive road network leads to an increase in the weight and especially in the value of trade; this suggests that, unlike in the United States, there is no evidence that more roads lead to specialization, but simply to more trade. Duranton (2015) justifies this discrepancy with the different distances at which trade takes place in Colombia; indeed, at short distances, also in the United States more roads in a city is found to lead to more value of trade in Duranton et al. (2014).

A somewhat different empirical approach has in turn been followed by Volpe M., Carballo, and Cusolito (2017) in a paper studying the effects of roads on international exports of differentiated products in Peru over the period 2003–10. In particular, they have information on the universe of transactions and, for each transaction, they know the municipality of

[19] He uses a road index which is the sum of the log of the number of principal roads, the log of the mileage of these roads, and the log of the number of exists from the municipality by principal roads.

[20] In the first step, Duranton (2015) finds a negative elasticity of trade with respect to distance between cities, with a smaller magnitude than that found by Duranton et al. (2014) for the US case.

origin, the port, airport, or territorial border (from now on, port in all cases) from which the shipment left the country, the identity of the firm as well as the type of product that was exported, and the export value in US dollars and the quantity in kilograms. Their main analysis rests on a diff-in-diff type of analysis because they exploit a massive road extension program that took place over the period 2003–10 and that substantially reduced the time to reach the nearest port for some firms but not for others. In other words, the change in exports for firms in locations that did not experience a reduction in the travel time to reach the nearest port is used as the counterfactual for the change in exports that would have faced those firms that did experience a reduction in travel time had the road expansion not taken place.

Moreover, because of the wealth of information in their data, Volpes M. et al. (2017) are able to control for a wide set of fixed effects. Indeed, they are able to estimate an equation like (7.3) below:

$$lnX_{frspc} = a_0 D_{frspc}(t) + \rho_{frspc} + \theta_{rs}(t) + \mu_{frspc}(t) \tag{7.3}$$

In Eq. (7.3), f stands for firm, r for region, s for sector, p for product category, c for destination country, and t is the year index. D is a binary indicator equal to 1 if a firm f in region r active in sector s ships a product p to a destination country c using a shortest route. In other words, D is equal to 1 for treated units, i.e., those that experienced a reduction in the distance to ship the product to the nearest port, and 0 otherwise.[21] Finally, ρ is a set of firm-region-sector-product fixed effects, and the $\theta_{rs}(t)$ are region-sector-year fixed effects.

Authors estimate Eq. (7.3) using only information for the first and the last year of the panel after taking first differences, so that they eliminate the ρ_{frspc}. Moreover, in the first difference specification they also include region-sector fixed effects and, in others, also province-sector or even municipality-sector fixed effects or product-destination fixed effects. In other words, their diff-in-diff specification should be able to take into account of various common trends that affects both the treated and the control units.

Moreover, they undertake a series of placebo tests (see Section 6.2.3). For instance, they compare their main results to an otherwise identical

[21] The authors show that results are robust to using actual distance to the nearest port as an alternative proxy of the effect of the lower transport costs associated with the road construction program.

regression for the period 1999–2002 when no massive road construction took place; reassuringly, they do not detect any significant effects of road construction. Note that this is a possible version of the test for the parallel trend assumption underlying the validity of diff-in-diff estimates, which was discussed in Section 6.2.3. Furthermore, they exploit the fact that many roads were planned but not built; using georeferenced data, authors are thus able to reconstruct such roads and assume they were in place; this allows them to build a fictitious treatment group. Again, no statistically significant effect is found. In addition to this, they check for possible remaining concerns for endogeneity of roads by using the "historical route approach"; in particular, they instrument road changes with distance from the geographical origin of exports to the nearest Inca road and the distance along the Inca roads between the origin of exports and the destination ports. They justify the validity of these instruments pretty much using arguments very similar to those of Duranton et al. (2014) and Duranton (2015). Of course, also in this case the instruments are valid conditionally on fixed effects and controls.

Volpe M. et al. (2017) find clear evidence of an increase in export value following the road construction program which is robust across specifications. Interestingly, they also find that the increase in value was largely driven by increasing in export quantity rather than unit values. Moreover, the effect they identify is essentially an intensive margin one, as they do not find evidence that road construction led to firm entry into the export market.

Finally, the authors show that the causal effect of roads on international trade is not a simple reorganization effect, i.e., they do not find evidence of negative spillovers to control units. Following the suggestions of Redding and Turner (2015), they construct three groups of observations: the treated ones, a group of observations in the same municipality/province and product category of the treated ones but that did not experience changes in road distances (untreated), and a residual category that includes observations in other province/municipalities which export different product categories and that did not experience a reduction in road distances (residual). If reorganization effects are important, one should find a lower treatment effect when comparing treated units with untreated, because the latter belong to the same area and export the same product category of the treated observations; however, the treatment effect is barely changed. Moreover, by comparing untreated and residual they do not find any statistically significant differences. All in all, the results in Volpe M. et al. (2017) suggest that, in their case, the road investment program has led to a net increase in international trade and not simply to a reorganization of production across firms in different areas of the country.

A similar analysis has been followed by Cosar and Demir (2016) who exploit the massive increase in the quality of road transport due to the conversion of roads from two-lines to four-line expressways occurring in Turkey over the period 2003–12. They have information on international trade flows from each province and the Turkish gateway port, as well data broken down by partner country and industry. Moreover, they are able, for each province–gateway combination, to reconstruct the share of expressways over the total road stock. They use this information to estimate the impact of the change in road capacity (as proxied by changes in the share of expressways) on the change in log trade flows. In particular, assuming that transportation costs incurred between each province and a gateway port depend on both distance and road capacity, they are able to derive an otherwise standard gravity equation (see Section 6.2.1, Box 6.1), where the change in trade flows occurring between the initial and the final year in the sample depends on the interaction between the province–gateway port distance and the increase in road capacity, plus a set of gateway port and province fixed effects. In some specifications, they also instrument the change in road capacity with the initial level of expressways at the beginning of the period. They consistently find across the various empirical specifications that the increase in road capacity is associated with a large and significant increase in trade flows. In particular, their estimates suggest that the cost of an average shipment falls by about 70% if the whole route is upgraded to a two-line per way. Cosar and Demir (2016) also find an increase in the probability that a trade link between a province and a gateway port is established; moreover, they find that most of their effect is due to the extensive margin, i.e., trade with new countries and industries.

All in all, the evidence discussed so far seems to suggest that roads matter for trade. Indeed, a part from Duranton et al. (2015), who find, for the US case, that, with the exceptions of the shortest distance shipments, the effects of road within a city are only that of fostering specialization in the production of heavy goods, the other studies find a positive effects of road quantity or quality on the value of both domestic and international trade, independently on the level of economic development of the country considered in the study. Moreover, there is little evidence of a spatial reorganization type of effect. These results are also confirmed by additional studies that we have not reviewed in this chapter.[22]

We now turn to consider the impact on trade of other modes of transport. In the case of airports, the evidence is really scant. Alderighi and Gaggero (2017) use half-yearly panel data on exports of 20 Italian regions toward 24 European countries over the period 1998–2010 as well as information on the number of nonstop scheduled flights from airports from each Italian region to estimate the impact of air transport services on exports.

To do so, they estimate a gravity equation very similar to that described in Box 6.1 of Section 6.2.1; they are therefore able to control for unobserved time-invariant determinants of both scheduled flights and exports by means of importer–exporter (i.e., country-by-region) fixed effects but also for a full set of region-by-year and country-by-year fixed effects. The gravity equation is estimated both with OLS and with the Poisson pseudo maximum likelihood estimator of Santos-Silva and Tenreyro (2006). Moreover, because there could still be concerns that unobserved time-varying shocks in some country-regions cell might drive both exports and the number of nonstop flights, Alderighi and Gaggero (2017) instrument the latter with its own 3 to 5 semester lags (see Box 6.2) and also with an external instrument which is a variant of the Bartik approach. They find that an increase in scheduled flights is associated with a positive and statistically significant increase in exports; in particular, a 10% increase in the number of scheduled flights would be associated with an increase in exports by about 0.2%–0.9%, depending on model specification.

Interestingly, the authors show that their effect stems only from traditional airlines; this is because low cost flights' business model is perhaps less attractive for businessmen, whereas, in turn, the possibility of having face-to-face meetings is sometimes referred to as one of the reasons underlying why airports can stimulate economic activity and trade (Cristea, 2011).[23]

[22] For instance, Volpe M. et al. (2013) use the earthquake that occurred in Chile in 2010, with the associated fall in the availability of infrastructure, as a quasi-natural experiment to estimate the impact of road networks on trade. In practice, the authors use a difference-in-difference design whereby the firms whose routes to their custom (port or airport) were not affected by the earthquake constitute the counterfactual for changes in export for firms that instead had been affected by the earthquake. They find that the damages to the road indeed resulted into lower trade, and that this effect is not associated with larger exports of Chilean unaffected firms; this last result suggests that spatial reorganization of economic activity may not play a key role in this case.

[23] Other reasons discussed in the literature are the reduction in transaction costs with the associated increase in the openness to trade, leading to product diversification, increased agglomeration, and higher productivity (Blonigen & Cristea, 2015).

There is some empirical evidence also that ports matter for trade.[24] In this case, one of the most important contributions is that of Clark, Dollar, and Micco (2004) who provide some empirical evidence consistent with the hypothesis that port efficiency is an important driver of trade. They use a rich dataset containing information on the costs of shipments of various categories of products from different ports around the world to US ports. Their analysis follows a two-step approach; first, they estimate a gravity equation where the charges per unit of weight for each product category k, which is transported between a foreign port located in a given country j and a US port located in district i, is regressed on the foreign country i's port efficiency. Port efficiency is measured either by a country-level index taken from a survey undertaken for the Global Competitiveness Report or additional crude proxies, such as the normalized total square number of the largest seaports in a country or even foreign country per capita GDP. The gravity equation is estimated with a set of product category and US districts fixed effects plus a set of controls. Unfortunately, Clark et al. (2004) cannot control for foreign ports fixed effects because it would essentially wipeout any variation to identify the impact of port efficiency. In the light of the discussion contained in Box 6.1 of Chapter 6, one can have doubts on the ability of this empirical specification to identify the causal effect of port efficiency on maritime costs. Nevertheless, a set of regressions show that higher port efficiency is correlated to lower transport charges. In a second step, authors find that a residual of transport costs derived from the gravity equation is negatively correlated with trade in a standard gravity equation.

Building on Clark et al. (2004), Bloningen and Wilson (2008) provide an interesting methodological improvement. They estimate an equation for import charges very similar to that estimated by Clark et al. (2004) in their first step for a panel covering the period 1991–2003; in practice, they regress charges in a given US port for goods which are shipped from a given foreign port, and that are relative to a particular product category, in a given year. A part from controlling for a series of drivers of charges, such as bilateral distance, share of containers, value, and weights of shipments, they separately control for US port, foreign port, product category, and year

[24] About 80% of international trade involves at some stage maritime services. Efficient and adequate port infrastructures might thus contribute to a reduction in transportation costs by fostering international connectivity and, being important nodes of multimodal transport networks, by also increasing the attractiveness and competiveness of host regions (Bottasso et al., 2018).

fixed effects. Their idea is to use US and foreign ports fixed effects as a proxy for the efficiency of each port; indeed, controlling for product category, year, and additional covariates, port fixed effects should pick up the costs in a given port.[25] They then aggregate the port efficiency at country level and run a standard gravity equation for bilateral trade across countries, controlling for year effects and country pairs fixed effects plus standard controls in gravity equations. They find that port efficiency is positively correlated with trade with a nonnegligible magnitude.

A somewhat different perspective is taken by Bottasso, Conti, Costacurta de Sa Porto, Ferrari, and Tei (2018) who estimate a gravity equation to evaluate the impact of port infrastructures on trade using information on a short panel data of bilateral exports between 27 Brazilian states and 30 of Brazil's main trade partners. In particular, the authors consider the impact of port infrastructures (measured by the total quay or pier extension in ports of each Brazilian state divided by that state's total area) on bilateral trade, controlling for Brazilian state-by-foreign country fixed effects, foreign country-by-year fixed effects, as well as Brazilian regions-by-year fixed effects[26] plus standard controls in gravity equations of trade. They find that increases in Brazilian port facilities have been associated with a large increase in exports and a smaller increase in imports. They also control for possible spillover effects, proxied by the weighted average of ports in adjacent Brazilian states, and they find evidence of positive spillovers (albeit not statistically significant).[27]

This section can be summarized as follows. There is empirical evidence showing that roads matter for international trade. This does not depend on the type of country, as positive effects are found for Turkey, Chile, Colombia, and Peru, neither on the research design. Moreover, with probably the exception of Duranton and Turner (2014) for the United States, the effects that are uncovered in the various empirical estimates seem

[25] Of course, they might also pick up unobserved heterogeneity in the districts where the port is located that might be correlated with port relative efficiency.

[26] Regions are the aggregates of a set of Brazilian states.

[27] Bensassi, Marquez-Ramos, Martinez-Zarzoso, and Suarez-Burguet (2015) estimate a gravity equation for a panel of Spanish regions and find that the efficiency of the port industry or a proxy for the extent of regional port facilities are positively correlated with trade, although the model fails to control for an appropriate set of fixed effects. Similarly, Wilson, Mann, and Otsuki (2005) find, for a large panel of countries, a positive correlation between bilateral exports and a composite indicator for air and port facilities. Similar results are also found in Marquez-Ramos (2016) for Spain.

to be consistent with a "trade creation" effect, rather than a spatial reorganization of economic activity story.

However, as far as the other modes of transport are concerned, it seems fair to say that there are fewer studies in the literature, and that their research design raises some concerns, as there is a lack both of convincing instruments and of quasi-natural experiments. In the case of ports, there are robust correlations between port infrastructures and port efficiency and international trade in the case of the United States, Brazil, and Spain, whereas, in the case of airports, one single study explores the relationship between the airport sector, proxied by traffic flows, and international trade, finding a positive effect.[28] Similarly, the evidence on railroads is even sparser; Duranton and Turner (2014) report some evidence for the United States which is consistent with railways fostering trade in weight but not in value, whereas Donaldson report evidence for 19th century India which is consistent with railways leading to more trade.[29]

7.2.2 Infrastructure and Productivity

In this section, we review the literature dealing with the impact of transport infrastructures on productivity. While we focus mainly on papers that have looked at total factor productivity (TFP), labor productivity, and innovation, we will also mention those that have brought some evidence on variables loosely related to productivity, such as per capita GDP or investment in fixed assets.

Transport infrastructures might affect productivity through different channels (see Chapter 3), both directly—by reducing transport time, and therefore reducing the costs of logistics and inventory—and indirectly—such as through specialization and division of labor, or by attracting new firms and increasing agglomeration externalities, or by reducing barriers to entry and leading to more competitive pressure on local incumbents, or by increasing communications and exchange of ideas which in turn lead to more innovation.

We start discussing the papers that have analyzed the impact of roads on productivity in strict sense. One important study is Ghani, Grover Goswami, and Kerr (2016) who evaluate the impact on productivity, employment, output, and number of establishments of a recent major

[28] See also the study by Wilson et al. (2005) already mentioned in 27.

[29] Jedwab and Moradi (2016) find that railways increased Cocoa production (which was destined to export) in early 20th century Ghana.

investment program in highways in India, the so-called Golden Quadrilateral (GQ) project,[30] which involved a massive upgrade (i.e., strengthening and expansion to four lines) of the GQ highways, which connects the four major cities of Delhi, Mumbai, Chennai, and Kolkata; works started in 2001, with 95% of works completed by the end of 2006. Ghani et al. (2016) have firm-level data (that they then aggregate into districts) before the beginning of construction works (1994) and then for 11 years following 1999. They conduct their empirical analysis on about 300 districts which account for about 90% of production in the formal Indian manufacturing sector.

Authors assess the impact of the GQ upgrade by considering distance of each district to the GQ network,[31] using a nonparametric specification, meaning that they build indicator variables for being a district located either at 0–10 km or 10–50 km from the network in their baseline specifications, with more than 50 km being the reference category.[32] In terms of econometric specification, they conduct a sort of long-difference analysis, as they regress the change in productivity (and other outcome variables) between 2000 (before upgrade works began) and the average of 2007 and 2009, on distance from the GQ indicators plus controls (district-specific characteristics such as access to other roads or railways, population, and economic characteristics) interacted with time trends, the initial level of economic activity in the district, state fixed effects, etc.

The identification is mainly achieved using the "incidental beneficiaries approach" discussed in Section 6.2.3. In particular, they do not focus on the major nodes of the GQ network, because the latter might have been the target of the transport scheme, creating endogeneity problems. In turn, the argument goes, the other districts, lying between any two of the major nodes, would have been incidental beneficiaries of the program, and therefore their proximity to the network is more likely to be exogenous. Moreover, as an important robustness check to OLS estimation, they also use IV techniques, where the distance indicators are instrumented with distance from an ideal straight-line network connecting the major nodes.

[30] The GQ project was part of a larger transport infrastructure program, which included, with different timings, the upgrade of the North–South and East–West corridors as well as the improvements of port connectivity (Ghani et al., 2016).

[31] They consider the shortest straight-line distance from the edge of the district to the network.

[32] Their results are robust to using, as controls, districts located more than 200 km from the GQ network.

Finally, they conduct a placebo analysis by exploring the impact of being close to the North–South and East–West corridors, whose upgrade had been planned together with that of the GQ but, unlike the latter, was not realized; unless major endogeneity issues exist, one should not find any statistical significant effect of being closer to a planned but not realized network.

As far as the main results are concerned, here we focus on productivity, while we refer to Sections 7.2.3 and 7.2.4 for a discussion of results related to firm dynamics and levels of economic activity. In the case of productivity, results turn out to be fairly robust across specifications; TFP is never statistically significant whenever nodal districts are dropped from the analysis. In turn, the impact of GQ on labor productivity is always positive but, unlike TFP, is generally statistically significant in districts located within 10 km from the network, whereas, in districts further away from the network (10–50 km), the impact is not significant (with respect to control districts located more than 50 km from the network). Moreover, the placebo test with NS-EW corridors is easily passed and, finally, estimates remain positive and significant when regressions are estimated with IV. Finally, their results do not seem to be driven simply by reallocation of economic activity from nearby areas.[33]

A study that uses a very different identification strategy is that of Li, Wu, and Chen (2017) who estimate the impact of roads on TFP in China over the period 1998–2007 using an approach à la Fernald (1999). This method, discussed at length in Section 6.2.3, Box 6.4, exploits the fact that some industries depend more on road services and so one should expect to find a relatively stronger impact of roads precisely in those sectors. Li et al. (2017) measure sectoral reliance on road transport by using the ratio between the value of inputs purchased from the transport equipment industry and the total value of inputs purchased in the sector, using input–output tables.[34] Authors estimate a firm-level version of the equation reported in Box 6.4 of Section 6.2.3:

$$dtfp_{it} = \theta s_{vj} dg_{nt} + \delta_{nt} + u_i + e_{it}. \tag{7.4}$$

[33] Melecky, Sharma, and Subhash (2018) use data over the period 1994–2011 and a diff-in-diff method and find that the GQ project led to a shift from the nonfarm to the farm sectors as well as to an increase in per capita GDP.

[34] Alternative proxies might have been the stock of autos and tracks used in an industry or, alternatively, the amount of services purchased in the road transport sectors as a fraction of total purchased inputs.

In Eq. (7.4), $dtfp_{it}$ is the rate of growth of TFP[35] for firms i in year t, δ_{nt} is the rate of growth of road length in province n in year t, δ_{nt} is a set of province-by-year fixed effects or other province level controls, and u_i is a set of firm fixed effects.[36]

The main result of the study is that θ is positive and statistically significant across the various empirical specifications. They conduct a large series of robustness checks. One of these rests on the possibility that a positive θ might simply reflect the effect of other variables which are correlated with roads growth and that, for various reasons, tends to have a stronger effect on TFP growth precisely in vehicle-intense industries; authors show that including an interaction of vehicle intensity with railways growth does not matter. An interesting additional result is that the effect of roads is smaller if the latter are measured at the prefecture level: because prefectures are smaller spatial units, this points toward the existence of positive spatial spillovers.[37]

As discussed in Section 6.2.3, it is important to bear in mind that the specification in Eq. (7.4) allows only to infer a differential effect between industries with high and low road intensities; only in the case of no general equilibrium effects one would be allowed to infer the impact on roads on a given industry by multiplying θ by s_{vj} and then use this information to weight-up the results across industries to gauge the overall effect of roads, as done by the authors.

[35] TFP is estimated in a first step.

[36] Note that Eq. (7.4) estimates the effects of the log level of highways on the log level of TFP. Being in first differences, the firm fixed effects are equivalent to a model with both firm fixed effects and firm specific linear time trends in a model in levels.

[37] Another interesting study on the impact of the massive investments in highways in China is Xu and Nakajima (2017). In particular, they apply a propensity score matching technique as well as a variant of the incidental beneficiaries' approach combined with a differences-in-differences research design to evaluate the impact of the expansion of highways in China over the period 1998–2007. They find a positive effect of highways construction on investment and output, with notable differences across types of regions and industries. Again, they do not find much evidence of spillover effects. Banerjee et al. (2012) use proximity to a straight-line ideal network between major Chinese cities and four historically important ports and using an incidental beneficiaries approach, to examine the impact of transport infrastructure (or, more properly, of being close to this ideal network) on counties per capita GDP levels and growth rates over the period 1986–2003. They find that closeness to the network is associated with modestly larger levels of per capita GDP and number of firms, but not to stronger growth rates.

Another study based on firm-level data is that by Holl (2016), who evaluates the impact of roads on TFP using Spanish panel data over the period 1997–2007, a time span characterized by a significant expansion in the Spanish highways network. Holl (2016) estimates TFP using the Levinshon and Petrin's (2003) approach and, in a second step, TFP is regressed on the (log) distance from the nearest highway, controlling for firms fixed effects plus a bunch of controls such as firm age and region-by-year fixed effects. Moreover, remaining concerns for endogeneity of highways distance—which, in this empirical setting, may stem both from nonrandom placement of highways and from self-selection of firms—are addressed using an IV approach based on the historical route approach. In particular, Holl (2016) considers distance from Roman roads and the 1760 Spanish postal routes. Again, conditional on controls, the identification assumption is that placement of Roman and old Spanish roads affects productivity only by influencing the position of current highways. An interesting feature of the identification assumption is that Holl (2016) is able to use a time-invariant instrument within a panel fixed effects analysis, which relies on within firm variation over time to identify the effect of interest, and therefore requires a time-varying instrument. To do so, she selects both postal routes and Roman roads that are within a 10-km corridor from the opening of a new highway each year.

The empirical estimates suggest a negative and statistically significant effect of distance from highways on firm TFP, with elasticities of about −0.02, with little variation between OLS and IV estimates. Moreover, another interesting feature of this study is that Holl (2016) controls for employment density, which can act as a mediating factor in her estimating equation; indeed, highways can increase productivity not only directly but also indirectly by fostering agglomeration. When she controls for employment or population density—which both enter with a positive and statistically significant coefficient into the analysis—the effect of distance from highways falls in absolute value, but remains statistically significant. This suggests that highways' effects on TFP do not pass only through agglomeration externalities.

Finally, Holl (2016) tackles the "reorganization versus growth effect" issue along the lines suggested by Chandra and Thompson (2000). First, she focuses on rural areas and she considers as "treated" only those firms in the 0–20 km range, or only firms in the 0–10 or 0–20 range; in this case, the effect of highways is never statistically significant. Interestingly, repeating the same exercise for suburban areas, only firms in the 0–10 range are positively affected by being close to a highway, whereas those in the 10–20 km range are negatively affected, suggesting that some reorganization of economic activity did take place in this case. The effect of being close (within 10 km) to a highway has a positive effect in the case of central cities and in suburban areas. Moreover, the effect is stronger in sectors characterized by low value/weight ratios, broadly confirming the results in Duranton et al. (2014).[38,39]

Agrawal, Galasso, and Oettl (2017) is instead the only paper to have explored the causal effect of roads on innovation (see also Section 3.6 for a discussion of models of growth, innovation, and geography). They do so by estimating the effects on innovation originating from the stock of interstate highways using a cross section of US MSAs. In particular, they regress the number of patents (or the number of citations-weighted patents) in a given patent class in a given US MSA in 1988 on the number of interstate highways in that US MSA in 1983, conditional on a set of controls. They deal with endogeneity issues using the 1947 Plan of the Interstate Highway System, the railroads routes in 1898 and the routes of major exploration expeditions already considered by various authors such as Duranton and Turner (2014).

They find that a larger stock of interstate highways leads to more innovation, with an elasticity of about 0.017. Interestingly, they do not find much evidence that this effect is the result of a spatial reorganization of economic activity; indeed, they include in the regression the spatial lag of highways, i.e., the weighted average of highways in other MSAs, using inverse of the distance as weights.[40] The spatial lag is never statistically significant, suggesting that the increase in patenting activity is probably not due to a displacement effect. Agrawal et al. (2017) reckons that, because of the nonrival nature of ideas, if a new highway reduces the cost of communication and collaboration, and therefore makes a more distant idea

[38] A positive effect on productivity, measured as output per worker, on incumbent firms affected by a road upgrade is found also by Gibbons et al. (2017), which we describe in Section 7.2.3.

[39] Similar results are also obtained by Holl (2012) who analyzes the impact of market potential on productivity for a panel of Spanish firms. Market potential for a firm depends on travel times to other nearby markets, and the travel times are directly affected by new highways. Holl (2012) finds a positive impact on improvements in market potential (induced by improvements in the availability of highways) on firm productivity.

[40] In the spatial econometrics terminology, they have estimated a Spatial Lag Model (SLM).

easier to be shared, it does not prevent inventors in other areas of the country from using that idea. Finally, they show that it is smaller firms that reap most of the benefits from the construction of highways in terms of higher innovation, and that highways tend to have a larger effect in those regions with lower population density because inventors are sparser and communication would have been more difficult in the absence of the road. With respect to the evidence presented in this paper, we believe it should be acknowledged that the data refer to the 1980s and it remains to be seen how useful will highways still be today, in the light of the IT revolution occurred in the past 20 years.

Turning to the effects of railways on productivity outcomes, we can mention the works by Ahlfeldt and Feddersen (2017) and Yu (2016). The first, already discussed in Box 6.5 of Section 6.2.3, is a counterfactual impact evaluation of the high-speed rail link connecting Cologne and Frankfurt in Germany. They evaluate the impact of the high-speed rail program by focusing on three counties that have been incidentally "treated"[41] by the high-speed railway.[42] They estimate a diff-in-diff type of analysis where not only do they control for county and year fixed effects but they also allow for a short- and a long-run impact on the level of the outcome variables, while controlling for pretrends in both treated and control counties by means of a full set of time trends interacted with treatment status.[43] The analysis is run using, as control units, either a large set of untreated counties or a synthetic control[44] for each treated county. The authors' preferred specification, which is based on the synthetic controls, finds a cumulative effect on GDP in the order of 8% after 6 years, with similar values for the three treated counties. The effect is very similar for GDP per worker, a proxy for labor productivity, suggesting that the additional GDP is due to the higher productivity of the labor force. As argued by the authors, the impact on growth can be

[41] Authors discuss also at length why the routing of the track is chiefly the results of geographical constraints, construction costs, as well as environmental concerns rather than regional development considerations.

[42] In this case, a city is treated when the high-speed railway stops in its area.

[43] In practice, they model the short-term impact of the high-speed rail on the level of the outcome variable through the interaction of an indicator variable for treated counties with a "posttreatment" dummy. Moreover, they model the long-run effect by interacting the posttreatment dummy with the indicator for treated counties multiplied by a linear time trend.

[44] See Box 6.5of Section 6.2.3.

explained by the fact that the availability of an intermediate stop of a high-speed rail leads to a large increase in the accessibility of formerly peripheral areas, which usually offer low land prices and thus become attractive for new firms. It is also possible that the impact occurs through higher productivity because of a composition effect; indeed, authors also show that the effects they find are due to financial services and other nonpublic services, which may have higher relative productivity.

In turn, Yu (2016) discusses the impact of recent high-speed rail upgrades in China that have improved the accessibility of important nodal districts but have left the peripheral areas bypassed by the new services. Yu (2016) does not use IV approaches, but rather employs a diff-in-diff type of specification for the period 2002–09 coupled with an incidental beneficiaries approach[45]; in particular, authors compare counties along the upgraded high-speed railways to a set of counties that were not affected, before and after the upgrade. They find a reduction in GDP and GDP per capita, largely driven by a fall in investment in fixed assets.[46] Yu (2016) explains this result arguing that transport investments that reduce the costs of moving people in some peripheral areas between large urban centers, as in the case of a high-speed rail upgrade, might turn out to increase the economic activity of core urban areas, at the expense of peripheral ones.[47] Moreover, empirical results show that most of the negative effect is concentrated in the service sector.

Somewhat different results are obtained by Lin (2017) who estimate a diff-in-diff model for a panel of Chinese prefecture cities over the period 2003–13. The sample is different from Yu (2016), given that the author focuses on the urban core and, to make treatment and control units more comparable, he focused only on cities with a high-speed rail that was built over the sample period or that was scheduled up to 2014. The study examines the impact of high-speed rail on a number of outcomes such as

[45] The authors focused on counties between major nodes that have been excluded from the analysis.

[46] They report a test à la Autor (2003), discussed in Section 6.2.3, which shows that pre-trends in the data, which could invalidate their diff-in-diff research design, are not likely to be important.

[47] Yu (2016) brings also some empirical evidence supporting this interpretation. Indeed, the negative effect on GDP is smaller in the case of counties with highways access; in these areas the commuting costs to large urban areas might have already been low and the availability of a high-speed rail connection might not have significantly changed commuting costs, unlike in counties with no highways connections.

employment, skilled employment, employment in different types of sectors, GDP, fixed investment, and patents. Another interesting novelty of the study is that not only does the author consider dummies for connection to high-speed rail but also a market access variable that depend on the presence of high-speed rail in other towns.[48] The study finds positive effects of high-speed railways on employment, particularly in skilled employment and tourism. There are important specialization effects associated with railways, because the effects are even stronger in industries with a larger share of nonroutine cognitive skill tasks. However, the authors also provide empirical evidence consistent with the idea that not only are there redistributive effects across sectors but also positive ones on overall GDP, employment, and even innovation (measured by patents), the latter, however, only after some years.

Turning to airports, the most complete and accurate empirical study is perhaps the counterfactual impact evaluation of Gibbons and Wu (2017). In particular, they assess the impact of airports by analyzing the impact on firm productivity due to reduced travel time as well as to the access to a wider market. They do not evaluate the impact of airports by simply proxying it with their presence in a given area or with their expansion in terms of passengers. Rather, the authors consider a treatment variable that is a continuous measure of access to population, often labeled as "market access" (Donaldson and Hornbeck, 2016). In particular, Gibbons and Wu (2017) compute, for a given county, an "air accessibility" index which computes the travel time from that county to the five nearest airports and, from that airport, to all other possible destination airports in China. As any market access index, it is a function of relative distances, population, and travel time. However, Gibbons and Wu (2017) constructs the index in such a way that its changes over time occur for two reasons only: first, because new airports are built, which in turn reduces the travel time that is necessary, in some counties, to get to the nearest airports; second, because a new airport changes the pattern of air–side linkages between airports.[49]

[48] Market access of a given city is given by the sum of population in other cities, weighted by the travel costs between any two pair of cities. See Lin (2017) for a description of the construction of various market access variables employed in the paper.

[49] See Gibbons and Wu (2017) for more details on how the index is computed.

Authors then estimate the impact of the air accessibility index on output by estimating a production function, where counties or county industries are the units. More in detail, they estimate their empirical model in long differences, so that they eliminate county fixed effects, which constitute one of the more likely sources of endogeneity. Nevertheless, also this diff-in-diff type of analysis might still be subject to endogeneity biases in the case of differences in pretrends across treatment and control units, or if shocks occurring at the same time of the change in the accessibility index are important. They deal with that endogeneity issue in two ways.

First, they employ a refined version of the by now well-known "incidental beneficiaries approach" and focus on counties that are within spatial buffer zones between existing airports at the beginning of the sample period and new airports built within the sample period. By doing this, they include in the sample two types of counties: those that are affected by the construction of the new airports both because they enjoy a reduction in distance to their nearest airports and because of a change in air—side network expansion and those counties which instead are affected only by a change in air—side network expansion, given their preferred airport is still the closest, even after the opening of the new airport. The authors follow this strategy because, by discarding the counties where new airports are located, they ensure that the counties included in the sample are not the target of the policy; moreover, by focusing on nearby airports they also make counties more comparable; third, changes in air accessibility is due to changes in the set of nearby airports, and these changes are essentially random because they depend on the distance relative to existing and newly constructed airports.

Second, Gibbons and Wu (2017) also implement an IV approach, using as instrument the location of military airports that were built before 1949 and that were subsequently converted to civil use. More in detail, distance from the nearest military airport converted to civil use is used as an instrument for the accessibility index; the validity of this instrument is justified on the grounds that both the construction of military airports pre-1949 and their conversion to civil ones in the post-Mao period were largely unrelated to economic development considerations.[50]

[50] They also carry out a placebo test using airports that had been planned but not subsequently opened to generate changes in the air accessibility index.

More in detail, Gibbons and Wu (2017) estimate various production functions augmented with the accessibility index, i.e., they control for inputs assuming a translog production function (see Section 6.1.1), which in turn allows the estimates to be interpreted as the impact of airport expansion on TFP. The main results show that improvements in air accessibility have large effects on output and therefore productivity. Interestingly, no effect is found in a larger sample that includes all units, suggesting that policy-makers tend to target underdeveloped areas. Positive impact of new airports is instead found neither on wages nor on urban consumption or employment, whereas a positive impact on GDP and fixed investment is found. There are also important heterogeneities in the estimated effects, as counties industries with a larger share of small firms, of nongovernment-owned firms and counties with higher population density are those benefiting the most from airport expansion.

Arbues, Banos, and Mayor (2015) have investigated the impact of airports on productivity in a panel of Spanish regions using spatial econometric techniques. Arbues et al. (2015) have estimated a production function augmented with the stock of airports, motorways, ports, and airports, and they attempt to deal with the endogeneity bias with a variant of the Bartik instrument approach, i.e., instrumenting the growth in the capital stock of a given transport mode in a region with the correspondent growth in Spain; they do not find any statistical significance direct or indirect impact of airports on productivity.[51]

Finally, a positive impact of airport activity on per capita income (a proxy for productivity in a local area) is reported by Blonigen and Cristea (2015), for a sample of US MSAs.[52]

In the case of ports, the empirical evidence on their impact on productivity is really scant and, by large, it is not framed into a causal setting. One study is the already-mentioned work by Arbues et al. (2015), who do

[51] Cohen and Morrison-Paul (2003) estimate a cost function with the share equations (See Section 6.1.2) for the manufacturing sector of the 50 US states over the period 1982–96 and find that states with a higher stock of airports tend to have lower costs associated with savings in material and labor costs. They also find evidence of positive spillovers, meaning that a higher stock of airport capital in nearby states is associated with lower costs. A study indirectly related to productivity is Fageda (2017) who finds evidence that the availability of direct flights with higher frequencies are correlated with more foreign direct investments to the region of Catalonia in Spain.

[52] See Section 7.2.4 for a discussion of this study.

not find strong evidence for a significant effect of ports on productivity.[53] In turn, using the cost function approach (see Section 6.1.2) for a panel of US states, Cohen and Monaco (2008) find evidence of a negative correlation between a state production costs and the stock of port infrastructure in that state. Interestingly, they also find some evidence of negative spillovers associated with the stock of ports in neighboring states, meaning that higher port infrastructures in neighboring areas are associated with higher costs in a given state. Similarly, Cohen and Monaco (2009) estimate a translog production function for the retail sector in a panel of counties in California and do not find any correlation with the stock of ports in the country, but positive spillovers from neighboring ones.[54]

The evidence surveyed in this section seems to point toward a positive impact of transport infrastructure on productivity. For instance, all papers that we have reviewed find a positive impact of roads on productivity or innovation, although Holl (2016) finds some evidence consistent with a spatial reorganization effect, unlike Ghani et al. (2016), Agrawal (2017) and Li et al. (2017) whose results seem more consistent with a net positive effect of roads on productivity.

In the case of railroads, we find conflicting results; indeed, while Ahlfeldt and Feddersen (2017) find a positive impact on per capita GDP in the case of three German cities that have been connected to large urban centers by means of a high-speed rail link, Yu (2016) finds, in the case of China, that the construction of a high-speed train has led to lower GDP per capita in counties connected to the network relatively to unconnected counties. By way of contrast, Lin (2017) finds, again for China, but this time for a sample of urban centers, a positive effect of high-speed rail on patenting activity.

Finally, the empirical evidence on both ports and airports is quite limited, although probably more geared toward finding a positive effect on productivity.

[53] Using a spatial econometric setting, they compute direct, indirect, and total effects; although they find some evidence for a negative direct impact, they cannot reject the hypothesis of a zero total effect of port infrastructures.

[54] Again in a spatial econometrics setting, Bottasso et al. (2014) find that port activity is positively and significantly correlated with regional per capita GDP using a sample of EU NUTS3 regions.

7.2.3 Infrastructure and Firm Dynamics

In this section, we analyze the impact of road infrastructure on firm dynamics, meaning the role that transport infrastructure plays on firm creation and relocation, on number of firms and probability of survival or on employment and growth in young versus more established firms.[55]

One relevant study is Gibbons, Lyytikainen, Overman, and Sanchis-Guarner (2017) who use UK firm-level data over the period 1997–2008 to investigate the impact of a series of road improvements on employment, firm formation, and labor productivity. They do this by considering the overtime variation in travel time in the electoral words that are located near the road improvement schemes; the idea of selecting the sample in this way is that the purpose of each individual road scheme was that of increasing the performance of the overall road network and not that of fostering the economic development of nearby words, which in fact, on average, account for about 6000 people only. Moreover, Gibbons et al. (2017) use very detailed data to construct a measure of road accessibility for each word, following a procedure similar to that outlined in Gibbons and Wu (2017) discussed above.

The identification strategy is not based on IV, but with OLS with word (or plant, depending on the empirical specification) fixed effects. They identify the effects of roads through within word changes over time in the accessibility index. However, Gibbons et al. (2017) argue that, conditional on various controls, they should be able to identify the causal effects of roads for various reasons. First, they focus on words that fall within 20 km from 1 of the 31 road schemes they were able to identify; in other words, all units considered in this study are "treated," because they are near the road

[55] We have not been able to identify recent studies on the impact of other modes of transport on firm dynamics. There are some exceptions in the case of airports. For instance, Blonigen and Cristea (2015)—that we review in Section 7.2.4—report a few regression results showing an increase in the growth rate of the number of firms following an increase in the activity of local airports. Similarly, McGraw (2017) estimates the effects of an airport hub on a panel of US MSAs observed over the period 1978–2012 using an event–study approach and finds positive effects of hub airports on regional income and number of firm creation using a panel fixed effects approach. Similarly, Bilotkach (2015) reports, for the US case, a significant effect of airport activity, measured by the number of destinations, on local employment and the number of firms using a GMM approach with internal instruments à la Arellano and Bover (1995). Moreover, Strauss-Khan and Vives (2009) find that the availability of good airport facilities significantly affects multinational firms' relocation decisions.

upgrade; however, the intensity of treatment can vary,[56] even if this variation is unlikely to be driven by local development policy considerations. Intuitively, the idea here is that being closer to a road scheme is essentially random, after controlling for differential trends in the outcome variable associated with each road scheme as well as for additional pretreatment controls. The identification approach pursued by Gibbons et al. (2017) is therefore yet another variation of the incidental beneficiaries' approach.

The baseline results using word-level regressions show that an increase in accessibility is associated with an increase in both employment and the number of plants; the effects are particularly strong in the manufacturing, producer services, and other service sectors in the case of the number of plants, and only in the last two industries in the case of employment. The microlevel data available to the authors allow them to test whether the increase in employment is generalized or whether it arises simply because of entry of new firms. The plant-level regressions, estimated with a full set of plant fixed effects, suggest that increases in accessibility are associated with lower employment. Because the plant fixed effects are location specific, changes in accessibility are due to road improvements, and not to firms changing location; this evidence suggests that road improvements lead to a reduction in employment by incumbents; however, the latter is more than counteracted by a strong increase in the number of plants. Moreover, additional results suggest that the reduction in employment by incumbent firms is associated with an increase in productivity, measured as output per worker, in wages and in the purchase of goods and services. These results suggest that road upgrades improve overall employment by fostering entry of firms that benefit from reductions in transport costs; however, incumbent firms, probably because of increases in wages, shed employment and increase productivity. Finally, results are robust to changing the distance from the road scheme: this in turn suggests again that results might not be simply driven by firm relocation. The paper by Gibbons et al. (2017) is important because it provides empirical evidence on various outcomes following minor improvements in the case of an already well-developed road

[56] Indeed, two words at the same distance from a road upgrade scheme could see a differential improvement in their road accessibility index, depending on whether the new scheme affects a node of the network that was already used by firms in a given word or not, because in the latter case the improvement in accessibility would only occur indirectly through a reduction in congestion in other nodes of the network.

network of a highly developed country, unlike in most studies that are reviewed in this chapter.

Another interesting study on the role played by highways construction on firm dynamics is Holl (2016) for Spain, which has been already reviewed in Section 7.2.2. In particular, she showed that the firms that have relocated into a 10-km highway corridor tend to be young ones if the relocation was to a central city location, older and with low productivity if relocating to a rural area and young and high productivity ones if relocating to a suburban location. Given the limited mobility of firms in her sample, Holl (2016) suggests that the effects on TFP uncovered in her main analysis are largely driven by incumbent firms.

Holl (2004a), using information on the number of manufacturing establishments for a panel of Spanish municipalities over the period 1980–94, estimates a set of Poisson fixed effects regression models showing that the construction of new motorways affects the spatial distribution of economic activity, leading firms to agglomerate near new motorway infrastructures; moreover, she reports evidence consistent with the possibility of negative spillovers in nearby areas. A similar result can be found also in Holl (2004b) for the case of a panel of Portuguese municipalities observed over the period 1986–97. The author estimates negative binomial models with fixed effects and finds a reduction in the number of firm births in 15 sectors in municipalities outside the 0–10 km corridor from a given highway. Interestingly, the author also finds important heterogeneities across sectors in the way transport infrastructures "diminish or increase the geographic concentration of firm birth in the economic core areas" (Holl, 2004a, 2004b).

Another relevant study which provides novel evidence on the relationship between transport networks and firm dynamics is Percoco (2016) who uses a sample of Italian municipalities observed over the period 1950–2001 to explore the impact of highways on employment and establishment counts. The author estimates a linear regression by OLS where he regresses changes in the outcome variable over the 1951–2001 period on changes in accessibility, the latter proxied by the existence of a highway exit within 15 km from the municipality, controlling for some covariates. Moreover, he run regressions where the unit of observations is a municipality sector, which in turn allows the author to estimate by OLS a regression with an interaction between highway exit and the sectoral dependence on road transport, in a differences-in-differences specification in the spirit of Fernald (1999). Finally, Percoco (2016) instruments the presence of a highway exit with the existence of a Roman road. Main results suggest that the presence of a highway exit fostered plants and employment growth, but not population growth, with a stronger effect in the 1951–81 period. The IV results confirm the OLS ones, although they point to somewhat stronger effects. Moreover, empirical results confirm Fernald (1999) and Li et al. (2017)'s results that the effect of roads is relatively stronger in the case of industries more reliant on transport.

Turning to non-European studies, the paper by Ghani et al. (2016), already described in Section 7.2.2, presents interesting evidence on the effects of a major highways upgrade project in India, the Golden Quadrilateral Project. Referring to Section 7.2.2 for a description of the sample and the identification strategy, we can note that Ghani et al. (2016) report a positive and significant effect of being close to the network upgrade on the overall number of plants in a district. Interestingly, for young establishments, they find a positive impact of the network upgrade on the number of plants and their employment and output levels, with very similar coefficients, suggesting that the Golden Quadrilateral Project has spurred entry into the affected districts. Ghani et al. (2016) also discuss the role of incumbents and new entrants on the levels of activity. They show that the activity carried out by firms older than 10 years (relative to total activity at the beginning of the period) increased following the network upgrade, both if we look at the number of entrants or to employment and, especially, output. However, the levels of activity due to young firms increased at an even faster rate, which in turn leads to a reduction in the share of activity at the end of the period associated with incumbent firms.

Ghani et al. (2016) show that the increase in entry and economic activity was particularly strong in the case of industries that are intensive users of land, suggesting that new firms in those industries might have located in the neighboring districts affected by the GQ upgrade; interestingly, there is no effect in far-away districts, whereas the positive effect on nodal districts (which represent the largest urban areas in India) is decreasing with the land intensity of production, suggesting some spatial sorting of industries. Finally, Ghani et al. (2016) show that allocative efficiency—measured as the negative of the standard deviation of TFP across plants in any given industry—increased the most in those sectors that were positioned along the GQ network before the upgrade.

An interesting study on Chinese data is that of Xu, Zhou, and Liang (2016) who consider a sample of Chinese rural counties to analyze the impact of expressways network (highways with toll stations) on a variety of economic outcomes. They measure treatment with the existence of at least one toll station in a given period in a given county. By focusing on non-nodal counties, they use the incidental treatment approach. Counties are divided into three groups, namely those that got the first toll station in the 2001–05 period, those that received the first toll station in the 2006–11 period, and those with no expressways as of 2011. The estimation is carried out on the period 1998–2005, but without considering those counties with no expressways as of 2011, to make the sample more comparable; indeed, in this way all counties in the sample had received one highway exit as of 2011, the only difference being that treated counties had received it before. They therefore use the diff-in-diff research design with an extensive set of controls; their identification thus comes from comparing changes over time in treated nonprimary counties versus changes in nonprimary untreated counties.[57]

They find a positive impact on the number of firms, employment in start-ups, as well as on both the overall employment levels and growth rates. Their baseline results on employment are confirmed by a placebo analysis, which consists in comparing the two groups of untreated counties in the period 1998–2005; if counties had been selected nonrandomly (conditional on covariates), one should see an increase in the outcome variables in the second group of counties (that had been selected for a highway exit although the latter had still to be constructed) in the 2001–05 period, even in the absence of a highway. The results confirm the absence of any significant pretrend. They also reestimate their baseline equation for employment by eliminating from the control group those counties whose neighbors in the same prefecture had received at least one expressway during the sample period. Results are unaffected and even stronger, suggesting that untreated counties that are closer to toll stations indirectly benefited from highways, suggesting positive spillovers rather than negative.

All in all, the above empirical results clearly suggest that road infrastructures matter as far as firm dynamics is concerned. New roads or road improvements seem to be associated with an increase in the number of firms and in the employment and output of new firms. Whether this is simply a reorganization effect is not completely clear. Indeed, a series of papers by Holl using Spanish and Portuguese data suggest that new highways are associated with a fall in the number of firms in areas that are not in the nearest neighboring of the highway, suggesting that relocation might be

[57] By primary we mean nodal cities.

important. However, in other studies conducted for diverse countries such as India, China, and the United Kingdom and for different typologies of road schemes (very large ones in the case of India and China, very marginal ones mainly to reduce bottlenecks in the UK case), there is no strong evidence that negative spillovers between local units are important.

7.2.4 Infrastructure and Local Economic Development

In this final section, we review a few studies that have examined the impact of transportation infrastructures on the size of the local economy or, said it differently, on local economic development, using GDP, employment, and, sometimes, population, as the main outcome variable.

Various studies have recently explored the impact of roads on local development, both in the case of rich and developing countries. One of such studies is the seminal contribution of Duranton and Turner (2012). They build a simple structural model where a representative consumer within a given city maximizes her utility subject to a budget constraint, which in turn suggests that the representative consumer can allocate her earnings to consumption, driving costs, and land. The cost of driving is assumed to inversely depend on the stock of roads in the city and positively on the total km traveled. Finally, the availability of land depends on the residents' willingness to drive, whereas earnings are a positive function of employment because of agglomeration economies. Given the usual conditions of equalization of utility between residents and nonresidents as well as equilibrium in all markets, the model yields a long-run equilibrium employment which is a function of the stock of roads. By assuming slow adjustment to the state–state, Duranton and Turner (2012) derive a dynamic equation for employment as a function of lagged employment, the initial stock of roads plus a set of city-invariant fixed effects, which capture the supply of land and other city amenities.

Duranton and Turner (2012) do not use panel data; rather, they regress employment growth in a given US MSA over the 1983–2003 period on initial employment levels as well as the stock of within city interstate highways at the beginning of the period plus a set of controls which should proxy for fixed city characteristics, such as population levels, geography, etc. The identification issue is addressed by using IV techniques and the same instruments as in Duranton et al. (2014).

OLS results suggest that a larger initial stock of highways significantly increases the growth of employment. Instrumental variable estimates confirm the OLS findings but point to a much higher effect of within city highways[58]; parameter estimates suggest that an increase in the stock of highways in the city leads to an increase in employment by about 1.5% after 20 years. Given the differentials in within city highways across US MSAs in 1983, a one standard deviation increase in the number of highways would account for an increase in 15% in MSA's employment, slightly less than two-thirds of the standard deviation in the period considered in the study by Duranton and Turner (2012).[59]

As noted above, the IV estimates are much larger than OLS ones; Duranton and Turner (2012) provide an interesting discussion of why they identify this pattern. They exclude measurement error because the same pattern is identified when they proxy the 1983 road stock with USGS major roads. However, Duranton and Turner (2012) note that the difference between IV and OLS might simply reflect the possibility that city experiencing negative shocks to employment growth also experience a positive shock to roads. They are able to check this conjecture by showing a negative correlation between the share of employment in the road construction industry in a given MSA and population growth; this suggests that roads are disproportionally built in areas facing negative economic shocks.

Finally, Duranton and Turner (2012) suggest that their result is unlikely to simply reflect the spatial reorganization of economic activity. Indeed, they show that, controlling for the stock of highways in neighbor MSAs, the impact of within city highways retains its sign, statistical significance, and magnitude, whereas the neighbor's stock is negative but insignificant, when controls are included.

The already-reviewed paper by Ghani et al. (2016) finds an increase in output, but not in employment, following the upgrade of the Indian GQ highways project; the size of the economy in districts along the upgraded GQ network significantly increased following the upgrade, but only thanks to an increase in productivity. Interestingly, the effect of the GQ expansion seems to have affected only nodal districts or districts within a 0–10 km distance from the network, with no effects (positive or negative) on districts laying in the

[58] First stage statistics are generally reasonably strong and the overidentifying restrictions are easily passed when control variables are included in the empirical specifications.

[59] Finally, Duranton and Turner (2012) conduct a similar empirical exercise as far as it concerns the employment effects of railways. Using OLS, they find a negative correlation between population growth between 1920 and 2000 and the stock of railroads in 1898.

10–50 km range; again, this evidence points toward the existence of a net effect of transport infrastructure on economic activity, and not simply a spatial reorganization type of effect.

Similar results are obtained by Gibbons et al. (2017) for a very different type of road upgrade (very minor compared with the massive investments associated with the GQ highways project) in the United Kingdom[60]; indeed, the authors find an increase in employment in areas around the small road projects considered in their study, with the increase in employment that derives entirely from new entrants, with incumbents that shed employment and increase their productivity. Also in this study there is little evidence of a spatial reorganization type of effect.

An expansion in the level of economic activity captured by an increase in employment growth following the construction of the Italian highways system over the period 1951–2001, particularly in transport-intensive sectors, is found by Percoco (2016).[61] Interestingly, he does not report any statistically significant increases in the rate of growth of population, which seems to suggest that the effect of the highways system might have worked through the creation of new jobs (also associated with the increase in the number of plants) and an increase in labor force participation rates rather than through an increase in city size.

A series of studies have recently investigated the impact of the major construction and upgrade programs undertaken in China in the past decades.

Faber (2014) examines the impact of the trunk highways system that was built in China between 1993 and 2003 on GDP, value added of various sectors, population, and government revenues over the period 1997–2006. Unlike other studies, he does not focus on large cities because their connection might have been the target of the road construction scheme, creating an endogeneity problem; by focusing on smaller cities, the author thus follows an incidental beneficiaries approach to identification. The presence of highways within a county is measured by the existence of a connection. As in many other studies, Faber uses not only OLS but also IV, where the highway connection is instrumented with distances from a hypothetical least cost path spanning tree network, that should tackle remaining

[60] See Section 7.2.3 for a discussion of the sample, methodology, and identification issues in Gibbons et al. (2017).

[61] See Section 7.2.3 above for a description of the methodology as well as the identification strategy.

concerns associated with nonrandom connections to the highway network.[62] In this study, the treated units are therefore peripheral counties that become randomly connected to the highway network simply because they happen to be placed between major nodes, whereas the control ones are peripheral nonconnected counties. Faber (2014) finds that, following the connection to the highways network, local GDP falls in the peripheral connected counties relative to the peripheral nonconnected ones, mainly because of a reduction in industrial output. Faber (2014) argues that his result might be consistent with two underlying theoretical explanations.

The first links the fall in output in connected peripheral counties to interregional trade integration. Indeed, various new-economic geography models have highlighted the existence, under certain conditions, such as increasing returns to scale, of core-periphery dynamics, whereby transport costs reduction leads to a strengthening of concentration forces toward the largest markets, mainly the urban ones. Similarly, as discussed by Faber (2014), in constant returns to scale neoclassical models of trade, in the presence of location-specific characteristics leading to comparative disadvantage in industrial production in peripheral areas, a fall in trade costs might lead to a shift of part of production toward large urban centers.

In turn, the same result found by Faber (2014) could be consistent with the (very) localized effects of a highways network expansion on the peripheral counties along the network, with respect to non—connected peripheral counties, along the lines of Baum-Snow (2007)—who, for the United States, found that an increase in the amount of interstate highways within metropolitan areas lead to a process of suburbanization, with a significant decline in central cities' population.

Faber (2014) shows that his results are more likely to be consistent with a reduction in trade costs story; indeed, connected peripheral counties in his sample do not experience any population decline or reduction in the urban share of population; moreover, he does not find evidence that unconnected counties near a connected one benefit from the highways expansion, as it would be implied, in both cases, by a suburbanization story á la Baum-Snow (2007). This lack of evidence indirectly backs the trade integration story, which is further supported by empirical evidence showing that the fall

[62] Faber (2014) builds a hypothetical road network that would have been constructed by central planners had their goal was only that of connecting, along a continuous network, the main city nodes, subject to a global construction cost minimization constraint.

in GDP is less strong in the case of peripheral counties with larger pretreatment market size and larger pretreatment trade costs.

A very recent study closely related to Faber (2014) is that of Baum-Snow, Henderson, Turner, Zhang, and Brandt (2017). They use data at a more aggregate level than Faber (2014) for 285 prefectures in Han China that account for about 90% of Chinese population and 50% of the land.[63] They analyze the impact of the stock of highways in 2010 and distance from the nearest international port in 2010 on the level of GDP, population, and wages of private firms. The services provided by highways are proxied by the number of highways km within a 450-km disk centered on each prefecture city in 2010, with higher weight given to limited access highways. They instrument 2010 highways and distance from the nearest international port with 1962 highways and 1962 travel time to the nearest international port, which they argue are valid instruments, conditional on an extensive set of controls. They find that more highways cause lower population and wages and lower population growth between 1990 and 2010 on average, but with strong heterogeneity across prefectures. In primary prefectures,[64] there is a statistically significant differential effect for all outcome variables, with a total effect of highways for primate prefectures that is positive, although poorly estimated. These empirical results are consistent with those of Faber (2014) because highways redistribute economic activity from periphery to core prefectures.[65] By way of contrast, a lower time to the nearest international port leads to higher GDP, wages, and population on average, with no differentials between primate and nonprimate prefectures.

Although the previous two studies suggest that the local economic effects of highways might be the result of nonnegligible spatial reorganization, the differences-in-differences study by Xu et al. (2016) that we have already reviewed in Section 7.2.3 finds different results. It is important to recall that Xu et al. (2016) focus on a group of nonnodal counties, i.e., a sample at a more disaggregate level than that in Baum-Snow et al. (2017), and without

[63] China is divided into provinces, which are further divided into prefectures and the latter into counties.

[64] Baum-Snow et al. (2017) defined a given prefecture as primate if, on the basis on 1982 population and travel time, it has the largest population within a 360-min drive over the 1962 road network at 90 kmph.

[65] Baum-Snow et al. (2017) show also some cross sector heterogeneity in the impact of highways. By way of example, highways have a positive impact in employment in agriculture of both types of prefectures, whereas employment in manufacturing and traded services reflect the aggregate effects.

the most important centers, which are often the nodes in a highway network. Their empirical results suggest that, in treated counties, defined as those receiving at least one highway exit, employment tends to grow, on average. However, unlike Baum-Snow et al. (2017) and Faber (2014), they do not find strong evidence in support of a spatial reorganization effect because, when they reestimate their equation after eliminating from the control groups those counties with a neighbor in the same region that had received at least one expressway exit during the sample period, results are unaffected and even stronger. This result suggests that untreated counties that are closer to toll stations benefited from highways indirectly, pointing toward the existence of positive spillovers across counties.

Positive effects of highways on Chinese local development are also uncovered by Xu and Nakajima (2015),[66] who analyze the effect of highways expansion on a sample of counties using a difference-in-difference approach combined with matching and an incidental beneficiaries approach. In general, they find positive effects on investment and industrial output, with the effect that varies depending on the distance from large cities. In particular, they find that the effect follows an inversed-U shape, as it is virtually zero for counties very near to large urban centers, where the agglomeration effects discussed by Faber (2014) dominates, quite large and positive for counties at intermediate distances (in the 250–400 km range), where dispersion forces are perhaps relatively more important than the agglomeration ones, to gradually fall to zero when distance further increases. Moreover, the authors test for spillover effects by focusing on counties that did not receive one highway connection during their sample period and test whether counties located in prefectures with at least one highways connection displayed stronger output growth with respect to other unconnected counties located in prefectures without any highway connection; interestingly, they do not find any statistical significant difference across these two types of untreated counties.[67]

A small number of studies have also analyzed the impact of railways and, in particular, high-speed railways on local development. Although most papers analyzing the impact of railways look at historical data, those on high-speed trains necessarily reflect contemporary data, both for the case of developed and developing countries. The role played by high-speed railways is interesting because, unlike highways, which usually reduce the costs of

[66] See Section 7.2.2 above.

[67] A positive impact of being close to a highway on municipal employment and population is also found by Holl (2016) for the case of Spain. See Section 7.2.1 above.

moving both people and goods, railways facilitate human interactions, but they barely affect trade costs, as noted by Ahlfeldt and Feddersen (2017). This might have important implications as far as the economic development of peripheral areas is concerned; indeed, as we have noted in several places in this and other chapters, the impact of transportation infrastructure improvements that follow from the reduction in trade costs in peripheral areas might either be positive or negative, depending on preexisting conditions associated with the size of the market, the importance of agglomeration economies, land prices, transportation costs, and so on.

Two recent studies have explored the economic effects of high-speed railways in China. The first is the paper by Qin (2017) that we have already reviewed in Section 7.2.2 above. This paper looks at the impact on counties that "received" an upgrade of their railways to high-speed level. The treated units are counties located along the upgraded lines, whereas those located along the unaffected railways lines constitute the control group. The study combines a diff-in-diff approach to identification together with the incidental treatment identification strategy. As we have already noted above, the upgrade of the railway network is associated with a drop in GDP, essentially because of a fall in fixed investment. Interestingly, the result is confirmed when the author drops from the control group all counties that are close to the upgraded railway. In general, this study lends some support to the hypothesis that the fall in GDP is due to a diversion of economic activities toward more populous urban districts. The second paper is that by Lin (2017) that we have already discussed in Section 7.2.2 above. Here we may recall that they focus on 278 prefecture level data (only relative to the urban core, not rural areas) using data from 2003 to 2013, and that they find evidence of reallocation effects across industries but also empirical results supporting the existence of net aggregate effects on GDP, employment, and house prices.[68]

[68] Zheng and Kahn (2013) present empirical evidence for China suggesting that the rate of growth in prefectures house prices over the period 2006–10 was positively affected by the rate of growth of market potential which, in their paper, can grow only because the city was connected to the high-speed rail network, by construction. Their empirical model, estimated with both OLS and IV (using connection to the railways network on 1961 and the presence of major troops in 2005 as instrument for market potential), suggests that once a city is connected to the high-speed rail network, that city becomes more attractive, which in turn leads to higher house prices. Other studies on the effects of high-speed railways on city prices are Diao, Zhu, and Zhu (2017), among the others.

As far as the case of developed countries is concerned, we can mention the study by Ahlfeldt and Feddersen (2017), which we have reviewed in both Section 7.2.2 and in Box 6.5 of Section 6.2.3, to which we refer for a description of the methodology and the sample. Here we can recall that the three German cities that have been connected with intermediate stops to the high-speed railways network experienced a large increase in GDP (but not in employment) in the order of 8.5% after 6 years. While not related to high-speed rail, Garcia-Lopez (2013) provide an interesting study on the long-run employment and population density effects of the regional express railways (RER) service in the Paris metropolitan area over the period 1968–2010. They first show, using IV and controlling for other modes of transportation, that the 2010 distance to the nearest RER service significantly reduces population and employment density in 2010, where distance to RER is instrumented with Roman roads and 1870 railroads; secondly, they report similar results for the growth rate of employment and population densities. The authors also show the existence of important heterogeneous treatment effects, as the effect decays with distance and is more pronounced in municipalities located in denser areas than in those located in the peripheries. The novelty of this study is that it provides interesting evidence on the causal effects of a transportation infrastructure network within a given metropolitan area and not across metropolitan areas as, by way of example, in Duranton and Turner (2012).

As previously noted, some recent studies have explored the very long-run impact of railways on the spatial organization of economic activity, by studying how current population depends on very early investments in rail infrastructures.[69] Berger and Enflo (2017) conduct such a study for the Swedish case. First, they estimate a difference-in-difference model with city fixed effects and region-by-year fixed effects, together with an instrumental variables strategy,[70] for the years 1840, 1855, and 1870, to evaluate the

[69] There is also a burgeoning literature on the impact that railways played on the economic development process of 19th century Germany, United States, and India that we do not consider here. See also footnote 10.

[70] The connection to a railway is instrumented through the use of a straight line connecting each set of endpoints that have been identified analyzing the network proposals. The authors then construct buffer zones of 10–20 km from these straight lines and build a dummy variable equal to one for cities that are located within these buffer zones and use that as instrument for having a railway connection. This is a variant of the incidental beneficiaries' approach that, instead of selecting the sample eliminating the nodal points, use distances from a sort of ideal network to instrument for railway connections. Additional instruments are two railways network proposals that did not materialize, yet another example of the planned route approach to identification.

short-term effects of having a rail connection in the first wave of railways investment in Sweden. Then they estimate a similar model using a fixed effects specification with decadal data on town population between 1800 and 2010. The short-run analysis finds that being connected to the railways network increased city population, with a stronger magnitude in the case of the IV regressions, suggesting that policy-makers might have selected cities with worse growth prospects. Berger and Enflo (2017) try to disentangle the effects due to spatial reorganization by comparing treated towns with control towns at a varying degree of distance from the treated ones; their empirical estimates show no positive effects when the treated cities are compared with control ones that located more than 70 kms from the network. The authors interpret this result as evidence that railways just reorganized the economic activity, although it is not immediately clear whether this result would also carry over to employment; moreover, as noted by the authors, the railways might have contributed to the urbanization of Sweden. Another interesting result of this study is that, despite massive increases in the network in successive decades, the short-term effects of having early access to the railways network in terms of city population are still existent in today Sweden, which the authors relate to important path-dependency effects.[71]

A very similar study has been conducted, for the case of Ghana, by Jedwab and Moradi (2016). The authors consider the 1901–31 period and analyze the short-run impact of being close to a railway constructed in the first two decades of the 20th century and then analyze the long-run effect of that railway. Their identification strategy works through a sort of spatial regression discontinuity design framework; indeed, their unit of analysis are very small cells of 11 km × 11 km, and they control for a fourth-degree polynomial in longitude and latitude; in this way, they are able to compare local areas that are very close to each other; moreover, Jedwab and Moradi (2016) instrument the distance from the railway with distance from an ideal straight-line network connecting the major nodes of the railways beside undertaking some placebo analysis. They find a strong and positive short-run effect of being close to the railway on population, the existence

[71] A similar result is found by Duranton and Turner (2012). Although the study is on the employment effect of highways, the authors report some regressions showing that the railways stock in a US metropolitan statistical area as of 1893 is positively correlated with population growth over the period 1920–2000, controlling for initial population and physical geography.

of cities, the urbanization rate, cocoa production,[72] and number of schools. As in Berger and Enflo (2017) for the Swedish case, they find that, in 2000, the rail connection completed in 1918 still has the same impact on population that the latter used to have in 1931, despite its de facto demise with the decolonization period. Similar long-run effects of railways are also confirmed for a sample of Sub-Saharan African countries, confirming the importance of path dependency associated with early connection to a railways network found for the case of Ghana and Sweden.[73]

We now turn to discuss the empirical evidence on the links between airports and local economic development. Two studies with different predictions refer to the United States. The first is the paper by Sheard (2014), who estimates the impact of airports on local employment for a sample of almost 300 US Core Based Statistical Areas in 2007. The author regresses the share of employment in various industries on airport size (proxied by the number of departing flights) plus an extensive set of controls and deals with endogeneity by instrumenting airport size with the 1944 National Airport Plan.[74] The main results suggest the existence of a reorganization effects across industries, with the share of employment that increased in the case of the tradable sector (mainly due to finance, retail trade, and real estate) and a relative contraction, albeit statistically insignificant, in the case of manufacturing. The absence of an effect in the case of manufacturing is quite surprising, in the light of the fact that airports should spur manufacturing activity by favoring business interactions among far-away partners. As far as total employment is concerned, the author finds inconclusive results on the level of employment in 2007 and generally positive but not statistically significant effects on the growth rate of employment over the period 1999–2011.

[72] The railway was built precisely with the aim of favoring the exporting of cocoa.

[73] They also discuss additional empirical evidence suggesting that displacement effects are probably not central in driving their empirical findings.

[74] The author uses information contained in the Plan to derive, for different types of airports considered by the Plan, a value of the replacement cost of each airport, which is then used as an instrument for the 2007 number of departing flights. The relevance of this instrument is justified on the basis of the path dependency associated with the sunk costs involved in airport constructions (Redding, Sturm, & Wolf, 2011). The validity is justified with the fact that the criteria specified for the selection of sites in 1944 were not associated with local development considerations and the choice of the site involved local authorities only marginally. This is yet another example of the "Planned Route Approach."

Somewhat contrasting results are in turn found by Blonigen and Cristea (2015) who, using data for about 260 US MSAs over a period of two decades, find a positive effect of airport service on population, employment, per capita income, and the number of firms. They use the growth in passengers as a proxy for the services provided by airports, and they deal with the endogeneity of the latter by exploiting the shock to the growth rate in airport passengers that occurred in certain MSAs following the airlines liberalization of 1978. Specifically, their identification strategy is a diff-in-diff one as they use data pre and post the 1978 shock and exploit the fact that the elimination of regulation in the aviation sector had a differential effect on various types of cities because small communities had been favored by the regulatory rules and, as a consequence, the boom in traffic that followed liberalization disproportionally affected large metropolitan areas. Blonigen and Cristea (2015) estimate a two-period panel and control for MSA fixed effects and time trends.[75] Moreover, they deal with possible remaining concerns of endogeneity by means of Bartik instruments.[76] They find a positive effect of airport passengers on population, per capita income, and, especially, employment.[77] Looking at the sectoral decomposition of the economy, Blonigen and Cristea (2015) suggest that wholesale and retail trade as well as other services account for the bulk of the employment effect, with zero effect on manufacturing employment, confirming in this case the results of Sheard (2015). Moreover, they find positive effects of airport passenger growth on the growth rate of the number of firms.

For the European case, we should mention the paper by Albalate and Fageda (2015), who investigate the impact of airports (proxied by flights of both network and nonnetwork airlines), highways (proxied by the density of highways km), and high-speed rail (proxied by the number of high-speed rail lines with at least one stop in the region) on employment in high technology sectors for a sample of 182 NUTS II regions of the

[75] In practice, they use the deviation in growth rates within a given MSA to identify the effect of airport passengers on each outcome variable. They also control for changes in local characteristics as well as for year fixed effects.

[76] They use airport traffic in cities within the same size category or information on neighboring cities as instruments.

[77] The authors suggest that, over a 20-year horizon, their OLS estimates correspond to an increase of 0.42%, 0.57%, and 1.6% in the population, per capita income and employment in the average city. The IV estimates are larger in the case of per capita income and population, again suggesting that policy-makers might be targeting local areas with poor development prospects.

European Union, Switzerland, and Norway over the period 2002–10. They use the GMM-SYS technique of Arellano and Bover (1995), which uses internal lagged values of endogenous variables as instruments,[78] and report a positive effect of passenger of network airlines and a nonsignificant one in the case of both highways and high-speed rail.[79] Finally, some empirical evidence for the Chinese case is provided by the already-reviewed study of Gibbons and Wu (2017), who report a positive effect of new airport openings on GDP and fixed investment, but not on employment or population.

Turning to the case of ports, only a few papers have explored the links between port activity and local economic development. In particular, Bottasso, Conti, Ferrari, Merk, and Tei (2013) estimate a set of dynamic employment equations for a panel of 560 regions located in 10 Western European countries over the period 2000–06 and proxy port activity with total port throughput. Endogeneity issues are dealt within the Arellano and Bover (1995) GMM-SYS framework. Authors report a positive and statistically significant correlation between the level of port activity and a region's total employment, with a very slightly larger effect in the case of manufacturing relative to service employment. Similar results are obtained, for the case of GDP, by a study of Bottasso, Conti, Ferrari, and Tei (2014) who estimate a Spatial Durbin Model using spatial econometric techniques. Keeping in mind the possible pitfalls associated with the estimation of spatial econometric models including the spatial lag of the dependent variable, the authors report strong spillover effects in neighboring regions, suggesting that port activity might be relatively more beneficial for the surrounding areas. Similar results are obtained also by Fageda and Gonzales-Aregall (2017) for the case of industrial employment in a panel of Spanish regions observed over the period 1998–2008.

The studies that we have reviewed in this section clearly suggest that transportation infrastructures do matter for local economic development. The evidence is perhaps stronger in the case of roads, railways, and, perhaps, airports, while, again, the effect of port activity on local development is

[78] We refer to Section 6.2.1 for a discussion of the limitations of the Arellano and Bover (1995) estimator.

[79] A positive correlation between sectoral employment and airport activity is also found for a sample of Italian provinces by Percoco (2010), who also report positive spillover effects from airport traffic in neighboring provinces. See also Bilotkach (2015) who finds positive employment effects of airport activity in a GMM setting.

unfortunately still a relatively underresearched theme, although the very few studies seem to point toward positive correlations between port activity and local employment and GDP. Moreover, Baum-Snow et al. (2017) find, for the Chinese case, that being closer to an international port has a positive and significant effect on local economic development. Finally, in the case of roads, most of the empirical evidence does not seem to favor the idea that spatial reorganization effects are important; however, in the case of railways, the evidence is perhaps more balanced.

7.3 THE EFFECTS OF TRANSPORT INFRASTRUCTURES ON PRODUCTION: A CONCLUSION

Transport infrastructure networks do have important economic effects; this is the unequivocal result of both the meta-analyses and our literature review. Indeed, the four meta-analyses that we have discussed in Section 7.1 report output elasticities with respect to public and transport infrastructure capital in the 0.1–0.2 range, which is definitely lower than the original estimates contained in Aschauer (1989), which gave rise to the modern debate on the productive effects of public capital, but also larger than the average values reported in the first literature reviews on the subject (Gramlich, 1994). Moreover, there is some evidence that roads are, on average, slightly more productive than other modes of transport (Melo et al., 2013), although with nonnegligible heterogeneity, depending on the industry under consideration (Holmgren and Merkel, 2017).

However, the bulk of studies that have been surveyed in the meta-analyses largely reflects the patterns in the empirical literature that prevailed over the period 1990–2010; those were often characterized by the estimation of production functions in a panel data setting, or by VAR-type of analysis in the case of time series studies, usually with relatively aggregated data. Indeed, the empirical analysis, with some relevant exceptions, was based on data at country, state, country–industry, or regional level, with fewer works that exploited data at a more spatially disaggregated level, i.e., MSAs or counties in the United States, NUTS III regions in the European Union, or firm-level data. Moreover, because most studies estimated production functions, the output elasticities might and should be more properly interpreted as TFP elasticities, because the effects of transport infrastructure capital on output which operate through private inputs is already controlled for in the regressions. In other words, the average elasticities reported in studies that estimate production or cost functions might be a lower bound for the total effect of transport infrastructure capital on production, if the latter tends to increase employment and lead to private capital accumulation.[80]

Finally, the meta-analyses suggest that elasticities tend to grow with the level of data aggregation; this result can be interpreted as evidence supporting the view that transport infrastructure networks generate significant positive spillovers across local areas that, however, are difficult to capture in studies conducted at a more spatially disaggregated level. However, establishing causality is difficult using more aggregate macroeconomic data because of the lack of either quasi-natural experiments or appropriate instrumental variables. For this reason, in the last decade or so, a rapidly increasing number of studies have explored the economic effects of transport infrastructures using spatially disaggregated data and have paid more attention to the research design and in general to identification issues than in the past.

The selective literature review that we have undertaken in Section 7.2 considers the effect of different categories of transport infrastructures on several economic outcomes, ranging from productivity to trade, firm dynamics, and level of economic development. Moreover, the survey deals overwhelmingly with studies that have put issues of research design and identification at the forefront of their empirical strategy.

The main message that arises from Section 7.2 largely confirms the conclusions we have drawn from the meta-analyses; indeed, there are few doubts that transport infrastructures matter as far as the level of economic activity, productivity, firm creation, and trade is concerned. The positive impact of transport infrastructure on both internal and international trade is particularly important because economic theory has highlighted that it is by stimulating trade that transport infrastructures ultimately exert most of their effect on the productivity and economic development of a region. From our survey, the broadly positive economic effects associated with transportation infrastructures do not seem to depend on the level of economic

[80] In practice, the existence of indirect effects occurring through increases in private inputs is closely associated with the existence of general equilibrium effects. Indeed, the additional workers might come from other sectors or might migrate from nearby areas; similarly, the stronger capital accumulation might occur at the expense of other sectors or local areas. Alternatively, the transport project might lead to a better utilization of poorly used resources, for example, in the presence of labor market frictions. The overall welfare effects of the two types of indirect effects are of course different. See Duranton and Venables (2018) for a clear discussion of this point.

development, and our survey has reviewed empirical evidence related not only to high-income countries such as United States, Germany, Italy, United Kingdom, Spain, and Portugal but also to middle-income countries or rapidly developing ones such as Turkey, China, Chile, Colombia, Brazil, and India. Overall, the fact that the level of economic development of the country does not seem to matter broadly confirms both the conclusions in Redding and Turner (2015), who reviewed a subset of the same papers that have been discussed in Section 7.2, and the metaanalysis by Melo et al. (2013).

As far as the individual modes of transport are concerned, there is little doubt about the positive effects of roads on economic development, trade, productivity, and firm creation. However, in the case of the other transport modes, the empirical evidence is less rich. In the case of airports, most studies identify positive effects on economic development, productivity, and trade. In turn, the few studies that have investigated the economic effects of port activity tend to report positive effects on trade, productivity, and local economic development, even if one should recognize that most of this small literature struggles to go beyond robust correlations in the data, given the difficulty of constructing convincing instruments or finding credible quasi-natural experiments. Finally, the evidence on the economic effects of railways is more mixed in the case of productivity and local economic development and perhaps more geared toward a positive effect in the case of trade.

One still hotly debated issue in this literature is the inherent difficulty in understanding whether the effects of transportation infrastructures reflect either a growth effect or simply a reorganization of economic activity. This is an important debate because it is obvious that, for a country, a growth effect would have different welfare implications with respect to a shift of economic activity from one region to another.[81] The most lucid account of this important topic is provided by Redding and Turner (2015), who are quite skeptical about the possibility that reduced-form equations estimated on data at very disaggregated spatial level are able to distinguish between

[81] However, if transport infrastructures could be used as a sort of "place-based" policy, i.e., as a tool to revitalize laggard regions, one might argue that it could still be worth investing in transportation infrastructure even if the investment only leads to a reorganization of economic activity. However, see Duranton and Turner (2012) for a somewhat skeptical view of this position. For a comprehensive account of place-based policies and the role of transport improvements, see Duranton and Venables (2018).

growth and reorganization effects. In other words, they think that it is a very challenging task to understand whether an increase in output in a given region, that is caused by the construction of a transportation network, is due to a pure growth effect or simply to a shift of existing economic activity from the neighboring untreated regions to the treated ones. Redding and Turner (2015) note, following Chandra and Thompson (2000), that one possible strategy to deal with this identification issue is to run separate regressions, one for the treated regions and one for the neighboring untreated ones, including in both regressions a control group of unaffected regions (i.e., untreated regions that are not neighbor of the treated ones) in each regression. Finding a negative effect of transport infrastructure in the untreated neighbor regions relatively to the unaffected ones is evidence of a reorganization effect.

However, Redding and Turner (2015) also argue that such an approach might fail too because of the complex spillover interactions existing not only between treated and neighbors but also between neighbors and their neighbors.[82] Authors think that this failure may have more important practical implications especially when researchers need to estimate the impact of large, national level, transportation projects; in this case, Redding and Turner (2015) argue that the general equilibrium effects can be impossible to pin down in reduced-form equations and call for structural general equilibrium models. However, it seems fair to say that these models are still in their infancy, and simulation based on them is valid conditional on the assumption that the proposed model is a correct and fairly precise representation of the functioning of the economy.

From an econometric point of view, the critique of Redding and Turner (2015) is equivalent to a violation of the SUTVA assumption, which is at the basis of counterfactual impact evaluation methods (see Section 6.3). In simple terms, what the SUTVA does is to rule out the possibility that the treatment of a given unit has an effect also on untreated ones, which in practice amounts, in our context, to rule out spillovers. Moreover, while the existence of reorganization effects implies a negative spillover arising from transport infrastructure investments, in practice also positive spillovers might occur, as the evidence in the meta-analyses

[82] Redding and Turner (2015) are also somewhat skeptical of the practice of including, into an individual regression, indicators related to transport infrastructures in nearby regions, as in Duranton and Turner (2012), who control for the growth in the highway stock in the nearest city.

suggests. Therefore, a positive effect of transport infrastructures uncovered in a reduced-form equation might either be an upper bound for the true overall economic effect (if reorganization is important) or instead a lower bound, if in turn positive spillovers are large.

While in the short literature review discussed in Redding and Turner (2015) only very few studies tried to test, perhaps imperfectly, for the importance of reorganization effects, the most recent works have started to take this issue more seriously than in the past. For instance, a few studies (e.g., Duranton & Turner, 2012 or Agrawal et al., 2017, among the others) control in the regressions for an indicator for the stock of highways in nearby MSAs in the United States, which however is not statistically significant in both studies and the authors interpret this result as prima facie evidence against the existence of important reorganization effects. By way of contrast, Volpe M. et al. (2017) follow an approach very similar to that advocated by Redding and Turner (2015), namely a distinction between treated, neighbor untreated, and a residual category, and they do not find evidence of reorganization effects. A similar approach has been followed by Xu et al. (2016), who eliminate from their control group the (untreated) Chinese counties whose neighbors in the same prefecture had received at least one expressway exit during the sample period and find even larger effects, possibly suggesting positive spillovers (see also Xu & Nakajima, 2015). A different test has been in turn employed by Ghani et al. (2016) who show that the GQ project in India positively affected districts in the nearby of the project (0–10 km), and that districts located more than 10 km away from it were neither positively nor negatively affected, providing prima facie evidence against a reorganization type of effect. A similar strategy has also been pursued by other authors, such as Gibbons et al. (2017), who do not find evidence that areas located at intermediate distance from a new road scheme have been negatively affected, and by Holl (2016), who analyzes the effects of highways on firm TFP in Spain by considering different degrees of distances from the highways and finds that the positive effects for firms that are located very close to the highway are de facto counterbalanced by the negative ones for those located in the 10–20 km range from the highway, in the case of suburban areas.

From these studies, there is no much evidence that reorganization effects are quantitatively important, at least as a first approximation. However, Faber (2014), Baum-Snow et al. (2017) and Yu et al. (2016) find negative impacts associated with the construction of highways and high-speed rails in China, respectively, which in turn points toward the existence of important reorganization effects. In particular, the evidence discussed in Faber (2014) lends some support to core-periphery dynamics, whereby a reduction in transportation costs might lead economic activity to shift toward the large urban centers; similarly, the finding of Baum-Snow et al. (2017) that the negative effect of highways on population and wages is not confirmed for the most important cities, is again consistent with a "core-periphery" effect. Xu and Nakajima (2015) in turn, again for the case of highways in China, find mixed evidence, as they show that the effect of highways is zero for spatial units very close to large urban centers, becomes positive for counties located at intermediate distances, and then falls again to zero at even larger distances.

Moreover, it is important to recall that not only might transport infrastructures lead to reorganization of economic activity across space but also across industries, and, indeed, a few papers have found some evidence of this type of reorganization.[83] This is the case, for example, of Duranton et al. (2014), who find that highways and railways within US MSAs tend to increase the weight but not the value of trade, thus implying a specialization-inducing effect in sectors producing heavier goods, although this result is not confirmed by Duranton (2015) for Colombia.[84] Similarly, Sheard (2014) finds that, for the United States, airports' activity tends to redistribute employment across sectors, with little, if any, effect on total employment, although Blonigen and Cristea (2015) for the United States finds not only a reorganization effect but also an overall net economic effect associated with airport expansion. Important reallocation effects across sectors are in turn also found by Holl (2016) for Spain an by Ghani (2016), who show that entry fostered by the GQ highway project in India has been particularly strong in those sectors that are intensive users of land.

It would also be extremely interesting to discuss the growth and reorganization effects for each mode of transport; however, with the exception of roads, there is not enough evidence so far and, moreover, it might not be

[83] This should be kept distinct from the existence of heterogeneous treatment effects across sectors. In other words, transport infrastructures might positively affect some sectors to a different degree or have a zero effect on others. With reorganization we mean that some sectors expanded at the expense of others, with a zero (or negative) total effect. Of course, this distinction is somewhat artificial because it is possible that some sectors experience a positive effect and others a negative one, with a positive aggregate effect for the economy as a whole, implying both reorganization and growth.

[84] See also Xu and Nakajima (2015) for a differential effect in "light" and "heavy" industries.

entirely correct to compare countries at different stages of economic development and samples at different levels of spatial disaggregation and with a different mix of rural and urban centers. However, the Chinese case is extremely interesting because China has been investing massive amounts of resources in both railways and roads (see Chapter 8), and a number of studies have exploited the construction and upgrade of the highway and high-speed railway networks as quasi-natural experiments. Again, the evidence is mixed; for instance, in the case of highways, two studies find evidence of important spatial reorganization effects (Baum-Snow et al., 2017; Faber, 2014), with four that point toward a net growth effect (Banerjee, Duflo, & Qian, 2012; Li et al., 2017; Xu & Nakajima, 2015; Xu et al., 2016). More mixed evidence in turn prevails in the case of railways, with Yu (2016) and Lin (2017) suggesting the existence of spatial reorganization and aggregate growth effects, respectively. It goes without saying that more research is still needed on this important issue.

All in all, our understanding of the literature is that reorganization effects are important, both across space and industries; nevertheless, we also believe that, in the empirical literature that we have surveyed, there is strong and clear evidence that the studies finding positive effects of transport infrastructures have not just been simply capturing the impact of reorganization. However, we agree with Redding and Tuner (2015) that structural general equilibrium models might be useful, especially in the evaluation of large infrastructure projects and hopefully one might see an expansion in their use over time. Two recent examples of such structural general equilibrium models can be found in Alder (2017) and Asturias, Garcia-Santana, and Ramos (2017), who use them to estimate the impact of the GQ highway project in India and found a positive effect on GDP and manufacturing income, respectively. This is reassuring, as they broadly confirm the results of the reduced-form single equation approach followed by Ghani et al. (2017).

CHAPTER 8
Application and Policies

Contents

8.1 TRANSPORT INVESTMENT POLICIES

Given the annual rate of growth of transport infrastructure investment (i.e., +5%), with some world regions accounting for more than 500bln USD per year (Oxford Economics, 2015), transport planning and appraisal activities are key elements connected to every country economic policy. Transport assessment, together with the evaluation of relevant impacts, has always been associated with relevant investment policies and national strategies. For this reason, several contributions have been published on these issues, by many associations and governments, to either maximize the positive impact of certain infrastructure investment (e.g., accessibility, income, and labor generation, trade) or to minimize potential negative effects (e.g., pollution, landscape transformation, congestion).

As seen in Chapter 7, several authors assessed the benefits generated by the transport infrastructure endowment. These benefits are linked to the optimal design of transport policies and planning activities that every country develops over the time. Because these planning activities are fundamental for better understanding transport development, this chapter focuses on the evolution of main international transport programs. Moreover, although the decision-making process involved in promoting transport investments is normally linked to strategic reasons, costs and benefits are normally evaluated at operational level. For this reason, it is important to highlight how the assessment processes described in Chapter 5 are embedded in major policy decisions.

Economic Role of Transport Infrastructure
ISBN 978-0-12-813096-4
https://doi.org/10.1016/B978-0-12-813096-4.00008-1

ITF (2011) discussed the importance of transport project appraisal in a special round table, trying to homogenize relevant practices at international level. Nevertheless, current appraisal techniques differ quite considerably across countries and different methods, such as cost–benefit analyses, multicriteria assessments, and I-O analysis, are sometime applied following different approaches. For instance, every country (or regional association) promotes differentiated appraisal practices to take into account national legislation and local market and business' conditions.

The need to reduce the heterogeneity of the appraisal process across countries has been recognized by the European Commission that has published the "Guide to Cost-Benefit Analysis of Investment Projects" (European Commission, 2014). The guide is a compulsory set of rules for the assessment of any EU-funded project, with a special chapter on transport projects. The document aims to introduce a homogenized approach among different recipients that are often using only national—and then different—appraisal methods. Similarly, the Australian government is promoting specific documents, such as the Australian guide for Cost–Benefit Analysis (Australian Government, 2016) to assure common practices within the Federation, as happens in many Federal countries and world regions that enjoy common source of funding, as in the case of the development banks.

The source of funding is another key element in the assessment of investment impacts and in understanding the decision-making process, often aligned to the national transport policy. An example is the exploitation of the public–private partnerships (PPPs) in the transport sector[1]; as discussed in Roumboutsos (2015), this form of funding is becoming extensively common to promote transport investment and is often shaping regional transport development (e.g., Ferrari & Tei, 2018). Moreover, different PPP's arrangements might have significant impact on the infrastructure management goals as well as in the assessment of the costs and benefits.

Transport investment appraisal is becoming a common practice, projects are often planned at strategic level (e.g., assessment of main corridors that

[1] For a general understanding of PPPs, Medda (2007) discussed the risk allocation among different players involved in PPPs using game theory; Li, Akintoye, Edwards, and Hardcastle (2005) discussed the success factors of PPPs in the UK transport sector; and Ghavamifar and Touran (2008) showed different alternatives in developing transport projects, comparing PPPs design with other solutions.

should be promoted), and costs and benefits are evaluated to better understand the feasibility and the attractiveness of alternative solutions. This multiple-step process (i.e., national framework plus specific appraisal) is often thought to increase the overall "outcome" of a certain investment and to reduce the potential lacks and subjectivity of different investment appraisal techniques. This double-layer process strongly influences the development of transport infrastructure and their conceptual planning; although in the past different infrastructure plans were developed separately, now the concept of logistics and integrated corridors is prevailing in the main national and international transport strategies. Thus, punctual projects (e.g., a rail connection, a highway) are normally interlinked with other projects, forming a complex interoperable network. Examples of this multiple-step approach are commonly found in the literature for all the main transport investment corridors, such as in China for the high-speed train development (e.g., World Bank, 2014), possibly increasing the benefits of the overall regional transport endowment (e.g., Tsamboulas, Vrenken, & Lekka, 2007 for the European transport policy).

Although the evaluation of an investment is done looking at the impact on a given region, or set of regions, the overall planning activity is normally linked to a wider perspective, incorporating specific evaluations at a later stage, also in relation to the funding schemes. Every country level and every transport corridors planning are normally characterized by this process that might also be affected by both sector related and intersector-related practices (e.g., in the case of intermodal transport corridors). Because the institutional link among public entities, local communities, and investment patterns increase the chances to achieve an optimal solution in terms of positive impact (e.g., Musso, Sillig, & Sanguineti, 2007), it is essential to study how transport policies have been developed worldwide and how the assessment of the investment (and related impacts) has been included within these transport policies. The focus of this chapter is to describe the main transport strategies of a set of countries, trying to identify how different public bodies have included the assessment of cost and benefits within their strategies. Thus, the following subsections will focus on the two main world transport investment examples, the European "Trans-European Network" and the Chinese "The Belt and Road Initiative", whereas the next section will discuss further elements, such as the funding process, that could influence the transport investment process and its economic impact.

8.1.1 The Transport European Network

The Trans-European Transport Network (TEN-T) is an ongoing infrastructural policy that aims at connecting all the European Union (EU) countries, through the implementation of several logistics corridors. The first version of the project (simply called Trans-European Network [TEN]) was included in the original European treaty (1957) and was a policy tool focused on promoting cohesion among the different European regions, boosting the internal market but without a specific focus on the transport sector. Nevertheless, during the 1990s, the TEN-T framework was introduced with the explicit aim of promoting common continental transport infrastructures and the related European transport market (European Commission, 1992). The duration of the policy and its aim has dragged relevant attention from many scholars willing to assess the effects of TEN-T projects on transport flows, investment characteristics, subsidies to transport, and environment (e.g., Burski, Mijalska-Szewczak, Wasilewski, & Szczepanik, 2016; Gutiérrez, Condeço-Melhorado, López, & Monzón, 2011; Proost et al., 2011). Moreover, the economic return of such extensive network has been often evaluated, also by comparing the impacts on different European regions (e.g., Crescenzi, Di Cataldo, & Rodriguez-Pose, 2016). These characteristics made the TEN-T policy a benchmark for many relevant regional transport strategies worldwide.

One of the main TEN-T factors of success is related to the duration of its strategic planning, started more than 30 years ago; most of the ongoing projects are foreseeing interventions until the 2030. Moreover, the initial project structure has changed considerably allowing the initial policy to adapt to the several market and economic changes; in the 1990s all the investments focused on specific infrastructures but, starting from 2004, the establishment of logistics corridors and the increased regional accessibility were seen as main goals of the policy. Eventually, starting from 2017 also EU partner countries can be involved in TEN-T projects, to increase the level of connectivity with main neighboring regions and make TEN-T strategy a key pillar of EU foreign policy. Because TEN-T projects are cofunded through the EU budget, the overall financial endowment is quite relevant and grew over the time, accounting for more than 8bln Euro for the period 2007–13 and for about 100bln in the period 2014–20 (European Commission, 2018). Nevertheless, the abovementioned TEN-T projects' value is relatively underestimated given that Member States need to cofund the relevant investments with internal budget allowing to achieve a multiplier effect in terms of actual investment and "*an estimated EUR 500 billion of financial investment is required for projects necessary for the implementation of the TEN-T in the current EU programming period, 2014 to 2020*" (European Commission, 2018).

As mentioned, the initial development of the TEN-T was linked to the reforms of the EU started in the 1990s that led to the introduction of the first 30 priority TEN-T projects. At that time, all the main continental investments were selected to increase the level of regional connectivity rather than looking at local costs and benefits, thus limiting the development of a formal assessment process of the investment impacts (at least in terms of regional benefits). During this first phase, road and rail transport played a major role with the upgrade of the main intra-European transport network. Among main examples of this first wave of investments, main funded projects were related to the development of road and rail connections between Ireland, United Kingdom, and the continent (i.e., France and Benelux); the bridges between Denmark and Scandinavia; road transport between Greece and other EU countries; and the current main Milan Airport in Italy. Only few projects were developed to create an overall European transport sector, among which were the initial phases of Galileo satellite system and the Motorways of the Sea. Nonetheless, at the beginning none of these latter policies could be classified as major infrastructure investments, but they were mainly research and business oriented. Starting from 2004, European strategy drastically changed with the introduction of the concept of logistics corridors that were aiming at developing "areas of coordinated transport development" where each country was supposed to lead the specific projects in respect to an agreed agenda. Thus, the 30 priority actions were embedded within a core network composed by nine corridors in which the priorities were acting as guidelines for further investment. Within each corridor, a series of infrastructure were included, taking into considerations ports as main import/export gateways, airports for the air traffic, and both railways and roadways for the internal EU connections. For this reason, this second phase of the TEN-T has been characterized by a strict collaboration among the EU departments and relevant stakeholders, also including the introduction of common appraisal processes as for the 2014 CBA guidelines. Moreover, EU agencies, such as the European Environmental Agency (EEA), and other institutions, such as the European Territorial Observatory Network (ESPON), have been also involved in the monitoring and planning of several projects, with the aim to further increase the awareness of the main problems and the beneficial effects of the planned investments.

In terms of funding—and taking into account that the most recent completed financial program is the 2007–13 one—Fig. 8.1 shows the chosen investments per sector.

Although the investments have been evenly developed among the EU countries, some priorities monopolized the community budget, with six of them attracting more than 50% of the overall expenditure. In particular, axes 6 (railway corridor Lyon–Trieste–Budapest–Ukraine) and 17 (railway corridor Paris–Strasbourg–Stuttgart–Wien–Bratislava) registered an investment of over 1 billion Euro during the period 2007–2013.

As said, current policy focuses on the creation of a core continental transport network, as illustrated in Fig. 8.2.

While the TEN-T budget continues to grow, the investment strategy has been aligned with relevant complementary actions, such as the collaboration with other EU and local initiatives, to better exploit the potential benefits of the growing transport network. In terms of evaluation process, all TEN-T projects include an overall policy evaluation done through specific research exercises at EU level, whereas each part of the corridors will have an *ad hoc* appraisal process developed locally by local authorities.

Concerning the evaluation at EU level, several documents (European Commission 2011, 2015) are released during the program duration to check both the progress of the construction process and the achievement of the overall policy. Thus, every 3 years the Commission promotes evaluation reports, assessing the use of the budget, the expected benefits, and the actual overall impact. This ongoing evaluation process is looking at different aspects

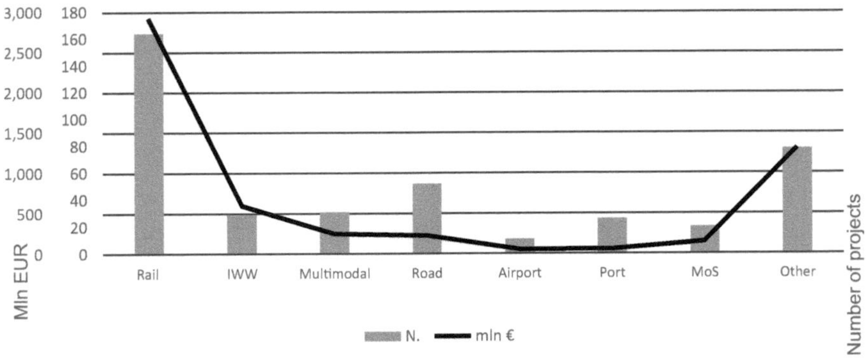

Figure 8.1 Trans-European Transport Network investment structure 2007–13 work program. *(Source: Own elaboration on EU TEN-T data, 2018.)*

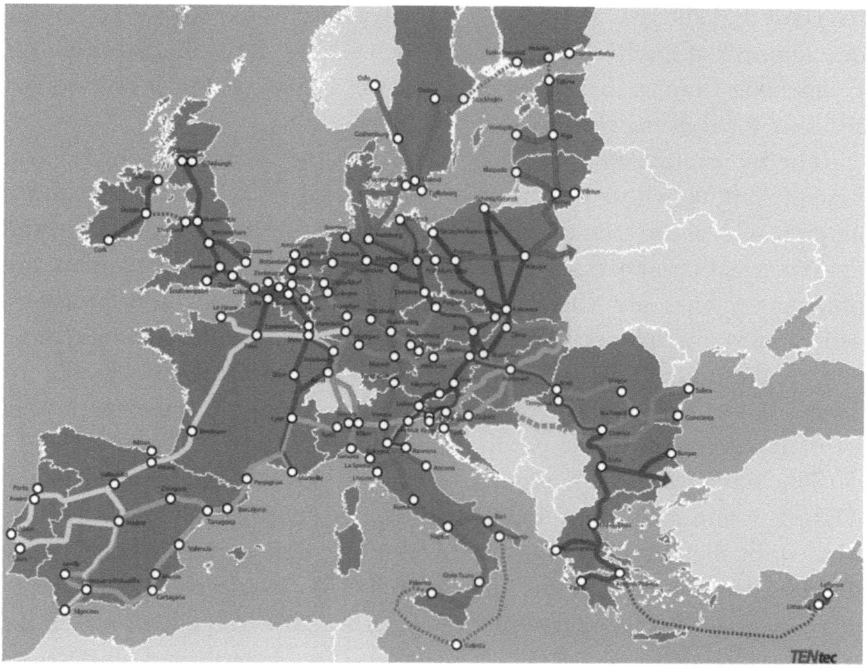

Figure 8.2 The European core transport corridors. *(Source: European Union, 2018.)*

and different sets of impacts. For this reason, EU evaluation is normally done in accordance with relevant continental institutions that represent either specialized agencies (e.g., EEA and ESPON) or industry representatives (e.g., UIC—world railway organization, ESPO—European Seaports Organisation). In particular, given the role of railway corridors within the TEN-T, special collaborations have been developed with the industry representatives to promote common standards and technologies within the EU countries not just within the TEN-T strategy but also through innovation funds, such as the Shift-to-Rail funding stream. Thus, to maximize the impacts of the TEN-T, EU introduced a series of complementary policies aiming at increasing the competitiveness of relevant transport solutions, especially taking into account environmental and social effects. Among these actions, while Shift-to-Rail is focusing on the railway sector, a series of other planning activities—like SESAR (Single European Sky ATM Research) and the European Aviation Strategy for the coordination of the air transport market and Marco Polo funding for the promotion of new Motorways of the Sea—have been introduced aiming at promoting policies and research actions to meet TEN-T goals. For this reason, also special research funding have been dedicated by the EU to solve challenges connected to the development of specific core corridors (such as the projects funded under the Connecting Europe Facility funding stream), increasing the overall budget available for realizing the TEN-T objectives.

The EU evaluation is normally focused on the achievement of relevant strategic results, whose performance is measured through general regional indexes, such as the connectivity level, the accessibility, the modal split, and the trade and transport costs. However, each of the involved partners and funding schemes are characterized by their own evaluation processes, generating a multiple set of assessments, often looking at different outcomes (e.g., pollution for EEA, accessibility for ESPON, potential modal split for Marco Polo), but with few integrated reports that could show the overall set of achievements of the corridor implementation.

The actual assessment process of every infrastructure included in the TEN-T is normally done locally during the different investment phases needed for the implementation of the relevant nine core corridors. This is possible because each of the nine corridors is characterized by a list of relevant projects that represent the actual infrastructures needed for the corridors to be completed. All these projects are characterized by different potential impacts and a different time frame in terms of investment, as well as different overall funding structures (e.g., partially EU funded, partially Member funded, and, possibly, also involving private funds). For this reason, in 2014 the EU promoted assessment guidelines as well as a methodology to identify the "correct" process to evaluate alternatives and to achieve the full implementation of the corridors by 2030. Thus, the overall framework provides the general impact assessment, but different projects will register discrepancies in the applied appraisal methods (e.g., elements included in the cost-benefit analysis) as well as in the evaluation of relevant appraisal outcomes. This two-step process partially slowed down some of the needed infrastructures due to discrepancies in the evaluation process that led to inconsistent results (e.g., the Lyon—Ukraine corridor) as well as to the lack of coordination among international partners (e.g., Lyon—Turn railway, Bratislava—Ukraine part). Moreover, the fact that these assessments were done separately provoked a misalignment in terms of construction time, often creating bottlenecks wherever only part of the corridor was completed, as for instance happened in urban nodes or within cross-border infrastructures. This latter element has also been the reason for political tensions whenever the completion of part of the corridor generated unexpected impacts in terms of competition, such as in the case of the

North–South corridors that are increasing the competitive advantage of Northern European ports due to the difficulties of the Southern part of the corridor to be built (Ferrari, Parola, & Gattorna, 2011).

Eventually, even if the TEN-T can be generally considered a success, the integration of a multistep assessment approach—often done by a plurality of actors—reduces the capability of comparing results of the assessment processes as well as of understanding the overall impact of the transport policy. Ex-ante assessment often includes flow-distribution studies as well as demand evaluations (e.g., wider economic benefits, new economic geography (NEG) approaches, demand forecasts), but only ex-post evaluation documents normally include a complete evaluation of specific impacts (e.g., I-O analysis, econometric modeling). Interestingly, none of the official documents includes spatial analysis, except from the economic geography approach.

The complexity of the inclusion of a plurality of elements in the evaluation is well defined by several studies that highlighted the lack, for instance, of health (e.g., Cavill, Kahlmeier, Rutter, Racioppi, & Oja, 2008) and energy consumption (e.g., Burski et al., 2016) considerations within transport appraisal process. Nevertheless, the most important aspect is the consideration of the overall external costs, as suggested by Maibach et al. (2008) and by the different updates of their "Handbook on estimation of external costs in the transport sector". This contribution represents the main source currently used within the EU to assess environmental (e.g., pollution, noise) and social (e.g., accidents, congestion, and risk) impacts determined by the transport industry. As stated in the Handbook, the authors registered substantial differences in the collection of relevant data, determining a structural weakness in generalizing the research results. Despite this, due to the need of standardized measures, the handbook is still considered an optimal tool to include external costs within different evaluations, potentially affecting the overall results. Similarly, the evaluation of positive impacts, as discussed in Chapter 5, might be distorted, explaining the delays and the critics of the infrastructure assessment process and the role played by the general EU strategy in promoting TEN-T, leaving the assessment of specific projects to the local authorities.

8.1.2 The Belt and Road Initiative

If the TEN-T strategy is based on a transport policy promoted by an international body to foster regional cohesion and transport integration, the Belt and Road Initiative (BRI) is something completely different. BRI evokes the development of a modern "Silk Road" connecting China with other major partner countries within and outside Asia. Launched in 2013 with the label of "One Belt, One Road" (OBOR) project, this integrated transport strategy has been substantially developed, thanks to the financial initiative of Chinese institutions. Starting from 2016, the initiative was opened to the support of international partners, mainly connected to the recently funded Asia Infrastructure Investment Bank. At 2017, more than 900 billion USD projects were already approved, and most of them already under development, demonstrating the effectiveness of the BRI policy (EBRD, 2018).

As a matter of fact, the BRI strategy will increase the connectivity through specific transport investment projects and long-term collaborations between China and several Asian, African, and European partners. Thus, the BRI differs from the TEN-T because it is not looking at increasing cohesion among different regions, but it focuses on boosting the connectivity of regions that are currently included in selected trade lanes. Moreover, main projects are strictly linked with integrated supply and logistics chains that are considered strategic to Chinese companies; and because of this, most of the projects have a substantial industrial link. Given its nature, BRI is mainly developed through land (i.e., both road and rail) and maritime integrated transport corridors, having a variety of specific international projects that will connect production and consumption sites.

Given the abovementioned premises, it is important to understand that the development of the projects is not homogenized because it strongly depends on bilateral—and in a few cases multilateral—agreements between Chinese institutions and other national authorities. Moreover, although specific corridors are identified, Chinese transport policies admit the introduction of differentiated solutions and *ad hoc* investment tools if market conditions allow for them. This was the case of the massive COSCO investment in Greek ports during the financial crisis (2012–16) as well as the foreseen investments in Sri Lanka container hub in 2016–17. Some of the abovementioned policies are also linked to new infrastructure solutions, such as the foreseen Kra Canal in Thailand (Lee, Hu, Lee, Choi, & Shin, 2018; Rahman, 2016), that will help bypassing the Malacca strait reducing shipping time between Europe and Asia of up to 5 days. Nonetheless, some of these investments are seen as politically driven rather than economically driven, given the potential threat that they could represent for competing countries (e.g., Singapore for the Kra Canal, Sri Lanka hub to bypass Indian ports) or the decision to limit collaboration with certain areas (e.g., India, Japan).

Despite the punctual interventions, BRI strategy is based on three main pillars: Intra-Asia connectivity (mainly through land infrastructures), Europe—Asia connectivity (mainly through maritime investments but also with an improvement of rail connections, especially with South East and Central Asia), and the Asia—Africa links (mainly through maritime investment and logistics improvements in African countries). Fig. 8.3 sums up these main corridors. As it is possible to check, Asia—Europe corridors are divided into three distinct investment projects: one rail corridor currently in operation that partially uses the Russian rail network, connecting Chinese main production sites with Eastern and Central European countries. The aim of this corridor is making competitive the rail solution for many added value trades, and it is currently operating low quantity of cargo reducing of more than half the transportation time between China and Europe. The second land corridor, which should pass through Iran and Turkey, is under development and international agreement is still to be signed. In principle, it should guarantee a competitive road and rail solution for the connection among Central Asian countries and both China and Europe. The other Europe—China corridor is the maritime one that will see an intensification of the flows between Chinese ports and European ports with Chinese

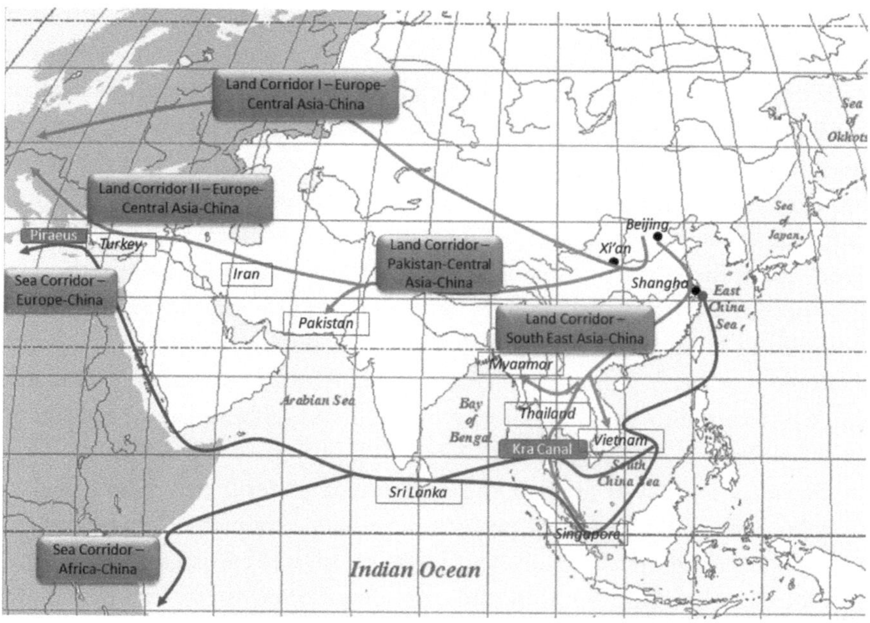

Figure 8.3 Belt and Road Initiative corridors. *(Source: Own elaboration from Xinhua data, 2018.)*

companies already involved in investment in transhipment hubs (such as Sri Lanka and Piraeus, in Greece) to acquire a regional competitive advantage in serving local regional traffic. The project of Kra Canal is also another element included in this part of the strategy.

The other two connectivity priorities relate to Africa and Asia. The African corridor will be partially overlapping with the Europe–China maritime route, apart from the final part of it. Most of the investments will be developed directly in African countries and will target port and logistics upgrades, fostering vertical integration among export-oriented companies that are currently exploiting African natural resources and production sites. Concerning port investments, several upgrades are currently under development, with Chinese companies already involved in several projects.

Internal Asian corridors are mainly land based, and they are currently under discussion due to political tensions among countries. Pakistan–China railway is in an advanced stage of development, whereas other solutions (e.g., China–Singapore railway) are still in an early stage of discussion with several countries that are not fully supporting the proposed solutions (e.g., routes within Thailand, Cambodia, and Vietnam).

When compared to the TEN-T, BRI is different not only for its objectives but also for the governance and the investment pattern. The governance of different projects is linked to the specific international agreement, allowing differentiated solutions that can go from a simple public–private collaboration (with Chinese companies normally leading the project in terms of capital investment and knowledge transfer) to a more top–down approach, where the foreign investors control all the construction and management of the project with no involvement of local partners. In this latter situation, Chinese companies normally provide also work force directly from mainland China (Tang, 2016), reducing the net benefits for the local community to the increased accessibility but then transferring most of the economic benefits to Chinese operators. This latter example has been particularly common in African investments that are strictly linked with the trade of raw material and differentiated production investments.

Another issue is related to the investment pattern; given the relative novelty of the BRI, only few projects have been completed, whereas most of them are either in a development phase or still in a bargaining phase with the local authorities. Most of the completed projects are actually pure monetary investment headed to control and/or expand existing infrastructures, as in the case of the port sector in both Asia and Europe.

Despite this, none of the foreseen integrated transport corridors has been actually developed, and this limits the possibility to evaluate the economic and social impact of the proposed solutions. Nevertheless, some authors (e.g., Herrero & Xu, 2017; Vinokurov & Tsukarev, 2018) discussed the economic value of some of the abovementioned projects for different communities, highlighting that some countries might not benefits from such increased connectivity, given either the increased competition from Chinese companies or their role as transit countries. In particular, as raised by several contributions (e.g., Du, 2016; Huang, 2016) no overall assessments have been done for most of the completed or planned investments, reducing the possibility to fully understand how this transport policy can work in the long run.

8.1.3 Other Transport Policy Initiatives

Different studies pointed out the role of local transport networks in fostering local development, as well as the potential benefits of improving the role of certain nodes (or regions) within the international networks (e.g., Ducruet, 2013). Thus, different national institutions promote transport assessment exercises together with relevant network expansions to increase the local presence in international trade and to promote local cohesion policies. For this reason, together with the two main examples of transport network investments, different countries have developed their own strategies and guidelines. Table 8.1 shows the committed amount of money (in Euro) in transport infrastructure investment for a panel of countries. As it is possible to observe from the table, road transport still attracts most of the investments, followed by the railway sector. Interestingly, China (CHN) concentrated more than a half of the investments recorded by ITF in both transport modes.

Most of these countries do follow a similar approach with an overall national strategy that assesses general foreseen costs and potential benefits of different investment choices and actual investment assessment done at microlevel by the authorities that will develop the different parts of the project. Before comparing different practices, it is important to highlight how this two-step approach, at national level, often brings a higher risk of uncertainty in the produced net benefits. In fact, it is associated with a higher uncertainty risk (e.g., Salling & Leleur, 2012) due to the overestimation of the benefits or the underestimation of certain costs at strategic level, as well as the risk of causing delays that again will impact on the actual

Table 8.1 Investments in Transport Infrastructure (2015 data)

	Rail	Road	Sea	Air	IWW
AUS	2755.64	10,513.37	1164.54	n.a.	n.a.
AZE	1.76	873.20	80.18	349.81	80.18
CAN	1056.72	5548.11	678.61	1053.19	n.a.
CHN	111,893.10	414,199.46	n.a.	26,633.22	n.a.
DEU	4750.00	11,690.00	460.00	850.00	1135.00
ESP	2631.00	4183.00	1101.00	293.00	n.a.
FRA	8569.90	8293.90	350.27	730.00	200.00
GBR	13,986.23	9046.83	n.a.	n.a.	n.a.
IND	11,462.49	15,107.53	77.29	356.35	n.a.
JPN	n.a.	n.a.	2106.10	1365.09	n.a.
KOR	8589.27	13,174.24	1326.33	83.01	n.a.
POL	340.44	2170.79	n.a.	302.43	n.a.
RUS	5022.32	6117.21	49.30	851.70	39.85
SWE	1387.67	1861.46	n.a.	131.27	n.a.
TUR	920.31	6729.76	5.96	132.70	n.a.
USA	15,687.64	85,436.19	n.a.	n.a.	n.a.

Source: Own elaboration from ITF data, 2018. Data in mln of EURO.

value of the project's net benefits. Moreover, large-scale transport projects are normally characterized by cost overruns due to several biases in the planning activity (e.g., Cantarelli et al., 2010), and this discrepancy can increase due to the differences between the corridor planner (e.g., National Strategy) and the actual project developer (e.g., private company or local authority). This normally limits the reliability of early evaluations and is discussed in all main national transport policy papers.

Thus, central governments normally introduce transport policy guidelines and general long-term strategies that will not include details of actual projects forming these large-scale strategies. Specific elements will then be added during the operational planning activity, together with the development of specific assessments. This is the scheme followed by most countries; for example, in Italy, the National Logistics Plan (formerly called National Transport Plan) includes priorities for all main transport modes, together with maritime, motorways, and railways upgrade (Consulta Nazionale per l'Autotrasporto e la Logistica, 2011).

The governance of transport infrastructure has a distinctive role in the development of the national network and in investing in different transport solutions. For instance, in United Kingdom different transport infrastructures are managed in different ways, so that the Department for

Transport releases a general document assessing national priorities in terms of investments (e.g., DfT, 2017a). Moreover, different groups within the Department release specific strategic plans for each mode of transport, such as the "Maritime 2050" report (DfT, 2018) or the "High Speed Two: From Concept to Reality" report (DfT, 2017b). This difference is needed because in United Kingdom, while the government is involved in most of the national planning, funding, and public–private involvement is different depending on the transport industry. Thus, port sector is highly privatized and investments are fully privately related; in this scenario, the government has a regulatory role and a lobbying role, but it is not normally involved in operational planning. On the other hand, in the railway sector, all the main infrastructures are owned by a public company that allows private companies to operate under a franchise system. Thus, government has the duty to plan and invest in the overall national network, as in the case of the new high-speed rail tracks.

Similar situations happen not only for the transport governance structure but also in the case of Federal jurisdictions. The Department for Transport in United States, for instance, dictates federal strategic goals for the transport investment plans for the 5-year period (i.e., current investment plan covers 2018-22) (Box 8.1) determining main goals that specific projects at both federal and state level should achieve (DoT, 2018a). Federal plans are then accompanied with relevant State plans that should act as complement to introduce local planning at both strategic and local levels. Thus, Federal countries do have a three-layer transport policy with both Federal and State strategic plans and then local operational planning. The specific project assessment is normally done at operational level, through public contractors. Similar processes can be observed in all the biggest Federations, such as Mexico, Brazil, Australia, and Germany. In some of them, the independent role of decentralized governments allows to introduce differentiated governance models (e.g., private port terminals in same Australian and Brazilian States against public ports in some other States and Federal public road infrastructures) that play a further role in the transport planning. Eventually, although the structure of the planning activity seems similar to most of the countries, the funding sources as well as the private interventions—together with the goals pursued through the investment—vary considerably. Public authorities are highly involved in the transport planning and actual investment activity in most of European and Asian countries, whereas private intervention is relatively high in the Anglo-Saxon tradition with infrastructure and service often fully privatized

Box 8.1 Transport planning in United States

US transport planning is organized in several layers; the United States Department of Transportation (DoT) is the federal agency in charge of planning (and funding) main national projects that represent the main core network within the country. Several policy papers and guidelines are then published (e.g., DoT, 2018a,b) as input for promoting federal projects. The main aim is to provide strategic resources for the development of United States in accordance with major government Acts. Despite the role of the DoT, states and local agencies are often in charge of the actual development and maintenance of most of the transport network. As underlined by Wiener (1984), most of the motorways—and in general the road network—are actually developed, planned, and maintained by states that are also in charge of the planning of the infrastructure.

This double-layered planning activity is sometime creating asymmetries within a country, with overall federal projects (as, for instance, described in the document "Beyond Traffic" [DoT, 2018b]) that should drive the future of transport in the country and several local applications. For example, in the case of driverless cars, several local heterogeneous legislations affect both the testing phase and risks involved in their development (as in the case of the tests in Arizona during winter 2018).

Moreover, the asymmetries in state regulations generate also the possibility of having different governance models among states for most of the infrastructures, with public (e.g., roads), private (e.g., rail), and mixed (e.g., franchise system in the port sector) models in the management of most of the infrastructure system. In these cases, Federal jurisdiction is normally limited in checking competition rules, whereas states are in charge of setting relevant legislation schemes as well as development plans.

(e.g., United Kingdom, United States, Australia). Asian countries are normally characterized by a mixed approach with some countries that promote publicly owned private companies that heavily invest in different economic and transport sectors (e.g., Cosco for China, Temasek for Singapore) and others that have a highly involvement of fully private companies in some transport sectors and fully publicly connected infrastructure for others (e.g., Japan, Korea, Taiwan). These differences obviously affect both the decision-making process and the planning activities together with the foreseen goals of different transport investors and the related impact evaluations.

8.2 THE ROLE OF FUNDING IN SHAPING THE TRANSPORT NETWORK

As depicted in the first chapters of this book, transport infrastructures are key factors in the developing strategy of a country (Banister-Berechman, 2000), contributing to the increase of the regional capital and increasing the investment attractiveness of a region (Stern, 2001). For this reason, investment in infrastructure affects not only the accessibility of the region but also determines higher GDP per capita and, if certain conditions are met, a more equal distribution of GDP among the population (as described in Chapter 7).

The research for a rapid economic development has been often linked to the enhancement of the local investment system. This kind of investment is highly capital intensive, and for this reason it is normally heavily linked with the need for specific funding streams. This has led several developing and emerging economies to attract private (foreign) companies to speed up the modernization of the main economic sectors, including transport (Ferrari & Tei, 2018). Moreover, different transport systems introduced specialized funding solutions to reduce investment risks or to maximize potential benefits, as underlined—for instance—by Meersman, Van de Voorde, & Vanelslander (2014) for the port sector.

Before the 1970s, most of the economies focused on national public resources to fund transport and related infrastructures. Nevertheless, starting from the US- and UK-based privatization processes, most economies have started looking for private funds to foster both infrastructural investment and to attract managerial skills to maximize efficiency. Both scientific literature (e.g., Araujo & Sutherland, 2010) and reports (e.g., IMF, 2016) highlighted the positive effects of attracting both the know-how and the capital of private companies through different funding schemes. As discussed earlier, TEN-T and BRI have partially followed this structure. Therefore, starting from the 1980s, most of the countries—especially in developing and emerging regions—have opened local markets to foreign companies, aiming at attracting relevant capitals and fostering new forms of collaborations through transfers of both technologies and know-how (Roumboutsos, 2015).

Despite these forms of partnerships helped the development of the transport sector, national interests have always influenced the real expansion of the network, such as in the example of the BRI. Moreover, different funding streams have often been connected to transnational investments, as in the case of Foreign Direct Investments (FDIs). Nevertheless, some authors (e.g., Bogliaccini, 2013) argued that international investments that increased market openness in certain world regions determined internal inequalities. Despite this, most of the studies recorded an average annual growth rates higher than before liberalization of the internal market (Wacziarg & Welch, 2008). Similarly, Wilsmeier et al. (2006) underline how the presence of specific transport infrastructure (i.e., seaports) may influence the international transport connectivity and the role of a region into the international trade network.

Thus, as discussed in Section 7.2.2, transport investments are generally considered a leverage to foster both international trade and to provide the basis for promoting internal growth (e.g., Crescenzi & Rodriguez-Pose, 2012; Ottaviano, 2008), and this issue is even more important wherever funding has been promoted through different and innovative kinds of investment policies, in accordance with specific institutional choices. In fact, although the causal relation between transport choices and government prescriptions has been often investigated by the literature (e.g., Verhoef, 2000), only recently the effects of institutions on transport investments and transport network have been considered (e.g., Ferrari & Tei, 2018 for Latin America or Gutiérrez et al., 2011 for the EU role within the TEN-T development).

In fact, the institutional choices related with the funding sources could also affect the outcome and the impact of the related investment. Traditionally, public initiative, private intervention, and international collaborations are normally the most common solutions used. Nevertheless, most countries—especially in their industrialization phase—need both funds and to fill in the missing know-how. This led most of them to promote PPPs as an important funding tool to develop public infrastructure and exploit the economic potential of a region (e.g., Makovsek, Hasselgren, & Perkins, 2014; OECD, 2013).

According to the World Bank definition (WB, 2007) and to several research papers (e.g., Hall, De la Motte, & Davies, 2003; Panayides, Parola, & Lam, 2015), PPPs are "agreements or contracts between the public and the private sector to jointly operate and/or own infrastructure projects". These forms of collaborations are often applied to several sectors (e.g., telecom, energy, health, transport) and are normally connected to the management and/or the construction (/renewal) of an infrastructure. Normally, the funding is partially assured by specialized funds, and the project developed through a specific company (i.e., Special Purpose Vehicle [SPV]) that will take care of the funding collection and of the organization and management of the project. Funding will be then at least partially privately collected, whereas the infrastructure will be managed following public authority prescription. Given the nature of the SPV, most of the project will be outsourced, generating differentiated impacts depending on the nature of collaboration with the outsourcing companies. As suggested by Hall et al. (2003), the fact that PPPs can involve also already existing infrastructure—and they might be related only to renewal or managerial issues—makes this tool an ideal substitute of the more traditional privatization processes, allowing private companies to fully control public infrastructure. Moreover, given the blurry distinction among different forms of collaborations, several reports (e.g., Araujo & Sutherland, 2010; UNESCAP, 2011; WB, 2007) treat PPP, Public–Private Investments (PPIs), Private Finance Initiative, or Private Sector Participation as the same policy tool without formal differences. On the contrary, the kind of private involvement in the projects may differ depending on the local context, affecting the nature of the partnership as well as the "ownership" of the final infrastructure that can be either completely private or public at the end of the funding agreement. Moreover, even though most of this partnership is normally linked to FDIs, the involvement of private companies is not normally only linked to this circumstance. Nevertheless, foreign partners are normally common in case of know-how exchange.

PPPs raised several critical issues mainly related to investment risk management, the relationship among the investors and the project governance organization (e.g., Chou, Tserng, Chieh, & Huang, 2015; Medda, 2007; Tang, Shen, & Cheng, 2010). Nevertheless, the importance of PPIs projects worldwide is given by Fig. 8.4 that shows the growing trend of the value of this kind of funding stream. Although the figure summarizes transport investment trend over different world regions, data highlight that Latin America and Caribbean account for the majority of the value (i.e., almost 900 mln USD), followed by South Asia and East Asia, respectively[2]. Concerning the role of single countries, Brazil accounts for the majority of the projects within the transport sector, with a share of about 22% of the invested amount, whereas India is attracting the majority of the projects. First three countries for both number of projects and invested amount (i.e., India, Brazil, and China) have a share of more than 60% of the market.

[2] Data are collected from the World Bank database. This database records all the information for the PPI projects in developing countries; for this reason, projects in advanced economies (e.g., United States, EU, Japan, Canada, Australia, and South Korea) are not included in the database. Nevertheless, this database is currently the only homogenized source of information on transport investment.

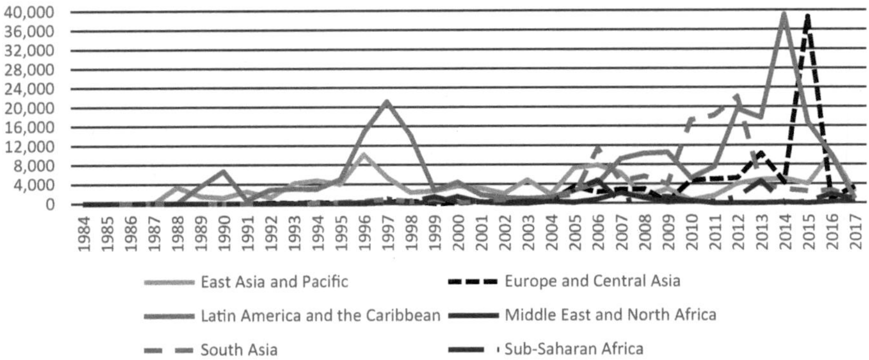

Figure 8.4 Evolution of public–private partnerships worldwide. *(Source: Own elaboration on World Bank PPIs Database, 2018. Data in millions of US$.)*

Concerning the different funded transport solutions, PPIs have been promoted often to enlarge national road networks, accounting for almost half of the value. This solution is often preferred for both knowledge transfer and for the need of relevant funding. All the other three transport modes register equal distribution of funding, as shown by the chart pie below (Fig. 8.5). It is interesting to underline that considering all the projects for which WB database gives access to full financial data, road projects register the higher private involvement in terms of provided funding (i.e., 92% of the capital invested), underlining the need for private money.

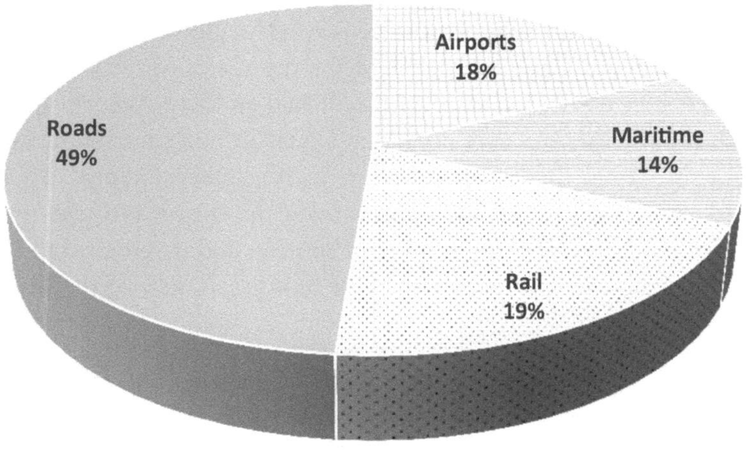

Figure 8.5 Funded projects per mode of transport. *(Source: Own elaboration on World Bank PPIs Database, 2018. Data in millions of US$.)*

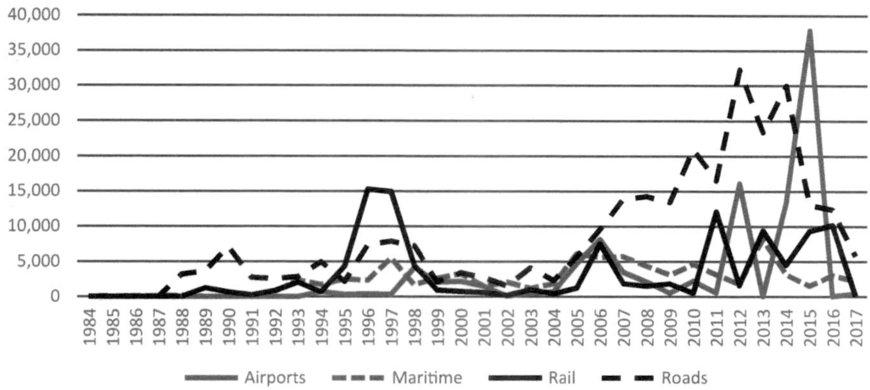

Figure 8.6 Trend in funded projects per mode of transport. *(Source: Own elaboration on World Bank PPIs Database, 2018. Data in millions of US$.)*

The concentration of PPIs in the road sector is also connected to the need for developing economies to speed up the industrialization process, increasing the overall regional accessibility through efficient motorways and paved roads. This explains the constant flow of money in expanding the road network (Fig. 8.6). Other transport infrastructures are experiencing differentiated trends with both rail and air infrastructures that are characterized by few peaks, whereas maritime infrastructures are normally collecting less financial support but with less volatility over the time.

8.3 THE LINK BETWEEN POLICY, RESEARCH, AND CURRENT INVESTMENTS

As discussed in the previous chapters (e.g., Chapter 7), several research contributions highlighted the regional benefits of transport infrastructure endowment. Several literature reviews (e.g., Deng, 2013; Kiel, Smith, & Ubbels, 2014) have underlined the link between transport and regional economies. Nevertheless, most of these contributions focused on the impact of different transport networks on regional competitiveness, in terms of trade, productivity, firm's dynamics, and general economic development, without the possibility of assessing the overall transport network of a certain region. Moreover, due to the contribution of NEG (Chapter 3), the inclusion of spatial distribution within research studies increased the understanding of the effects of the transport system. NEG allowed scholars to include the location of economic activities as well as the potential spillover effects within the relevant analysis. These combined effects are often not just limited to economic values but also in relation to both social and environmental impacts (Chapter 5). Nevertheless, the difficulty of merging different perspectives and kinds of analysis explains the current misalignment between transport policy practices and research outcomes. During the description of the main studies and transport planning activities, a clear discrepancy came out wherever macroeconomic values and assessments were not taken into consideration in the actual assessment developed for transport infrastructure investments. This fact has been investigated for all major transport policies. For instance, Purwanto et al. (2017) discussed the discrepancies between TEN-T corridor planning activities, expected goals, and performed assessment analyses. The authors highlight that current guidelines and software packages used for the evaluations of more than 25 reviewed projects—within the same TEN-T corridor—were not implementing any macroeconomic analysis nor incorporating relevant variables (e.g., GDP) to their evaluation exercise. Different studies (e.g., Lakshmanan, 2011) then highlighted the benefits of incorporating WEIs within the general assessments; nevertheless, the current practice of the evaluation processes seems to be the avoidance of full estimation of network improvement impacts, limiting the calculation of the benefits to simplified versions of the full methodologies. One of the reasons of these simplifications is often related to the difficulties in collecting reliable and consistent datasets (Chapter 4) to allow the evaluator to achieve the desired result. This problem is normally similar to the one connected to the estimation of the induced effects, often solved through the application of the so-called "rule of half", as described in relevant literature (e.g., Grimaldi & Beria, 2013; Salling & Leleur, 2011) and also included in several policy guidelines (EU Commission, 2014).

Thus, given the difficulties in including such elements within the planning activity, the ex-post evaluations—as well as the compulsory ex-ante appraisal activities—become crucial in the assessment of the foreseen investments. As seen in Chapter 7, every infrastructure network, also depending on regional characteristics, differently affects the economic environment of the studied region. For this reason, different approaches can be developed, also in connection with the differentiated transport users.

Fig. 8.7 sums up the general structure of the transport policy process, as described above. The general strategic planning is usually connected with network analyses and demand forecasts that lead the decision-making process, together with other strategic evaluations, such as the general

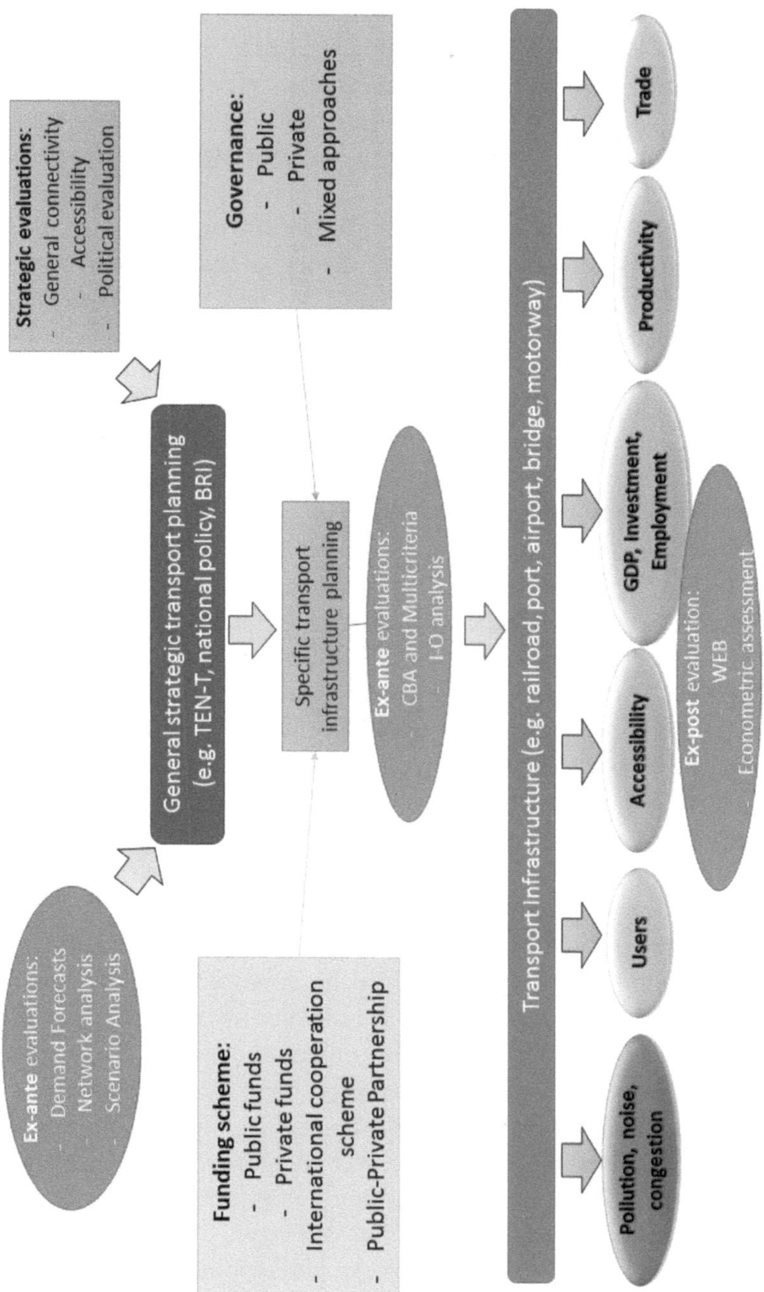

Figure 8.7 Transport investment process.

political framework. The overall strategy is normally linked to the specific planning of different project alternatives. This phase is often done locally, and it is linked with the funding and the governance characteristics of the project. Only after the project planning phase, relevant assessments are organized (e.g., CBA). Ex-post evaluations will be the only ones that include all the registered effects on the economy, the users, and the environment.

Apart from the evaluations, a key element for the understanding of the different impacts of the planned infrastructure is the funding scheme, together with the chosen governance model. As underlined earlier, PPPs are becoming particularly important within the transport sector. These forms of funding are relevant not only for the developing countries but has raised several questions in industrialized countries too, mainly in relation to their duration and the different goals pursued by the private companies involved (e.g., Ortiz & Buxbaum, 2008). This latter element is of particular importance if linked with the value of PPPs around the world. In addition to the WB database, other international statistics confirm the growing value of PPP projects, with the OECD that estimated a value of the overall infrastructure assets funded via PPPs equal to 0.8 trillion USD in 2012, just within the OECD countries (OECD, 2012). The same report highlighted how many OECD countries are registering a growing private involvement in "public" transport infrastructures, with 11 countries (out of 20) that were registering a partial private ownership of relevant national assets higher than 5% of the total public capital endowment.

Funding schemes are then crucial not only in respect to the source of the funds but also because they directly affect the foreseen governance structure of the infrastructure, normally linked to an SPV that will manage the critical operations of the projects. The governance will then affect the level of productivity and the efficiency of the infrastructure as well as the relevant impacts of the transport network itself. For instance, Bottasso et al. (2013) registered a higher impact of private ports on the regional employment in respect to public or landlord ports in a set of European countries. This finding was justified by the higher integration along the supply chain of private terminals in respect to other kinds of port. This element has been highlighted for many other transport modes (e.g., Cowie, 2009 for the rail sector or Christodoulou & Finger, 2012 for the urban transport) determining a discussion among opposed points of view between increased efficiency level due to a market-oriented approach and the benefits, mainly in terms of community impacts, of a more public-oriented governance. Although it is not the goal of this book to assess governance issues, it is important to underline that the choices made by the regulator of the market—either in a private or a public governance model—normally have a great effect on the potential impact of the transport infrastructure. This latter fact has been observed in different countries, normally linked to the development of integrated transport networks, such as in the case of Australian export chain of raw material (e.g., Robinson, 2006) or in the case of differentiated systems within the same market, as in the case of the rail sector in Europe (Cantos & Maudos, 2001; Friebel, Ivaldi, & Vibes, 2010). In this latter situation, the two studies show an increased productivity within the sector due to the deregulation but differentiated results if comparing different approaches to the deregulation itself (e.g., different forms of sequential privatization against immediate privatization), highlighting the role of the regulators to achieve planned results.

Eventually, it is worth noting that the tendency of planning integrated transport networks and logistics corridors, instead of separated parts of it, is affecting the capability of further increasing the impact of those infrastructural investments. Thus, while the infrastructure appraisal is performed taking into consideration only the specific investment, strategic planning, as well as relevant impact assessments, should take into consideration wider intraregional and interregional effects.

CHAPTER 9

Conclusions

Almost every action of our life implies the use of some transport services. Indeed, they are essential not only for the production process of most goods and services but also for their consumption; however, transport services need proper infrastructures to be performed. By way of contrast, an insufficient access to the transport network undermines the efficiency of firms and reduces consumers' surplus (e.g., because of the higher firm prices induced by the inefficient provision of infrastructure) and utility (e.g., because of the additional time individuals spend in congested infrastructure and which is no longer available for leisure). It is not an overstatement saying that the current economic system, as we are used to know it, would not exist without transport infrastructures and related services.

Concerning both freight and passenger, infrastructural nodes—seaports and airports, in particular—are fundamental for international transport; for instance, it is often quoted that nearly 80% of international trade is supported by ocean shipping services transiting through ports. Instead, liner infrastructure—railways, highways, and the other roads—supports trades at a smaller, typically regional, but not less important, scale. Therefore, infrastructure may facilitate exchange of goods and people, but, at the same time, depending on particular conditions, they may also set apart some communities and places.

It is important to keep in mind that infrastructures systems do not evolve to simply satisfy a growing demand of transport, but they can and have been used by policy-makers as a strategic tool to address the development of several countries and the distribution of wealth across space. Indeed, investments made by the European Union in the Trans-European Transport Network (TEN-T) and, more recently, by China in the Belt and Road Initiative have been explicitly designed to reduce spatial disparities, improve regional cohesion, and foster integration. The nonrandomness of transport infrastructures complicates the measurement of their impact on the local economy, as we have noted in various parts of this book and in particular in Chapters 6 and 7.

In 2016, the McKinsey Global Institute published a report stating that nearly 50 trillion of US dollars should be invested over the next 20 years to

Economic Role of Transport Infrastructure
ISBN 978-0-12-813096-4
https://doi.org/10.1016/B978-0-12-813096-4.00009-3

bridge the current global infrastructure gaps. Even if the term infrastructure is not restricted to transport, it is a figure sufficiently high to renew the interest of academics and practitioners alike on the economic contribution of an additional provision of, or the update of the existing, transport infrastructure.

Scientific literature on transport infrastructure is extremely large[1] also in the light of the multiplicity of points of view that may be adopted to study their contribution to both the economy and society. Indeed, transport infrastructure is a trending topic for a wide community of scientists grouping economists, engineers, geographers, sociologists, regional scientists, and planners, among others.

At the same time, the impact of transport infrastructure on economic growth and productivity is disputed. Since the seminal work of Aschauer (1989), this issue has been investigated using several different models and types of data and a consensus probably has not yet been settled.

The present volume seeks to critically summarize and discuss the recent evolution of the literature on these topics by providing the readers with a description and discussion of the theories and models that have been used to investigate the economic effects of transport infrastructure.

The first part of this book has shown that transport infrastructures are strategic elements that influence firms and workers' location decisions, as well as the movement of goods across space. Improvements in the transport system are important policy instruments that might be able to affect the distribution of economic activities across regions. However, the theoretical literature suggests that the reduction of regional disparities might, under certain circumstances, conflict with the realization of long-run growth, so that policy interventions need to be carefully designed and accompanied by nontransport policies aimed at balancing the achievement of different objectives.

The second part of this book is mostly dedicated to discuss the importance of the availability of proper and reliable data in connection with the several appraisal and econometric models developed to estimate the economic effects associated with the provision of transport infrastructure. In particular, Chapter 4 assesses the difficulties that are encountered in the collection of a clear set of reliable information that could be used to effectively and efficiently describe the infrastructure

[1] For instance, the Scopus database records more than 5,000 documents using "transport infrastructure" as keyword.

regional system. The existence of discrepancies among different sources, as well as the possibility to measure and represent the transport system using different (and sometime conflicting) concepts, is a crucial issue that should be solved to improve our comprehension of the economic effects of transport networks.

The third part of this book shows the lack of a clear consensus on the magnitude, if not on the direction, of the economic impact of transport infrastructure due to the heterogeneity of the empirical approaches adopted in the literature, combined with the great diversity of data in respect to specific countries and transport modalities as well. Having said this, the existing meta-analysis as well the most recent studies employing rigorous counterfactual impact evaluation techniques, that have been critically discussed in Chapter 7, point toward positive effects of transportation infrastructure investments on various economic outcomes, although with some exceptions. Moreover, the relative importance of spatial reallocation effects versus net growth effects is still an area of active research.

The third part ends with an overview on the main transport integrated projects, recently developed in some of the most important world regions. The last chapter is then dedicated to discuss differences in how transport assessment is included in the regional planning activity and how funding streams and regional governance have been indeed deeply influencing the possibility to develop both ex-ante and ex-post assessments.

The long list of references, most of them quite recent, testifies that there is room for further research work in the future. Among the several possible avenue for further research, three ideas attract our interest: the inclusion of the so-called wider economic impacts in cost—benefit analysis, the construction and refinement of structural general equilibrium models, and a further application of ex-post impact assessment based on counterfactual impact evaluation techniques.

The relevance of some of the topics discussed in this book is also dependent of the particular economic and political conditions existing in that particular moment and place. For instance, in economic downturns it may be crucial to avoid an infrastructure supply redundancy to allocate resources efficiently; however, it is well known that in the past most of the radical changes in the economic structure of several countries had been deeply influenced by the availability of an excessive provision of infrastructure; moreover, due to the sunk nature of most infrastructure investments, the latter tend to have persistent long-run effects on the structure and evolution of local economies. Hence, it is quite easy to argue that the economic role played by transport infrastructures as well as the most convincing way to measure their costs and benefits will ever attract the discussion of academics all over the world. This book simply represents our contribution to this ever-going debate; for sure, many others will follow.

REFERENCES

Abadie, A., Diamond, A., & Hainmuller, J. (2010). Synthetic control methods for comparative case studies: Estimating the effect of California's tobacco control program. *Journal of the American Statistical Association, 105*(490), 493–505. Applications and Case Studies.

Abadie, A., & Garzeadabal, J. (2003). The economic costs of conflict: A case study of the basque country. *American Economic Review, 93*(1), 113–132.

Abadie, A., Diamond, A., & Hainmueller, J. (2015). Comparative politics and the synthetic control method. *American Journal of Political Science, 59*(2), 495–510.

Acciaro, M., & Vasileios, K. (2018). Environmental port charges reduction schemes: An economic analysis. In *Proceedings of WCTR SIGA2 conference, 3rd-4th May 2018, Antwerp*.

Ackergerg, D. A., Caves, K., & Frazer, G. (2015). Identification properties of recent production function estimators. *Econometrica, 83*(6), 2411–2451.

Adler, N., Fu, X., Oum, T. H., & Yu, C. (2014). Air transport liberalization and airport slot allocation: The case of the Northeast Asian transport market. *Transportation Research Part A, 62*, 3–19.

Afraz, N., Aquilina, M., Conti, M., & Lilico, A. (2006). *Impact of transport infrastructure on economic growth. Annex 6 to Final Report of COMPETE Analysis of the contribution of transport policies to the competitiveness of the EU economy and comparison with the United States.* Karlsruhe, Germany: Funded by the European Commission-DG TREN.

Agrawal, A., Galasso, A., & Oettl, A. (2017). Roads and innovation. *The Review of Economics and Statistics, 99*(3), 417–434.

Agenor, P. (2010). A theory of infrastructure-led development. *Journal of Economic Dynamics and Control, 34*, 932–950.

Aghion, P., & Howitt, P. (1992). A model of growth through creative destruction. *Econometrica, 60*, 323–351.

Agrawal, A., Galasso, A., & Oettl, A. (2017). Roads and innovation. *The Review of Economics and Statistics, 99*(3), 417–434.

Ahlfeldt, G., & Feddersen, A. (2017). From periphery to core: Measuring agglomeration effects using high-speed rail. *Journal of Economic Geography, 15*(6), 1–26.

Ahlfeldt, G., Moeller, K., & Wendland, N. (2015). Chicken or egg? The PVAR econometrics of transportation. *Journal of Economic Geography, 15*(6), 1169–1193.

Albalate, D., & Bel, G. (2009). Regulating concessions of toll motorways: An empirical study on fixed vs. variable term contracts. *Transportation Research Part A, 43*(2), 219–229.

Albalate, D., & Fageda, X. (2015). High-tech employment and transportation: Evidence from the European regions. *Regional Studies, 50*(9), 1564–1578.

Alder, S. (2017). *Chine roads in India: The effect of transport infrastructure on economic development*, mimeo.

Alderighi, M., & Gaggero, A. (2017). Fly and trade: Evidence from the Italian manufacturing industry. *Economics of Transportation, 9*, 51–60.

Anderson, J. E., & Van Wincoop, E. (2003). Gravity with gravitas: A solution to the border puzzle. *The American Economic Review, 93*(1), 170–192.

Angrist, J., & Pischke, J. (2009). *Mostly Harmless econometrics*. Princeton: Princeton University Press.

Araujo, S., & Sutherland, D. (2010). *Public-private partnerships and investments in infrastructure*. OECD Economics Department WP n. 803. Paris: OECD publishing.

Arbues, P., Banos, J., & Mayor, M. (2015). The spatial productivity of transportation infrastructure. *Transportation Research Part A, 75*, 166–177.

Arellano, M., & Bond, S. (1991). Some tests of specification for panel data models: Monte Carlo evidence and an application to employment equations. *The Review of Economic Studies, 58*, 277–297.

Arellano, M., & Bover, O. (1995). Another look at the instrumental variables estimation of error-components models. *Journal of Econometrics, 88*, 29–51.

Arellano, M., & Bover, O. (1995). Another look at the instrumental variables estimation of error-components models. *Journal of Econometrics, 88*, 29–51.

Aschauer, D. A. (1989). Is public expenditure productive? *Journal of Monetary Economics, 23*, 177–200.

Asteris, M., & Collins, A. (2007). Developing Britain's port infrastructure: Markets, policy, and location. *Environment and Planning A, 39*, 2271–2286.

Asturias, J., Garcia-Santana, M., & Ramos, R. (2017). *Competition and the welfare gains from transportation infrastructures: Evidence from the Golden Quadrilateral of India.* mimeo.

Australian Government. (2016). *Cost benefit analysis, Department for the Prime Minister and the Cabinet.* Retrievable at https://www.pmc.gov.au/regulation/guidance-policymakers/cost-benefit-analysis.

Autor, D. (2003). Outsourcing at will: The contribution of unjust dismissal doctrine to the growth of employment outsourcing. *Journal of Labour Economics, 21*(1), 1–42.

Bagloee, S. A., Tavana, M., Asadi, M., & Oliver, T. (2016). Autonomous vehicles: Challenges, opportunities, and future implications for transportation policies. *Journal of Modern Transportation, 24*(4), 284–303.

Baldwin, R. (1999). Agglomeration and endogenous capital. *European Economic Review, 43*, 253–280.

Baldwin, R., Forslid, R., Martin, P., Ottaviano, G., & Robert-Nicoud. (2003). *Economic geography and public policy.* Princeton University Press.

Baldwin, R., & Martin, P. (2004). Agglomeration and regional growth. In J. V. Henderson, & J. F. Thisse (Eds.), *Handbook of regional and urban economics* (Vol. 4, pp. 2671–2711). Amsterdam: Elsevier.

Baldwin, R., Martin, P., & Ottaviano, G. (2001). Global income divergence, trade and industrialization: The geography of growth take-off. *Journal of Economic Growth, 6*, 5–37.

Baldwin, R., & Taglioni, D. (2006). *Gravity for dummies and dummies for gravity, NBER WP 12516.*

Banerjee, A., Duflo, E., & Qian, N. (2012). *On the road: Access to transportation infrastructure and economic growth in China.* NBER. w 17897.

Banister, D., & Berechman, J. (2001). Transport investment and the promotion of economic growth. *Journal of Transport Geography, 9*, 209–218.

Barro, R. (1990). Government spending in a simple model of endogenous growth. *Journal of Political Economy, 98*, 103–125.

Barro, R., & Sala I Martin, K. (1992). Public finance in models of economic growth. *The Review of Economic Studies, 59*, 645–661.

Barro, R., & Sala I Martin, K. (2004). *Economic growth.* MIT Press.

Barros, C. P., & Athanassiou, M. (2004). Efficiency in European seaports with DEA: Evidence from Greece and Portugal. *Maritime Economics and Logistics, 6*, 122–140.

Basile, R., Durban, M., Minguez, R., Montero, J., & Mur, J. (2014). Modeling regional economic dynamics: Spatial dependence, spatial heterogeneity and nonlinearities. *Journal of Economic Dynamics and Control, 48*, 229–245.

Baum-Snow, N. (2007). Did highways cause suburbanization? *The Quarterly Journal of Economics, 122*(2), 775–805.

Baum-Snow, N., & Ferreira, F. (2015). Causal inference in urban and regional economics. In G. Duranton, J. Henderson, & W. Strange (Eds.), *Handbook of regional and urban economics* (Vol. 5). Amsterdam: Elsevier.

Baum-Snow, N., Henderson, J. V., Turner, M. A., Zhang, Q., & Brandt, L. (2017). *Does investment in national highways help or hurt hinterland city growth?* mimeo.

Baum Snow, N., Vernon-Handersen, J., Turner, M., Zhang, Q., & Brandt, L. (2018). Does investment in national highways help or hurt hinterland city growth? *Journal of Urban Economics, in press.*

Bede, B. (2013). *Mathematics of fuzzy sets and fuzzy logic.* Heidelberg: Springer.

Bektas, T., & Crainic, T. G. (2007). *A brief overview of intermodal transportation. University of Montreal, Interuniversity research centre on Enterprise Networks, Logistics and transportation (CIRRELT).* Montreal: CIRRELT.

Belotti, F., Hughes, G., & Piano Mortari, A. (2017). Spatial panel data models using Stata. *STATA Journal, 17*(1), 139–180.

Benfratello, L., Iozzi, A., & Valbonesi, P. (2003). Technology and incentive regulation in the Italian motorways industry. *Journal of Regulatory Economics, 35*, 201–221.

Ben-Horin, M., & Kroll, Y. (2012). The limited relevance of the multiple IRRs. *The Engineering Economist, 57*(2), 101–118.

Bensassi, S., Marquez-Ramos, L., Martinez-Zarzoso, L., & Suarez-Burguet, C. (2015). Relationship between logistic infrastructure and trade: Evidence from the Spanish regional exports. *Transportation Research Part A, 72*, 47–71.

Berg, A., Buffie, E., Pattillo, C., Portillo, F., Presibitero, A., & Zanna, L. F. (2015). Some misconceptions about public investment efficiency and growth. *IMF Working Paper, 15*, 272.

Bergantino, A., & Goetz, A. (2013). Infrastructure, accessibility and growth: Some open issues. *International Journal of Transport Economics, 40*(3), 301–311.

Berger, T., & Enflo, K. (2017). Locomotives of local growth: The short and long term impacts of railroads in Sweden. *Journal of Urban Economics, 98*, 124–138.

Beria, P., Giove, M., & Miele, M. (2012). A comparative analysis of assessment approaches: Six cases from Europe. *International Journal of Transport Economics, 39*(2), 185–217.

Beria, P., & Grimaldi, R. (2013). Open issues in the practice of cost benefit analysis of transport projects. In *Proceedings of the 13th World Conference on Transport Research, Rio de Janeiro (Brazil).*

Beria, P., Grimaldi, R., Albalate, D., & Bel, G. (2018). Delusions of success: Costs and demand of high-speed rail in Italy and Spain. *Transport Policy, 68*, 63–79.

Van Beveren, I. (2012). Total factor productivity estimation: A practical review. *Journal of Economic Surveys, 26*(1), 98–128.

Bilotkach, V. (2015). Are airports engine of economic development? A dynamic panel data approach. *Urban Studies, 52*(9), 1577–1593.

Bismark, A. (2014). An empirical analysis of three econometric frameworks for evaluating economic impacts of transport infrastructure expenditures across countries. *Transport Policy, 35*, 304–310.

Black, D., & Henderson, V. (1999). A theory of urban growth. *Journal of Political Economy, 107*, 252–284.

Blauwens, G., De Baere, P., & Van de Voorde, E. (2008). *Transport economics* (3rd ed.). Antwerp: Uitgeverij De Boeck.

Blonigen, B., & Cristea, A. (2015). Air service and urban growth: Evidence form a quasi-natural experiment. *Journal of Urban Economics, 86*, 128–146.

Blonigen, B., & Wilson, W. (2008). Port Efficiency and Trade Flows. *Review of International Economics, 16*(1), 21–36.

Blum, U. (1998). Positive externalities and the public provision of transportation infrastructure: An evolutionary perspective. *Journal of Transportation and Statistics, 1*(3), 81–88.

Blundell, R., & Bond, S. (1998). Initial conditions and moment restrictions in dynamic panel data models. *Journal of Econometrics, 87*, 115–143.

Bocarejo, J., & Oviedo, D. (2012). Transport accessibility and social inequities: A tool for identification of mobility needs and evaluation of transport investments. *Journal of Transport Geography, 24*, 142–154.

Bogliaccini, J. A. (2013). The effect of economic liberalization on inequality: Evidence from Latin American middle-income countries. *Latin America Research Review, 48*, 79–105.

von Böhm-Bawerk, E. (1889). *Positive Theorie des Kapitales*. Innsbruck: Wagner.

Bom, P., & Ligthart, J. (2014). What have we learnt from three decades of research on the productivity of public capital? *Journal of Economic Surveys, 28*(5), 889–916.

Bonnafous, A. (1987). The regional impact of the TGV. *Transportation, 14*(2), 127–137.

Bonnafous, A., & Jensen, P. (2005). Ranking transport projects by their socioeconomic value or financial internal rate of return? *Transport Policy, 12*, 131–136.

Bottasso, A., Castagnetti, C., & Conti, M. (2013). And yet they co-move! Public capital and productivity in the OECD. *Journal of Policy Modelling, 35*(5), 713–729.

Bottasso, A., & Conti, M. (2010). The productive effect of transport infrastructures: Does road transport liberalization matter? *Journal of Regulatory Economics, 38*(1), 27–48.

Bottasso, A., & Conti, M. (2012). The cost structure of the UK airport industry. *Journal of Transport Economics and Policy, 46*(3), 313–332.

Bottasso, A., & Conti, M. (2017). The cost structure of the airport industry: Methodological issues and empirical evidence. In J. D. Bitzan, & J. H. Peoples (Eds.), *The economics of airport operations, advances in airline economics* (Vol. 6, pp. 181–212). Emerald Publishing Limited.

Bottasso, A., Conti, M., Costacurta de Sa Porto, P., Ferrari, C., & Tei, A. (2018). Port infrastructures and trade: Empirical evidence from Brazil. *Transportation Research Part A, 107*, 126–139.

Bottasso, A., Conti, M., & Ferrari, C. (2011). Efficiency and productivity growth in a sample of italian container terminals. *International Journal of Transport Economics, XXXVIII*(2), 107–122.

Bottasso, A., Conti, M., Ferrari, C., Merk, O., & Tei, A. (2013). The impact of port throughput on local employment: Evidence from a panel of European regions. *Transport Policy, 27*, 32–38.

Bottasso, A., Conti, M., Ferrari, C., & Tei, A. (2014). Ports and local development: A spatial analysis on a panel of European regions. *Transportation Research Part A, 65*, 44–55.

Boucekkine, R., Camacho, C., & Zou, B. (2009). Bridging the gap between growth theory and the new economic geography: The spatial Ramsey model. *Macroeconomic Dynamics, 13*, 20–45.

Brady, K. L. (2008). The value of human life: A case for Altruism. *Natural Resources Journal, 48*(3), 541–564.

Braun, B. B. (1990). Measuring the influence of public authorities through economic impact analysis: The case of Port Canaveral. *Policy Studies Journal, 18*(4), 1032–1044.

Brighouse, H., & Robeyns, I. (2010). *Measuring justice: Primary goods and capabilities*. Cambridge (Mass.): Cambridge University Press.

Brock, W., & Xepapadeas, A. (2008). Diffusion-induced instability and pattern formation in infinite horizon recursive optimal control. *Journal of Economic Dynamics and Control, 32*, 2745–2787.

Brock, W., & Xepapadeas, A. (2010). Pattern formation, spatial externalities and regulation in coupled economic-ecological systems. *Journal of Environmental Economics and Management, 59*, 149–164.

Bronzini, F., & Piselli, P. (2009). Determinants of long-run regional productivity with geographical spillovers: The role of R&D, human capital and public infrastructures. *Regional Science and Urban Economics, 39*(2), 187–199.

Burgess, D. F., & Zerbe, R. O. (2011). Appropriate discounting for benefit-cost analysis. *Journal of Benefit-Cost Analysis, 2*(2), 1–20.

Burski, Z., Mijalska-Szewczak, I., Wasilewski, J., & Szczepanik, M. (2016). Evaluation of energy consumption of vehicles in EU trans-European transport network. *Transportation Research Part A, 92*, 120–130.

Button, K. J. (1982). *Transport economics*. Aldershot: Gowen Publishing Company.

Button, K. J., & Keeler, T. E. (1993). The regulation of transport markets. *The Economic Journal, 103*(419), 1017–1027.

Cadot, O., Roller, L. H., & Stephan, A. (2006). Contribution to productivity or pork barrel? The two faces of infrastructure investment. *Journal of Public Economics, 90*(6–7), 1133–1153.

Calatayud, A., Palacin, R., Mangan, J., Jackson, E., & Ruiz-Rua, A. (2016). Understanding connectivity to international markets: A systematic review. *Transport Reviews, 36*(6), 713–736.

Calderon, C., Moral-Benito, E., & Serven, L. (2015). Is infrastructure capital productive? A dynamic heterogeneous approach. *Journal of Applied Econometrics, 30*, 177–198.

Cameron, A. C., & Miller, D. L. (2015). A practioneer's guide to cluster-robust inference. *Journal of Human Resources, 50*(2), 317–372.

Canning, D., & Pedroni, P. (2008). Infrastructure, long run economic growth and causality tests for cointegrated panels. *The Manchester School, 76*, 504–527.

Canterelli, C. C., Flyvbjerg, B., Molin, E. J. E., & van Wee, B. (2010). Cost overruns in large-scale transportation infrastructure projects: Explanations and their theoretical embeddedness. *European Journal of Transport and Infrastructure Research, 10*(1), 5–18.

Cantos, P., & Maudos, J. (2001). Regulation and efficiency: The case of European railways. *Transportation Research Part A, 35*, 459–472.

Card, D., & Krueger, A. B. (1995). Time-series minimum wage studies: A meta-analysis. *The American Economic Review, 85*(2), 238–243.

Cavill, N., Kahlmeier, S., Rutter, H., Racioppi, F., & Oja, P. (2008). Economic analyses of transport infrastructure and policies including health effects related to cycling and walking: A systematic review. *Transport Policy, 15*, 291–304.

Chandra, A., & Thompson, E. (2000). Does public infrastructure affect economic activity? Evidence from the rural interstate highway system. *Regional Science and Urban Economics, 30*, 457–490.

Chang, V., & Tovar, B. (2014). Efficiency and productivity changes for Peruvian and Chilean ports terminals: A parametric distance functions approach. *Transport Policy, 31*, 83–94.

Chen, Z., & Haynes, K. (2013). Public surface transportation and regional output: A spatial panel approach. *Papers in Regional Science, 94*(4), 727–752.

Chou, J. S., Tserng, P. H., Chieh, L., & Huang, W. H. (2015). Strategic governance for modelling institutional framework of public-private partnerships. *Cities: The International Journal of Urban Policy and Planning Part B, 42*, 204–211.

Christodoulou, A., & Finger, C. (2012). *The governance of urban public transport systems: The case of Zurich (ZVV)*. Netherlands: Delft University of Technology.

CIA – Central Intelligence Agency. (2017). *The world factbook*. Retrievable at https://www.cia.gov/library/publications/the-world-factbook/geos/uk.html.

Clark, X., Dollar, D., & Micco, A. (2004). Port efficiency, maritime transport costs, and bilateral trade. *Journal of Development Economics, 75*, 417–450.

Cohen, J., & Monaco, K. (2008). Ports and highways infrastructure. An analysis of intra and inter-state spillovers. *International Regional Science Review, 31*(3), 257–274.

Cohen, J., & Morrison-Paul, C. (2003). Airport infrastructure spillovers in a network system. *Journal of Urban Economics, 54*, 459–473.
Cohen, J., & Morrison-Paul, C. (2004). Public infrastructure investment, interstate spatial spillovers, and manufacturing costs. *The Review of Economics and Statistics, 86*(2), 551–560.
Cole, S. (2005). *Applied transport economics* (3rd ed.). London: Kogan Page.
Combes, P., Duranton, G., Gobillon, L., Puga, D., & Roux, S. (2012). The productivity advantages of large cities: Distinguishing agglomeration from firm selection. *Econometrica, 80*(6), 2543–2594.
Coppens, F., Lagneaux, F., Meersman, H., Sellekaerts, N., Van de Voorde, E., van Gastel, G., et al. (2007). *Economic impact of port activity: A disaggregate analysis. The case of Antwerp*. Working paper document no. 110 (February). Antwerp: National Bank of Belgium.
Cosar, A., & Demir, B. (2016). Domestic road infrastructure and international trade: Evidence from Turkey. *Journal of Development Economics, 118*, 232–244.
Cowie, J. (2009). The British Passenger rail privatisation: Conclusions on subsidy and efficiency from the First Round of Franchises. *Journal of Transport Economics and Policy, 43*, 85–104.
Crescenzi, R., Di Cataldo, M., & Rodriguez-Pose, A. (2016). Government quality and the economic returns of transport infrastructure investment in European regions. *Journal of Regional Science, 56*(4), 555–592.
Crescenzi, R., & Rodriguez-Pose, A. (2012). Infrastructure and regional growth in the European Union. *Papers in Regional Science, 91*, 487–513.
Cristea, A. (2017). Buyer-seller relationship in international trade: Evidence from the US states' exports and business class travel. *Journal of International Economics, 84*(2), 207–220.
Crozet, Y. (2004). European railway infrastructure: Towards a convergence of infrastructure charging? *International Journal of Transport Management, 2*, 5–15.
Cullinane, K. P. B., & Wang, T.-F. (2006). The efficiency of European container ports: A cross-sectional data envelopment analysis. *International Journal of Logistics: Research and Applications, 9*(1), 19–31.
Danielis, R., & Gregori, T. (2013). An input-output-based methodology to estimate the economic role of a port: The case of the port system of the Friuli Venezia Giulia Region, Italy. *Maritime Economics and Logistics, 15*(2), 222–255.
de Jong, J., Ferdinandusse, M., Funda, J., & Vetlov, I. (2017). The effect of public investment in europe: A model-based assessment. *ECB WP*, 2021.
Deaton, A. (2010). Instruments, randomization, and learning about development. *Journal of Economic Literature, 48*, 424–455.
De la Fuente, A. (2010). *Infrastructure and productivity: An updated survey*, mimeo.
De la Fuente, A., & Vives, X. (1995). Infrastructure and education as instruments of regional policy. *Economic Policy, 20*, 13–51.
Del Bo, C., & Florio, M. (2012). Infrastructure and growth in a spatial framework: Evidence from the EU regions. *European Planning Studies, 8*(1), 1393–1414.
Del Bo, C., & Florio, M. (2013). Infrastructure and growth in a spatial framework: Evidence from the EU regions. *European Planning Studies, 20*(8), 1393–1414.
Del Gatto, M., Di Liberto, A., & Petraglia, C. (2011). Measuring productivity. *Journal of Economic Surveys, 25*, 952–1008.
Deng, T. (2013). Impacts of transport infrastructure on productivity and economic growth: Recent advances and research challenges. *Transport Reviews, 33*(6), 686–699.
Derrible, S., & Kennedy, C. (2011). Applications of graph theory and network science to transit network design. *Transport Reviews, 31*, 495–519.
Desmet, K., & Rossi-Hansberg, E. (2014). Spatial development. *The American Economic Review, 104*, 1211–1243.

DfT – Department for Transport. (2017a). *Transport investment strategy - Moving Britain ahead.* London: Department for Transport.

DfT – Department for Transport. (2017b). *High speed two from concept to reality - Moving Britain ahead.* London: Department for Transport.

DfT – Department for Transport. (2018). *Maritime 2050 call for evidence - Navigating the future.* London: Department for Transport.

Diao, M., Zhu, Y., & Zhu, J. (2017). Intra-city access to inter-city transport nodes: The implications of high-speed-rail station locations for the urban development of Chinese cities. *Urban Studies, 54*(10), 2249–2267.

Dimitriou, H. T., Ward, E. J., & Dean, M. (2016). Presenting the case for the application of multi-criteria analysis to mega transport infrastructure project appraisal. *Research in Transportation Economics, 58*, 7–20.

Dixit, A., & Stiglitz, J. (1977). Monopolistic competition and optimum product diversity. *The American Economic Review, 67*, 297–308.

Donaldson, D. (2018). Railroads of the Raj: Estimating the impact of transportation infrastructure. *The American Economic Review, 108*(4), 899–934.

Donaldson, D., & Hornbeck, R. (2016). Railroads and American economic growth: A "market access" approach. *The Quarterly Journal of Economics, 131*(2), 799–858.

DoT - Department of Transportation. (2018a). *Strategic Plan for FY 2018-2022.* Washington: US Department of Transportation.

DoT - Department of Transportation. (2018b). *Beyond Traffic.* Washington: Department of Transportation.

Drewello, H., & Scholl, B. (2016). In *Integrated spatial and transport infrastructure development.* Berlin: Springer.

Drèze, J., & Stern, N. (1990). Policy reform, shadow prices, and market prices. *Journal of Public Economics, 42*(1), 145.

Du, M. (2016). China's "One Belt, One road" initiative: Context, focus, institutions, and implications. *The Chinese Journal of Global Governance, 2*, 30–43.

Ducruet, C. (2013). Network diversity and maritime flows. *Journal of Transport Geography, 30*, 77–88.

Ducruet, C., & Lugo, I. (2013). Structure and dynamics of transport networks: Concepts, models, and applications. In J. P. Rodrigue, T. Notteboom, & J. Shaw (Eds.), *The SAGE handbook of transport studies* (pp. 347–364). SAGE Publications Ltd.

Duggal, G., Saltzmana, C., & Kleinb, L. (1999). Infrastructure and productivity: A non-linear approach. *Journal of Econometrics, 92*(1), 47–74.

Duranton, G. (2007). Urban evolutions: The fast, the slow, and the still. *The American Economic Review, 97*, 197–221.

Duranton, G. (2015). Roads and trade in Colombia. *Economics of Transportation, 4*, 16–36.

Duranton, G., Morrow, P., & Turner, M. (2014). Roads and trade: Evidence from the US. *The Review of Economic Studies, 81*, 681–724.

Duranton, G., & Turner, M. (2012). Urban growth and transportation. *Review of Economic Studies, 1*, 1–36.

Duranton, G., & Puga, D. (2004). Micro-foundations of urban increasing returns: Theory. In J. V. Henderson, & J.-F. Thisse (Eds.), *Handbook of regional and urban economics. Cities and geography* (pp. 2063–2117). Amsterdam: Elsevier.

Duranton, G., & Turner, M. (2012). Urban growth and transportation. *The Review of Economic Studies, 1*, 1–36.

Duranton, G., & Venables, A. J. (2018). *Place-based policies for development.* CEPR Discussion Paper Series, n. 12889.

Eaton, J., & Kortum, S. (2002). Technology, geography, and trade. *Econometrica, 70*, 1741–1779.

EBRD – European Bank for Reconstruction and Development. (2018). *The belt and road initiative*. Retrievable at http://www.ebrd.com/what-we-do/belt-and-road/overview.html.

Economic Commission for Europe. (2003). *Cost benefit analysis of transport infrastructure projects*. New York and Geneva: United Nations.

ECORYS – CE Delft. (2005). *Infrastructure expenditures and costs*. Final Report. Retrievable at http://ec.europa.eu/ten/transport/studies/doc/2005_11_30_guidelines_infrastructure_report_en.pdf.

EEA – European Environmental Agency. (2018). https://www.eea.europa.eu/.

Elburz, Z., Nijkamp, P., & Pels, P. (2017). Public infrastructure and regional growth. *Journal of Transport Geography, 58*, 1–8.

Elhorst, J. P., & Oosterhaven, J. (2008). Integral cost-benefit analysis of Maglev Rail projects under market imperfections. *Journal of Transport and Land Use, 1*(1), 65–87.

Eliasson, J., & Lundberg, M. (2012). Do cost–benefit analyses influence transport investment decisions? Experiences from the Swedish Transport Investment Plan 2010–21. *Transport Reviews, 32*(1), 29–48.

EU - European Union. (2014). *Commission delegated regulation N. 480/2014 of 3 March 2014*. Brussels: European Union.

EU – European Union. (2017). *Connecting Europe report*. Retrievable at https://ec.europa.eu/transport/themes/infrastructure_en.

European Commission. (1992). *The future development of the common transport policy. COM(92) 494*. Brussels: European Commission.

European Commission. (2011). *Mid-term evaluation of the TEN-T Programme (2007-2013)*. Brussels: Directorate General Mobility and Transport.

European Commission. (2014). *Guide to cost-benefit analysis of investment projects*. Brussels: European Commission.

European Commission. (2015). *Assessment of TEN-T Programme implementation*. Brussels: European Commission.

European Commission (2018). https://ec.europa.eu/transport/themes/infrastructure/ten-t-guidelines/project-funding_en.

Faber, B. (2014). Trade integration, market size and industrialization: Evidence from China's national trunk highway system. *The Review of Economic Studies, 81*, 1046–1070.

Fageda, X. (2017). International air travel and FDI flows: Evidence from Barcelona. *Journal of Regional Science, 57*(5), 858–883.

Fageda, X., & Gonzales-Aregall, M. (2017). Do all transport modes impact on industrial employment? Empirical evidence from the Spanish regions. *Transport Policy, 55*, 70–78.

Fally, T. (2015). Structural gravity and fixed effects. *Journal of International Economics, 97*, 76–85.

Farhadi, M. (2015). Transport infrastructure and long run economic growth in OECD countries. *Transportation Research Part A, 74*, 73–90.

Fernald, G. (1999). Roads to prosperity? Assessing the link between public capital and productivity. *The American Economic Review, 89*(3), 619–638.

Ferrari, C. (2016). *The rationale for the colonial train: An economic perspective*, mimeo.

Ferrari, C., Parola, F., & Gattorna, E. (2011). Measuring the quality of port hinterland accessibility: The ligurian case. *Transport Policy, 18*, 382–391.

Ferrari, C., & Tei, A. (2018). PPIs and transport infrastructure: Evidence from Latin America and the Caribbean. *Journal of Transport Geography, 71*, 204–212.

Fisher, I. (1930). *The theory of Interest*. New York: MacMillan.

Flyvbjerg, B. (2007). Policy and planning for large infrastructure projects: Problems, causes, cures. Environment and planning B: *Planning and Design, 34*, 578–597.

Flyvbjerg, B., Bruzelius, N., & Rothengatter, W. (2003). *Megaprojects and risk: An anatomy of ambition*. Cambridge: Cambridge University Press.

Fridstrøm, L., & Elvik, R. (1997). The barely revealed preference behind road investment priorities. *Public Choice, 92*(1/2), 145–168.

Friebel, G., Ivaldi, M., & Vibes, C. (2010). Railway (De)Regulation: A European efficiency comparison. *Economica, 77*(305), 77–91.

Fujita, M., & Krugman, P. (1995). When is the economy monocentric? Von Thunen and Chamberlin unified. *Regional Science and Urban Economics, 25*, 505–528.

Fujita, M., Krugman, P., & Venables, A. (1999). *The spatial economy. Cities, regions and international trade*. Cambridge: MIT Press.

Fujita, M., & Thisse, J. (2002). *Economics of Agglomeration*. Oxford: Oxford University Press.

Fujita, M., & Thisse, J. (2003). Does geographical agglomeration foster economic growth? And who gains and looses from it? *The Japanese Economic Review, 54*, 121–145.

Fujita, M., & Thisse, J. (2013). *Economics of Agglomeration. Cities, industrial location and globalization*. Cambridge: Cambridge University Press.

Garcia-Lopez, M., Holl, A., & Viladecans-Marsal, E. (2015). Suburbanization and highways in Spain when the Romans and the Bourbons still shape its cities. *Journal of Urban Economics, 85*, 52–67.

Geurs, K. T., Boon, W., & van Wee, B. (2009). Social impacts of transport: Literature review and the state of the practice of transport appraisal in The Netherlands and the United Kingdom. *Transport Reviews, 29*(1), 69–90.

Geurs, K. T., & Östh, J. (2016). Advances in the measurement of transport impedance in accessibility modelling. *European Journal of Transport and Infrastructure Research, 16*(2), 294–299.

Geurs, K. T., Patuelli, R., & Dentinho, T. P. (2016). *Accessibility, equity and efficiency. Challenges for transport and public services*. Cheltenham: Edward Elgar Publishing.

Geurs, K. T., & van Wee, B. (2004). Accessibility evaluation of land-use and transport strategies: Review and research directions. *Journal of Transport Geography, 12*, 127–140.

Ghani, E., Grover Goswami, A., & Kerr, W. (2016). The impact of the golden quadrilateral project for the location and performance of Indian manufacturing. *The Economic Journal, 126*(591), 317–357.

Ghavamifar, K., & Touran, A. (2008). Alternative project delivery systems: Applications and legal limits in transportation projects. *Journal of Professional Issues in Engineering Education and Practice, 134*(1), 106–111.

Gibbons, S., Lyytikainen, T., Overman, H., & Sanchis-Guarner, R. (2017). New road infrastructure: The effect on firms. In *SERC Discussion Paper, 214*.

Gibbons, S., & Overman, H. (2012). Mostly pointless spatial econometrics. *Journal of Regional Science, 52*(2), 172–191.

Gibbons, S., & Wu, W. (2017). Airports, market access and local economic performance: evidence from China. In *SERC Discussion Paper, 211*.

Glancy, D. J. (2015). Sharing the road: Smart transportation infrastructure. *Fordham Urban Law Journal, 41*(5), 1617–1664.

Goh, A., & Olivier, J. (2002). Learning by doing, trade in capital goods and growth. *Journal of International Economics, 56*, 411–444.

Golden, M. A., & Picci, L. (2008). Pork-barrel politics in post-war Italy, 1953-94. *American Journal of Political Science, 52*(2), 268–289.

Gramlich, E. (1994). Infrastructure investment: A review essay. *Journal of Economic Literature, 32*(3), 1176–1196.

Grimaldi, F., & Beria, P. (2013). *Open issues in the practice of cost-benefit analysis of transport projects*. MPRA Paper No. 53766.

Grossman, G., & Helpman, E. (1991). *Innovation and growth in the World economy*. Cambridge: MA: MIT Press.

Gühnemann, A., Laird, J. J., & Pearman, A. D. (2012). Combining cost-benefit and multi-criteria analysis to prioritise a national road infrastructure programme. *Transport Policy, 23*, 15–24.

Gutiérrez, J., Condeço-Melhorado, A., López, E., & Monzón, A. (2011). Evaluating the European added value of TEN-T projects: A methodological proposal based on spatial spillovers, accessibility and GIS. *Journal of Transport Geography, 19*, 840–850.

Gutierrez, J., Monzon, A., & Pifiero, J. M. (1998). Accessibility, network efficiency, and transport infrastructure planning. *Environment and Planning A, 30*, 1337–1350.

Haimes, Y. Y., Horowitz, B. M., Lambert, J. H., Santons, J. R., Lian, C., & Crowther, K. G. (2005). Inoperability input-output model for interdependent infrastructure sectors. I: Theory and Methodology. *Journal of Infrastructure Systems, 11*(2), 67–79.

Haimes, Y. Y., & Jiang, P. (2001). Leontief-based model of risk in complex interconnected infrastructure. *Journal of Infrastructure Systems, 7*(1), 1–12.

Hall, P. (2004). "We'd have to sink the ships": Impact studies and the 2002 West Coast port Lockout. *Economic Development Quarterly, 18*, 354–367.

Hall, D., De la Motte, R., & Davies, S. (2003). *Terminology of public-private partnerships* (Psiru research paper).

Hamilton, J. D. (1994). *Time series analysis*. Princeton: Princeton University Press.

Hansen, W. G. (1959). How accessibility shapes land use. *Journal of the American Institute of Planners, 25*(1), 73–76.

Hanson, G. (1998). *Market potential, increasing returns, and geographic concentration*. Working Paper No. 6429. National Bureau of Economic Research.

Haralambides, H. (2002). Competition, excess capacity, and the pricing of port infrastructure. *International Journal of Maritime Economics, 4*, 323–347.

Head, K., & Mayer, T. (2015). Gravity equations: Workhorse, toolkit, and codebook. In G. Gopinath, H. Helpman, & K. Rogoff (Eds.), *Handbook of international economics* (Vol. 4). Oxford: BV.

Hamilton, J. (1994). *Time Series Analysis*. Princeton University Press.

Helm, D. (2009). Infrastructure investment, the cost of capital, and regulation: An assessment. *Oxford Review of Economic Policy, 25*, 307–326.

Helm, D., & Thompson, D. (1991). Privatised transport infrastructure and incentives to invest. *Journal of Transport Economics and Policy, 25*(3), 231–246.

Helpman, E. (1998). The size of regions. In D. Pines, E. Sadka, & I. Zilcha (Eds.), *Topics in public economics. Theoretical and applied analysis*. Cambridge: Cambridge University Press.

Henneberry, J. (1997). Transport investment and house prices. *Journal of Property Valuation and Investment, 16*(2), 144–158.

Herrero, A. G., & Xu, J. (2017). China's Belt and road initiative: Can Europe Expect trade gains? *China and World Economy, 25*, 84–99.

Hickford, A. J., Nicholls, R. J., Otto, A., Hall, J. W., Blainey, S. P., Tran, M., et al. (2015). Creating an ensemble of future strategies for national infrastructure provision. *Futures, 66*, 13–24.

Hicks, J. R. (1940). The valuation of social income. *Economica, 7*, 105–124.

Holl, A. (2004a). Manufacturing location and impacts of road transport infrastructure: Empirical evidence from Spain. *Regional Science and Urban Economics, 34*, 341–363.

Holl, A. (2004b). Transport infrastructure, agglomeration economies and firm birth: Empirical evidence from Portugal. *Journal of Regional Science, 44*(4), 693–712.

Holl, A. (2016). Highways and productivity in manufacturing firms. *Journal of Urban Economics, 93*, 131–151.

Holmgren, J., & Merkel, A. (2017). Much ado about nothing? A meta-analysis of the relationship between infrastructure and economic growth. *Research in Transportation Economics, 63*, 13–26.

Hornung, E. (2015). Railroads and growth in Prussia. *Journal of the European Economic Association, 13*(4), 699–736.

Huang, Y. (2016). Understanding China's belt & road initiative: Motivation, framework and assessment. *China Economic Review, 40*, 314–321.

Imbens, G., & Wooldridge, J. (2009). Recent developments in the econometrics of programme evaluation. *Journal of Economic Literature, 47*(1), 5–86.

Imbens, G. (2019). Better LATE than nothing: Some commetns on Deaton (2009), Heckman and Urzua (2009). *Journal of Economic Literature, 48*, 399–423.

IMF – International Monetary Fund (2016). www.imf.org.

ITF - International Transport Forum. (2011). *Improving the practice of transport project appraisal.* Paris: OECD publishing. Retrievable at https://www.keepeek.com//Digital-Asset-Management/oecd/transport/improving-the-practice-of-transport-project-appraisal_9789282103081-en#.WraDFYe7KUk#page11.

ITF - International Transport Forum. (2018). *Transport infrastructure investment and maintenance.* Paris: ITF Transport Statistics (database). https://doi.org/10.1787/g2g55573-en. Retrievable at.

Janic, M. (2007). Modelling the full costs of an intermodal and road freight transport network. *Transportation Research Part D, 12*, 33–44.

Jansson, J. O., & Shneerson, D. (1979). Charging what the traffic can bear — alternative rule to the value of service principle. *International Journal of Transport Economics, 6*(3), 347–355.

Jara-Diaz, S. (1986). On the relation between users' benefits and the economic effects of transportation activities. *Journal of Regional Science, 26*(2), 379–391.

Jedwab, R., & Moradi, A. (2016). The permanent effects of transportation revolutions in poor countries: Evidence from Africa. *The Review of Economics and Statistics, 98*(2), 268–284.

Jiwattanakulpaisarn, P., Noland, R., & Graham, D. (2009). Marginal productivity of expanding highway capacity. *Journal of Transport Economics and Policy, 46*(3), 333–347.

Jiwattanakulpaisarn, P., Noland, R., Graham, D., & Polack, J. (2009). Highways infrastructure investments and county employment growth: A dynamic panel regression analysis. *Journal of Regional Science, 49*(2), 263–286.

Jiwattanakulpaisarn, P., Noland, R., Graham, D., & Polack, J. (2012). Highways infrastructure investments and county employment growth: a dynamic panel regression analysis. *Journal of Regional Science, 49*(2), 263–286.

Jones, H., Moura, F., & Domingos, T. (2014). Transport infrastructure project evaluation using cost-benefit analysis. In *Procedia - social and behavioral sciences, Proceedings of EWGT2013 – 16th Meeting of the EURO Working Group on Transportation* (pp. 400–409).

Kahn, A. E. (1988). Surprises of airline deregulation. *The American Economic Review, 78*(2), 316–322.

Kahneman, D., & Tversky, A. (1979). Prospect theory: An analysis of decision under risk. *Econometrica, 47*(2), 263–292.

Kaldor, N. (1939). Welfare propositions and interpersonal comparisons of utility. *Economic Journal, 49*, 549–552.

Kalhoefer, C. (2010). Ranking of mutually exclusive investment projects – how cash flow differences can solve the ranking problem. *Investment Management and Financial Innovations,* 7(2), 81–86.

Kamps, C. (2004). *The dynamics effects of public capital: VAR evidence from 22 OECD countries.* Kiel Working Paper, 1224.

Keeney, R. L., & Raiffa, H. (1976). *Decision analysis with multiple conflicting objectives, preferences and value tradeoffs.* New York: John Wiley.

Kelejian, H., & Prucha, I. R. (1998). A generalized spatial two-stage least squares procedure for estimating a spatial autoregressive model with autoregressive disturbances. *The Journal of Real Estate Finance and Economics, 17*(1), 99–121.

Keynes, J. M. (1936). *The general theory of employment, interest, and money*. New York: Macmillan.

Kiel, J., Smith, R., & Ubbels, R. (2014). The impact of transport investments on competitiveness. *Transportation Research Procedia, 1*, 77–88.

Klijn, E. H., & Teisman, G. R. (2003). Institutional and strategic barriers to public-private partnership: An analysis of Dutch cases. *Public Money and Management, 23*(3), 137–145.

Knitter, C., & Sandler, R. (2015). *The welfare impact of second best uniform-Pigouvian taxation: Evidence from transportation*. Cambridge: MIT working paper.

Koopmans, T. (1965). *On the concept of optimal economic growth. The economic approach to development planning* (pp. 225–287). Chicago: Rand McNally.

Koopmans, T. C. (1965). On the concept of optimal economic growth. In T. C. Koopmans (Ed.), *The economic approach to development planning* (pp. 225–287). Chicago: Rand McNally.

Krugman, P. (1991a). Increasing returns and economic geography. *Journal of Political Economy, 99*, 483–499.

Krugman, P. (1993). On the number and location of cities. *European Economic Review, 37*, 293–298.

Krugman, P. (1994). Complex landscapes in economic geography. *The American Economic Review, 84*, 412–416.

Krugman, P. (1998). What is new about the new economic geography? *Oxford Review of Economic Policy, 4*, 7–17.

Krugman, P., & Venables, T. (1995). Globalization and the inequality of nations. *Quarterly Journal of Economics, 110*, 857–880.

Krugman, P., & Venables, T. (1996). Integration, specialization, and adjustment. *European Economic Review, 40*, 959–968.

Laird, J. J., & Venables, A. J. (2017). Transport investment and economic performance: A framework for project appraisal. *Transport Policy, 56*, 1–11.

Lakshmanan, T. R. (2011). The broader economic consequences of transport infrastructure investments. *Journal of Transport Geography, 19*, 1–12.

Lechner, M. (2010). The Estimation of Causal Effects by Difference-in-Difference Methods. *Foundations and Trends R in Econometrics, 4*(3), 165–224.

Lee, P. T. W., Hu, Z. H., Lee, S. J., Choi, K. S., & Shin, S. H. (2018). Research trends and agenda on the Belt and Road (B&R) initiative with a focus on maritime transport. *Maritime Policy and Management, 45*(3), 282–300.

Lee, L. F., & You, J. (2010). Estimation of spatial autoregressive panel data models with fixed effects. *Journal of Econometrics, 154*(2), 165–185.

Leontief, W. (1986). *Input-output economics* (2nd ed.). New York: Oxford University Press.

LeSage, J., & Pace, K. (2009). *Introduction to spatial econometrics*. New York: CRC Press.

Levinshon, J., & Petrin, A. (2003). Estimating production functions using inputs to control for unobservables. *The Review of Economic Studies, 70*, 317–342.

Li, B., Akintoye, A., Edwards, P. J., & Hardcastle, C. (2005). Critical success factors for PPP/PFI projects in the UK construction industry. *Construction Management and Economics, 23*(5), 459–471.

Li, Z., Wu, M., & Chen, B. (2017). Is infrastructure investment in China excessive? Evidence from productivity of firms. *Regional Science and Urban Economics, 65*, 116–126.

Lin, Y. (2017). Travel costs and urban specialization patterns: Evidence from China's high speed rail system. *Journal of Urban Economics, 98*, 98–123.

Litman, T. (1995). Evaluating transportation land use impacts. *World Transport Policy and Practice, 1*(4), 9–16.
Little, I. M. D., & Mirrlees, J. A. (1974). *Project appraisal and planning*. London: Heinemann.
Little, I. M. D., & Mirrlees, J. A. (1991). Project appraisal and planning twenty years on. In *Proceedings of the World bank Annual conference on development economics 1990*. The International Bank for Reconstruction and Development.
Livas-Elizondo, R., & Krugman, P. (1996). Trade policy and the third-world metropolis. *Journal of Development Economics, 49*(1), 137–150.
Lucas, R. (1988). On the mechanics of economic development. *Journal of Monetary Economics, 22*, 3–42.
Lynde, C., & Richmond, J. (1992). The role of public capital in production. *The Review of Economics and Statistics, 74*(1), 37–44.
Macharis, C., & Bernardini, A. (2015). Reviewing the use of multi-criteria decision analysis for the evaluation of transport projects: Time for a multi-actor approach. *Transport Policy, 37*, 177–186.
Mackie, P., Worsley, T., & Eliasson, J. (2014). Transport appraisal revisited. *Research in Transportation Economics, 47*, 3–18.
Maibach, M., Schreyer, C., Sutter, D., van Essen, H. P., Boon, B. H., Smokers, R., et al. (2008). *Handbook on estimation of external costs in the transport sector, IMPACT Project*. Delft.
Makovšek, D. (2014). Systematic construction risk, cost estimation mechanism and unit price movements. *Transport Policy, 35*, 135–145.
Makovsek, D., Hasselgren, B., & Perkins, S. (2014). *Public private partnerships for transport infrastructure renegotiations, how to approach them and economic outcomes*. ITF Discussion Paper, n. 2014-25.
Mankiw, N. G., Romer, D., & Weil, D. N. (1992). A contribution to the empirics of economic growth. *The Quarterly Journal of Economics, 107*(2), 407–437.
Manski, C. (1993). Identification of endogenous social effects: The reflection problem. *The Review of Economic Studies, 60*(3), 531–542.
Manyika, J., Chui, M., Bughin, J., Dobbs, R., Bisson, P., & Marrs, A. (2013). *Disruptive technologies: Advances that will transform life, business, and the global economy*. New York: McKinsey Global Institute.
Mao, J. C. (1969). *Quantitative analysis of financial decisions*. New York: Prentice Hall.
Marchese, U. (1996). *Lineamenti e problemi di Economia dei Trasporti (in Italian)*. Genova: ECIG.
Marquez-Ramos, L. (2016). Port facilities, regional spillovers and exports: Empirical evidence from Spain. *Papers in Regional Science, 95*(2), 329–351.
Marshall, A. (1920). *Principles of economics* (8th ed.). London: MacMillan.
Martin, P., & Ottaviano, G. (1999). Growing locations: Industry location in a model of endogenous growth. *European Economic Review, 43*, 281–302.
Martin, P., & Ottaviano, G. (2001). Growth and agglomeration. *International Economic Review, 42*, 947–968.
Martin, P., & Rogers, C. A. (1995). Industrial location and public infrastructure. *Journal of International Economics, 39*, 335–351.
Martin, J. C., & Voltes Dorta, A. (2011). The econometric estimation of airports' cost function. *Transportation Research Part B, 45*(1), 112–127.
Mas Colell, A., Whinston, M., & Green, J. (1995). *Microeconomic theory*. Oxford: Oxford University Press.
McGraw, M. J. (2017). *Does airport size matter? Hub airports and local economic outcomes*. Mimeo.
McMillen, D. (2012). Perspectives on spatial econometrics: Linear smoothing with structured models. *Journal of Regional Science, 52*(2), 192–209.

Medda, F. R. (2007). A game theory approach for the allocation of risks in transport public private partnerships. *International Journal of Project Management, 25*, 213–218.

Medda, F. R., & Nijkamp, P. (2003). A combinatorial assessment methodology for complex transport policy analysis. *Integrated Assessment, 4*(3), 214–222.

Meersman, H., & Nazemzadeh, M. (2017). The contribution of transport infrastructure to economic activity: The case of Belgium. *Case Studies on Transport Policy, 5*, 316–324.

Meersman, H., Van de Voorde, E., & Vanelslander, T. (2014). In *Port infrastructure finance*. London: Informa Law from Routledge.

Melecky, M., Sharma, S., & Subhash, H. (2018). *Wider economic benefits of investments in transport corridors and the role of complementary policies*. World Bank Policy Research Working Paper, n. 8350.

Melitz, M., & Ottaviano, G. (2008). Market size, trade, and productivity. *The Review of Economic Studies, 75*(1), 295–316.

Melo, P., Graham, D., & Brage-Ardao, R. (2013). The productivity of transport infrastructure investment: A meta-analysis of empirical evidence. *Regional Science and Urban Economics, 43*, 695–706.

Mid-term evaluation of the TEN-T Programme. (2007-2013). Brussels: Directorate General Mobility and Transport.

Miller, R. E., & Blair, P. D. (2009). *Input–output analysis. Foundations and extensions* (2nd ed.). Cambridge: Cambridge University Press.

Minerva, G., & Ottaviano, G. (2009). Endogenous growth theories: Agglomeration benefits and transportation costs. In R. Capello, & P. Nijkamp (Eds.), *Handbook of regional growth and development theories*. Cheltenham: Edward Elgar.

Mishan, E. J. (1972). *Elements of cost benefit analysis*. London: George Allen and Unwin.

Mogridge, M. J. H., Holden, D. J., Bird, J., & Terzis, G. C. (1987). The Downs-Thomson Paradox and the transportation planning process. *International Journal of Transport Economics, 14*, 283–311.

Mohring, H. (1993). Maximizing, measuring, and not double counting transportation-improvement benefits: A primer on closed-and open-economy cost-benefit analysis. *Transportation Research Part B, 27*(6), 413–424.

Musso, E., Sillig, C., & Sanguineti, S. (2007). Socio-economic impact of transport policies: An institutional approach. In E. Haezendonck (Ed.), *Transport Project evaluation: Extending the social cost-benefit approach* (pp. 95–114). Edward Elgar Publishing.

Nash, N. (2005). Rail infrastructure charges in Europe. *Journal of Transport Economics and Policy, 39*(3), 259–278.

Nijkamp, P., & Rienstra, S. A. (1995). Private sector involvement in financing and operating transport infrastructure. *The Annals of Regional Science, 29*(2), 221–235.

Nijkamp, P., Rietveld, P., & Voogd, H. (1990). *Multicriteria evaluation in physical planning*. Amsterdam: Elsevier Science Publishers.

Nijkamp, P., & Ubbels, B. (1999). How reliable are estimates of infrastructure costs? A comparative analysis. *International Journal of Transport Economics, 26*, 23–53.

Notteboom, T., Coeck, C., & van Den Broeck, J. (2000). Measuring and explaining the relative efficiency of container terminals by means of Bayesian stochastic frontier models. *International Journal of Maritime Economics, 22*, 83–106.

Notteboom, T., De Langen, P., & Jacobs, W. (2013). Institutional plasticity and path dependence in seaports: Interactions between institutions, port governance reforms and port authority routines. *Journal of Transport Geography, 27*, 26–35.

Notteboom, T., & Rodrigue, J. P. (2008). Containerization, box logistics and global supply chains: The integration of ports and liner shipping networks. *Maritime Economics and Logistic, 10*, 152–174.

NSW – New South Wales Government. (2016). *Principles and guidelines for economic appraisal of transport investment and initiatives.* Chippendale: New South Wales Government. Retrievable at www.transport.nsw.gov.au.

Nunez-Serrano, J., & Velaszquez, F. (2017). Is public capital productive? Evidence from a meta-analysis. *Applied Economics Perspectives and Policy, 39*(2), 313–345.

Odlyzko, A. (2010). *Collective hallucinations and inefficient markets: The British Railway Mania of the 1840s.* Retrievable at http://www.dtc.umn.edu/~odlyzko.

OECD – Organisation for the Economic Cooperation and Development. (2012). *Public governance of public-private partnerships - recommendation of the Council on principles for, Paris.* OECD publishing.

OECD – Organisation for the Economic Cooperation and Development. (2013). *Better Regulation of public-private partnerships for transport infrastructure.* ITF Roundtable 151, Paris.

Olivier, G., Songhi, J., & Zhou, N. (2014). *High-speed railways in China: A look at construction costs.* World Bank reports, China Transport Topics No. 9.

Olley, S., & Pakes, A. (1996). The dynamics of productivity in the telecommunications equipment industry. *Econometrica, 64*, 1263–1295.

Ortiz, I. N., & Buxbaum, J. N. (2008). Protecting the public interest in long-term concession agreements for transportation infrastructure. *Public Works Management and Policy, 13*, 126–137.

Osborne, M. J. (2010). A resolution to the NPV–IRR debate? *The Quarterly Review of Economics and Finance, 50*, 234–239.

Ott, I., & Turnovsky, S. S. (2006). Excludable and non-excludable public inputs: Consequences for Economic Growth. *Economica, 73*, 725–748.

Ottaviano, G. G. (2008). Infrastructure and economic geography: An overview of theory and evidence. *European Bank of Investments Papers, 13*, 8–35.

Oxford Economics. (2015). *Assessing the global transport infrastructure market: Outlook to 2025.* London: Price Waterhouse Cooper.

Pallis, A. A., Notteboom, T., & De Langen, P. W. (2008). Concession agreements and market entry in the container terminal industry. *Maritime Economics and Logistics, 10*(3), 209–228.

Panayides, M. P., Parola, F., & Lam, J. S. L. (2015). The effect of institutional factors on public–private partnership success in ports. *Transportation Research Part A, 71*, 110–127.

Pandey, I. M. (2015). *Essentials of financial management* (4th ed.). New Delhi: Vikas Publishing House.

Park, J., & Seo, Y. (2016). The impact of seaports on the regional economies in South Korea: Panel evidence from the augmented solow model. *Transportation Research Part E, 85*, 107–119.

Pedrycz, W., Ekel, P., & Parreiras, R. (2011). *Fuzzy multicriteria decision-making: Models, methods and applications.* New York: John Wiley & Sons.

Percoco, M. (2010). Airport activity and economic development: Evidence from Italy. *Urban Studies, 47*(11), 2427–2443.

Percoco, M. (2016). Highways, local economic structure and urban development. *Journal of Economic Geography, 16*, 1035–1054.

Pereira, A., & Andraz, J. (2004). Public highway spending and state spillovers in the USA. *Applied Economics Letters, 11*(12), 785–788.

Pereira, A., & Andraz, J. (2005). Public investment in transportation infrastructures and economic performance in Portugal. *Review of Development Economics, 9*, 177–196.

Pereira, A., & Andraz, J. (2013). On the economic effects of public infrastructure investment: A survey of the international evidence. *Journal of Development Economics, 38*(4), 1–37.

Perez, I., Trujillo, L., & Gonzalez, M. M. (2016). Efficiency determinants of container terminals in Latin American and the Caribbean. *Utilities Policy, 41*, 1–14.

Pickrell, D. H. (1990). *Urban rail transit projects: Forecasts versus actual ridership and cost.* Washington: US Department of Transportation.

Pigou, A. C. (1929). *The economics of welfare*. London: Macmillan.

Pilegaard, N., & Fosgerau, M. (2008). Cost benefit analysis of a transport improvement in the case of search unemployment. *Journal of Transport Economics and Policy, 42*(1), 23–42.

Pinske, J., & Slade, M. (2010). The future of spatial econometrics. *Journal of Regional Science, 50*(1), 103–117.

Priemus, H., & Zonneveld, W. (2003). What are corridors and what are the issues? Introduction to special issue: The governance of corridors. *Journal of Transport Geography, 11*(3), 167–177.

Profillidis, V., Botzoris, G., & Galanis, A. (2014). Environmental effects and externalities from the transport sector and sustainable transportation planning – a review. *International Journal of Energy Economics and Policy, 4*(4), 647–661.

Proost, S., Dunkerley, F., De Borger, B., Gühneman, A., Koskenoja, P., Mackie, P., et al. (2011). When are subsidies to trans-European network projects justified? *Transportation Research Part A, 45*, 161–170.

Proost, S., & Thisse, J. F. (2015). *Skilled cities, regional disparities, and efficient transport: The state of the art and a research agenda.* CEPR Discussion Papers, n. 10790.

Puffert, D. (2002). Path dependence in spatial networks: The standardization of railway track gauge. *Explorations in Economic History, 39*, 282–314.

Purwanto, A. J., Heyndrickx, C., Kiel, J., Betancor, O., Socorro, P., Hernandez, H., et al. (2017). Impact of transport infrastructure on international competitiveness of Europe. *Transportation Research Procedia, 25*, 2877–2888.

Qin, Y. (2017). "No county left behind"? The distributional impact of high-speed rail upgrades in China. *Journal of Economic Geography, 17*(3), 489–520.

Quah, D. (2002). Spatial agglomeration dynamics. *The American Economic Review, 92*, 247–252.

Quinet, E. (1998). *Principes d'Economie des Transports*. Paris: Economica.

Quinet, E., Touzery, L., & Triebel, H. (1982). *Économie des Transports*. Paris: Economica.

Quinet, E., & Vickerman, R. (2004). *Principles of transport economics*. Cheltenham: Edward Elgar.

Ramsey, F. P. (1928). A mathematical theory of saving. *Economic Journal, 38*(152), 543–559.

Rawls, J. (1971). *A theory of Justice*. Cambridge: Harvard University Press.

Redding, S. (2016). Goods trade, factor mobility and welfare. *Journal of International Economics, 101*, 148–167.

Redding, S. J., Sturm, D. M., & Wolf, N. (2011). History and industry location: Evidence from German airports. *The Review of Economics and Statistics, 93*(3), 814–831.

Redding, S., & Turner, M. (2015). Transportation costs and the spatial organization of economic activity. In G. Duranton, J. Henderson, & W. Strange (Eds.), *Handbook of regional and urban economics* (Vol. 5). Amsterdam: Elsevier.

Rietveld, P. (1994). Spatial economic impacts of transport infrastructure supply. *Transportation Research Part A, 28*(4), 329–341.

Rietveld, P. (2003). Winners and losers in transport policy: On efficiency, equity, and compensation. In. In D. A. Hensher, & K. J. Button (Eds.), *Handbook of transport and the environment* (Vol. 4, pp. 585–601).

Rietveld, P., & Boonstra, J. (1995). On the supply of network infrastructure. *The Annals of Regional Science, 29*, 207–220.

Rietveld, P., & Bruinsma, F. (1998). *Is transport infrastructure effective?* Heidelberg: Springer.

Robinson, R. (2006). Regulating efficiency into port-oriented chain systems: Export coal through the Dalrymple Bay terminal. In *Australia. Proceeding of the 2006 IAME conference, Melbourne, Australia.*

Rodrigue, J. P., Comtois, C., & Slack, B. (2006). *The Geography of transport systems.* Abingdon: Routledge.

Romer, P. (1986). Increasing returns and long-run growth. *Journal of Political Economy, 94*, 1002–1037.

Romer, P. (1990). Endogenous technological change. *Journal of Political Economy, 90*, 71–102.

Romp, W., & de Haan, J. (2007). Public capital and economic growth: A critical survey. *Perspektiven der Wirtschaftspolitik, 8*, 6–52.

Roodman, D. (2009). How to do xtabond2: An introduction to difference and system GMM. *STATA Journal, 9*(1), 86–136.

Rosenthal, S. S., & Strange, W. C. (2003). Geography, industrial organization and agglomeration. *The Review of Economics and Statistics, 85*, 377–393.

Rothengatter, W. (2015). Approaches to internalisation of transport externalities. In C. Nash (Ed.), *Handbook of research methods and applications in transport economics and policy.* Cheltenham: Edward Elgar Publishing.

Rothengatter, W. (2017). Wider economic impacts of transport infrastructure investments: Relevant or negligible? *Transport Policy, 59*, 124–133.

Roumboutsos, A. (Ed.). (2015). *Public private partnerships in transport. Trends and theory.* Abingdon: Routledge.

Rouwendal, J. (2012). Indirect effects in cost-benefit analysis. *Journal of Benefit-Cost Analysis, 3*(1), 1–27.

Rovolis, A., & Spence, N. (2002). Duality theory and cost function analysis in a regional context: The impact of public infrastructure capital in the Greek regions. *The Annals of Regional Science, 36*, 55–78.

Roy, B. (1975). Vérs une méthodologie générale de l'aide à la décision. *Revue METRA, 14*(3), 459–497.

Saaty, T. L. (1988). *The analytic hierarchy process.* New York: McGraw Hill.

Salling, K. B., & Banister, D. (2009). Assessment of large transport infrastructure projects: The CBA-DK model. *Transportation Research Part A, 43*, 800–813.

Salling, K. B., & Leleur, S. (2011). Transport appraisal and Monte Carlo simulation by use of the CBA-DK model. *Transport Policy, 18*, 236–245.

Salling, K. B., & Leleur, S. (2012). Modelling of transport projects uncertainties: Risk assessment and scenario analysis. *European Journal of Transport and Infrastructure Research, 12*, 21–38.

Samuelson, P. (1952). Spatial price equilibrium and linear programming. *The American Economic Review, 42*, 283–303.

Samuelson, P. (1954). A pure theory of public expenditure. *The Review of Economics and Statistics, 36*, 387–389.

Sánchez, P. C. (2000). A subadditivity test for the cost function of the principal European railways. *Transport Reviews, 20*(3), 275–290.

Santos, M. G., & Santos, B. F. (2012). Shadow-tolls in Portugal: How we got here and what were the impacts of introducing real tolls. In *European Transport conference 2012, Glasgow, Scotland.*

Santos-Silva, J., & Tenreyro, S. (2006). The log of gravity. *The Review of Economics and Statistics, 88*(4), 641–658.

Schuckmann, S. W., Gnatzy, T., Darkow, I. L., & von der Gracht, H. A. (2012). Analysis of factors influencing the development of transport infrastructure until the year 2030 — a Delphi based scenario study. *Technological Forecasting and Social Change, 79*, 1373–1387.

Scotchmer, S., & Thisse, J. (1992). Space and competition: A puzzle. *The Annals of Regional Science, 26*, 269–286.

Sen, A. (1990). Justice: means versus freedoms. *Philosophy and Public Affairs, 19*(2), 11–121.

Sen, A. (2000). The discipline of cost-benefit analysis. *The Journal of Legal Studies, 29*(2), 931–952.

Sentence, A. (2003). Airport slot auctions: Desirable or feasible? *Utilities Policy, 11*(1), 53–57.

Serebrisky, T., Sarriera, J. M., Suárez-Alemán, A., Araya, G., Briceño-Garmendía, C., & Schwartz, J. (2016). Exploring the drivers of port efficiency in Latin America and the Caribbean. *Transport Policy, 45*, 31–45.

Shan, J., Yu, M., & Lee, C. (2014). An empirical investigation of the seaport's economic impact: Evidence from major ports in China. *Transportation Research Part E, 69*, 41–53.

Sheard, N. (2014). Airports and urban sectoral employment. *Journal of Urban Economics, 80*, 133–152.

Shioji, E. (2001). Public capital and economic growth: A convergence approach. *Journal of Economic Growth, 6*, 205–227.

Smith, A. S. J. (2006). Are Britain's railways costing too much? Perspectives based on TFP comparisons with British Rail 1963–2002. *Journal of Transport Economics and Policy, 40*(1), 1–44.

Solomon, E. (1956). The arithmetic of capital budgeting decisions. *Journal of Business, 29*(2), 124–129.

Song, L., & van Geenhuizen, M. (2014). Port infrastructure investment and regional economic growth in China: Panel evidence import regions and provinces. *Transport Policy, 36*, 173–183.

Stanley, T. D. (2001). Wheat from chaff: meta-analysis as quantitative literature review. *The Journal of Economic Perspectives, 15*, 131–150.

Stern, N. (2001). *A strategy for development.* Washington: The World Bank Publications.

Stone, R. (1962). *A social accounting matrix for 1960. Volume 2S in A Programme for growth.* London: Chapman and Hall.

Straub, S. (2011). Infrastructure and development: A critical appraisal of the macro-level literature. *Journal of Development Studies, 47*(5), 683–708.

Strauss-Khan, V., & Vives, X. (2009). Why and where do headquarters move? *Regional Science and Urban Economics, 39*, 168–186.

Sturm, J. E., Kuper, G. H., & de Haan, J. (1998). Modelling government investment and economic growth on a macro level: A review. In S. Brackam, H. van Ees, & S. K. Kuipers (Eds.), *Market behaviour and macroeconomic modelling* (pp. 359–406). London: MacMillan.

Sue, W. P., Anderson, W. P., & Lakshmanan, T. R. (2008). *The broader benefits of transport infrastructure. The wider economic benefits of transport.* Paris: OECD-International Transport Forum.

Sunstein, C. R. (2004). Valuing life: A plea for disaggregation. *Duke Law Journal, 54*, 385–445.

Szymanski, S. (1991). The optimal timing of infrastructure investment. *Journal of Transport Economics and Policy, 25*(3), 247–258.

Tabuchi, T., Thisse, J. F., & Zhu, X. (2015). *Does technological progress affect the location of economic activity?*. CORE Discussion Paper, N°2015/11.

Tang, X. (2016). Does Chinese employment benefit Africans? Investigating Chinese enterprises and their operations in Africa. *African Studies Quarterly, 16*, 107–128.

Tang, L., Shen, G. Q., & Cheng, E. W. L. (2010). A review of studies on Public–Private Partnership projects in the construction industry. *International Journal of Project Management, 28*, 683–694.

Tanino, T., Tanaka, T., & Inuiguchi, M. (2003). In *Multi-objective programming and goal programming*. New York: Springer.

Tavasszy, L. A., Behdani, B., & Konings, R. (2015). *Intermodality and synchromodality*. https://doi.org/10.2139/ssrn.2592888. Retrievable at SSRN.

Tillema, T., Hamersma, M., Sussman, J., & Arts, J. (2012). Extending the scope of highway planning: Accessibility, negative externalities and the residential context. *Transport Reviews, 32*, 745–759.

Torrisi, G. (2009). *Infrastructures and economic performance: A critical comparison across four approaches*. MPRA Paper, n. 25849.

Triantaphyllou, E. (2000). *Multi-criteria decision making methods: A comparative study*. New York: Springer.

Tripathi, S., & Gautam, V. (2011). Road Transport Infrastructure and Economic Growth in India. *Journal of Infrastructure Development, 2*, 2.

Trujillo, L., Quinet, E., & Estache, A. (2002). Dealing with demand forecasting games in transport privatization. *Transport Policy, 9*, 325–334.

Tsamboulas, D. A. (2007). A tool for prioritizing multinational transport infrastructure investments. *Transport Policy, 14*(1), 11–26.

Tsamboulas, D., Verma, A., & Moraiti, P. (2013). Transport infrastructure provision and operations: Why should governments choose private-public partnership? *Research in Transportation Economics, 38*, 122–127.

Tsamboulas, D., Vrenken, H., & Lekka, A. M. (2007). Assessment of a transport policy potential for intermodal mode shift on a European scale. *Transportation Research Part A, 41*, 715–733.

UNCTAD – United Nations Conference on Trade and Development. (2018). *Liner shipping connectivity index*. Retrievable at http://unctadstat.unctad.org/wds/TableViewer/tableView.aspx?ReportId=92.

UNECE – United Nations Economic Commission for Europe. (2003). *Cost benefit analysis of transport infrastructure projects*. Geneva: United Nations.

UNESCAP – United Nation Economic and Social Commission for Asia and the Pacific. (2011). *A guidebook on public-private partnership in infrastructure*. Bangkok: United Nation report.

Vega, S., & Elhorst, J. (2015). The SLX model. *Journal of Regional Science, 55*(3), 339–363.

Verhoef, E. (2000). The implementation of marginal external cost pricing in road transport. *Papers in Regional Science, 79*, 307–332.

Vickerman, R. (2008). Recent evolution of research into the wider economic benefits of transport infrastructure investments. In *OECD-international transport forum*. Paris: The Wider Economic Benefits of Transport.

Vinokurov, E., & Tsukarev, T. (2018). The belt and road initiative and the transit countries: An economic assessment of land transport corridors. *Area Development and Policy, 3*, 93–113.

Volpe, M. C., Carballo, J., & Cusolito, A. (2017). Roads, exports and employment: Evidence from a developing country. *Journal of Development Economics, 125*, 21–39.

Wacziarg, R., & Welch, K. H. (2008). Trade liberalization and growth: New evidence. *The World Bank Economic Review, 22*, 187–231.

Walz, U. (1996). Transport costs, intermediate goods and localized growth. *Regional Science and Urban Economics, 26*, 671–795.

Wanke, P. F. (2013). Physical infrastructure and shipment consolidation efficiency drivers in Brazilian ports: A two-stage network-DEA approach. *Transport Policy, 29*, 145–153.

WB – World Bank. (2007). *Private participation in infrastructure database methodology*. Washington: WB reports.

WB - World Bank. (2016). Private Participation in Infrastructure (PPI). *Annual Update*. Retrievable at https://ppi.worldbank.org.

WB - World Bank. (2017). *Logistics performance Index*. https://lpi.worldbank.org/.

WB - World Bank. (2018a). *DoingBusiness report*. http://www.doingbusiness.org/.

WB - World Bank. (2018b). *Transport projects*. Retrievable at http://www.worldbank.org/en/topic/transport.

WB - World Bank. (2018c). *PPI database*. Retrievable at http://ppi.worldbank.org/.

Weber, A. (1929). *Theory of the location of industries*. Chicago, US: The University of Chicago Press.

Weber, T. A. (2014). On the (non-)equivalence of IRR and NPV. *Journal of Mathematical Economics, 52*, 25–39.

van Wee, B. (2007). Large infrastructure projects: A review of the quality of demand forecasts and cost estimations. *Environment and Planning B: Planning and Design, 34*, 611–625.

van Wee, B. (2011). *Transport and ethics. Ethics and the evaluation of transport policies and projects.* Cheltenham: Edward Elgar Publishing.

van Wee, B. (2012). How suitable is CBA for the ex-ante evaluation of transport projects and policies? A discussion from the perspective of ethics. *Transport Policy, 19*, 1–7.

Wilmsmeier, G., & Hoffmann, J. (2008). Liner shipping connectivity and port infrastructure as determinants of freight Rates in the Caribbean. *Maritime Economics and Logistics, 10*, 130–151.

Wilmsmeier, G., Hoffmann, J., & Sanchez, R. (2006). The impact of port characteristics on international maritime transport costs. *Research in Transportation Economics, 16*, 117–140.

Wilson, J. S., Mann, C. L., & Otsuki, T. (2005). Assessing the benefits of trade facilitation: A global perspective. *The World Economy, 28*, 841–871.

Wooldridge, J. (2010). *Econometric analysis of cross section and panel data*. Cambridge: The MIT Press.

World Bank. (1998). The effects of pollution on health: The economic toll. In *Pollution prevention and abatement handbook*. Washington: World Bank Reports.

World Bank. (2014). *Regional economic impact analysis of high speed rail in China*. Report n. ACS9734. Washington, US: China and Mongolia Sustainable Development Sector Unit.

Xu, H., & Nakajima, K. (2015). Highways and industrial development in the peripheral regions of China. *Papers in Regional Science, 96*(2), 325–357.

Xu, H., Zhou, H., & Liang, L. (2016). The locational dynamics of manufacturing in China's counties: Influence of expressway investment. *Journal of Regional Science, 56*(3), 522–543.

Xu, H., & Nakajima, K. (2017). Highways and industrial development in the peripheral regions of China. *Papers in Regional Science, 96*(2), 325–357.

Yamamoto, K. (2003). Agglomeration and growth with innovation in the intermediate goods sector. *Regional Science and Urban Economics, 33*, 335–360.

Yard, A. (2012). Cost-benefit analysis according to Sen: An application in the evaluation of transport infrastructures in France. *Transportation Research Part A, 46*, 707–719.

Yu, N., de Jong, M., Storm, S., & Mi, J. (2013). Spatial spillover effects of transport infrastructure: Evidence from Chinese regions. *Journal of Trnasport Geography, 28*, 56–66.

Yu, Q. (2016). 'No county left behind?' The distributional impact of high-speed rail upgrades in China. *Journal of Economic Geography*, 1–32.

Zheng, S., & Kahn, M. E. (2013). China's bullet trains facilitate market integration and mitigate the cost of megacity growth. *Proceedings of the National Academy of Science of the United States of America*, 1248–1253.

Zhu, X., Van Ommeren, J., & Rietveld, P. (2009). Indirect benefits of infrastructure improvement in the case of an imperfect labor market. *Transportation Research Part B, 43*, 57–72.

FURTHER READING

Arduino, G., Aronietis, R., Crozet, Y., Frouws, K., Ferrari, C., Guihéry, L., et al. (2013). How to turn an innovative concept into a success? An application to seaport-related innovation. *Research in Transportation Economics, 42*, 97–107.

Aviles Zugasti, A., Gomez Garcia, R., & Sanchez Maldonado, J. (2002). The effects of public infrastructure on the cost structure of Spanish industries. *Spanish Economic Review, 3*(2), 131–150.

Banister, D., & Berechman, J. (2000). *Transport investment and economic development*. London: UCL Press.

Berg, A., Buffie, E., Pattillo, C., Portillo, F., Presibitero, A., & Zanna, L. F. (2015). *Some misconceptions about public investment efficiency and growth*. IMF Working Paper, 15, 272.

Bom, P., & Ligthart, J. (2014). What have we learnt from three decades of research on the productivity of public capital? *Journal of Economic Surveys, 28*(5), 889–916.

Breinlich, H., Ottaviano, G., & Temple, J. (2014). Regional growth and regional decline. In S. Durlauf, & P. Aghion (Eds.), *Handbook of economic growth* (Vol. 2A, pp. 683–779). Amsterdam: North Holland. https://www.safaribooksonline.com/library/view/handbook-of-economic/9780444535467/xhtml/CHP012.html - AF005.

Button, K. J., & Perman, A. D. (Eds.). (1983). *The practice of transport investment appraisal*. Aldershot: Gower Publishing Company.

Calatayud, A., Palacin, R., Mangan, J., Jackson, E., & Ruiz-Rua, A. (2016). Understanding connectivity to international markets: A systematic review. *Transport Reviews, 36*(6), 713–736.

Chen, Z., & Haynes, K. (2013). Public surface transportation and regional output: A spatial panel approach. *Papers in Regional Science, 94*(4), 727–752.

Consulta Nazionale per l'Autotrasporto e la Logistica. (2011). *National logistics plan 2011-2020*. Rome: Italian Ministry of Transport.

Cristea, A. (2017). Buyer-seller relationship in international trade: Evidence from the US states' exports and business class travel. *Journal of International Economics, 84*(2), 207–220.

Desmet, K., & Rossi-Hansberg, E. (2010). On spatial dynamics. *Journal of Regional Science, 50*(1), 43–63.

ESPO – European SeaPort Organization. (2018). *Facts and figures*. Retrievable at https://www.espo.be/fact-and-figures.

Farhadi, M. (2015). Transport infrastructure and long run economic growth in OECD countries. *Transportation Research Part A, 74*, 73–90.

Garcia-Lopez, M., Hémet, C., & Viladecans-Marsal, E. (2017). How does transportation shape intrametropolitan growth? An answer from the Regional Express Rail. *Journal of Regional Science, 57*, 758–780.

Holtz-Eakin, D., & Lovely, M. (1996). Scale economies, returns to variety, and the productivity of public infrastructure. *Regional Science and Urban Economics, 26*, 105–123.

Imbens, G. (2015). Matching methods in practice: Three examples. *Journal of Human Resources, 50*(2), 373–419.

Jalili, M., Salehzadeh-Yazdi, A., Gupta, S., Wolkenhauer, O., Yaghmaie, M., Resendis-Antonio, O., et al. (2016). Evolution of centrality measurements for the detection of essential proteins in biological networks. *Frontier in Physiology, 7*, 1–4.

Krugman, P. (1991b). *Geography and trade*. Cambridge: MIT Press.

Michaels, G. (2008). The effect of trade on the demand for skill: Evidence from the interstate highway system. *The Review of Economics and Statistics, 90*(4), 683–701.

Nadiri, M. I., & Mamuneas, T. (1994). The effects of public capital infrastructure and R&D capital on the cost structure and performance of US manufacturing industries. *The Review of Economics andStatistics, 76*(1), 22–37.

Rahman, N. S., Salleh, N. H., Najib, A. F., & Lun, V. (2016). A descriptive method for analysing the Kra Canal decision on maritime business patterns in Malaysia. *Journal of Shipping and Trade*, 1–13.

Solow, R. (1956). A Contribution to the theory of economic growth. *Quarterly Journal of Economics, 70*, 65–94.

Volpe, M. C., & Blyde, J. (2013). Shaky roads and trembling exports: Assessing the trade effects of domestic infrastructure using a natural experiment. *Journal of International Economics, 90*, 148–161.

Walz, U. (1996). Transport costs, intermediate goods and localized growth. *Regional Science and Urban Economics, 26*(6), 671–795.

Wangness, P. B., Rødseth, K. L., & Hansen, W. (2017). A review of guidelines for including wider economic impacts in transport appraisal. *Transport Reviews, 37*(1), 94–115.

Weiner, E. (1984). Urban transportation planning in the U.S.: An historical overview. Part 1. *Transport Reviews, 4*(4), 331–358.

Xie, F., & Levinson, D. (2009). Modeling the growth of transportation networks: A comprehensive review. *Network Spatial Economics, 9*, 291–307.

INDEX

'*Note:* Page numbers followed by "f" indicate figures, "t" indicate tables and "b" indicate boxes.'

J

K

L

T

U

V

W

FSC
www.fsc.org
MIX
Papier | Fördert
gute Waldnutzung
FSC® C083411

Kolibri 360 GmbH
Ferdinand-Jühlke-Straße 7
99095 Erfurt, Deutschland
produktsicherheit@kolibri360.de